MW00450626

FREE DVD FREE FREE DVD

From Stress to Success DVD from Trivium Test Prep

Dear Customer,

Thank you for purchasing from Cirrus Test Prep! Whether you're looking to join the military, get into college, or advance your career, we're honored to be a part of your journey.

To show our appreciation (and to help you relieve a little of that test-prep stress), we're offering a **FREE *Praxis Biology Essential Test Tips DVD**** by Cirrus Test Prep. Our DVD includes 35 test preparation strategies that will help keep you calm and collected before and during your big exam. All we ask is that you email us your feedback and describe your experience with our product. Amazing, awful, or just so-so: we want to hear what you have to say!

To receive your **FREE *Praxis Biology Essential Test Tips DVD***, please email us at 5star@cirrustestprep.com. Include "Free 5 Star" in the subject line and the following information in your email:

1. The title of the product you purchased.

2. Your rating from 1 – 5 (with 5 being the best).

3. Your feedback about the product, including how our materials helped you meet your goals and ways in which we can improve our products.

4. Your full name and shipping address so we can send your **FREE *Praxis Biology Essential Test Tips DVD*.**

If you have any questions or concerns please feel free to contact us directly at 5star@cirrustestprep.com.

Thank you, and good luck with your studies!

* Please note that the free DVD is <u>not included</u> with this book. To receive the free DVD, please follow the instructions above.

Praxis II Biology Content Knowledge (5235) Study Guide 2019-2020

Exam Prep and Practice Test Questions for the Praxis 5235 Exam

Copyright © 2018 by Cirrus Test Prep

ALL RIGHTS RESERVED. By purchase of this book, you have been licensed one copy for personal use only. No part of this work may be reproduced, redistributed, or used in any form or by any means without prior written permission of the publisher and copyright owner.

ETS was not involved in the creation or production of this product, is not in any way affiliated with Cirrus Test Prep, and does not sponsor or endorse this product. All test names (and their acronyms) are trademarks of their respective owners. This study guide is for general information only and does not claim endorsement by any third party.

Table of Contents

Online Resources

To help you fully prepare for your Praxis Biology exam, Cirrus includes online resources with the purchase of this study guide.

PRACTICE TEST

In addition to the practice test included in this book, we also offer an online exam. Since many exams today are computer-based, getting to practice your test-taking skills on the computer is a great way to prepare.

FLASH CARDS

A convenient supplement to this study guide, Cirrus's e-flash cards enable you to review important terms easily on your computer or smartphone.

FROM STRESS TO SUCCESS

Watch *From Stress to Success*, a brief but insightful YouTube video that offers the tips, tricks, and secrets experts use to score higher on the exam.

REVIEWS

Leave a review, send us helpful feedback, or sign up for Cirrus's promotions—including free books!

   To access these materials, please enter the following URL into your browser: **www.cirrustestprep.com/praxis-biology-online-resources**.

Introduction

Congratulations on choosing to take the Praxis Biology: Content Knowledge (5235) test! By purchasing this book, you've taken the first step toward becoming a science teacher.

This guide will provide you with a detailed overview of the Praxis Biology test, so you know exactly what to expect on test day. We'll take you through all the concepts covered on the test and give you the opportunity to test your knowledge with practice questions. Even if it's been a while since you last took a major test, don't worry; we'll make sure you're more than ready!

WHAT IS THE PRAXIS BIOLOGY TEST?

The Praxis Biology test measures aptitude in biology for teacher candidates looking to certify as biology teachers. This test must be taken *in addition* to the assessments in reading, writing, mathematics, and professional knowledge required in your particular state. The Praxis Biology test does not replace these other exams.

WHAT'S ON THE PRAXIS BIOLOGY TEST?

The Praxis Biology test gauges college-level content knowledge in biology, as well as the necessary skills for biology. Candidates are expected to demonstrate thorough and extensive conceptual knowledge of subjects including cell biology, organismal biology, human biology, biochemistry, genetics, evolution, biological diversity, and ecology. You will also be expected to demonstrate mastery of key skills related to scientific inquiry. The content is divided into six subareas.

You will have two hours and thirty minutes to answer 150 multiple-choice questions.

What's on the Praxis Biology: Content Knowledge (5235) Test?

Content Category	Objectives	Number of Questions	Percentage
I. Molecular and Cellular Biology	A. Important molecules—chemical structures and properties B. Importance of chemical principles to biological processes C. Enzymes D. Biochemical pathways and energy flow in an organism E. Prokaryotes and eukaryotes F. Structure and function of cells and organelles G. Cell function and activity H. Cellular division, cell cycle and regulation I. Nucleic acids J. Protein synthesis K. Regulation of gene expression L. Differentiation and specialization of cells M. Nature of mutations N. Basic laboratory techniques O. DNA technologies and genetic engineering	30	20%
II. Genetics and Evolution	A. Mendel's laws B. Non-Mendelian inheritance C. Common human genetic disorders and their chromosomal and genetic causes D. Sources of genetic variation E. Population genetics F. Hardy-Weinberg Equilibrium G. Mechanisms of evolution H. Evidence supporting evolution I. Genetic basis of speciation J. Models of evolutionary rates K. Scientific explanations for the origin of life on Earth L. Factors that lead to extinction	30	20%

Content Category	Objectives	Number of Questions	Percentage
III. Diversity of Life and Organismal Biology	A. Living versus nonliving things B. Classification systems of organisms C. Viruses, bacteria, protists, fungi, plants, and animals D. Major animal phyla E. Organizational hierarchy of multicellular organisms F. Major organ systems in animals G. Homeostasis H. Reproduction, development, and growth in animals I. Major plant divisions J. Structures and functions of major plant tissues and organs K. Plant life cycles and reproduction L. Transportation of water in plants M. Photosynthesis	30	20%
IV. Ecology: Organisms and Environments	A. Hierarchy of the biosphere B. Components of ecosystem that impact population size (biotic and abiotic) C. Models of population growth D. Relationship between reproductive strategies and mortality rates E. Relationships within and among species F. Ecological succession G. Biomes H. Energy flow in the environment I. Biogeochemical cycles J. Effects of natural disturbances on ecosystems K. Human impact on ecosystems and biodiversity L. Interconnectedness of ecosystems	24	16%

What's on the Praxis Biology: Content Knowledge (5235) Test? (continued)

Content Category	Objectives	Number of Questions	Percentage
V. Science, Technology, and Social Perspectives	A. Environmental impact of science and technology	15	10%
	B. Impact of human activity and natural phenomena on society		
	C. Management of natural resources and social impact		
	D. Ethical and societal issues associated with science and technology use		
VI. History and Nature of Science	A. Processes involved in scientific inquiry	21	14%
	B. Interdisciplinary nature of science		
	C. How facts, hypotheses, theories, and laws differ		
	D. Historical shifts in science		
	E. Scientific measurement and notation systems		
	F. Reading and interpretation of data in tables, graphs, and charts		
	G. Use of scientific models		
	H. Safe preparation, storage, use, and disposal of laboratory and field materials		
	I. Use and care of laboratory equipment		
	J. Safety and emergency procedures in labs and science classrooms		

Category I emphasizes scientific processes. Specifically, this includes the process of formulating and investigating scientific questions and the proper design and implementation of experiments, from proper handling of data to mastery of key equipment. This subarea also assesses your understanding of the larger context of science from both the historical and current perspective.

Category II assesses your understanding of the chemical aspects of biology as well as your understanding of cellular biology. You must demonstrate mastery of the key molecules and chemical processes involved in life. You should also be able to identify the structures and functions of cells, compare different types of cells, and explain their major processes. Finally you must demonstrate an understanding of relevant basic laboratory techniques and the ways in which DNA technologies and genetic engineering are used and applied.

Category III assesses your understanding of genetic processes. You should be able to demonstrate an understanding of the basic principles of classical, molecular, and population genetics. You must demonstrate a mastery of evolution. Topics include sources of genetic variation, mechanisms of evolution, supporting evidence, and significant scientific explanations for the origins of life, speciation, and extinction.

Category IV assesses your understanding of all living things including plants, prokaryotes, protists, fungi, invertebrates, and vertebrates. You must be able to explain the life cycles, reproductive strategies, and significant processes of each category of life. You must also be able to identify their major classifications and how the living creatures maintain homeostasis. Finally, you should know the major organs and systems of animals and plants.

Category V covers the relationships between living organisms and the environment and the role of these relationships in shaping specific ecosystems. You should know the relationships within and among species and the factors that influence population size. You should also understand the changes that occur during ecological succession, the different types of biomes and how energy flows within them, and the biogeochemical cycles, as well as how scientists organize and model this information. Finally, you should demonstrate an understanding of how natural phenomena can impact biodiversity and ecosystems, how ecosystems connect to each other, and how humans impact ecological systems.

Category VI assesses your societal perspective on science and technology. Specifically, you must demonstrate an understanding of the ethical, legal, economic, and social implications of scientific research. You must also demonstrate comprehension of the major challenges in biology today, including the environment, management of natural resources, and globalization.

How is the Praxis Biology Test Scored?

Your scores on your Praxis Biology test will become available online on a predetermined release date ten to eleven days after the close of your testing window. For more information, check https://www.ets.org/praxis. Your scores will be available for one year after your test date. In order to have your scores sent out to a particular institution, you must make a request when you register for the exam. You can select up to four institutions.

Each multiple-choice question is worth one raw point. The total number of questions you answer correctly is added up to obtain your raw score, which is then converted to a scale of 100 – 300. The passing score is determined by each state; requirements can be found here: https://www.ets.org/praxis/states.

There will be some questions on the test that are not scored; however, you will not know which ones these are. ETS uses these to test out new questions for future exams.

There is no guess penalty on the Praxis, so you should always guess if you do not know the answer to a question.

How is the Praxis Biology Test Administered?

The Praxis Biology test is a computer-based test offered in pre-determined testing windows at a range of universities and testing centers. Check out https://www.ets.org/praxis/ for more information.

You will need to print your registration ticket from your online account and bring it, along with your identification, to the testing site on test day. No pens, pencils, erasers, printed or written materials, electronic devices, or calculators are allowed. You also may not bring any kind of bag or wear headwear (unless for religious purposes). You may take the test once every twenty-one days.

About Cirrus Test Prep

Cirrus Test Prep study guides are designed by current and former educators and are tailored to meet your needs as an incoming educator. Our guides offer all of the resources necessary to help you pass teacher certification tests across the nation.

Cirrus clouds are graceful, wispy clouds characterized by their high altitude. Just like cirrus clouds, Cirrus Test Prep's goal is to help educators "aim high" when it comes to obtaining their teacher certification and entering the classroom.

About This Guide

This guide will help you master the most important test topics and also develop critical test-taking skills. We have built features into our books to prepare you for your tests and increase your score. Along with a detailed summary of the test's format, content, and scoring, we offer an in-depth overview of the content knowledge required to pass the test. Our sidebars provide interesting information, highlight key concepts, and review content so that you can solidify your understanding of the exam's concepts. Test your knowledge with sample questions and detailed answer explanations in the text that help you think through the problems on the exam and practice questions that reflect the content and format of the Praxis Biology test. We're pleased you've chosen Cirrus to be a part of your professional journey!

Molecular and Cellular Biology

All organisms share a set of common properties. Organisms can be single celled or multicellular and survive and persist through a system of chemical reactions called metabolism. Homeostasis is necessary for coordinating the biological processes of the cell, and all organisms grow, replicate, and carry hereditary information that can be passed on to their offspring or daughter cells by some form of reproduction.

To understand these properties and how organisms function, it's necessary to understand many different molecular and cellular processes, including the biochemistry and functions of macromolecules, anabolic and catabolic pathways, the structure and organization of both prokaryotic and eukaryotic cells, cell division, and the processes of meiosis.

BIOLOGICAL MOLECULES

An understanding of chemistry is critical to understanding living organisms. The chemicals that comprise life have structure, which often influences their functions, and the properties of these chemicals allow them to bind to form the biomolecules of a cell. All of this chemistry is organized by water. Therefore life requires water. The human body, for instance, is about two-thirds water.

ATOMIC STRUCTURE

Life is composed of matter, which is any substance that has mass and occupies space. One of the smallest and most fundamental units of matter is the **atom**. The center of an atom is called the **nucleus**, which is composed of two subatomic particles: (1) **neutrons**, which carry no electrical charge, and (2) **protons**, which are positively charged particles. The atomic number of an atom refers to the number of protons in its nucleus, while the mass number of an atom equals the number of protons and neutrons in the nucleus.

Atoms also contain negatively charged particles called **electron**s that orbit the nucleus. Electrons are located in **shells** whose energy level varies with their distance from the nucleus: shells close to the nucleus have less energy than those farther away. An atom's outermost shell is its **valence shell**; the electrons in this shell are involved in chemical reactions with other atoms.

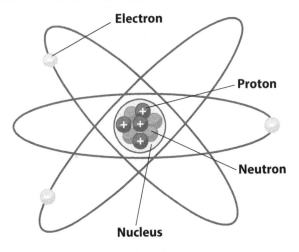

Figure 1.1. Structure of an Atom

SAMPLE QUESTIONS

1) If the atomic number of a neutral atom is 6, how many protons and electrons does the atom have?

   A. 0 protons and 6 electrons

   B. 3 protons and 3 electrons

   C. 6 protons and 0 electrons

   D. 6 protons and 6 electrons

   Answer:

   D. Correct. The atomic number of this atom is 6, so it must have 6 protons. For the atom to be neutral, it must have the same number of protons and electrons.

2) The mass number of an atom is 23, and its atomic number is 11. How many protons, electrons, and neutrons does this atom have?

   A. 11 protons, 11 electrons, and 12 neutrons

   B. 11 protons, 11 electrons, and 1 neutron

   C. 11 protons, 1 electron, and 11 neutrons

   D. 6 protons, 5 electrons, and 12 neutrons

Answer:

A.   **Correct.** The number of protons in the nucleus of an atom equals the atomic number (in this case, 11). The number of protons and neutrons in the nucleus of an atom equals the mass number (23 – 11 protons = 12 neutrons). And the number of protons and electrons in an atom are equal, because atoms are electrically neutral.

CHEMICAL BONDING

Atoms will share, gain, or lose electrons to fill their valence shell with eight electrons. These processes result in the **chemical bonds** that hold atoms together. A group of atoms joined by chemical bonds forms a **molecule**. A **compound** is defined as a molecule made of at least two different atoms. All compounds, therefore, are molecules, but not all molecules are compounds. For example, oxygen (O_2) is a molecule that consists of two chemically bonded oxygen atoms, but it is not a compound because the atoms are the same. A macromolecule, however, contains carbons and hydrogens—because a macromolecule is an organic compound.

An **ionic bond** forms when one atom donates an electron to another atom. The classic example is the ionic bond that forms between an atom of sodium (Na) and an atom of chlorine (Cl). A sodium atom donates its outermost electron to a chlorine atom; in losing its electron, the sodium atom becomes a positively charged ion (Na^+)—called a cation—resulting in a full outer valence shell. The chlorine atom on the other hand gains an electron to become a negatively charged ion (Cl^-)—called an anion—and this interaction fills its outer valence shell. These charged ions are attracted to each other and form an intricate molecule of ionic bonds commonly known as table salt.

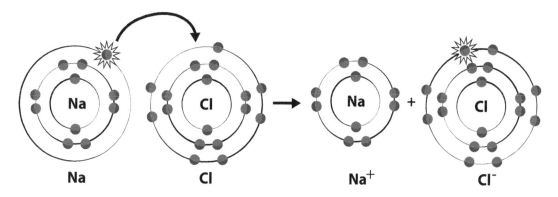

Figure 1.2. Ionic Bonds of Table Salt

A **covalent bond** is the stronger of the two main chemical bonds; it is also the most common bond holding biological molecules together. Covalent bonds form when two atoms share electrons. Atoms share electrons in order to fill their outermost electron, or valence, shell. Generally, this is made up of eight electrons in the outermost shell for most atoms and two electrons for the atoms of hydrogen and helium. Hydrogen gas is an example of a molecule held together by a covalent bond that forms between two hydrogen atoms. A hydrogen atom carries a single electron in its outermost electron shell. However when one atom of hydrogen shares its electron with a second atom of hydrogen, the two atoms carry two electrons, which give each atom a full and stable outermost electron shell.

Figure 1.3. The Covalent Bond Between Two Atoms of Hydrogen

SAMPLE QUESTIONS

3) **Which of the following terms describes an atom that has donated an electron to become a positively charged particle?**

   A.   anion

   B.   cation

   C.   compound

   D.   molecule

   Answers:

   A.   Incorrect. an anion is a negatively charged ion.

   B.   Correct. An atom that loses an electron becomes a positively charged ion called a cation.

   C.   Incorrect. A compound is composed of two or more different atoms joined together.

   D.   Incorrect. A molecule is composed of two more of the same type of atom.

4) **A carbon atom has four electrons in its valence shell, while a hydrogen atom has one electron in its valence shell. How many atoms of hydrogen can be covalently bonded to carbon?**

   A.   two

   B.   three

   C.   four

   D.   five

   Answer:

   C.   Correct. When carbon shares its four electrons with four hydrogen atoms, the outermost electron shell of each atom becomes full. (The resulting compound is methane, CH_4.)

ORGANIC AND INORGANIC MOLECULES

The cells and bodies of all living organisms contain many different kinds of molecules. These molecules are usually held together by covalent bonds and often consist of carbon atoms in rings or long chains. Other atoms—such as hydrogen, oxygen, and nitrogen—can attach to these carbon atoms. If a molecule contains carbon and hydrogen atoms, it is called an **organic molecule**. Large organic molecules that contain many atoms and repeating units are often called **macromolecules**. Life is built from four main macromolecules: proteins, lipids, nucleic acids, and carbohydrates.

In contrast, **inorganic molecules** usually contain a small number of atoms held together by ionic bonds. Unlike organic molecules, inorganic molecules do not have carbons attached to hydrogens. These molecules often contain metals and nonmetals, and although most inorganic molecules are not as common in living organisms as organic molecules, organisms still require certain inorganic molecules for survival. Water, for instance, does not contain carbon, so it is not classified as an organic molecule. Yet, to persist, all life needs water.

SAMPLE QUESTION

5)   Which of the following is an organic molecule?

A. CO_2

B. CH_4

C. NH_3

D. H_2

Answers:

A.   Incorrect. This molecule has carbon but not hydrogen, so it is not organic.

B.   Correct. By definition, an organic molecule contains atoms of both carbon and hydrogen.

C.   Incorrect. This molecule does not contain carbon.

D.   Incorrect. This molecule does not contain carbon.

PROPERTIES OF WATER

Unlike most inorganic molecules, the two hydrogen atoms and single oxygen atom that comprise water (H_2O) are held together by covalent bonds. These atoms do not share electrons equally, however. Oxygen attracts electrons more strongly than hydrogen atoms; therefore, oxygen carries a partial negative charge, while the hydrogen atoms carry partial positive charges. This type of covalent bond is called a **polar bond**, which makes water a polar molecule. When the negative end of one polar molecule binds to a hydrogen atom on another polar molecule, a **hydrogen bond** forms.

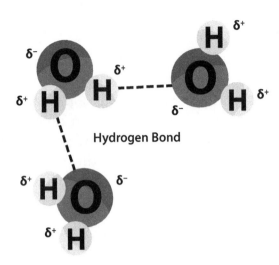

Figure 1.4. Hydrogen Bonds of Water

Although an individual hydrogen bond is a weak chemical bond, water contains many hydrogen bonds. Together, these bonds give water the properties that make it essential for life. Polar molecules, for instance, are attracted to each other; **cohesion** is the attraction between two water molecules. Cohesion creates the high **surface tension** of water, which is the force that allows certain insects to stride across the surface of a pond or lake and organizes biomolecules into cellular structures like membranes and organelles. Water molecules are also very attracted to other types of molecules, a property called **adhesion**. This property allows water to "climb" against gravity via **capillary action.**

Hydrogen bonds also influence the **specific heat** of water. Water molecules are held tightly together by hydrogen bonds, which means that a lot of energy is needed to heat water; therefore, water heats slowly but also maintains its temperature longer.

Lastly, water is often referred to as the "universal solvent" because its polarity allows it to dissolve other polar substances, such as salts. However, nonpolar substances, such as oils, will not dissolve in water.

SAMPLE QUESTIONS

6) **Which of the following properties of water causes water droplets to form beads on surfaces, such as on a leaf?**

   A.   adhesion
   B.   specific heat
   C.   surface tension
   D.   ability to dissolve substances

Answer:

C.   **Correct.** Surface tension pulls together the molecules on the surface of water, forcing them to form a sphere, or bead.

7)   **Which of the following bonds gives rise to the properties of water that make it essential for life?**

A.   the ionic bonds between water molecules

B.   the ionic bonds within a water molecule

C.   the hydrogen bonds between water molecules

D.   the hydrogen bonds within a water molecule

Answers:

A.   Incorrect. Water molecules do not bond to each other through ionic bonds.

B.   Incorrect. Hydrogen atoms are bound to the oxygen atom in water by covalent bonds.

C.   **Correct.** The hydrogen bonds that form among water molecules hold these molecules together tightly and influence all the important properties of water.

D.   Incorrect. Hydrogen bonds form between (and within) polar molecules.

MACROMOLECULES

The covalent bonds that join each subunit of a macromolecule form when one subunit loses a hydroxyl group (OH), while the other subunit loses an atom of hydrogen (H). Since water is lost to form the bond, this process is called **dehydration synthesis**. The four macromolecules are: proteins, carbohydrates, lipids, and nucleic acids. **Proteins** are built from amino acids; enzymes are important proteins that catalyze the chemical reactions of a cell. **Carbohydrates** are polymers made of carbon, hydrogen, and oxygen atoms; they are also known as sugars, and one of their most important functions is to store energy. **Lipids** are built from fatty acids and glycerol and play important roles in the cell, including in energy storage and in the structure of membranes. Long chains of nucleotides form the two types of **nucleic acids**—DNA (deoxyribonucleic acid) and RNA (ribonucleic acid)—which store the genetic information of a cell. (Nucleic acids are covered in more detail later in this chapter.)

> **HELPFUL HINT**
>
> Dehydration synthesis is easily distinguished from hydrolysis (when water reacts with a molecule and chemical bonds are broken), because the prefix *de–* means removal, loss, or separation; *hydro* means water. Loss of water creates a bond between two atoms; the addition of water breaks a bond between two atoms.

SAMPLE QUESTION

8) Proteins are built from which of the following monomers?

   A. monosaccharides

   B. nucleotides

   C. amino acids

   D. fatty acids

   Answers:

   A. Incorrect. Monosaccharide are the monomers of carbohydrates.

   B. Incorrect. Nucleotides are the monomers of nucleic acids.

   C. Correct. Amino acids are the building blocks of proteins.

   D. Incorrect. Fatty acids are the monomers of lipids.

CHEMICAL PRINCIPLES

Every biological process—from the synthesis of a sugar molecule to the insertion of that molecule into the cell membrane of an organism—is dependent on the principles of molecular chemistry. These principles govern the movement of electrons from one molecule to another, the formation of a chemical gradient that drives the production of cellular energy, the degradation or synthesis of molecules, and many more essential processes of a cell or organism.

CHEMICAL AND PHYSICAL GRADIENTS

A **gradient** refers to a change—usually the **rate** of increase or decrease—in the value of a **variable** that influences the growth or persistence of a cell. Physical gradients, like **pressure gradients** or **temperature gradients**, form when changes in physical variables occur over a specified distance.

Chemical **gradients** are an integral part of cell processes. For example, the difference in the concentration of protons inside and outside a cell gives the membrane an electrical charge and creates a **potential gradient** across the membrane. Cell signaling and cell-to-cell communication are driven by changes in membrane potential.

SAMPLE QUESTION

9) Which of the following scenarios would most likely result in a membrane potential?

A.   The concentration of potassium ions inside the cell is the same as the concentration of hydrogen ions outside the cell.

B.   The concentration of potassium inside the cell is the same as the concentration of oxygen outside the cell.

C.   The concentration of potassium inside the cell is greater than the concentration of potassium outside the cell.

D.   The concentration of potassium ions inside the cell is greater than the concentration of potassium ions outside the cell.

Answer:

D.   **Correct.** Membrane potentials generally form in response to differences in the concentration of a charged particle—an ion—across a cell membrane. The other options would not create a difference in charge across the membrane.

THERMODYNAMICS

All the work an organism does, from metabolizing food to walking, requires **energy**. The source of energy for all life is sunlight. Photosynthetic organisms, like plants, algae, and some bacteria, convert light energy into chemical energy, which then becomes available to all other organisms.

Thermodynamics is the study of energy and its transformations. The **first law of thermodynamics** is the conservation law. This law states that energy can change from one form to another (for example, from light energy to chemical energy) but energy can never be created or destroyed and that the total amount of energy in a system, such as the universe, is constant. The **second law of thermodynamics** governs the direction that energy flows or changes. Energy flows through a system, or changes, until it reaches a state of **equilibrium**. For example, energy will flow from a higher temperature to a lower temperature or from a higher pressure to a lower pressure. And as this spontaneous energy flow or transformation occurs, **entropy**—the measure of disorder in a system—increases.

SAMPLE QUESTION

10) **Which of the following statements about thermodynamics explains why energy is required to move a hydrogen atom against a chemical gradient?**

A.   The first law of thermodynamics states that energy can neither be created nor destroyed.

B.   The second law of thermodynamics states that energy must be conserved.

C.   The first law of thermodynamics states that entropy increases.

D.   The second law of thermodynamics states that entropy increases.

Answers:

A.   Incorrect. The conservation law refers to the amount of energy in the universe, whereas this question refers to the movement or transformation of energy.

B.   Incorrect. The first law of thermodynamics, not the second law of thermodynamics, refers to the conservation of energy.

C.   Incorrect. The second law of thermodynamics, not the first law of thermodynamics, refers to the tendency for the entropy of a system to increase.

D.   Correct. Without an input of energy, a hydrogen atom will move to areas of lower (not higher) concentration because this movement increases the entropy of the system.

ANABOLIC AND CATABOLIC REACTIONS

Cells are dynamic entities; they consume and release energy. The sum of all of the constantly occurring chemical reactions of a cell is called **metabolism**. There are two types of **metabolic reactions**: **anabolic reactions** and **catabolic reactions**. Enzymes catalyze both of these types of reactions. **Anabolism** can also be referred to as biosynthesis, because anabolic reactions use energy to build, or synthesize, complex molecules—like proteins, lipids, carbohydrates, and nucleic acids—from simpler molecules. Energy drives dehydration synthesis, which forms covalent bonds between these simple subunits. **Catabolism**, in contrast, releases energy. Catabolic reactions, therefore, can be thought of as degradation reactions or hydrolytic reactions because, to release energy, the bonds of a molecule must be broken. **Hydrolysis**, or the addition of water to a molecule, is one way to break a covalent bond between two atoms.

SAMPLE QUESTION

11)   **Which of the following equations is an anabolic reaction?**

A. $6CO_2 + 6H_2O \rightarrow C_6H_{12}O_6 + 6O_2$

B. $2H_2O_2 \rightarrow 2H_2O + O_2$

C. $C_6H_{12}O_6 + 6O_2 \rightarrow 6CO_2 + 6H_2O$

D. $2NH_3 \rightarrow N_2 + 3H_2$

Answers:

A.   Correct. This is the equation for photosynthesis, whereby sugars are synthesized from carbon dioxide and water.

B.   Incorrect. The degradation of hydrogen peroxide is a catabolic reaction.

C.   Incorrect. This is the equation for aerobic respiration: glucose is broken down—or catabolized—completely to carbon dioxide and water, and energy is released in the process.

D.   Incorrect. The degradation of ammonia is a catabolic reaction.

OXIDATION–REDUCTION REACTIONS

To survive and persist, a cell must continuously extract energy from the chemical bonds in food sources like carbohydrates. When a chemical bond is broken, electrons are harvested and used to synthesize adenosine triphosphate (ATP), the molecule that stores energy. When ATP is degraded, energy is subsequently released and used for biosynthesis.

The degradation of a food source—like glucose—to release electrons is called an oxidation reaction. When a molecule is oxidized, or loses an electron (or a hydrogen atom), that electron (or hydrogen atom) is accepted by another molecule. The molecule that accepts the electron (or hydrogen atom) is reduced, and this transfer of electrons (or hydrogen atoms) from one molecule to another is called an **oxidation-reduction (redox) reaction**. The oxidation state—or oxidation number—of an atom indicates how many electrons the atom can gain or lose in a redox reaction. For instance, the oxidation state of the oxygen ion (O^{-2}) is –2, because it can donate two electrons to form a chemical bond.

QUICK REVIEW

What is a reduction potential and how does it relate to the tendency of a molecule to be a good reducing agent versus a good oxidizing agent?

SAMPLE QUESTION

12) If the iron ion Fe^{+3} has an oxidation number of +3, which TWO of the following are true?

  A. Fe^{+3} can donate three electrons to form a chemical bond.

  B. Fe^{+3} can accept an electron to form a chemical bond.

  C. Fe^{+3} is an oxidizing agent.

  D. Fe^{+3} is a reducing agent.

Answers:

  A. Incorrect. An oxidation number—or oxidation state—of +3 indicates that the iron ion can gain three electrons.

  B. Correct. The iron ion can accept, or gain, three electrons from another molecule.

  C. Correct. When the iron ion accepts electrons from another molecule, it becomes reduced, and the other molecule becomes oxidized, which makes the iron ion an oxidizing agent.

  D. Incorrect. Reducing agents lose, or donate, electrons to another molecule in a redox reaction.

Enzymes

Enzyme Function

Enzymes are the proteins of a cell that catalyze, or speed up, chemical reactions. Enzymes are complex, three–dimensional, globular proteins with folds and twists that form a groove into which another molecule(s) fits. Enzymes act by binding molecules, also known as **substrates**, and bringing atoms close together to catalyze a change to those molecules by, for example, breaking or synthesizing a covalent bond between two atoms. The tendency of an enzyme to bind a certain substrate(s) and catalyze a certain set of reactions is known as **specificity**.

> **DID YOU KNOW?**
>
> A **coenzyme** is a nonprotein molecule that binds to an enzyme and helps the enzyme do its job.

The **active site** of an enzyme consists of grooves or depressions on the enzyme surface that bind to the substrate(s) of a chemical reaction. The substrate(s)—or reactant(s)—fits into the enzyme like a key fits into a lock to form an **enzyme-substrate complex**.

The active site of some enzymes changes shape when bound to a substrate(s). This is called **induced fit** because the substrate(s) induces the enzyme to mold itself around the substrate(s). This change in the shape of the enzyme aligns the catalytic groups of the enzyme.

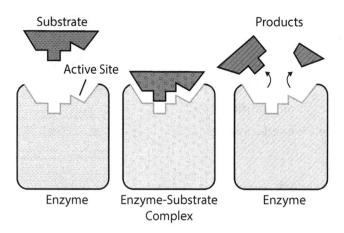

Figure 1.5. Enzyme–Substrate Complex

Any factor that changes the shape of an enzyme will influence the activity of that enzyme. Two key environmental factors that influence enzyme activity are **pH** and **temperature**. A change in pH may alter the shape or charge of an enzyme; therefore, most enzymes work best within a specific pH range. An increase in temperature weakens the bonds that hold an enzyme together and may ultimately cause the enzyme to unfold or denature.

Chemicals called **inhibitors** can also interfere with the function of an enzyme. In competitive inhibition, for instance, a molecule of a shape similar to the substrate of an enzyme competes with the substrate for the active site of the enzyme. If the enzyme binds the non-substrate molecule, the chemical reaction slows or even stops. Drugs used to treat infectious diseases are often enzyme inhibitors; likewise, some pesticides use enzyme inhibitors.

SAMPLE QUESTION

13) **Which of the following terms describes a molecule that inhibits the function of an enzyme by altering the shape of the enzyme's active site?**

   A.   coenzyme

   B.   repressor

   C.   activator

   D.   substrate

   Answers:

   A.   Incorrect. A coenzyme binds an enzyme to form an active enzyme that can catalyze a chemical reaction.

   B.   **Correct.** A repressor molecule inhibits an enzyme from binding its substrate(s) by binding to the enzyme and changing the shape of the active site.

   C.   Incorrect. An activator binds an enzyme and changes the shape of the active site in a way that it can recognize and bind to the substrate(s).

   D.   Incorrect. The substrate bonds to the enzyme's active site during the normal functioning of an enzyme.

REGULATION

When an enzyme binds a substrate(s), it catalyzes a change in that substrate(s), which results in a product that is released from the enzyme. Enzymes are not used up in the reactions they catalyze. In addition, some enzymes bind more than one substrate. For these reasons, cells have evolved strategies for regulating the activities of enzymes. Two of these strategies are feedback inhibition and cooperative binding.

In **feedback inhibition**, the product of the enzymatic reaction can bind the enzyme to repress the action of the enzyme. If the product of the reaction blocks the active site of the enzyme, then the repressor is called a competitive inhibitor. Some repressors, however, force a change in the shape of the enzyme by binding to the enzyme at a site other than the active site; this conformational change in the enzyme prevents the enzyme from binding a substrate, and this repressor is called a noncompetitive inhibitor.

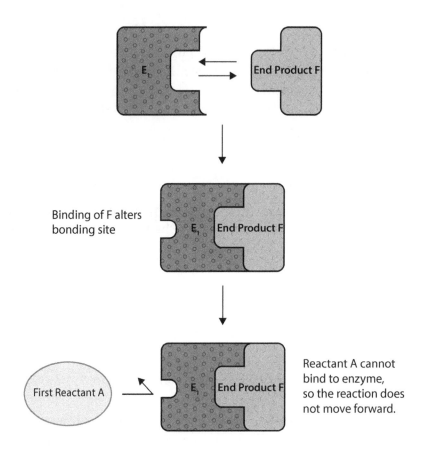

Binding of F alters
bonding site

Reactant A cannot
bind to enzyme,
so the reaction does
not move forward.

Figure 1.6. Feedback Inhibition

Cooperative binding is an important regulation strategy for enzymes that bind more than one substrate. In cooperative binding, a substrate bound to one active site effects a change in the other active sites to either increase the affinity of those sites for the substrate (in positive cooperativity) or decrease the affinity of the remaining sites for the substrate (in negative cooperativity).

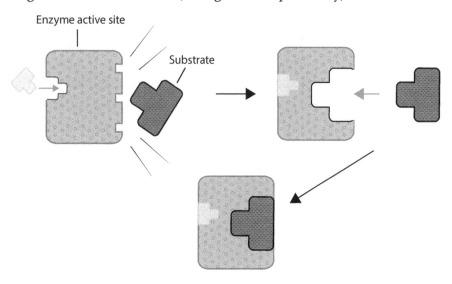

Figure 1.7. Cooperative Binding

SAMPLE QUESTION

14) Which of the following types of regulation is described below?

Enzyme *X* catalyzes the metabolism of Amino Acid *G*. When Amino Acid *G* is bound to Enzyme *X*, the affinity for Amino Acid *G* increases at the other active sites on Enzyme *X*.

A.   competitive inhibition

B.   noncompetitive inhibition

C.   positive cooperativity

D.   negative cooperativity

Answers:

A.   Incorrect. Competitive inhibition is a type of feedback inhibition, which represses the action of the enzyme.

B.   Incorrect. Noncompetitive inhibition is a type of feedback inhibition, which represses the action of the enzyme.

C.   Correct. In positive cooperativity, when substrate binds one of the active sites on an enzyme, the affinity for the substrate at the other active sites increases.

D.   Incorrect. In negative cooperativity, a substrate bound to one active site on the enzyme decreases the affinity for the substrate at the other active sites on the enzyme.

BIOCHEMICAL PATHWAYS

Living things require energy to do cellular work, for example, to maintain membranes, to build proteins, and to carry out cell division. The sun is the source of energy that flows through most biological systems. Plants, algae, and photosynthetic bacteria capture this light energy and—through a series of chemical reactions—transform this energy into chemical energy, namely the sugars used by the cells of a living organism.

A chemical reaction occurs when a chemical bond forms between two atoms or when a chemical bond between two atoms breaks. Chemical reactions are catalyzed by enzymes and often occur in a series, where the product of one reaction becomes the substrate for the next reaction, and so on. A set sequence of chemical reactions is called a **biochemical pathway**.

Biochemical pathways drive the various forms of metabolism, including photosynthesis, cellular respiration, and chemosynthesis.

> **HELPFUL HINT**
>
> The enzymes that catalyze some biochemical pathways are often situated near each other in a cell membrane. Because the enzymes are close together, the chemical reactions of the pathway proceed faster.

PHOTOSYNTHESIS

The sun powers nearly all biological systems on this planet. Prokaryotic organisms, including certain bacteria, and eukaryotic organisms, like plants and algae, harness the energy of sunlight and transform it into chemical energy through biochemical pathways called **photosynthesis**.

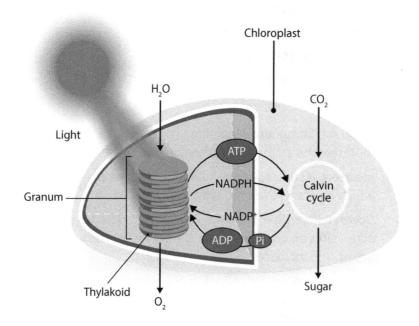

Figure 1.8. Photosynthesis

This discussion will focus on how photosynthesis works in eukaryotic cells—complex cells with membrane-bound compartments called organelles. An example of an organelle is the nucleus. A maple tree is an example of a eukaryotic, photosynthetic organism. When light shines on a maple leaf, it penetrates the interior mesophyll cells, which are filled with green organelles called **chloroplasts**.

Inside each chloroplast are stacks of flat, interconnected sacs called thylakoids, and within the membrane of each thylakoid sac are light-absorbing pigments called chlorophyll. Proteins anchor chlorophyll molecules to the thylakoid membrane so as to form a **photosystem**, or network of chlorophyll and protein molecules.

Two photosystems comprise the light-dependent reactions of photosynthesis. A cell captures photons of energy when light strikes a chlorophyll molecule in **photosystem II**; some of the electrons of the chlorophyll molecule become "excited" as they are boosted to a higher energy level. This excitation energy is passed from one chlorophyll molecule to another until it reaches a special chlorophyll molecule at the reaction center. Here, the excited electron is released from photosystem II to an electron transport system. As this electron is lost from photosystem II, an enzyme-catalyzed reaction splits water to release O_2, which is one of the products of photosynthesis.

In **electron transport**, an electron cascades through a series of protein carriers embedded in the thylakoid membrane. At one protein molecule, the energy of the electron is used to pump protons into the thylakoid space. The concentration of these protons increases until the protons flow down their concentration gradient and out of the thylakoid space through a protein called ATP synthase.

In addition to producing ATP, the electron transport system transfers an electron from photosystem II to **photosystem I**. Although photosystem I accepts an electron from photosystem II, photosystem I also has an antenna complex of chlorophyll molecules that captures photons. And, like photosystem II, photosystem I passes its electrons to an electron transport system. Instead of ATP, however, NADPH (an electron carrier) is produced from this transport.

The ATP from photosystem II and the NADPH from photosystem I enter the Calvin cycle, which occurs in the stroma (interior, liquid part of the chloroplast). The energy stored in ATP and the hydrogen atoms of NADPH power the chemical reactions of the Calvin cycle that produce carbohydrates, specifically glucose ($C_6H_{12}O_6$). The Calvin cycle is also called C_3 **photosynthesis**; in this biochemical pathway, the carbon from atmospheric CO_2 is "fixed" to an organic molecule to form glucose. This is also called carbon fixation.

The balanced chemical equation for photosynthesis then is:

$$6CO_2 + 6H_2O \rightarrow C_6H_{12}O_6 + 6O_2$$

In hot, dry climates, plants like corn and grasses fix carbon by a pathway called C_4 **photosynthesis**. Before CO_2 enters the Calvin cycle in C_4 plants, it is generated in a two-step process: first, malate (malic acid) is produced in mesophyll cells; then in bundle-sheath cells, malate is degraded to release CO_2.

> **HELPFUL HINT**
>
> Chemosynthetic microbes and photosynthetic organisms are similar in that they are autotrophs. The prefix *auto-* means self, and *-troph* means to obtain food or to eat. The self-feeding autotrophs make their own food (sugar) by reducing carbon dioxide.

SAMPLE QUESTIONS

15) **Why do some photosynthetic structures, like leaves, appear green?**

   A.   The epidermis of the leaf absorbs red and blue light.

   B.   The epidermis of the leaf absorbs green light.

   C.   The chlorophyll of the leaf absorbs red and blue light.

   D.   The chlorophyll of the leaf absorbs green light.

Answer:

   C.   **Correct.** Light passes through the epidermis and strikes the pigment chlorophyll, which absorbs the wavelengths of light that humans see as red and blue and reflects the wavelengths of light that the human eye perceives as green.

16) The Calvin cycle produces one molecule of glucose from which of the following three molecules?

   A.   ATP, NADPH, and O_2

   B.   ATP, NADPH, and CO_2

   C. CO_2, H_2O, and ATP

   D. CO_2, H_2O, and O_2

   Answers:

   A.   Incorrect. Although ATP and NADPH are substrates of the Calvin cycle, O_2 is not. O_2 is a product of photosystem II.

   B.   **Correct.** Glucose is produced from CO_2 by the energy stored in ATP and the hydrogen atoms associated with NADPH.

   C.   Incorrect. ATP and CO_2 are needed for the Calvin cycle, but H_2O is not; H_2O is a substrate in photosystem II.

   D.   Incorrect. When H_2O is split in photosystem II, O_2 is released; in contrast, CO_2 is a substrate in the Calvin cycle.

CELLULAR RESPIRATION

In cellular respiration, food molecules, such as glucose, are oxidized, and electrons harvested from these molecules are used to make ATP. The first stage of cellular respiration is an **anaerobic** (does not require oxygen) process called **glycolysis**. Glycolysis takes place in the cytoplasm of a cell and comprises ten enzyme-catalyzed reactions that transform glucose into two molecules of pyruvate. In the process, two molecules of ATP are produced by substrate-level phosphorylation and two molecules of NAD^+ (an electron carrier) are reduced to two molecules of NADH. Under anaerobic conditions, pyruvate is reduced to acids and sometimes gases and/or alcohols in a process called fermentation. NAD^+ is recycled to drive more glycolysis.

Under aerobic conditions, however, pyruvate enters the second stage of cellular respiration—the **Krebs cycle**. The Krebs cycle takes place in the mitochondria, or tubular organelles, of a eukaryotic cell. Here, pyruvate is oxidized completely to form six molecules of carbon dioxide; two more molecules of ATP are produced by substrate-level phosphorylation, and ten molecules of NADH and two molecules of $FADH_2$ (an electron carrier) carry electrons into the final stage of cellular respiration—the electron transport chain.

Similar to the electron transport system in photosynthesis, electron transport in the mitochondria is a series of oxidation-reduction reactions, whereby electrons are transferred from electron carriers like NADH and $FADH_2$ to other carrier molecules, which continue to pass the electrons from carrier to carrier. This sequential movement of electrons drives the formation of a proton (H^+) gradient across the inner mitochondrial membrane. These protons eventually move back across the membrane-bound ATP synthase, which catalyzes the synthesis of ATP.

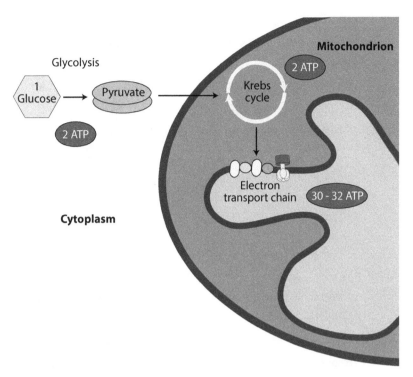

Figure 1.9. Cellular Respiration

Electron transport is responsible for the majority of ATP made during cellular respiration: thirty-four molecules of ATP are produced during electron transport, which means thirty-eight molecules of ATP are produced per molecule of glucose in cellular respiration. But this is the ideal scenario; the process is a bit less efficient than this because some ATP is needed to move NADH from the cytoplasm to the mitochondria in eukaryotic cells. The balanced chemical equation for cellular respiration is:

$$C_6H_{12}O_6 + 6O_2 \rightarrow 6CO_2 + 6H_2O$$

SAMPLE QUESTIONS

17) In the balanced chemical equation for cellular respiration, $C_6H_{12}O_6 + 6O_2 \rightarrow 6CO_2 + 6H_2O$, which molecule is oxidized and which is reduced?

   A. $C_6H_{12}O_6$ is oxidized and CO_2 is reduced

   B. $C_6H_{12}O_6$ is oxidized and O_2 is reduced

   C. O_2 is oxidized and H_2O is reduced

   D. O_2 is oxidized and $C_6H_{12}O_6$ is reduced

Answers:

   A.   Incorrect. Although the first part of this answer is correct—glucose *is* oxidized—the second part of this answer is incorrect. Carbon dioxide is a product of cellular respiration.

   B.   Correct. In cellular respiration, glucose serves as the electron donor, and oxygen serves as the final electron acceptor.

C.   Incorrect. Oxygen is the final electron acceptor in cellular respiration; therefore, oxygen is reduced. Water is the product of the reduction of oxygen.

D.   Incorrect. This is the opposite of what happens in cellular respiration.

18) **Which of the following molecules is the final electron acceptor in lactic acid fermentation?**

A. NAD^+

B.   NADH

C.   pyruvate

D. O_2

Answers:

A.   Incorrect. NAD+ is produced during fermentation and recycled into glycolysis.

B.   Incorrect. NADH is oxidized during fermentation.

C.   **Correct.** Pyruvate is reduced during fermentation; therefore, it serves as the final electron acceptor.

D.   Incorrect. Fermentation usually occurs in the absence of oxygen.

CHEMOSYNTHESIS

Although the source of energy for most living organisms is the sun, there are ecosystems on Earth that are devoid of sunlight. One of these ecosystems is found deep in the sea around cracks in the ocean floor. These cracks, or fissures, are called hydrothermal vents. These fissures spew hot, acidic fluid full of inorganic molecules, like hydrogen sulfide (H_2S). Bacteria and other microbes associated with these vents oxidize H_2S—and other inorganic electron donors—and use the electrons to reduce carbon dioxide (CO_2) to organic molecules, namely sugars. These microbes, and the organic molecules they produce, serve as the base of the food chain that supports the growth and persistence of deep-sea creatures like vent crabs, squat lobsters, and giant tubeworms.

SAMPLE QUESTION

19) **Which of the following is NOT a similarity between photosynthesis and chemosynthesis?**

A.   The electron donor in photosynthesis and chemosynthesis is water.

B.   The final electron acceptor in photosynthesis and chemosynthesis is carbon dioxide.

C.   Carbon dioxide is reduced to sugars in both processes.

D.   An inorganic molecule is a product of both processes.

Answers:

A. **Correct.** This is a difference between the two processes. Water is the electron donor in photosynthesis, but an inorganic molecule like hydrogen sulfide (H_2S) is the electron donor in chemosynthesis.

B. Incorrect. In both processes, carbon dioxide is reduced to organic molecules like sugars, so this is a similarity between the two processes.

C. Incorrect. This is also a similarity between the two processes.

D. Incorrect. Oxygen is produced during photosynthesis. In chemosynthesis, when a molecule like H_2S serves as an electron donor, sulfur is produced in the process.

STRUCTURE AND FUNCTION OF CELLS

The word **cell** comes from the Latin word *cella*, which means a small room or chamber. A cell, therefore, is the smallest unit of life. The cells of some organisms contain special compartments that carry out specific functions of the cell. These compartments are called **organelles**. Not all cells, however, carry organelles. Organelles are typically found in **eukaryotic cells** (complex cells with a membrane-bound nucleus) but not in **prokaryotic cells** (relatively simple cells that do not possess a membrane-bound nucleus).

ORGANELLES

Most organelles are membrane-bound structures, and each performs an important cellular process. The **nucleus**, for instance, is a spherical structure that houses the genetic information of an organism. The **Golgi apparatus** collects, packages, and distributes the proteins produced by ribosomes, which are found either free in the cytoplasm or attached to the **endoplasmic reticulum**. The Krebs cycle and electron transport chain are carried out in various parts of **mitochondria**; therefore, much of the energy-producing metabolism of a cell takes place in these organelles. A **lysosome** is an organelle that contains enzymes that degrade other molecules; these enzymes often catalyze hydrolytic reactions. **Chloroplasts** are plant organelles; the reactions of photosynthesis are catalyzed in these compartments. A chloroplast is a kind of **plastid**; plastids are organelles that synthesize or store sugars. **Vacuoles** are also typically found in plant cells; these organelles carry water and collect the metabolic waste products of a cell.

SAMPLE QUESTION

20) Which of the following structures is NOT bound by a cellular membrane?

    A.   nucleus

    B.   chloroplast

    C.   ribosome

    D.   lysosome

Answer:

C.   Correct. Ribosomes can be found free in the cytoplasm and not bound a cellular membrane. The other organelles are bound by cellular membranes.

PROKARYOTIC AND EUKARYOTIC CELLS

Prokaryotes are simple, single-celled organisms and include the bacteria and archaea. All other organisms on the planet are **eukaryotes**. Prokaryotic cells are generally smaller than eukaryotic cells and the DNA of a prokaryotic cell, which exists as a single circle of genetic material, is found in the cytoplasm. In contrast, the DNA of a eukaryotic cell is associated with protein and organized into linear chromosomes, which are housed in a membrane-bound nucleus. The lack of a membrane-bound nucleus is one of the defining features that set prokaryotic cells apart from eukaryotic cells.

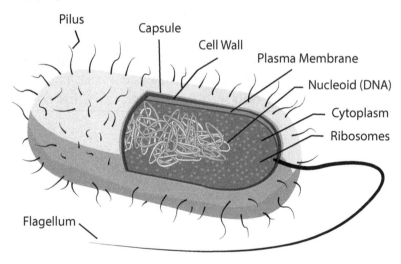

Figure 1.10. Prokaryotic Cell

The nucleus is just one of many organelles found in the eukaryotic cell. Prokaryotes, on the other hand, rarely carry internal compartments or possess internal membrane systems. Prokaryotes and certain eukaryotic cells are surrounded by a cell wall, but the prokaryotic cell wall is structurally more complex than the cell wall of a plant cell, for example. The primary compound in the prokaryotic cell wall is peptidoglycan, while the main structural component of plant cell walls is cellulose.

HELPFUL HINT

The diameter of a typical prokaryotic cell is about one micrometer, whereas the diameter of a typical eukaryotic cell is greater than ten micrometers.

Cell division also differs between prokaryotic cells (which divide by binary fission) and eukaryotic cells (which divide by mitosis). Finally, the metabolic pathways observed in prokaryotes differ from those of eukaryotic cells. In fact, the metabolic diversity of prokaryotic cells is much greater than that of eukaryotic cells and includes different forms of aerobic and anaerobic photosynthesis, chemosynthesis, and nitrogen fixation.

SAMPLE QUESTION

21) **Which of the following features distinguishes prokaryotic cells from eukaryotic cells?**

   A.   division by binary fission

   B.   the presence of DNA

   C.   an organized cell membrane

   D.   a rigid cell wall

Answer:

A.   **Correct.** Binary fission is characteristic of all prokaryotic cells but does not occur in eukaryotic cells. The other choices can be found in both prokaryotic and eukaryotic cells.

PLANTS VERSUS ANIMAL CELLS

Plant cells and **animal cells** are eukaryotic cells that have many similarities, including the following organelles: a nucleus, mitochondria, Golgi bodies, endoplasmic reticulum, and ribosomes. A cell membrane surrounds the cytoplasm of both cell types, but plant cells possess a cell wall of cellulose, whereas animal cells do not have a cell wall. Plant cells are, therefore, rectangular in shape, while animal cells are typically circular but can take on many different, irregular shapes.

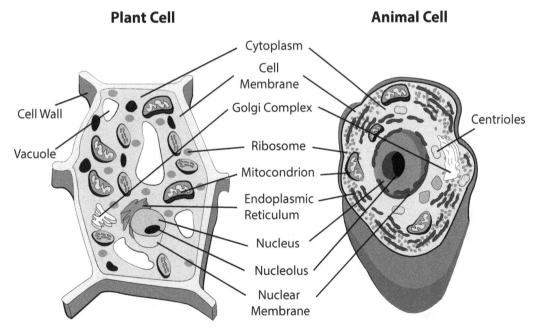

Figure 1.11. Plant Cell versus Animal Cell

Plant and animal cells differ in other ways. Animal cells carry lysosomes and plant cells do not. Plant cells carry chloroplasts and a large, central vacuole, while animal cells do not perform photosynthesis, so they do not possess chloroplasts. Animal cells also have either no vacuoles or have small vacuoles. Another difference is that flagella (whip-like structures that mediate movement of a cell) are typically found anchored to the cell membrane of an animal cell, but flagella are only found on plant gametes. Finally, plants are autotrophs; their primary metabolic strategy is photosynthesis, whereby they make their own food using sunlight to reduce carbon dioxide to sugar and oxidize water to oxygen. Animals, in contrast, are heterotrophs, which means they must get their food from another source.

SAMPLE QUESTION

22) **Which TWO of the following metabolic reactions occur in plants?**

A. $6CO_2 + 6H_2O \rightarrow C_6H_{12}O_6 + 6O_2$

B. $C_6H_{12}O_6 + 6O_2 \rightarrow 6CO_2 + 6H_2O$

C. $N_2 + 8H^+ + 8e^- \rightarrow 2NH_3 + H_2$

D. $CO_2 + 4H_2S + O_2 \rightarrow CH_2O + 4S + 3H_2O$

Answers:

A.   **Correct.** This is the balanced equation for photosynthesis, which is the metabolic lifestyle common to plant cells but not animal cells.

B.   **Correct.** This is the balanced equation for cellular respiration. Plants synthesize sugars via photosynthesis and, like most other eukaryotic cells, extract energy from those sugars via cellular respiration and store that energy as ATP.

C.   Incorrect. This is the balanced equation for nitrogen fixation, whereby prokaryotic cells convert atmospheric nitrogen into ammonia, which plant cells can use to grow.

D.   Incorrect. This is a chemosynthetic reaction carried out by hydrothermal vent bacteria.

CELL MEMBRANES

The **cytoplasm** of all cells, whether prokaryotic or eukaryotic, is surrounded by a **cell membrane**—or plasma membrane—made of two layers of phospholipids. A phospholipid molecule is composed of two parts: a polar head, and a chemical group containing phosphate (which makes the polar region hydrophilic) that is attached to two nonpolar, hydrophobic, fatty acid tails made of carbon and hydrogen. Because the long, nonpolar tails are repelled by water, the lipid bilayer of the cell membrane forms with the fatty acid tails on the inside of the membrane and the hydrophilic, phosphate heads on the outside.

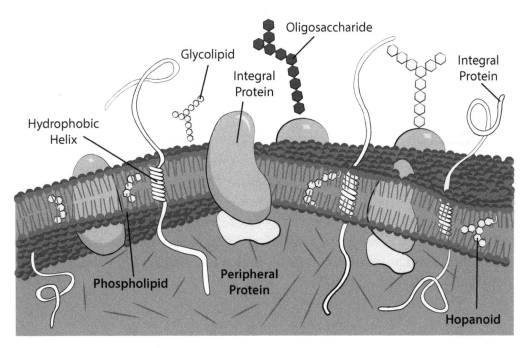

Figure 1.12. Lipid Bilayer of a Cell Membrane

In addition to the two layers of phospholipids, a cell membrane houses proteins that float within the bilayer structure, which is why the fluid mosaic model is the name given to the description of a plasma membrane. Some of these proteins reside on the surface of the membrane and bind molecules like hormones; some membrane proteins span the lipid bilayer and serve as bridges, or transmembrane channels, for molecules to get into or out of the cell. These protein channels do not let every kind of molecule into or out of the cell. Instead, each channel controls the passage of a specific molecule, which is called **selective permeability**. A cell membrane, therefore, is defined as a **semipermeable phospholipid bilayer**.

> **DID YOU KNOW?**
>
> Phospholipids and proteins are not the only components of a cell membrane. Molecules of cholesterol, a kind of lipid, and certain carbohydrates are scattered throughout the phospholipid bilayer.

SAMPLE QUESTION

23) **Which of the following is true about the phospholipids that make up the cellular membrane?**

   A. The phosphate heads of the bilayer interact with the extracellular environment and the cytoplasm.

   B. The phosphate heads of the bilayer interact with the cytoplasm only.

   C. The fatty acid tails of the bilayer interact with the extracellular environment and the cytoplasm.

   D. The fatty acid tails of the bilayer interact with the cytoplasm only.

Answer:

A.   **Correct.** The bilayer forms with the polar heads on the outside and the fatty acid tails on the inside; therefore, the polar heads are exposed to both the external environment of the cell as well as the cytoplasm.

CYTOSKELETON

Attached to proteins embedded in the plasma membrane of a eukaryotic cell is a web of protein fibers called the **cytoskeleton**. This internal scaffolding gives an animal cell its shape, and certain enzymes and organelles, like mitochondria, are found anchored to this structure. The cytoskeleton is built from three types of protein fibers: thick fibers of intertwined proteins called **intermediate filaments**; hollow tubes, or **microtubules**, made of a protein called *tubulin*; and long, thin fibers of actin called **microfilaments**.

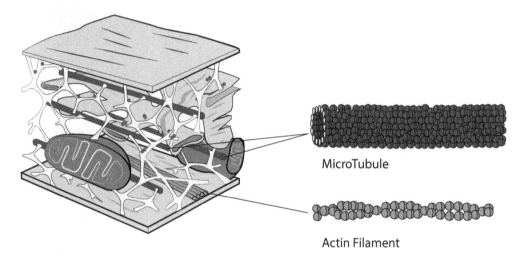

MicroTubule

Actin Filament

Figure 1.13. Protein Fibers of the Cytoskeleton

The cytoskeleton is a dynamic structure. The protein fibers assemble and disassemble continuously, and each type of fiber plays an important role in cell structure and function. Intermediate filaments, for instance, give the cell strength and prevent the cell from stretching too much. Microtubules, which are assembled by the centrioles of a cell, play a role in the separation of chromosomes during cell division and are a key structural component in the flagella of eukaryotic cells. The rapid assembly and disassembly of microfilaments drives distortions in cell shape and cell movement.

SAMPLE QUESTION

24)   **Which of the following protein fibers of the cytoskeleton are primarily responsible for the crawling movement of cells such as white blood cells?**

A.   flagella

B.   intermediate filaments

C.   microtubules

D.   microfilaments

Answers:

A.   Incorrect. Flagella are rich in microtubules; these structures protrude from the cell surface.

B.   Incorrect. These thick, ropelike fibers give the cell strength.

C.   Incorrect. Although these structures can play a role in movement, microfilaments drive the crawling movement of cells such as white blood cells.

D.   Correct. These fibers are made of actin, and it is the arrangement of microfilaments that allows for crawling—a phenomenon observed in inflammation, clotting, wound healing, and in the spread of cancer cells.

CELL EQUILIBRIUM AND COMMUNICATION

The cell membrane mediates several processes to maintain **cell equilibrium** and responds to signals released by neighboring cells. These processes include **selective permeability**, **osmosis**, **exocytosis** and **endocytosis**, and **intercellular communication**. These processes ensure the stable internal cellular environment necessary for each cell to function efficiently and for cells to interact and communicate with each other properly.

SELECTIVE PERMEABILITY

The cell membrane is selectively permeable: transmembrane proteins regulate the movement of molecules into and out of the cell. The survival of a cell is dependent on this movement: the cell must acquire nutrients and eliminate waste molecules. The movement of molecules across the cell membrane, therefore, influences the proper functioning of the cell.

Diffusion describes the movement of a molecule down its **concentration gradient**—its movement from an area where the molecule is at a high concentration to an area where the molecule is at a low concentration. When diffusion occurs across a semipermeable membrane, equilibrium is reached when there is no net movement of molecules into or out of a cell. In other words, the molecule moves into the cell at the same rate as it moves out of the cell.

Diffusion can occur passively, or without an input of energy. Two types of passive diffusion that occur across the cell membrane are simple and facilitated diffusion. In **simple diffusion**, small and/or hydrophobic molecules, such as O_2, slip down their concentration gradient and through the phospholipid bilayer of the cell membrane. Large molecules, like glucose, and/or charged or hydrophilic molecules move across a cell membrane by facilitated diffusion. **Facilitated diffusion** is mediated by a carrier protein which binds the molecule to be transported and moves it across the membrane—or a channel protein—which creates pores in the membrane through which molecules move.

Simple and facilitated diffusion are types of passive diffusion, whereby a molecule moves down its concentration gradient to cross into or out of a cell. In **active transport**, however, a molecule is pushed up or against its concentration gradient to an area of higher concentration. This movement is driven by the oxidation, or hydrolysis, of ATP. For example, gradients of Na^+ and K^+ are maintained by a protein called the $Na^+ - K^+$ pump. This pump keeps the concentration of Na^+ outside the cell about ten times higher than the concentration of Na^+ inside the cell. A gradient of K^+, on the other hand, is found at a higher concentration inside the cell. To maintain these concentrations, the pump must move these ions against their concentration gradients. This is driven by ATP hydrolysis, whereby ATP phosphorylates the pump and induces a conformation change in this protein. One cycle of hydrolisis moves three Na^+ ions outside the cell and two K^+ ions from inside the cell.

> **HELPFUL HINT**
>
> A human cell puts about one-third of its energy into driving sodium-potassium pumps. Two functions of these pumps are to help the cell draw sugars and amino acids into the cell and conduct electrical signals in a nerve cell.

SAMPLE QUESTIONS

25) **Which of the following statements about the sodium-potassium pump is true?**

   A.   Sodium ions are pumped into the cell; potassium ions are pumped out of the cell.

   B.   The formation of ATP drives the action of the sodium-potassium pump.

   C.   The sodium-potassium pump uses facilitated diffusion to move ions across the membrane.

   D.   The sodium-potassium pump is powered by the oxidation of ATP.

   Answers:

   A.   Incorrect. Sodium ions are pumped out of the cell; potassium ions are pumped into the cell.

   B.   Incorrect. ATP is broken down to provide energy for active transport in the pump.

   C.   Incorrect. Facilitated diffusion is a form of passive diffusion that does not require energy inputs.

D.   Correct. Hydrolysis of one molecule of ATP drives one cycle of the sodium-potassium pump and moves three ions of sodium versus two ions of potassium.

26)   **Which of the following statements about diffusion is true?**

A.   Facilitated diffusion is the movement of molecules from areas of low to high concentration.

B.   Small molecules may move through the membrane by the process of simple diffusion.

C.   ATP drives the facilitated diffusion of molecules across the cell membrane.

D.   The movement of molecules by facilitated diffusion does not require a carrier protein.

Answers:

A.   Incorrect. In facilitated diffusion, molecules move down their concentration gradient.

B.   Correct. In simple diffusion, small molecules pass through the membrane without the help of embedded proteins.

C.   Incorrect. ATP drives active transport, not diffusion.

D.   Incorrect. A carrier protein is required to move molecules across the cell membrane in facilitated diffusion.

MOVEMENT OF WATER

The passive diffusion of water molecules from an area of high water concentration to an area of low water concentration is called **osmosis**. Aquaporins are channels in the cell membrane that mediate the free movement of water molecules into and out of a cell by osmosis. Because water molecules are polar and react with solutes—such as other polar molecules, sugars, and proteins—the solute concentration, which is also called osmotic concentration or **osmolarity**, impacts the movement of water molecules through a system: water molecules move from an area of high water concentration/low solute concentration to an area of low water concentration/high solute concentration.

As the solute concentration of a solution increases, the **water potential**—a measure of the free water molecules in a solution and the tendency for those molecules to move into a solution—decreases. If a cell is placed in a solution with a greater water potential

> **DID YOU KNOW?**
>
> Salting meats creates a hypertonic environment that dehydrates microbes, including disease-causing bacteria. This food preservation technique exploits the movement of water in a hypertonic environment: the bacterial cell loses water until it can no longer carry out essential functions like metabolism; the growth of the cell is inhibited, and the cell may eventually die.

than the water potential of the cell itself, then the solution is **hypotonic**, and there is a net movement of water molecules into the cell. The cell then expands and may eventually burst, which is called plasmoptysis. In the opposite scenario in which a cell is placed in a solution with a lesser water potential than the water potential of the cell itself, the solution is **hypertonic**. This means that there is a net movement of water molecules out of the cell; the cell shrinks, which is called plasmolysis.

SAMPLE QUESTIONS

27) Which TWO of the following statements are true of a solution with a high water potential?

    A.   The solution consists of more free water molecules than a solution with a low water potential.

    B.   The solution consists of fewer free water molecules than a solution with a low water potential.

    C.   The concentration of solutes is high compared to a solution with a low water potential.

    D.   The concentration of solutes is low compared to a solution with a low water potential.

Answers:

    A.   **Correct.** A high water potential means a solution has a lot of free water molecules.

    B.   Incorrect. A solution with a high water potential has many free water molecules.

    C.   Incorrect. A solution with a high water potential has many free water molecules; therefore, the osmotic concentration of the solution is low.

    D.   **Correct.** A high water potential means a solution has a lot of free water molecules, indicating that the solution has low osmotic concentration.

28) Which of the following will occur when a cell is placed in a hypotonic solution?

    A.   Water will move from outside the cell to inside the cell.

    B.   Water will move from inside the cell to outside the cell.

    C.   Solute will move from outside the cell to inside the cell.

    D.   Solute will move from inside the cell to outside the cell.

Answer:

    C.   **Correct.** The solute concentration inside the cell will be higher than the solute concentration of a hypotonic solution; therefore, water moves into the cell.

ENDOCYTOSIS AND EXOCYTOSIS

In addition to the active transport of molecules through transmembrane proteins, ATP is used to bring large materials, like organic molecules or bacteria, into the cell and excrete wastes from the cell by the processes of **endocytosis** and **exocytosis**, respectively. When a large particle like a bacterium or a molecule like a sugar binds to specific receptors on the cell surface of a eukaryote, the plasma membrane forms extensions that grow around the molecule and engulf it in a vesicle that is transported into the cell. When the cell ingests large particles (for example, a bacterial cell), the process is called **phagocytosis**. When the ingested material is liquid or a macromolecule dissolved in a liquid, the process is called **pinocytosis**.

Exocytosis can be thought of as the reverse of endocytosis. Molecules to be released from the cell are carried to the cell surface in a secretory vesicle. The secretory vesicle fuses with the plasma membrane and forms a pore through which the molecules are released from the cell. Examples of molecules that are released from a cell via exocytosis are hormones, digestive enzymes, and the molecules needed to build the cell wall of a plant cell.

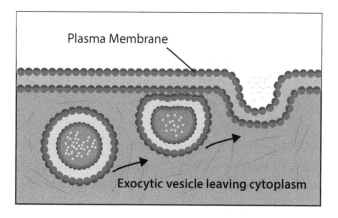

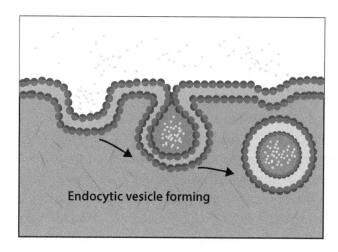

Figure 1.14. Endocytosis versus Exocytosis

SAMPLE QUESTION

29) **Which of the following facilitates exocytosis in a cell?**

A.   carrier proteins

B.   vesicles

C.   pores in the cell membrane

D.   cell-surface receptors

Answers:

A.   Incorrect. Carrier proteins are necessary for facilitated diffusion.

B.   **Correct.** Secretory vesicles carry the cellular material that needs to be excreted from the cell; these structures fuse with the cell membrane.

C.   Incorrect. The pores through which materials are released from the cell form when the secretory vesicle fuses with the cell membrane.

D.   Incorrect. Cell surface receptors mediate the interaction between the cell membrane and the large materials that are brought into the cell via endocytosis.

INTERCELLULAR COMMUNICATION

In multicellular organisms, the proper functioning of each cell is necessary for the health and survival of the organism. To carry out its tasks efficiently, a cell is tuned to its environment. Its internal properties—like temperature and pH—are held at ideal levels, or set points, and its ability to interact with other cells and respond to signals from those cells or changing environmental conditions is mediated by **cell surface proteins**, or **receptors**. These cell surface proteins, or receptors, allow the cell to communicate with the world of molecules, cells, and tissues that exists outside the plasma membrane.

When each variable that defines the internal environment of the cell is at its set point, allowing the cell to function properly, that constancy is called **homeostasis**. Internal constancy is regulated by feedback mechanisms, or control systems, that detect changes in the level of an internal variable and respond to that change by increasing or decreasing the level of that variable.

When the response is opposite to the change—for instance, if the variable increases and the response is to decrease the level of the variable—then the feedback mechanism is called **negative feedback**. Many variables are regulated by negative feedback, including temperature and the secretion of **hormones**. In the negative feedback loop that regulates the internal temperature of an animal cell, for example, an increase in body temperature that exceeds the set point triggers nerve cells to release **neurotransmitters**, which are molecules that transmit signals, or messages, from neuron to neuron. The message eventually reaches the brain, and the brain responds by sending a message that activates the sweat glands, because sweating cools the body.

Because the increase in temperature results in a feedback mechanism that leads to a decrease in temperature, this loop is called negative feedback. Most feedback loops involved in homeostasis are negative feedback loops. There are, however, important **positive feedback** mechanisms; blood clotting is one example. Platelets—small cell fragments that play a key role in clotting—are attracted to damaged blood vessels. As they attach to the injury, they release chemicals that signal other platelets to the site, which pile onto the injured vessel and release chemicals that draw more platelets to the site. The loop continues until the blood clots.

The blood-clotting example highlights how cells communicate with one another. In cell-to-cell communication, signaling molecules like **hormones** and neurotransmitters are released by one cell and recognized by another cell. This recognition is mediated at the cell membrane where the signaling molecule binds to cell surface proteins or receptors. The binding of the signal molecule triggers a series of chemical reactions called a **signal transduction cascade** that eventually effects a change in a target molecule, reaction, or process.

SAMPLE QUESTION

30) During labor, the body releases oxytocin, a hormone that speeds up the time between contractions. As contractions increase, more oxytocin is released, which speeds up the contractions, resulting in the release of more oxytocin. This cycle continues until the baby is born.

The phenomenon described is an example of

A. positive feedback.

B. negative feedback.

C. homeostasis.

D. signal transduction.

Answers:

A. **Correct.** The release of oxytocin ultimately leads to the release of more oxytocin, which is the definition of positive feedback.

B. Incorrect. If this process was regulated by negative feedback, then an increase in oxytocin would ultimately lead to a decrease in oxytocin.

C. Incorrect. Homeostasis is the maintenance of a stable condition.

D. Incorrect. Signal transduction is a cascade of chemical reactions triggered when an extracellular-signaling molecule binds a receptor on the cell membrane (or occasionally inside the cell).

THE CELL CYCLE AND CELL DIVISION

All cells reproduce in a process of **cellular division** that passes genetic information from the parent cell to daughter cells. The **cell cycle** in prokaryotes is simple: DNA is copied, and the parent cell splits into two daughter cells. This process is called binary fission. Eukaryotic cells carry much more DNA than prokaryotic cells, and this genetic material is wound around proteins and packaged into chromosomes that are housed in the nucleus of the cell. The cell cycle in eukaryotic cells, therefore, is much more complex than the cell cycle in prokaryotic cells.

THE STAGES OF THE CELL CYCLE

The DNA of a eukaryotic cell divides in one of two ways: nonreproductive cells divide by **mitosis**, while reproductive cells divide by **meiosis**. **Interphase** is the first stage of the cell cycle in a eukaryotic cell. There are three phases of interphase: In the G_1 phase, where G stands for *Gap*, the cell is growing, transcribing genes into messenger RNA (mRNA) and translating mRNA into protein. In the S, or *synthesis*, phase of interphase, two copies of each chromosome are produced. In the G_2 phase of interphase, chromosomes condense, mitochondria replicate, and microtubules are synthesized. The four stages of mitosis (or M phase)—**prophase**, **metaphase**, **anaphase**, and **telophase**—follow interphase. The final stage of cell division is **cytokinesis**, which is also referred to as C phase.

SAMPLE QUESTION

31) **A cell spends most of its life in which of the following phases?**

   A. G_1 phase

   B.   S phase

   C. G_2 phase

   D.   M phase

Answers:

   A.   **Correct.** In this phase, cells do much of their growing, carrying out processes like metabolism and gene expression.

   B.   Incorrect. A cell gears up for cell division in the S phase by synthesizing new DNA.

   C.   Incorrect. Chromosomes condense in the G_2 phase; mitochondria are replicated and microtubules are produced.

   D.   Incorrect. The M phase stands for mitosis.

CELL CYCLE CHECKPOINTS

The cell cycle is regulated at various **checkpoints**—or transitions—from one phase of the cycle to the next to ensure that cell division occurs under favorable conditions. At the G_1 **checkpoint**, for instance, the cell either commits to division or not. The cell will not enter S phase if the cell: is not large enough to divide; has limited nutrients; lacks positive environmental signals, like growth factors, from neighboring cells; is too crowded by other cells; or has DNA damage of any kind.

Interphase
G_1
S
G_2
Mitosis

MOLECULAR AND CELLULAR BIOLOGY   35

A cell that passes the G_1 checkpoint begins replicating its DNA. This is an irreversible commitment to divide, but there is an additional checkpoint before mitosis begins: the **G_2 checkpoint**. The focus of this checkpoint is the DNA of the cell. If the DNA is damaged or not completely copied during S phase, repair mechanisms are triggered. If the issue is resolved, then the cell moves into mitosis. If the problems are not fixed, then the cell self-destructs in a process called apoptosis.

SAMPLE QUESTION

32) **Apoptosis prevents a cell from transitioning to which of the following phases of cell division?**

   A. G_1 phase

   B. S phase

   C. G_2 phase

   D. M phase

Answers:

   A. Incorrect. There is no checkpoint before the G_1 phase.

   B. Incorrect. Cells that fail at the G_1 checkpoint often go into a G_0 phase, which is a kind of resting state.

   C. Incorrect. There is no checkpoint between S phase and the G_2 phase.

   D. **Correct.** Apoptosis destroys damaged cells at the G_2 checkpoint before they enter M phase.

MITOSIS

Chromosomes replicate in interphase and are therefore made of two genetically identical sister chromatids, which are divvied up in mitosis (nuclear division) to form two **daughter cells**. Because the parent cell is a **diploid (2n)** cell, and each daughter cell is identical to the parent cell, each daughter cell is also a diploid (2n) cell. In contrast, the process of meiosis results in four **haploid (1n)** cells; each cell carries only one set of chromosomes.

The four phases of mitosis are prophase, metaphase, anaphase, and telophase. In **prophase**, the chromosomes continue to coil and thicken as they become shorter, becoming increasingly visible under a microscope. This is a process called condensation, which began in interphase. The nuclear envelope begins to degrade in prophase. In an animal cell, two centrosomes—each composed of two centrioles—migrate to opposite sides of the cell. This begins the formation of the **mitotic spindle**, a network of microtubules that will, ultimately, separate the two sister chromatids.

HELPFUL HINT

The n in 2n or 1n represents a set of chromosomes; a diploid (2n) cell has two sets of chromosomes, while a haploid (1n) cell carries only one set.

The two sister chromatids are attached by a structure called the centromere, which is composed of two kinetochores. In **metaphase**, microtubules—or spindle fibers—from one centriole attach to the kinetochore of one sister chromatid, while fibers from another centriole attach to the other sister chromatid. The spindle fibers draw the chromosomes to the middle of the cell where they align along an imaginary plane or plate called the equatorial plate, the metaphase plate, or the **cell plate**.

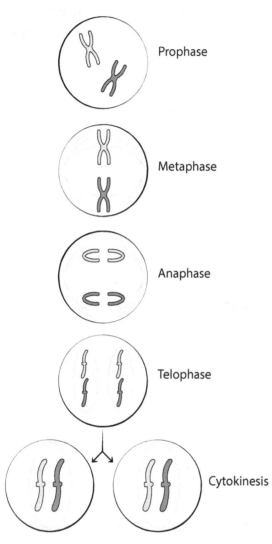

The spindle pulls the sister chromatids apart during **anaphase**. As the microtubules shorten, the sister chromatids, or daughter chromosomes, are pulled to opposite poles of the cell.

In the final stage of mitosis—called **telophase**—the mitotic spindle degrades, each set of chromosomes becomes surrounded by a nuclear envelope, and the chromosomes decondense, or start to uncoil.

The final stage of cell division is **cytokinesis**. In an animal cell, actin filaments contract to form a **cleavage furrow**, or indentation, which pinches inward until the cytoplasm is completely divided, and the cell is cleaved into two daughter cells.

Figure 1.15. Phases of Mitosis

SAMPLE QUESTIONS

33) **At the end of which of the following phases are chromosomes first clearly visible under a light microscope?**

A.   interphase

B.   prophase

C.   metaphase

D.   anaphase

Answers:

A.   Incorrect. The DNA just begins to condense into chromosomes during interphase.

B.   **Correct.** The DNA replicated during interphase condenses into chromosomes, which are clearly visible under a light microscope by the end of prophase.

C.   Incorrect. The chromosomes align at the center of the cell during metaphase.

D.   Incorrect. Sister chromatids are separated and drawn to opposite poles of the cell during anaphase.

34)   **In which of the following phases of mitosis does the nucleolus reappear?**

A.   prophase
B.   metaphase
C.   anaphase
D.   telophase

Answers:

A.   Incorrect. Prophase prepares the sister chromatids for binding by the spindle fibers.

B.   Incorrect. Metaphase prepares the sister chromatids for separation.

C.   Incorrect. Anaphase prepares the daughter chromosomes for the division of the cytoplasm.

D.   **Correct.** A new nuclear envelope, hence a new nucleus and nucleolus, forms in telophase.

MEIOSIS

In contrast to mitosis, **meiosis** describes the process of sexual reproduction, or the formation of **gametes** (**egg** and **sperm** cells) and the fusion of these gametes to form a new cell called a zygote. Gamete-forming cells are diploid, or 2n, cells. Gametes, however, are haploid cells; an egg cell (1n) and a sperm cell (1n) fuse to form a diploid (2n) zygote. Meiosis, therefore, is a cell division process that results in gametes that carry a reduced set of chromosomes.

One similarity between mitosis and meiosis is the first phase in the cell division process: interphase. The chromosomes replicate before the cell transitions into a set of cell division phases called meiosis I. The four stages of meiosis I are: prophase I, metaphase I, anaphase I, and telophase I. **Prophase I** proceeds like prophase in mitosis until chromosomes begin to adhere to each other to form homologous pairs of chromosomes called tetrads, and nonsister chromatids exchange chunks of chromosome in a process called **crossing over**. In **metaphase I**, these tetrads migrate to the metaphase plate, and spindle fibers begin to attach to the centromeres of each chromosome.

Then, in **anaphase I**, the homologous chromosomes are pulled apart and toward opposite poles of the cell. **Telophase I** and cytokinesis occur as in mitosis, and two daughter cells are formed.

These cells enter into a second set of meiosis phases called meiosis II, which is also divided into four stages: prophase II, metaphase II, anaphase II, and telophase II. A new spindle forms in **prophase II**; in **metaphase II**, these new microtubule fibers attach to the centromeres of each chromosome and guide the chromosomes to align in the center of the cell. The sister chromatids are divided in **anaphase II**, and nuclear envelopes re-form to enclose the four sets of daughter chromosomes in **telophase II**. Division of the cytoplasm results in four haploid (1n) gamete cells.

QUICK REVIEW

Cell division in plants has some noticeable differences from division in animal cells. In plant cells, mitosis is induced by the hormone cytokinin. Plant cell reproduction also does not use centrosomes, and the daughter cells split using the cell plate method.

SAMPLE QUESTIONS

35) **Which of the following processes occurs during anaphase I of meiosis?**

   A.   The spindle pulls homologous chromosomes to either side of the cell.

   B.   The spindle pulls sister chromatids to either side of the cell.

   C.   Chromosomes align along the metaphase plate.

   D.   Two diploid (2n) daughter cells are formed.

   Answers:

   A.   **Correct.** It is the separation of homologous chromosomes in meiosis I that leads to the formation of four diploid (1n) cells in meiosis II.

   B.   Incorrect. This describes what happens in anaphase of mitosis.

   C.   Incorrect. This occurs during metaphase in both mitosis and meiosis.

   D.   Incorrect. This only occurs during mitosis.

36) **Which of the following statements about meiosis is true?**

   A.   The process of meiosis includes one nuclear division.

   B.   Recombination occurs during the first phases of meiosis.

   C.   Chromosomes replicate prior to meiosis II.

   D.   Meiosis results in four diploid (2n) daughter cells.

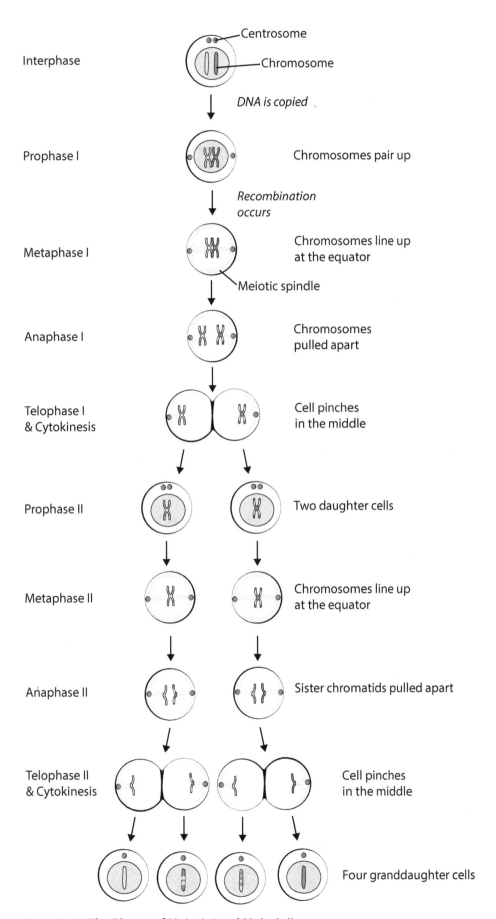

Figure 1.16. The Phases of Meiosis I and Meiosis II

Answers:

A.   Incorrect. Mitosis involves only one nuclear division; meiosis involves two nuclear divisions.

B.   Correct. Recombination—the chromosome swapping that happens between homologous chromosomes—occurs in prophase I.

C.   Incorrect. No DNA replication occurs between meiosis I and meiosis II.

D.   Incorrect. Meiosis results in four haploid (1n) daughter cells.

NUCLEIC ACIDS

All cells, whether prokaryotic or eukaryotic, carry genetic information that is replicated and passed on to daughter cells when the parent cell divides. The macromolecule that carries this hereditary information is **DNA** (deoxyribonucleic acid). DNA is a type of nucleic acid, a complex molecule built from subunits called **nucleotides**. Certain sequences of nucleotides direct the synthesis of proteins. **RNA** (ribonucleic acid) is the second type of nucleic acid. RNA plays a key role in deciphering the information stored in DNA.

THE STRUCTURE OF NUCLEIC ACIDS

Although DNA and RNA are structurally and functionally different, at their most basic level, both DNA and RNA are built from nucleotides, which consist of three parts: a single or two-ringed organic molecule containing nitrogen, a sugar containing five carbon atoms, and a phosphate group. One structural difference between DNA and RNA is the five-carbon monosaccharide: the nucleotides of DNA are made of **deoxyribose sugar**, while the nucleotides found in RNA are made of **ribose sugar**.

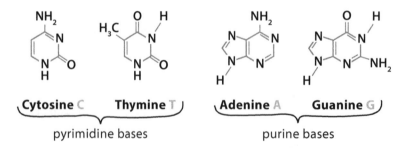

Figure 1.17. Structure of a Nucleotide

Nucleotides are joined through dehydration reactions that bind the sugar molecule of one nucleotide to the phosphate group of another nucleic acid. In this way, a long, **single strand** structure with a **sugar-phosphate backbone** forms. The nitrogen-containing organic molecule (called a nitrogenous base) attached to each nucleotide extends from the sugar-phosphate backbone. In DNA, two strands of nucleotides wrap around each other to form a **double helix**, or twisted structure. The sugar-phosphate backbone lies on the outside of this structure, and the nitrogenous bases of each strand are joined by hydrogen bonds on the inside of the double helix.

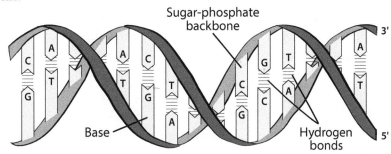

Figure 1.18. The Double Helix of DNA

Nitrogenous bases pair in specific ways called **complementary base pairing**. There are four nitrogenous bases found in DNA: **adenine (A)**, **thymine (T)**, **guanine (G)**, and **cytosine (C)**. These are the four bases that define the **genetic code** of a cell. In a double helix, adenine and thymine align in a way that favors the formation of a hydrogen bond; likewise, hydrogen bonds form between guanine and cytosine. Therefore, A – T pairs and G – C pairs hold together each molecule of DNA.

SAMPLE QUESTION

37) **Which of the following nucleotides are two-ringed nitrogenous bases?**

A.   adenine and thymine

B.   cytosine and thymine

C.   adenine and guanine

D.   guanine and cytosine

Answers:

A.   Incorrect. Although A and T are complementary bases, their ring structures are different.

B.   Incorrect. C and T are single-ringed bases.

C.   **Correct.** A and G are made from a two-ringed, nitrogen-containing organic molecule.

D.   Incorrect. Although G and C are complementary bases, their ring structures are different.

DNA VERSUS RNA

DNA and RNA differ in chemical, structural, and functional ways. First, the sugar component of the nucleotides of RNA is a ribose sugar, and the sugar in DNA nucleotides is deoxyribose. Second, RNA forms as a single strand of nucleotides, whereas DNA forms as a double helix. And third, DNA and RNA only share three nitrogenous bases: adenine, guanine, and cytosine. Thymine is found only in DNA, and the fourth base found in RNA—which is only found in RNA and not in DNA—is uracil (U). Finally, DNA and RNA differ in their cellular functions. The sequence of nucleotides that defines each DNA double helix carries all the information a cell needs to survive, while RNA is the molecule that reads the code and carries it to the parts of the cell that produce proteins.

SAMPLE QUESTION

38) **Which of the following statements about RNA are true? Select all that apply.**

   A.   Hydrogen bonds form between A – T and G – C bases.

   B.   A sequence of RNA will not contain T bases but will contain U bases.

   C.   RNA is single stranded.

   D.   RNA is double stranded

   Answers:

   A.   Incorrect. These are the complementary base pairs that form in DNA.

   B.   Correct. This is true; RNA does not carry thymine bases but does carry uracil bases.

   C.   Incorrect. This is true; a molecule of RNA exists as one long chain of nucleotides, not as a double helix.

   D.   Incorrect. RNA does not form a double helix; DNA exists as a double helix.

CHROMOSOMES

In eukaryotic cells, DNA coils around proteins, called **histones**, to form tight, linear structures called chromosomes. The **nucleosome** is a precise structure—approximately 150 to 200 nucleotides wrapped around eight histones—that results from this coiling. Another structure, the **telomere** (found at the tip of a chromosome) consists of a repeated sequence of DNA.

Chromosomes are more easily packaged into the nucleus than are long strands of DNA. Eukaryotic cells tend to carry between ten and fifty chromosomes. Prokaryotic cells, in contrast, usually have a single, circular (or nonlinear) chromosome found in the cytoplasm.

In the nonreproductive (somatic) cells of a eukaryote, two chromosomes that carry the same genes—one chromosome from one parent and one chromosome from the other parent—pair to form homologous chromosomes. During cell division, each homolog replicates. The two identical chromosomes are called sister chromatids. Sister chromatids are joined at the **centromere**, a junction often at the center of each chromosome.

SAMPLE QUESTION

39) **All of the following properties are shared by chromosomes in an individual somatic cell EXCEPT**

    A.   size.

    B.   shape.

    C.   location of the centromere.

    D.   presence of telomeres.

Answers:

    A.   Incorrect. A chromosome will vary in size depending on the length of its DNA molecule.

    B.   Incorrect. Although all chromosomes are generally linear, chromosomes do differ in shape.

    C.   Incorrect. The centromere is not always located in the middle of a chromosome.

    D.   **Correct.** All chromosomes have telomeres.

DNA REPLICATION

Before a cell divides by binary fission (in prokaryotes) or mitosis or meiosis I (in eukaryotes), it must replicate its DNA, which is then split between each daughter cell. DNA is formed from two **complementary strands** of nucleotides that twist to form a double helix. The sugar-phosphate backbone of each strand has distinct ends: a phosphate group at one end (the 5' end) and a 5-carbon sugar group at the other end (the 3' end). Since the double helix is held together by the hydrogen bonds that form between complementary base pairs (A pairs with T; G pairs with C) on the inside of the structure, the sugar-phosphate backbones of the two strands are found on the outside of the helix, aligned in opposite orientations. In other words,

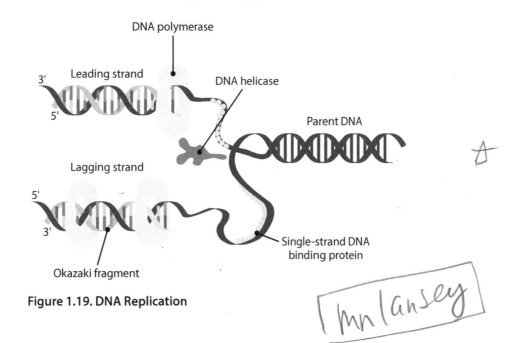

Figure 1.19. DNA Replication

one strand runs 5' to 3', while the other strand is joined to the structure in the 3' to 5' orientation. This directionality plays a key role in **DNA replication**.

DNA replication begins when an enzyme called **helicase** separates the two strands of the double helix, forming a **replication fork**. The two strands are referred to as the **leading strand** (which is oriented 3' to 5') and the **lagging strand** (which is oriented 5' to 3'). An enzyme attaches a short chain of nucleotides, called a **primer**, to the leading strand, and **DNA polymerase** works *toward* the replication fork, catalyzing the addition of appropriate nucleotides as it grows a strand complementary to the leading strand. The leading strand is built by joining the 3' sugar group of one nucleotide to the 5' phosphate group of a new nucleotide that is added to the chain. In this way, the new DNA strand grows 5' to 3'.

The orientation of the lagging strand (5' to 3') is opposite that of the leading strand. Because DNA polymerase synthesizes a new strand of nucleotides by joining the 3' sugar to the 5' phosphate of the new nucleotide, it must move away from the replication fork to catalyze the formation of a strand of nucleotides complementary to the lagging strand. Therefore, as the DNA molecule is unzipped by helicase, the lagging strand is built in segments: a primer is attached to the lagging strand at the replication fork, and DNA polymerase builds a complementary strand by adding nucleotides in a 5' to 3' direction, moving *away* from the replication fork, until it bumps up against a previous segment. DNA ligase joins each segment on the lagging strand before the two new DNA molecules twist to form two identical double helices.

SAMPLE QUESTIONS

40) If a strand of DNA has the base sequence 5' AAGCCCTATAC 3', the corresponding base sequence in the complementary strand of DNA would be

   A. 3' UUCGGGAUAUG 5'

   B. 3' TTCGGGATATG 5'

   C. 3' GTATAGGGCTT 5'

   D. 3' GUAUAGGGCUU 5'

Answers:

   A. Incorrect. DNA does not contain uracil.

   B. Correct. The orientation of a complementary strand of DNA is opposite that of its template.

   C. Incorrect. The sequence of bases is correct, but the indicated orientation is wrong.

   D. Incorrect. Uracil is a base found only in RNA.

41) **DNA is replicated during which of the following cell phases?**

A. C phase

B. M phase

C. S phase

D. G_1 phase

Answers:

A. Incorrect. Cytokinesis is the last phase of mitosis when the cytoplasm is split between two daughter cells. There is no C phase.

B. Incorrect. Mitosis is also referred to as M phase.

C. **Correct.** The *S* stands for *synthesis*. This is the stage of interphase when DNA is replicated.

D. Incorrect. This is also an interphase stage. In G_1, cells prepare for mitosis by transcribing and translating genes.

PROTEIN SYNTHESIS

A **gene**, in essence, is a segment of DNA nucleotides that carries the directions for the synthesis of a protein. Gene expression, then, is the **transcription** of a gene into mRNA and the **translation** of that mRNA into protein. The process of gene expression in prokaryotes versus eukaryotes has many similarities but also some important differences.

> **HELPFUL HINT**
>
> All proteins are made from 22 common amino acids.

RNA TRANSCRIPTION

In prokaryotes, genes are transcribed into a length of mRNA. Since a prokaryotic cell does not possess a nucleus, transcription occurs in the cytoplasm. The genes of eukaryotic cells are found in the nucleus, and transcription takes place in this organelle.

Transcription occurs in three steps: initiation, elongation, and termination. In the **initiation** step, RNA polymerase binds to a promoter site on the DNA double helix, pulls the two strands apart, and begins assembling a strand of RNA complementary to the template strand of DNA. The growth of the mRNA transcript is called **elongation**. Like in DNA replication, RNA polymerase adds complementary RNA nucleotides to the growing, single strand of mRNA in the 5' to 3' direction. The opposite strand of the original gene is called the **coding strand** because the mRNA will have the same sequence of nucleotides as the coding strand except that uracil (U) will be inserted into the strand of RNA nucleotides instead of thymine (T). The final step is **termination** and occurs when the RNA polymerase reaches a sequence of DNA that directs the enzyme to release itself from the template strand of DNA nucleotides and stop transcribing.

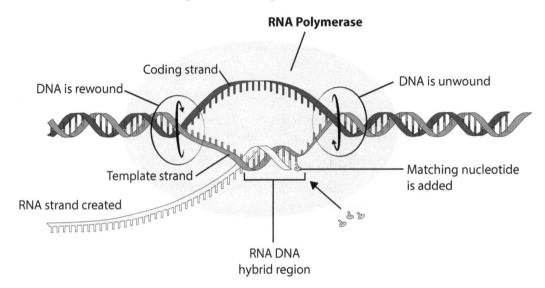

Figure 1.20. Transcription and the Action of RNA Polymerase

SAMPLE QUESTIONS

42) **Which of the following best describes the processes of transcription and translation?**

A.   RNA → protein → DNA

B.   DNA → protein → RNA

C.   protein → DNA → RNA

D.   DNA → RNA → protein

Answers:

A.   Incorrect. Gene expression starts with a gene, and genes are made of DNA, not RNA.

B.   Incorrect. Genes are stretches of DNA; proteins are produced in the last stage of gene expression.

C.   Incorrect. Proteins are the end products of gene expression.

D.   **Correct.** DNA must first be transcribed into a special kind of RNA before that piece of RNA can be translated into protein.

43) **If a strand of DNA has the base sequence 5' AAGCCCTATAC 3', the corresponding base sequence on the mRNA transcript would be**

A.   3' UUCGGGAUAUG 5'

B.   3' TTCGGGATATG 5'

C.   3' GTATAGGGCTT 5'

D.   3' GUAUAGGGCUU 5'

Answers:

A.   **Correct.** RNA polymerase transcribes DNA in the 5' to 3' direction.

B.   Incorrect. RNA molecules do not carry thymine bases.

C.   Incorrect. RNA and DNA share the adenine, guanine, and cytosine bases, but the fourth base in RNA molecules is uracil, while in DNA it is thymine.

D   Incorrect. Although the sequence is correct, the orientation is incorrect.

mRNA PROCESSING

The structure of the eukaryotic gene differs from the structure of prokaryotic genes: the genes of eukaryotes are called exons, which are interrupted by stretches of noncoding DNA nucleotides called introns. Exons and introns are first transcribed into a piece of RNA. Enzymes add a cap to the 5' end of the RNA molecule, which includes a methylated molecule of guanosine triphosphate (GTP). A tail of several hundred adenine nucleotides is added to the 3' end of most eukaryotic mRNAs. An enzyme called poly(A) polymerase catalyzes the addition of the tail; the process is called polyadenylation, and the tail is called a poly A tail. The **5' cap** and **poly A tail** protect the RNA from degradation as it is further processed: the introns are removed and the exons are joined together to form a mature transcript of mRNA.

QUICK REVIEW

Exons account for about 1.5 percent of the genetic material in a human cell, while introns make up about 24 percent. Are there any advantages to noncoding introns? Why does the human genome carry these stretches of DNA nucleotides?

SAMPLE QUESTIONS

44)   RNA processing in a eukaryotic cell occurs in which of the following locations?

A.   ribosomes

B.   cell membrane

C.   cytoplasm

D.   nucleus

Answer:

D.   **Correct.** DNA is transcribed into a primary RNA transcript in the nucleus of a eukaryotic cell; here, the RNA is processed into a mature length of mRNA.

45) The process of removing introns from the pre-mRNA molecule in a eukaryotic cell is called

    A.   ligation.

    B.   splicing.

    C.   polyadenylation.

    D.   initiation.

Answers:

    A.   Incorrect. Ligation is the joining of exons after the introns have been removed.

    B.   **Correct.** Splicing is the process whereby the introns are removed from the pre-mRNA.

    C.   Incorrect. Polyadenylation is the addition of a long stretch of A bases to the 3' end of the pre-mRNA transcript.

    D.   Incorrect. Initiation is the step in transcription when RNA polymerase binds the promoter of a gene.

TRANSLATION

In the final step in gene expression, the mRNA copy of a gene directs the synthesis of a chain of amino acids called a polypeptide. This process is called translation, and it takes place in the cytoplasm of both prokaryotic and eukaryotic cells. Because

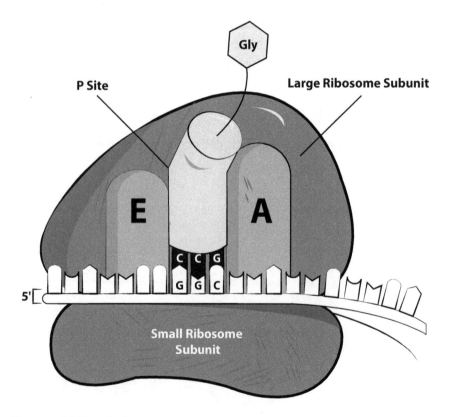

Figure 1.21. Translation

mRNA is produced in the nucleus of a eukaryotic cell, it must be transported across the nuclear envelope before it can be translated.

Ribosomes are the organelles that join amino acids into a polypeptide chain. Ribosomes are made of protein and ribosomal RNA (rRNA), and each ribosome consists of a small subunit and a large subunit that fit together. The mRNA transcript binds to a short piece of rRNA exposed on the small subunit. Next to this binding site are three pockets—the A, P, and E sites—that bind another kind of RNA called transfer RNA (tRNA).

Molecules of tRNA carry a three-nucleotide sequence called an **anticodon**, which is complementary to a three-nucleotide sequence on the mRNA called a **codon**. The anticodon is read by activating enzymes, which attach each amino acid to its proper tRNA. Ribosomes translate mRNA in three-nucleotide bursts, starting at an AUG codon, which is the start codon. A tRNA with a UAC anticodon, which carries an amino acid called methionine, binds to the codon. This step in translation is called **initiation**.

In the next step, **elongation**, tRNAs sequentially bring their amino acids to the mRNA and bind to the appropriate codon. A new tRNA binds to the codon at the A site; at the P site, each new amino acid is joined to the previously inserted amino acid by a peptide bond, and tRNAs are eventually released from the ribosome at the E site. **Translocation** is the process by which the mRNA advances on the ribosome, revealing the next codon and allowing the next tRNA to bind and add its amino acid to the growing chain.

The final step in translation is **termination**. The protein-making machinery eventually reaches a stop codon—the three-nucleotide sequence that directs translation to stop. The polypeptide chain is released from the tRNA, and the ribosome splits into its subunits and dissociates from the mRNA.

SAMPLE QUESTIONS

46) **Which of the following is the site at which the tRNAs are released from the ribosome?**

   A.   P site

   B.   E site

   C.   elongation site

   D.   termination site

Answers:

   A.   Incorrect. The P site is where new amino acids are joined to the previously inserted amino acid by a peptide bond.

   B.   Correct. The E site is where tRNAs exit the ribosome.

   C.   Incorrect. Elongation is a process, not a site.

   D.   Incorrect. A stop codon at this site signals the end of translation.

47) At an ACU codon, the amino acid threonine will be inserted in the growing polypeptide. What is the anticodon of the tRNA molecule that brings threonine to the ribosome?

A.   ACU

B.   UCA

C.   TGA

D.   UGA

Answer:

D.   Correct. Anticodons and codons are complementary.

REGULATION OF GENE EXPRESSION

Not all genes are transcribed and translated at all times. To conserve energy and to make sure only the genes that are needed are being used at any given moment, each cell regulates the timing of **gene expression**. Gene expression in prokaryotes is often controlled by changing environmental conditions. Prokaryotes generally evolve and divide quickly and must respond to their environments quickly, so the **regulation of gene expression** usually involves turning genes on or turning them off.

A collection of genes transcribed and translated in a cluster is called an **operon**. Transcription starts at a sequence on the operon called the **promoter**. This is where RNA polymerase binds. To turn transcription on, therefore, an **activator** protein can bind to make the promoter more available. Next to the promoter is a sequence of DNA called the **operator**. To turn transcription off, a **repressor** protein can bind the operator and block RNA polymerase from reaching the promoter.

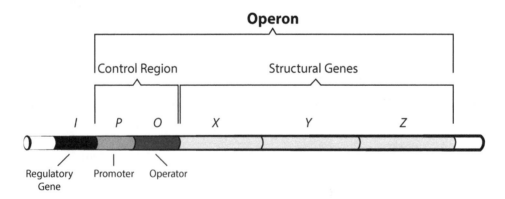

Figure 1.22. An Operon

Gene expression in eukaryotic organisms is regulated to benefit the survival of the whole organism rather than individual cells. **Transcription factors** are proteins that bind DNA and can influence whether RNA polymerase binds a promoter and transcribes a gene. One of the sites at which transcription factors bind to activate transcription is a sequence of DNA nucleotides called an **enhancer**; these sequences are often located far from the promoter.

Modifying gene expression in these ways can cause changes in an organism, including phenotypic variations, that are not caused by mutations or changes in the sequence of DNA nucleotides in a gene. **Epigenetics** is the study of gene regulation and the changes in an organism that result from this regulation.

SAMPLE QUESTIONS

48) **Which of the following is true of an enhancer?**

A. Enhancers are a form of promoter in a bacterial cell.

B. Enhancers are enzymes that help in the transcription of DNA.

C. Enhancers are located at a distance to the promoter.

D. Enhancers are proteins that bind and activate RNA polymerase.

Answers:

A. Incorrect. In bacteria, transcription is initiated at a promoter, not an enhancer.

B. Incorrect. Enhancers are sections of DNA, not enzymes.

C. **Correct.** Enhancers can exert their influence at a distance because the DNA bends to form a loop.

D. Incorrect. Enhancers are sections of DNA, not proteins.

49) **In both prokaryotes and eukaryotes, the regulation of gene expression most commonly occurs at which point?**

A. post-transcription

B. post-translation

C. transcription

D. translation

Answer:

C. **Correct.** Most gene expression is controlled at the initiation of transcription.

CELL DIFFERENTIATION AND SPECIALIZATION

Although all the somatic cells of some multicellular organisms carry the same genome, a multicellular organism is made of many different cell types with many different shapes, sizes, and functions. These **specialized cells** originate from **unspecialized cells** called **stem cells**, and **cell differentiation** describes the process by which a stem cell divides to form specialized cells like a nerve cell, blood cell, or sperm cell. Many of these cells form tissues. Tissues are the building blocks of organs, such as the skin or the stomach, and organs comprise the systems of an organism—the digestive system, for example.

DIFFERENTIAL GENE EXPRESSION

A muscle cell and an exocrine cell of the pancreas carry all the same genes, such as the genes for the production of myosin, actin, amylase, and lipase. For a muscle cell to carry out its specific functions, however, it expresses only the genes for myosin and actin production, but will likely not express the genes for the production of amylase and lipase. The exocrine cell, in contrast, will express the genes for amylase and lipase but will likely not express the genes for myosin or actin. This is called **differential gene expression**, and studies show that only a small number of the genes carried by a cell are actually expressed by that cell.

Many steps and changes in cell structure and function are involved in the transformation of an unspecialized cell into a specialized cell. Certain internal, cellular signals and external, extracellular **signals** trigger and/or control each of these steps. An internal signal that regulates differential gene expression might be a transcription factor, while an external signal might be a chemical secreted by another cell that attaches to a cell receptor of the differentiating cell.

SAMPLE QUESTION

50) Cell A and Cell B carry the same genes, including Gene 1, Gene 2, Gene 3, and Gene 4. Which of the following scenarios best describes differential gene expression?

A.   Cell A expresses all four genes; Cell B expresses all four genes.

B.   Cell A expresses only Genes 1 and 2; Cell B expresses only Genes 1 and 2.

C.   Cell A expresses only Genes 3 and 4; Cell B expresses only Genes 3 and 4.

D.   Cell A expresses only Genes 1 and 2; Cell B expresses only Genes 3 and 4.

Answer:

D.   **Correct.** Differential gene expression describes how specialized cells transcribe and translate only certain genes, even though all specialized cells carry all the same genes.

STEM CELLS

Stem cells—the unspecialized cells of some multicellular organisms—play key roles in the early life and growth of that organism. When induced by certain physiological or experimental conditions, stem cells differentiate into the specialized cells of specific tissues and organs. The two types of stem cells are **adult stem cells** and **embryonic stem cells**.

Adult stem cells are usually found in a specific organ or differentiated tissue and usually only give rise to the cells of that organ or tissue. For example, the adult stem cells found in bone marrow differentiate into the various types of blood cells but are unlikely to produce a liver cell or a skin cell. Embryonic stem cells, meanwhile, originate from embryos.

A stem cell can also be described by its potency—the number of different cell types the stem cell can differentiate into. A **totipotent** cell can differentiate into all the cells of an organism and can, therefore, produce all the structures, tissues, and organs of an organism. A **pluripotent** cell, like most embryonic stem cells, can differentiate into any cell type except the cells of certain structures of the placenta. The other terms that describe the differentiation of an unspecialized cell are: **multipotent**, which describes an unspecialized cell that can differentiate into several different cell types, but these cell types are usually similar or closely related (most adult stem cells are multipotent); **oligopotent**, meaning a stem cell can differentiate into only a few different cell types; and **unipotent**, when a stem cell only produces one cell type.

SAMPLE QUESTION

51) If a fertilized egg can develop into every cell in an organism, it is classified as which type of cell?

    A.   totipotent cell

    B.   pluripotent cell

    C.   multipotent cell

    D.   unipotent cell

Answers:

    A.   **Correct.** If a cell can differentiate to produce all the cells of an organism, then that cell is totipotent.

    B.   Incorrect. Most of the cell types of an organism are produced by a pluripotent cell, but not all cell types are produced.

    C.   Incorrect. Only similar or related cell types are produced by multipotent cells.

    D.   Incorrect. A unipotent cell will only differentiate into one cell type.

GENETIC MUTATIONS

The rare but permanent changes in the DNA sequences of genes are known as **mutations**. Some mutations cause harm to a cell and may lead to the death of that cell; some mutations have no effect on the cell. Other mutations, however, are beneficial to a cell, and if these changes are **germ-line mutations**, or mutations that occur in a cell that will become a gamete, then these mutations can be passed on to the **offspring** of an organism. These are the changes in a cell or organism that are inherited. These are also the changes that, through natural selection, might result in the evolution of an organism. If the mutation in the DNA sequence of an organism occurs in a cell other than a germ-line cell, then this change is called a **somatic mutation** because it happens to a somatic cell, which is a body cell, not a germ-line cell. Somatic mutations cannot be passed on to the offspring of an organism.

CAUSE OF MUTATIONS

Although rare, mutations can be caused by mistakes made during DNA replication as a cell prepares to divide. Likewise, exposure to certain chemicals or radiation, which are types of **mutagens**, can damage DNA by causing mutations in that DNA. Mutations are generally small-scale changes in a DNA sequence, while a rearrangement or a restructuring of a chromosome is a larger-scale change called **recombination**.

Both mutation and recombination can change the genetic information of a cell and play a role in the evolution of an organism, but mutation and recombination are not related and should not be confused. Recombination is a cellular process catalyzed and regulated by enzymes and other molecules. An example of recombination occurs during meiosis, when **homologous chromosomes** swap a piece of DNA in the event called *crossing over* (discussed earlier in the chapter). **Translocation** is another example of recombination, whereby a segment of DNA moves from one position in a chromosome to another position in the same chromosome, or to a position in a separate chromosome. Nonhomologous chromosomes could exchange segments of DNA in this way.

SAMPLE QUESTION

52)   **Ultraviolet light is known to cause which of the following?**

    A.   crossing over

    B.   translocation

    C.   recombination

    D.   a mutation

Answer:

    D.   **Correct.** Ultraviolet (UV) radiation is a mutagen. Recombination, including translocation, is a cellular process.

TYPES OF MUTATIONS

One way a gene can be changed permanently is through a **point mutation**, where a single base in the sequence of a gene changes. This can happen through a single base substitution, insertion, or deletion. If one base (or a few bases) in the sequence changes, this is called a **base substitution**. For example, a sequence that was originally ATC might now be ATG, where the original cytosine (C) base has been substituted for a guanine (G) base. A base substitution can lead to a **missense mutation**, in which one amino acid is substituted for another in the polypeptide chain. It can also lead to **nonsense mutations**, in which a substitution causes a codon to be changed to a stop codon, or **silent mutations**, in which changes are made to non-coding regions and cause no change.

QUICK REVIEW

Of the mutation types described here, which one would likely cause major changes in the cell?

When one base (or a few bases) is added to the sequence, this is called an **insertion**. And, when one nucleotide (or a few nucleotides) is lost from the sequence, this is called a **deletion**. Adding or removing nucleotides from a stretch of DNA changes the total amount of DNA, which can influence how the gene is read by RNA polymerase and, ultimately, by ribosomes. This type of mutation is called a **frame-shift mutation**. Occasionally, two breaks may occur in a chromosome, and the fragment that breaks away flips around and reattaches. This type of mutation is called a **chromosome inversion**.

SAMPLE QUESTIONS

53) **If the sentence below represents a chromosome, which of the following answers represents a chromosome inversion?**

This is a chromosome inversion.

   A.   This is chromosome inversion.

   B.   This is emosomorhc a inversion.

   C.   This is a inversion chromosome.

   D.   This is a emosomorhc noisrevni.

Answers:

   A.   Incorrect. In an inversion, the segment that breaks away rotates 180 degrees and then rejoins the chromosome. In this example, *a* and *is* are swapped, but there is not a 180-degree rotation.

   B.   **Correct.** The segment that broke away from the sentence was *a chromosome*, which, in this answer, has reinserted after a 180-degree flip.

   C.   Incorrect. Again, this is a swap of two segments, but the pieces have not inverted.

   D.   Incorrect. This could only occur if two segments broke away from the chromosome (requiring at least three breaks in the chromosome), inverted, and reinserted, but an inversion is generally described as two breaks in a chromosome that release a segment of DNA that flips and reinserts.

54) **Which of the following mutations results when an adenine base is added before the first C in the DNA sequence CTGGGAATC?**

   A.   base substitution

   B.   deletion

   C.   insertion

   D.   inversion

Answers:

   A.   Incorrect. In a base substitution, one base is deleted and one is added; therefore, there is no change in the total number of nucleotides in the sequence.

   B.   Incorrect. A deletion mutation results in the loss of a nucleotide.

   C.   **Correct.** This is an insertion and might also lead to a frame-shift mutation.

   D.   Incorrect. In an inversion, a piece of a chromosome breaks off, inverts, and reinserts in the chromosome.

STUDYING CELLULAR PROCESSES

Gel electrophoresis, **microscopy**, and **spectrophotometry** are laboratory techniques that scientists use to study the genetic differences in organisms, the structures of cells, and biological processes like transcription and translation.

GEL ELECTROPHORESIS

Scientists use a method called gel electrophoresis to separate and learn about the size of proteins or pieces of DNA or RNA. The *gel* in gel electrophoresis refers to the porous, jelly-like substance through which the segments of DNA, RNA, or proteins move. The gel is placed in a compartment filled with a salt solution. The fragments of DNA, RNA, or the proteins to be separated are loaded into the top part of the gel, and an **electrical field** is applied across the gel; this is where the "**electrophoresis**" part of the name comes from. The salt solution conducts the electricity and draws the DNA, RNA, or the proteins to the bottom of the gel.

DNA and RNA are negatively charged and are drawn to the positive charge at the bottom of the gel. Shorter fragments of nucleic acid will snake through the pores of the gel more quickly than larger fragments; therefore, over a given period of time, fragments of DNA and RNA are separated by size. To separate proteins, scientists must give the proteins a negative charge by soaking them in a detergent.

SAMPLE QUESTION

55) Nucleic acids carry an overall negative charge due to

    A.   nucleotides.

    B.   sugar molecules.

    C.   phosphate groups.

    D.   nitrogenous bases.

Answers:

    A.   Incorrect. Nucleic acids are built from many nucleotides, but nucleotides carry three parts: a sugar, a phosphate group, and a nitrogenous base.

    B.   Incorrect. The sugar molecule of a nucleotide does not confer a net negative charge.

    C.   **Correct.** It is the phosphate group of a nucleotide, specifically the negatively charged oxygen atoms of the phosphate group, that confers the negative charge.

    D.   Incorrect. The nitrogenous base of a nucleotide does not confer the net negative charge that is characteristic of nucleic acids.

MICROSCOPY

Microscopy is the study of organisms and structures that are too small to be seen without the aid of a special instrument that magnifies small things. These tiny cells or structures are said to be **microscopic**, and the special instrument used to see them is called a **microscope**. There are several different types of microscopes that can be used in a variety of ways across many different scientific disciplines. For instance, microscopes are used to do the following things: study tissues and cells, including single-celled organisms like bacteria; inspect microscopic evidence in forensic science; monitor the number and diversity of organisms in a river or sample of soil as a way to monitor ecosystem health; study protein function in a living cell; and, with a very powerful microscope, investigate the surface of an atom.

Optical microscopes (light microscopes) and **electron microscopes** are two common categories of microscopes. An optical microscope focuses visible light, or sometimes UV light, through a series of magnification lenses to view a **specimen**. Electron microscopes can magnify even smaller cells, structures, or particles, because these microscopes use a beam of electrons rather than light to magnify a specimen. A **scanning electron microscope**, for instance, passes a beam of electrons over the surface of a cell or structure, and the electrons reflected back are used to capture a three-dimensional image of the cell, protein, amino acid, atom, etc.

SAMPLE QUESTION

56) **To study the structure of a virus particle, which of the following microscopes should be used?**

A. optical microscope

B. electron microscope

C. scanning electron microscope

D. any of the above

Answers:

A. Incorrect. Viruses are typically much smaller than bacteria and usually impossible to see with a light microscope.

B. Incorrect. An electron microscope would work, but this question specifically asks about the structure of the virus; therefore, the scanning electron microscope would be the best choice.

C. **Correct.** This is the best choice for the studying the structure of an organism.

D. Incorrect. Option C is the best answer.

SPECTROPHOTOMETRY

Spectrophotometry is the study of how much light a molecule absorbs. The tendency of a molecule to be **light absorbing** (or **light transmitting**) can be used to learn many things, including: the concentration and purity of samples of DNA and RNA, the concentration and chemical composition of proteins, and the cell density and growth curve of a culture (usually a bacterial culture). Spectrophotometry is also used to gather information about other molecules of interest to the food and pharmaceutical industries and in wastewater treatment.

The instrument used to detect these things is called a **spectrophotometer**. A spectrophotometer passes a stream of **photons** (particles of light or electromagnetic radiation) through a sample; some of the photons will be absorbed by the molecule and reduce the intensity of the light, so the concentration of the molecule is the

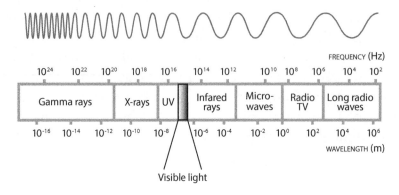

Figure 1.23. The Electromagnetic Spectrum

difference in the intensity of the light before passing through the sample and after passing through the sample.

The light transmitted by a spectrophotometer is of a certain **wavelength**. The **electromagnetic spectrum** describes the various wavelengths of electromagnetic radiation and how they relate to each other. For example, the wavelengths of visible light are shorter than the wavelengths of infrared light but longer than the wavelengths of ultraviolet light.

SAMPLE QUESTION

57) **A spectrophotometer can be used to do which of the following tasks?**

  A.   distinguish between pigments in a plant cell

  B.   measure enzymes in the blood of a heart attack patient

  C.   determine how fast a pathogen grows in liquid culture

  D.   all of the above

Answers:

  A.   Incorrect. The concentrations and types of molecules in a sample can indeed be determined with a spectrophotometer. There is a better answer choice, however.

  B.   Incorrect. While a spectrophotometer is often used to calculate the concentration of a protein in a sample, there is a better answer choice.

  C.   Incorrect. Microbial growth curves are commonly determined using a spectrophotometer. However, a better answer choice is available.

  D.   **Correct.** All of these are applications of spectrophotometry.

DNA TECHNOLOGIES

A greater understanding of DNA has been made possible by advancements in technologies for manipulating and studying DNA, like DNA sequencing technologies and the polymerase chain reaction. Knowledge about the structure and function of DNA has led to the growth of new scientific disciplines, such as gene therapy, cloning, and genetic engineering.

DNA SEQUENCING AND PCR

DNA sequencing is the process scientists use to identify the precise order of A, C, G, and T bases in a molecule of DNA. Before a DNA molecule can be sequenced or analyzed, it must be amplified. **Amplification** is the process used to quickly make many copies of a DNA sequence; the method used to amplify DNA is called the **polymerase chain reaction (PCR)**. There are three basic steps in PCR: A segment of DNA is denatured with heat. Then, short segments of complementary DNA called primers anneal to the separated DNA strands. Finally, DNA polymerase synthesizes new double-stranded DNA. To obtain many copies of this DNA fragment, the three steps in PCR are repeated many times.

Genome sequencing provides information about the entire genetic code of a cell or organism. By comparing the genome sequence of one cell or organism to the genetic codes of other cells or organisms, scientists can begin to understand the genetics of cancer, development of disease, and how organisms develop and evolve, among many, many other things. To do this, however, the entire genome must first be broken into smaller pieces; those pieces must be sequenced separately, and each bit of sequence is then pasted into a complete genome sequence, which is called the **genome assembly**. These genome assemblies are organized in databases with **genome annotations**, which describe the genes identified in the genome sequence and their likely functions.

Some of the large, interdisciplinary, and often international projects that aim to sequence whole genomes are the **Human Genome Project**, which was launched over twenty-five years ago, the **Neanderthal genome project**, which published a full sequence of a Neanderthal genome in 2010, and the **Influenza Genome Sequencing Project**, which is sequencing the genomes of thousands of viruses that cause the flu in humans and birds.

SAMPLE QUESTION

58) **Which of the following is/are NOT required to amplify a segment of DNA (by PCR) for further analysis?**

 A. forward and reverse primers

 B. heat

 C. RNA polymerase

 D. DNA polymerase

Answers:

 A. Incorrect. Primers are added to attach to the denatured DNA and provide a place for DNA polymerase to start growing a new strand of complementary DNA.

 B. Incorrect. To replicate a segment of DNA, the two strands of the segment must first be separated, or denatured, with heat.

 C. Correct. This is the enzyme that catalyzes the synthesis of mRNA, not complementary DNA.

 D. Incorrect. This is a key enzyme in PCR amplification of DNA; DNA polymerase adds nucleotides to the primers and thereby synthesizes a complementary strand of DNA.

GENE THERAPY

Genetic disorders like cystic fibrosis, which are passed from parent to offspring, result from some sort of change or damage to a gene(s) or chromosome(s). If that "unhealthy" gene or chromosome could be replaced with a "healthy" gene or chromosome, then in principle the disorder should be cured. The process of transferring a functional gene into the cells of a patient in an effort to treat or prevent a disease by replacing a defective gene is called **gene therapy**. Instead of replacing a gene, gene therapy can also be used to silence, or **knock out**, a troublesome gene or introduce a completely new gene into the cells of a patient to help those cells fend off a disease.

Although the first successful gene therapy procedure in humans was demonstrated in 1990, gene therapy is still considered **experimental** and controversial because some patients of gene therapy have developed cancer after treatment. There are also ethical concerns about using gene therapy to treat germ-line cells. Finally, it is unclear how the immune system might respond to certain gene therapy treatments.

SAMPLE QUESTION

59) **All of the following are reasons why gene therapy is still considered experimental and controversial EXCEPT**

   A.   If gene therapy is performed on a germ-line cell, the effects on a future fetus are not known.

   B.   Patients in some gene therapy trials have experienced serious side effects.

   C.   The immune system may attack new materials inserted into a cell.

   D.   It is unknown whether gene therapy is effective in preventing the expression of a gene.

Answers:

   A.   Incorrect. While it is correct that the effects of gene therapy on a germ-line cell may have unknown effects on a future fetus, there is a better answer choice.

   B.   Incorrect. Serious side effects are potential problems that gene therapy procedures must overcome. When a virus is used to insert a new gene or a functional gene into the cells of an organism, that insertion event might cause some other mutation that could potentially cause cancer.

   C.   Incorrect. Possible unwanted immune system responses are a risk in gene therapy, but there is a better answer choice.

   D.   **Correct.** Gene therapy has been shown to be successful in treating genetic conditions.

CLONING

Cloning is to take a cell, cell product, or entire organism and produce a genetically identical copy of the original. When the original template for cloning is a gene, then the process is called **gene cloning**. To clone and analyze a segment of DNA, that fragment is first ligated to a cloning **vector**—a plasmid, for example—and then inserted into a host cell like a bacterium or yeast. As the vector replicates inside the host, the target DNA is cloned.

In **reproductive cloning**, an individual organism is cloned, and the nucleus from an adult cell is removed from that cell and inserted into an enucleated egg cell. The egg is then stimulated to form an embryo, which develops into a blastocyst. At this stage, the blastocyst is implanted in a surrogate mother, and the offspring is a reproductive clone of the original organism.

Therapeutic cloning follows the same trajectory as reproductive cloning until the blastocyst stage; at that point, embryonic stem cells are extracted, grown, and induced to differentiate into a specific cell type. These cells are then transferred to a patient.

> **HELPFUL HINT**
>
> Somatic cell nuclear transfer, which is abbreviated SCNT, is the process of taking a nucleus from a body (somatic) cell and implanting it into an egg cell that carries no nucleus.

SAMPLE QUESTION

60) **Which of the following types of cloning is NOT considered controversial?**

A.   gene cloning

B.   reproductive cloning

C.   therapeutic cloning

D.   All of the above are considered controversial.

Answers:

A.   Correct. Generating identical copies of a gene is the basis of DNA sequencing and analysis and is not generally considered a controversial area of research.

B.   Incorrect. Reproductive cloning of animals is very controversial because humans are animals, and the cloning of humans raises all sorts of ethical, social, psychological, and biological issues.

C.   Incorrect. Therapeutic cloning is controversial because it involves the formation of an embryo and the use of embryonic stem cells.

D.   Incorrect. Not all of the above are controversial types of cloning.

GENETICALLY ENGINEERED CELLS

Genetic engineering involves the manipulation of the genetic information of a cell or organism. This manipulation can include taking a gene or sequence of DNA from one organism and introducing this **foreign DNA** or **exogenous DNA** into an unrelated organism. Splicing DNA from one organism and inserting it into the genome of another organism is often carried out by restriction enzymes. These proteins recognize short, symmetrical, specific sequences of DNA and cut the DNA at those sites. The cuts result in either "blunt ends," which terminates the base pair and cannot easily join to other DNA, or "sticky ends" that can be joined to another segment of DNA with complementary sticky ends. The manipulated cell is called a **genetically engineered cell**, and the altered organism is often referred to as a genetically modified organism (GMO). When genetic engineering confers a new property on an organism that the organism can pass along to its offspring, the process is called **transgenesis**.

SAMPLE QUESTION

61) Which of the following proteins make it possible to cut DNA from the genome of one cell and transfer that DNA to another cell?

A. DNA polymerases

B. RNA polymerases

C. restriction enzymes

D. ligases

Answers:

A. Incorrect. These enzymes play a role in DNA replication.

B. Incorrect. These enzymes catalyze the synthesis of mRNA from a DNA template.

C. Correct. These proteins are also called restriction endonucleases.

D. Incorrect. These are the enzymes that join together two fragments of DNA.

2

Genetics and Evolution

MENDELIAN GENETICS

Genetics is the study of heredity—how characteristics are passed from parents to offspring. These characteristics, or **traits**, are determined by genes, which are located on chromosomes and are the basic units of heredity. Each individual has two versions of the same gene, called **alleles**. Parents each contribute one set of alleles to their offspring. The combination of genes that make up individual traits are known as **genotypes**. A genotype is a full set of genetic material and differs from an organism's **phenotype**, which is the set of observable traits in an organism. An example of a phenotype is brown hair; the genotype of this trait is a set of alleles that contain the genetic information for brown hair.

Different combinations of alleles result in different traits that are expressed in offspring. If an individual has identical alleles from each parent for a given trait, he or she is considered to be **homozygous**. The resulting phenotype is straightforward—if an individual inherits the same blood type from each parent, then he or she will express that same blood type.

If the individual inherits one type of allele for a given trait from one parent but a different allele from the other parent, then he or she is considered to be **heterozygous**. The resulting phenotype is more complicated for heterozygous traits. In this case, the more **dominant** allele will be expressed, while the **recessive** (less dominant) allele will not be expressed.

These basic ideas are considered to be the foundation of Mendelian genetics and are named after the man who is considered to be the founder of modern genetics, Gregor Mendel. Mendel, an Austrian monk who lived in the 1800s, carefully observed the variation of traits that exists among pea plants. He deliberately cross-pollinated plants with one trait with plants that contained another trait, observing the variations in offspring along the way. This led him to determine that inheritance stems from different possible traits inherited from each parent, laying the foundation of the modern understanding of genetics. Mendel's further experiments expanded upon these ideas and eventually gave rise to other basic principles of genetics: the laws of independent assortment, segregation, and dominance; the concept of mono-hybrid and dihybrid crosses; and the development of pedigree analysis to determine inheritance patterns.

Mendelian genetics is dependent upon the principles found in three major laws. The **law of segregation** states that genes separate into distinct alleles during gamete formation; **the law of independent assortment** states that these genes separate and recombine independently of one another, with every combination of alleles having the same likelihood of occurring; and the **law of dominance** states that the dominant allele will be expressed in the resulting offspring.

Segregation of genes occurs as cells undergo meiosis. These cells are **diploid**, meaning that each contains a full set of DNA, or genetic information, from both parents. This information is found on genes in the cell's chromosomes. The process of meiosis creates a **haploid** reproductive cell, or gamete. These cells each contain one half of a cell's genetic information. As a result, each gamete contains one allele for each gene.

But which allele is found in each gamete? This is determined by **independent assortment**. According to this law, the division of genes during meiosis happens randomly and independently of gene division in other gametes. This means that no two gametes will contain the exact same combination of genetic information, and all combinations of genetic information have an equal chance of occurring.

During fertilization, the gametes from two different parents unite and combine alleles, giving each offspring a full genetic set that contains two versions of every gene. Each allele that makes up a gene is either dominant or recessive. According to the law of dominance, if a dominant allele is paired with another dominant allele or a recessive allele, then the dominant allele will be expressed in the corresponding trait.

The individual still carries this genetic information in his or her genotype, which can then be passed on to future offspring. If the individual has inherited two recessive alleles from both parents, then the resulting genotype is homozygous and the recessive phenotype will be expressed. For example, if both parents of a pea plant contribute recessive alleles that result in wrinkled seeds, then the offspring will also have wrinkled seeds.

HELPFUL HINT

When writing the genetic information for a genotype, the dominant allele is written as a capital letter (B) while the recessive is written in a lowercase (b). A genotype that is homozygous can be written as (BB) or (bb), and a genotype that is heterozygous can be written as (Bb).

SAMPLE QUESTIONS

1) Which one of the following laws states that genes separate into distinct alleles during gamete formation?

 A. law of inheritance

 B. law of dominance

 C. law of independent assortment

 D. law of segregation

Answers:

 A. Incorrect. All of Mendel's laws are collectively referred to as the laws of inheritance.

 B. Incorrect. The law of dominance states that the dominant allele of a pair will be expressed as a trait.

 C. Incorrect. The law of independent assortment states that genes divide and recombine independently of one another.

 D. Correct. The law of segregation states that alleles segregate independently during meiosis.

2) Which of the following is NOT a scenario in which the dominant allele will be expressed as a trait?

 A. a recessive allele from the father paired with another recessive allele from the mother

 B. a dominant allele from the father paired with another dominant allele from the mother

 C. a recessive allele from the mother paired with a dominant allele from the father

 D. a recessive allele from the father paired with a dominant allele from the mother

Answers:

 A. Correct. This genotype is homozygous, and the recessive trait is the only trait that can be expressed.

 B. Incorrect. This genotype is homozygous, and the dominant trait is the only trait that can be expressed.

 C. Incorrect. This dominant allele will be expressed over the recessive allele in this heterozygous combination.

 D. Incorrect. This dominant allele will be expressed over the recessive allele in this heterozygous combination.

MONOHYBRID AND DIHYBRID CROSSES

A **genetic cross** is a method in genetic experimentation in which a scientist intentionally breeds two individual parent organisms in order to produce an offspring that carries genetic material from both parents. The pair of parents is called the parental generation, or **P generation**. The offspring of this initial breeding is known as the first filial generation, or **F1 generation**. If the F1 generation is intentionally bred as well, the offspring of this generation is known as the second filial generation, or **F2 generation**. This pattern of naming continues on as more generations are bred during experimentation.

The purpose of these genetic crosses is to isolate and study traits as they are passed through the generations. In **monohybrid** crosses, the P generation is selected based on one particular trait—one parent possesses the dominant trait, while the other possesses the recessive trait. For example, in one of Mendel's pea experiments, he selectively bred one plant with the dominant yellow seed trait with another plant that had the recessive green seed trait. The parent with the dominant trait can have a genotype that is either homozygous (YY) or heterozygous (Yy), while the parent with the recessive trait has a homozygous genotype (yy).

The phenotype of the resulting F1 generation can be predicted using a **Punnett square**. This diagram determines the probability that an offspring will inherit a particular genotype. For monohybrid crosses, the Punnett square only has four possible combinations for a genotype.

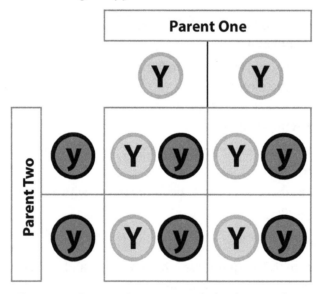

Figure 2.1. Punnett Square: Monohybrid Cross of Seed Color

The probability that a certain genotype combination will occur is the Punnett ratio. For example, if a homozygous yellow (YY) pea plant is crossed with a homozygous green (yy) pea plant, then the Punnett square will reveal that there is a 4/4 probability that the offspring will be Yy and yellow. This gives this monohybrid cross a Punnett ratio of 4:0.

In a **dihybrid cross**, the P generation is selected for two traits that differ between the two parents. One of Mendel's pea experiments included the dihybrid cross of a P generation that bred one parent with the two dominant traits (yellow and smooth, RRYY) with a parent that had two recessive traits (green and wrinkled, rryy). The Punnett Ratio for the F1 generation is 16:0, as an RRYY crossed with an rryy results in 16 RrYy offspring. The Punnett ratio for the F2 generation, in which an RrYy is crossed with another RrYy, is 9:3:3:1, with the following phenotypes:

- 9/16 probability that the second generation of offspring will be yellow and smooth

- 3/16 probability that the offspring will be yellow and wrinkled

- 3/16 probability that the offspring will be green and smooth

> **QUICK REVIEW**
>
> If the parent with the dominant yellow seed trait has a homozygous trait of YY and the second parent has a homozygous trait of yy, then there is a 100 percent chance that the F1 generation will express the yellow seed trait. How does this change if the YY parent instead has a Yy genotype?

- 1/16 probability that the offspring will be green and wrinkled.

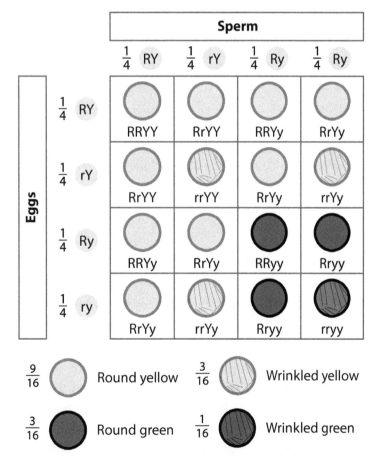

Figure 2.2. Punnett Square: Dihybrid Cross of Seed Color and Shape

SAMPLE QUESTIONS

3) **Which of the following describes the purpose of genetic crosses?**

A. to determine the probability of an expressed phenotype

B. to isolate and study inherited traits through generations

C. to manipulate the traits of offspring

D. to create a new set of traits

Answers:

A. Incorrect. This describes the purpose of a Punnett square.

B. Correct. This is the experimental purpose of genetic crosses.

C. Incorrect. This could be an application of information learned from a genetic crossing but is not the purpose of the experiment as defined.

D. Incorrect. This could be an application of information learned from a genetic crossing but is not the purpose of the experiment as defined.

4) **What is the probability that the offspring of a cross between two parents who are heterozygous for a particular trait will express the recessive trait?**

A. 100 percent

B. 75 percent

C. 50 percent

D. 25 percent

Answer:

D. Correct. One box of the Punnett square shows the (aa) genotype which is the only genotype that is capable of expressing the recessive trait.

PEDIGREE ANALYSIS

When studying genetics, it is not always possible to perform monohybrid and dihybrid crosses in order to determine how genes are passed through generations. In these instances, a **pedigree** analysis is used in place of a breeding experiment. A pedigree is a diagram of a familial genetic history, tracing inherited traits as they are passed on from generation to generation.

Similar in structure to a family tree, a pedigree chart shows relationships between mating pairs and their offspring. Circles are used to represent females; squares are used to represent males. If a family member has a homozygous genotype for a dominant trait, his or her pedigree symbol is completely filled in. Family members who have a heterozygous genotype for a dominant trait have their symbols partially filled in.

A close examination of a pedigree chart will help researchers determine if a particular trait is dominant or recessive. If the trait is dominant, then every individual with the trait will also have a parent with the same trait. If the trait is recessive, then it is possible for parents without the trait to produce offspring who exhibit the trait, indicating that parents are heterozygous carriers of the trait.

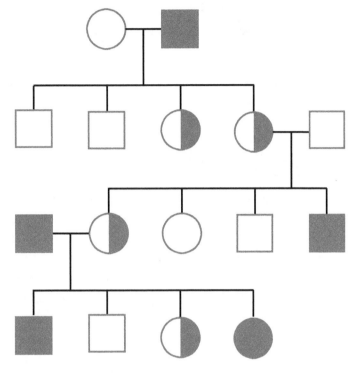

Figure 2.3. Pedigree Analysis

SAMPLE QUESTION

5) The pedigree analysis below shows the inheritance of the gene for cystic fibrosis through three generations. Which of the following is true about this genetic condition?

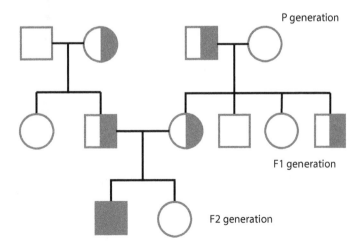

A. The trait is dominant.

B. Only the P generation carries the trait.

C. Only the F2 generation carries the trait.

D. The trait is recessive.

Answers:

A. Incorrect. A dominant trait would be expressed in all three generations; this trait is only expressed in the F2 generation.

B. Incorrect. The trait is carried by all three generations.

C. Incorrect. The trait is carried by all three generations.

D. **Correct.** This chart indicates a recessive trait, as it is carried by all three generations but only is expressed in the F2 generation.

Non–Mendelian Genetics

Non-Mendelian genetics refers to any processes or patterns of inheritance that do not follow Mendel's laws. Mendel's laws apply to traits that are controlled by one gene that has two possible alleles that have a dominant/recessive relationship. Many traits have alleles that do not have a dominant/recessive relationship. Other traits have many different kinds of possible alleles which also do not follow the traditional rules of dominance. Other traits are controlled by more than one gene which can be combined in many different arrangements and express different phenotypes.

Linkage

As previously discussed, chromosomes are the cell components that carry genes. Diploid cells have two copies of each chromosome. Each matching pair are called **homologous** chromosomes. Humans have 23 homologous pairs; 46 total chromosomes. During meiosis, the homologous pairs are split and divided into two distinct haploid cells. Genes that are situated close together on a chromosome are more likely to be inherited together. This relationship is known as **gene linkage**. Genes that are not found close together on a chromosome are not considered linked; genes that exist on separate chromosomes in the cell are also not considered linked.

Although these gene combinations are more likely to be transmitted together on the same chromosome, they do not always travel in tandem. This is due to a process called **recombination**. Recombination occurs during the prophase I stage of meiosis. During this stage, the chromosomes condense and separate into distinct **chromatids, each aligned with its homologue**. The chromatids of the duplicated, intertwined chromosomes

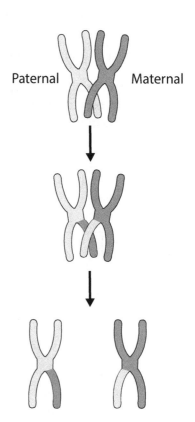

Figure 2.4. Recombination During Prophase I

swap alleles at random with each other by crossing over. The resulting chromosome has all the same genes but contains alleles from both chromosomes.

Tracking the frequency of linked genes being transmitted together can help researchers develop a **recombination map**. All genes have a 50 percent chance of being inherited with any other gene. Genes that are paired with another gene more than 50 percent of the time are more likely to be linked; the higher the percentage, the closer the genes are in distance to one another. This information is used to develop physical maps of genes, which help researchers further study and understand where genes, particularly disease-causing genes, are found.

Genetically linked traits that differ between males and females are called **sex linked**. Sex-linked genes are located on the **sex chromosome** of each individual. All females have two **X chromosomes**, while all males have both an X and a **Y chromosome**. Genes that are located on the Y chromosome result in traits that are expressed only in the males of a species. The Y chromosome is smaller and contains fewer genes than other chromosomes, so there are few examples of Y-linked traits or diseases.

HELPFUL HINT

The X and Y chromosomes that determine sex of the offspring are known as allosomes. The remaining chromosomes that determine the rest of an individual's genetic makeup are called autosomes. Humans have one pair of allosomes and twenty-two pairs of autosomes.

The X chromosomes are much larger and are found in both the males and females of a species. Since females have two X chromosomes, this means that they also have two possible alleles, and the dominant allele will express itself for X-linked traits. Males, however, only have one allele for every X gene. As a result, this is the trait that will be expressed, regardless of whether it is a dominant or recessive allele. This phenomenon accounts for several X-linked traits and disorders—such as colorblindness and hemophilia—that are carried by females but primarily expressed in males.

SAMPLE QUESTIONS

6) **Which of the following is true about recessive X-linked genetic traits?**

   A.   They are carried by females but primarily expressed in males.

   B.   They are only expressed in females.

   C.   They are only expressed in males.

   D.   They are carried by males but primarily expressed in females.

   Answers:

   A.   **Correct.** Females carry recessive X-linked traits but do not necessarily express them, while males express a disproportionate number of these traits.

B.   Incorrect. Recessive X-linked traits can be expressed by both males and females, but are more common in men.

C.   Incorrect. Recessive X-linked traits can be expressed by both males and females, but are more common in men.

D.   Incorrect. Both males and females carry X-linked traits, but males express a disproportionate number of these traits.

7)   **Which of the following is true about the relative locations of linked genes?**

A.   They are located near each other on the same chromosome.

B.   They are located at opposite ends of the same chromosome.

C.   They are located near each other on separate chromosomes.

D.   They are located at opposite ends of separate chromosomes.

Answers:

A.   **Correct.** Genes must be located near one another on the same chromosomal structure in order to be linked.

B.   Incorrect. The further apart the genes are found on the chromosome, the less likely they will be linked.

C.   Incorrect. Genes that are on separate chromosomes cannot be linked.

D.   Incorrect. Genes that are on separate chromosomes cannot be linked.

CODOMINANCE AND INCOMPLETE DOMINANCE

Mendelian genetics are rooted in the notion that there are two alleles possible for every gene—a dominant allele and a recessive allele. Further scientific developments have determined that many genes have **multiple alleles**. When multiple alleles exist in a population, there is a much greater genetic diversity, more complex rules of dominance, and many more combinations of phenotypes that can be expressed.

A classic example of multiple alleles in a human population are the alleles that determine the **human blood type**. Blood type is determined by a type of protein called an **antigen** that is found on the surface of red blood cells. The most common antigens that determine blood type are the A and B antigens. Humans can have one of four different blood types based on the appearance or lack of antigens: A (A antigens only), B (B antigens only), AB (A and B antigens), and O (no antigens). A person's blood genotype is determined by which pairing of the three different blood type alleles they inherit from their parents: A (dominant), B (dominant), or O (recessive). Type A blood results from a pairing of either two Type A alleles or a Type A and a Type O allele. Similarly, Type B blood results from a pairing of either two Type B alleles or a Type B and a Type O allele. If an individual inherits Type O blood, it is the result of receiving two recessive O alleles from both parents. These patterns of inheritance follow Mendel's law of dominance.

When an individual inherits a dominant Type A and a dominant Type B allele, the law of dominance becomes more complex. The appearance of two dominant alleles creates an effect called **codominance**, in which both dominant genes are expressed in the individual. In this case, the individual that inherits both Type A and Type B blood would have Type AB blood, with red blood cells covered in both A and B antigens.

Parent Alleles	A	B	O
A	AA (A)	AB (AB)	AO (A)
B	AB (AB)	BB (B)	BO (B)
O	AO (A)	BO (B)	OO (O)

genotype of child → AO (A)

phenotype of child → BO (B)

Figure 2.5. Punnett Square: Human Blood Type

In some cases of inheritance, such as patterns involving eye color or flower color, one allele is not completely dominant over the other. When this occurs, **incomplete dominance** is expressed. One example of this is the flower pigmentation of snapdragon plants. In these plants, the red color is incompletely dominant over the recessive white color. In order for a red phenotype to be expressed, the plant needs contribution from both dominant alleles. Without this contribution from a second red allele, the plant will only produce a partial amount of red pigment. Therefore, when a plant inherits a red allele (R) and a white allele (W), the resulting phenotype is a pink flower.

QUICK REVIEW

The pink flower is heterozygous (RW), which means that it can pass on either allele to the next generation. Homozygous combinations of genotypes (RR, WW) will follow traditional Mendelian laws of dominance. What color offspring would pink flowers produce with red flowers? With white flowers? With other pink flowers?

	W	W
R	RW	RW
R	RW	RW

Figure 2.6. Punnett Square: Snapdragon Color

SAMPLE QUESTION

8) Type AB blood—the expression of both A and B antigens on a red blood cell surface—occurs as the result of which of the following?

A.   incomplete dominance

B.   recombination

C.   codominance

D.   independent assortment

Answers:

A.   Incorrect. Incomplete dominance occurs when one gene is not completely dominant over another, resulting in an impartial expression of the dominant allele.

B.   Incorrect. Recombination is the process of chromosomes exchanging genetic information during meiosis.

C.   Correct. Type AB blood occurs when two equally dominant alleles (A and B) are inherited. Since they are both dominant, one does not mask the other; instead, both are expressed.

D.   Incorrect. Independent assortment refers to the notion that all genes divide independently of one another.

GENE INTERACTION

The basic laws of Mendelian genetics seem to imply that most traits are governed by a single gene. However, the opposite of this is true. The majority of traits are determined by multiple genes in an inheritance pattern known as **polygenic inheritance**. Traits that are controlled by multiple genes include human height, eye color, and hair color. These traits can be determined by dozens to hundreds of different genes. Unlike the traits observed in Mendel's pea plants, these traits do not come in only a select number of varieties. Instead, traits such as height, are observed in **continuous variation**, meaning that heights exist along a continuum.

Genes that are found at different **loci** (placements on the chromosome) can also interact and have an impact upon one another. **Epistasis** occurs when one gene suppresses the expressed phenotype of another gene. This differs from a dominant/recessive relationship because these are not alleles for the same trait. Instead, the phenotype expressed by one gene is dependent upon a **modifier gene** that can mask the trait. This is common in the genes that influence the pigment of eye color, hair or fur color, or feather color. Modifier genes do not always have a masking effect on the genes they modify; they can also diminish or augment the expression of another gene. For example, modifier genes can impact the amount of pigment produced by genes that control fur color in mammals.

The influence of a single gene is not limited to one trait. Through a process known as **pleiotropy**, one gene can have multiple effects. This can be viewed as the opposite of polygenic inheritance: rather than many genes influencing one trait, one gene influences many different traits. This can be seen in Mendel's experiments on pea plants, where Mendel noted that the gene that controlled the color of the seed coat also had an impact on the color of the plant's flowers and axils.

SAMPLE QUESTION

9)   **Which of the following is NOT true about epistasis?**

   A.   Epistasis results in a certain phenotype being hidden.

   B.   Epistasis is an interaction between genes on two different loci.

   C.   Epistasis is a dominant/recessive relationship between alleles.

   D.   In epistasis, one gene is modified by another.

   Answers:

   A.   Incorrect. Epistasis results in one gene masking the phenotypic expression of another gene.

   B.   Incorrect. The genes interacting during epistasis are found on different chromosomal locations.

   C.   Correct. Epistasis differs from dominance because the two interacting genes are not alleles of the same gene at the same loci.

   D.   Incorrect. The modifier gene masks the trait of the other gene.

ORGANELLE INHERITANCE

The majority of DNA is found within a cell's nucleus. Short strands of DNA make up genes, which are found in chromosomes and are the source of most of an organism's genetic variability. But there is some DNA that can be found outside the nucleus within other specialized cell structures, or organelles—such as the mitochondria and chloroplasts—which is passed on from parent to offspring. This process is called **organelle inheritance**. The primary type of organelle inheritance from extranuclear organelles is called **uniparental inheritance** because the genetic material of these organelles comes only from the mother. This type of inheritance most commonly occurs in eukaryotic animals that undergo sexual reproduction.

HELPFUL HINT

There are two other types of organelle inheritance. Biparental inheritance, (organelle inheritance from both parents), is less common than uniparental inheritance but can occur among organisms that reproduce by fusing two organisms during their haploid life stage. Vegetative segregation—the random replication of organelles during cell division and the partitioning of cytoplasmic organelles—is another example of organelle inheritance that occurs among organisms that reproduce asexually.

The most prominent example of uniparental organelle inheritance among humans is maternal **mitochondrial inheritance**. The mitochondria are the major energy producers of a cell and will often replicate in response to an organism's increasing energy needs. The genetic material within the mitochondria replicates independently of the genetic material in the cell nucleus. At fertilization, the egg provides a copy of the mother's mitochondrial DNA, with no paternal influence. As a result, mitochondrial traits—along with any genetic variation or disorders—are passed only from mother to offspring.

SAMPLE QUESTION

10) **Which of the following is the inheritance of DNA that is contained outside the nucleus?**

    A.   biparental inheritance

    B.   organelle inheritance

    C.   mitochondrial inheritance

    D.   polygenic inheritance

Answers:

    A.   Incorrect. Biparental inheritance is one specific type of organelle inheritance.

    B.   **Correct.** Organelle inheritance refers to DNA that is replicated and passed on to offspring outside of the nucleus.

    C.   Incorrect. Mitochondrial inheritance refers to inheritance from that one particular organelle.

    D.   Incorrect. Polygenic inheritance refers to the process of many genes contributing to the expression of one particular trait.

SOURCES OF GENETIC VARIATION

The genome of each individual organism is composed of DNA sequences that are quite similar across a population of organisms. Alterations, or **mutations**, to this common strand of DNA are a primary source of genetic variation within a population. DNA is composed of a sequence of bases (adenine, thymine, guanine, and cytosine) that contain instructions for genes to create traits. Although most mutations have no effect on the expressed genes of an individual, some can cause a variation in traits, such as change in face shape or eye color. If a DNA mutation occurs in the cells that eventually become gametes, then these mutations can be inherited by the offspring.

Genetic variation is made more complex and varied among eukaryotes that undergo sexual reproduction. Asexually reproducing organisms create offspring by replicating exact copies of DNA from one parent, which limits genetic variation. However, if two parents contribute a set of genetic information, then there are many more possible combinations of genetic information that can occur in offspring. In sexual reproduction, parent cells undergo meiosis to create haploid cells—gametes that will fuse with other gametes during fertilization. The law of independent assortment asserts that genetic information divides at random, which ensures that each gamete contains slightly different genetic information. When gametes fuse during fertilization, each gamete is providing a unique combination of genetic information that increases genetic diversity in the population.

Recombination, or **crossing-over** during meiosis, is another source of genetic variation among eukaryotic organisms. As previously discussed, recombination occurs during the prophase I stage of meiosis as gametes are forming. During this process, homologous chromosomes will come together and swap sections of genetic information to create a chromosome that contains genetic information from both parents. The new chromosome will contain genetic codes that vary from the parent generation and will be passed on in the offspring, contributing genetic variation to the gene pool.

Prokaryotic organisms do not undergo meiosis to reproduce and therefore do not cross over or reproduce sexually to create variety in genetic information among a population. Instead, bacteria and archaebacteria exchange genetic information via **transduction**, **transformation**, and **conjugation**. These three genetic exchanges allow bacteria to create new DNA sequences without forming gametes or undergoing sexual reproduction.

Transduction occurs when a host bacterium is infected by a bacterial virus, or **phage**, that absorbs genetic information from the host cell into its own genetic code. This genetic information is transferred to another bacterium when the phage moves on to another host cell.

In transformation, a bacterium uptakes DNA from a source outside the cell. This **exogenous** DNA, which can come from a closely related dead bacteria cell, is absorbed through the membrane of the transforming bacteria. In order to absorb and express the new genetic information, the receiving bacteria must be in a state of **competence**, meaning that it is sufficiently permeable to receive new genetic information.

Conjugation is the only one of the three methods of genetic exchange in bacteria that require cell-to-cell contact. During this process, **plasmids** are exchanged over a connection between two different bacterial cells. Plasmids are small, extrachromosomal DNA molecules contained within a bacteria that carry genes. These circular-shaped structures replicate independently from the DNA within a chromosome. Conjugation begins when a bacterium produces a **pilus**—a thin appendage that connects to another cell. A portion of plasmid DNA is then transferred over the pilus to the new cell. Once plasmid DNA is successfully transferred to a new host cell, its genetic information can recombine with the genetic information found in the host. This process can occur within species of protozoa and algae, in addition to bacteria.

SAMPLE QUESTIONS

11) Homologous chromosomes swap pieces of genetic information in which of the following processes?

   A.   crossing over

   B.   reproduction

   C.   inheritance

   D.   variation

Answers:

   A.   Correct. Crossing over (recombination) happens during meiosis in eukaryotic cells.

   B.   Incorrect. Genetic information is not swapped when cells fertilize and reproduce.

   C.   Incorrect. Inheritance is the process of receiving genes from parent organisms.

   D.   Incorrect. Variation is the result of crossing over but not the process itself.

12) Which of the following terms describes a permanent change to a base found in a DNA sequence?

   A.   variation

   B.   recombination

   C.   mutation

   D.   duplication

Answers:

   A.   Incorrect. Variation is a result of a mutation but not the act of mutating itself.

   B.   Incorrect. Recombination results in an altered chromosome, not an altered DNA strand.

   C.   Correct. A mutation is an alteration of one of the bases (A, C, G, or T) of a DNA sequence.

   D.   Incorrect. A mutation may occur as genetic information duplicates during cell division, but duplication is not the correct term for this process.

GENETIC DISORDERS

Mutations to chromosomes can lead to a number of complications in humans. If the mutation is lethal, the resulting zygote or embryo will be miscarried. Other chromosomal mutations and changes lead to physical abnormalities or genetic disorders. Still others have little to no effect on the resulting offspring but add to genetic diversity among a population. The primary mutations occur with the number of chromosomes within a cell and the order and structure of genetic information on the chromosome itself.

CHANGES IN CHROMOSOME NUMBERS

Humans reproduce by producing haploid egg and sperm cells, which each have one full set of chromosomes. Their chromosomal number—n—is 23. Gametes meet and fuse during fertilization to form a diploid zygote, which has a chromosomal number of $2n$, or 46. The state of having an equal number of chromosomes that is an exact multiple of the haploid number is called **euploidy**. An alteration to chromosomal numbers in an individual changes the ploidy state and causes a variety of different genetic disorders.

A **monoploid** is an organism that has half the normal number of chromosomes. This differs from haploid cells, which are gametes that fuse with other haploid cells. There are examples of organisms that exist as monoploid in their adult state. These include some species of fungi and plants, as well as insects, such as bees and ants. These cases are rare and result in sterile, non-reproducing adults.

Polyploids have more than two pairs of chromosomes. This includes triploids (three sets), tetraploids (four sets), hexaploids (five sets), and so on. There are multiple groups of organisms that exist normally in a state of polyploidy. Flowering plants, which constitute the largest group of plants on Earth, obtained their state of genetic diversity and speciation by existing and reproducing in increasingly higher ploidy levels. Some modern crops, such as watermelon and bananas, are bred specifically for a triploid state in order to produce seedless produce for human consumption. Polyploidy in humans is rare and usually lethal. Most polyploid embryos are triploids, with an extra set of chromosomes coming from either the mother or the father, and result in miscarriages.

Chromosome number abnormalities occur as a result of **nondisjunction**—the failure of one or more chromosomes to fully separate during meiosis. This results in gametes with abnormal numbers of chromosomes, with one gamete receiving an extra chromosome and the other forming without one. **Monosomy** occurs when nondisjunction results in the loss of a single chromosome. The chromosome number of this cell then becomes $2n - 1$. **Trisomy** occurs when a chromosome is added to the cell, making the chromosome number $2n + 1$.

Most cases of monosomy are not survivable and result in miscarriage. One exception is **Turner syndrome**. This disorder occurs among females who are missing an X chromosome, giving them a total of 45 chromosomes instead of the normal 46. The missing chromosome leads to a wide array of possible abnormalities, although these are varied and rarely all occur in one individual. Potential abnormalities include growth reduction, webbed neck, and heart disorders.

Excess genetic material found on chromosome 21 in humans leads to a disorder called **Down syndrome**. An individual with Down syndrome has 47 chromosomes, instead of the normal number of 46. The presence of these additional genes on the extra chromosome leads to genetic abnormalities such as growth reduction and decreased mental ability.

SAMPLE QUESTIONS

13) **Which of the following is a type of ploidy in which the organism has half the normal number of chromosomes?**

   A. euploid

   B. diploid

   C. monoploid

   D. polyploid

   Answers:

   A. Incorrect. Euploids have normal amounts of chromosomes.

   B. Incorrect. Diploids have two sets of chromosomes, which is normal for most organisms.

   C. Correct. Monoploids have one set of chromosomes, or half of the normal amount.

   D. Incorrect. Polyploids have multiple sets of chromosomes.

14) **Which of the following occurs when a gamete is formed with a chromosome number of $2n + 1$ following nondisjunction?**

   A. monoploidy

   B. trisomy

   C. polyploidy

   D. monosomy

   Answers:

   A. Incorrect. Monoploidy occurs when there is only one set of chromosomes with no homologous pairs (number n).

   B. Correct. Trisomy results in a gamete forming with extra genetic material due to an additional chromosome (number $2n + 1$).

   C. Incorrect. Polyploidy occurs when there are more than two full sets of chromosomes, not just a single extra chromosome ($3n$, $4n$, etc.)

   D. Incorrect. Monosomy occurs when a gamete is formed without one of its chromosomes (number $2n - 1$).

CHANGES IN CHROMOSOME STRUCTURE

Abnormalities can occur as chromosomes duplicate, recombine, and divide during meiosis. Sections of chromosomes can break off, be deleted, or be otherwise mutated during this process. This alters the DNA sequence found within the chromosome and can lead to genetic disorders, physical deformities, or other abnormalities.

Chromosome **deletion** occurs when a section of chromosome is lost during cell division. Small or large sections of a chromosome can become deleted; if the section is large enough, the zygote is usually miscarried. Zygotes that survive will have a disorder or physical abnormalities at birth. Examples of chromosome deletion disorders include Cri du Chat syndrome and Wolf-Hirschhorn syndrome.

A second form of mutation to chromosome structure is called **duplication**. Just as sections of chromosomes can be deleted, there is also a possibility that sections can be duplicated. This can occur when homologous chromosomes exchange unequal amounts of information during recombination or when DNA is copied onto the incorrect DNA strand. Duplication is not always a harmful event; in fact, much of the genetic diversity that gives rise to species' evolution stems from gene duplication. In other cases, genetic disorders, such as Huntington's disease, can occur as a result.

HELPFUL HINT

When the end of a chromosome structure is deleted, it is possible for a **ring chromosome structure** to form. Depending on which chromosome it appears, ring formations can cause different kinds of disorders.

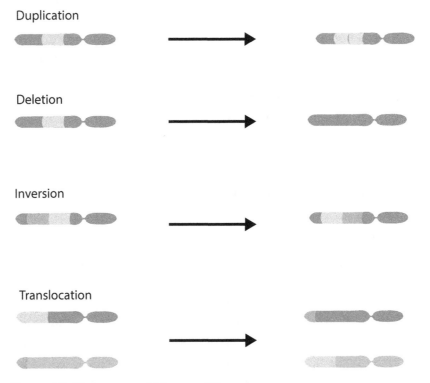

Figure 2.7. Chromosomal Abnormalities

Abnormalities can occur even when all pieces of a chromosome are present. **Translocation** occurs when nonhomologous chromosomes exchange information within a cell. The resulting cells often express a normal set of traits but can lead to infertility within the offspring. **Inversion** occurs when a section of a chromosome breaks off of the main chromosome, becomes inverted, and then reattaches to the same chromosome structure. As seen with translocation, inversions usually do not lead to any genetic abnormalities unless they coincide with chromosome deletion or duplication.

SAMPLE QUESTION

15) **Which of the following types of chromosome structure changes can lead to a ring chromosome being formed?**

A. deletion

B. translocation

C. inversion

D. duplication

Answers:

A. **Correct.** When one or both end sections of a chromosome become deleted, it increases the likelihood that one end of the chromosome will attach to the other to form a ring.

B. Incorrect. Ring structures are unlikely to form on a chromosome that has experienced translocation, unless it is accompanied by deletion on one end.

C. Incorrect. Ring structures are unlikely to form on a chromosome that has experienced inversion, unless it is accompanied by deletion on one end.

D. Incorrect. Ring structures are unlikely to form on a chromosome that has experienced duplication, unless it is accompanied by deletion on one end.

COMMON GENETIC DISORDERS

Cystic fibrosis is a genetic disorder caused by the deletion of protein-producing genetic material on the CFTR gene. This is an **autosomal recessive disorder** that is inherited by having two parents who are carriers of the mutated gene. It is characterized by a thick buildup of mucus lining the lungs, pancreas, and other major organs, which can cause infection, prevent food digestion, and respiratory failure.

Huntington's disease is a degenerative disease that breaks down nerve cells in the brain and causes cognitive and psychiatric impairment. Signs and symptoms of the disease do not present themselves until later in life, when the individual is in his or her thirties or forties. It is caused by the duplication of genetic material, causing excess amounts of the huntingtin protein. Huntington's disease is an **autosomal**

dominant disorder. Parents have a 50 percent chance of passing the disorder on to their children.

Sickle cell anemia is a recessive autosomal disorder that occurs when a single protein subunit of the hemoglobin gene, called beta-globin, is substituted with the incorrect unit. This abnormality causes the individual's red blood cells to be distorted from a round shape to a sickle shape. The shape distortion causes the cells to break down easily, resulting in low blood cell counts, jaundice, infections, and repeated bouts of pain.

Many different types of **muscular dystrophy** exist among humans, all of which are caused by a mutation to a gene unique to the type of disease. In general, these mutations cause the degeneration of skeletal muscle tissue. All forms are caused by a mutation to a gene that prevents the proper production of **dystrophin**—a protein that repairs and builds muscle tissue. The gene defect that causes muscular dystrophy is commonly found on the X chromosome and is an X-linked recessive disorder, but other kinds of disorders are passed on through both parents and are either autosomal dominant or autosomal recessive disorders.

PKU, or phenylketonuria, is caused by a gene defect that increases phenylalanine levels in the body. Phenylalanine is an amino acid found in proteins; a buildup of this substance can cause intellectual disability, seizures, and developmental delays. The disorder is autosomal recessive and caused by a mutation to the PAH gene that prevents phenylalanine from being broken down properly in the body.

Tay-Sachs disease is a degenerative nerve disease that destroys brain and spinal cord cells, leading to severe motor and intellectual disability and loss of life in early childhood. It is an autosomal recessive disease caused by a mutation to the HEXA gene, which is responsible for producing enzymes that break down and remove toxic substances in nerve cells.

Albinism occurs when an individual lacks the proper amount of melanin pigment found in the skin, hair, and eyes, causing him or her to have partial or no pigmentation. There are several different kinds of albinism. Most cases are autosomal recessive disorder, but others are passed on through the X chromosome. Albinism is most commonly caused by a mutation to the TYR gene, which produces an enzyme found in melanin-producing cells.

Polydactyly is a genetic defect that causes the appearance of extra fingers or toes on an individual. There are many different possible mutations to the GLI3 gene that can lead to this condition. Polydactyly can be either autosomal recessive or dominant, depending on the specific genetic mutation, and the symptoms can express themselves in different numbers or body locations in different family members who inherit the trait.

Hemophilia is an X-linked recessive genetic disorder that primarily appears in males. It is linked to a deleted or defected gene that produces a blood-clotting protein. Without this protein, individuals with hemophilia experience prolonged bleeding, which can lead to excessive blood loss or death if not treated properly.

Red-green color blindness is another example of an X-linked genetic disorder. This condition arises when there is a mutation among the genes that produces proteins in the retina to detect certain colors.

SAMPLE QUESTIONS

16) **Which of the following is NOT an example of a genetic disorder that can be inherited through an X-linked recessive gene?**

   A.   red-green color blindness

   B.   hemophilia

   C.   PKU

   D.   muscular dystrophy

   Answers:

   A.   Incorrect. Red-green color blindness arises from several gene mutations on the X chromosome.

   B.   Incorrect. Hemophilia is an example of a recessive X-linked disorder.

   C.   Correct. PKU is an example of an autosomal recessive disorder.

   D.   Incorrect. Different kinds of muscular dystrophy are inherited in different ways, including through X-linked genes.

17) **Which of the following genetic disorders arises as a result of a mutation to the TYR gene, which produces melanin?**

   A.   muscular dystrophy

   B.   albinism

   C.   polydactyly

   D.   Tay-Sachs

   Answers:

   A.   Incorrect. Muscular dystrophy arises from a defect to genes that produce dystrophin, which is a protein that repairs and builds muscle tissue.

   B.   Correct. Albinism is a genetic condition in which the melanin-producing protein is inhibited, thus causing lack of pigmentation.

   C.   Incorrect. Polydactyly is a result of a mutation to the GLI3 gene, which is responsible for shaping embryonic material into patterns.

   D.   Incorrect. Tay-Sachs arises due to a mutation to the HEXA gene, which is responsible for producing enzymes that break down and remove toxic substances in nerve cells.

POPULATION GENETICS

Population genetics examines how genes are distributed and move within and between different species **populations**. A population is a group of organisms of the same species that are all located in the same geographic area. The **gene pool** is the complete set of genetic information that exists within a population. **Allele frequency** refers to how often a particular allele occurs in the gene pool of a population. Population geneticists study how the allele frequency of a population's gene pool shifts over time, integrating essential concepts of Mendelian genetics with the concepts of natural selection and evolution.

DISTRIBUTION AND MOVEMENT OF ALLELES IN POPULATIONS

There are several different mechanisms that allow alleles to move within and between populations of species. One of these mechanisms is **gene flow**—the movement of alleles from one population to another. Genes move from population to population via **migration**, which is the movement of the individual organism from one population to another. Gene flow can result from migration if the migrating individuals successfully reproduce with members of the new population. If the populations are genetically distinct from one another, then the migrating individuals introduce new alleles and gene combinations into the population. This accomplishes two things: it increases the genetic diversity of the gene pool, and it also alters the frequency with which certain alleles appear in the population.

Changes to allele distribution can also happen within a population. One of these mechanisms is called **genetic drift**. Genetic drift is the variation in gene frequency within a population and accounts for the random nature in which traits are passed on. Sometimes, due to random external events, an individual that does not possess desirable adaptations can reproduce more successfully than others. For example, a population of mice with black fur may not reproduce due to a random external factor unrelated to the fitness of the black fur trait, such as all black mice happened to get caught in mouse traps. This alters the relative frequency of a particular allele in a population. Genetic drift can affect all populations, but is most effectual in populations that are small in size. Populations that are reduced due to chance events, such as natural disaster or disease, will see changes in allele frequency as the surviving population members contribute a small number of alleles to the gene pool.

Another mechanism that leads to a change in allele frequency is **nonrandom mating**. This means that the probability that two members of a population will mate is not equal to other pairs in the population. A form of nonrandom

QUICK REVIEW

In general, animal species are mobile and are capable of physically moving from one population to another. Plants, however, are not mobile organisms and rely on seed and pollen dispersal in order to increase genetic diversity through gene flow. What plant mechanisms could cause migration among plants?

mating that directly leads to changes in allele frequency is **sexual selection**. This means that individuals are actively choosing their mate based on certain advantageous characteristics, which means that some members of a population mate more than others. Mates can be chosen due to superior physical characteristics or physical accessibility. In either case, the gene frequencies are altered in a population as a result.

SAMPLE QUESTIONS

18) Which of the following is the type of nonrandom mating that leads to changes in allele frequency?

   A.   sexual selection

   B.   genetic drift

   C.   reproduction

   D.   migration

   Answers:

   A.   **Correct.** Sexual selection changes allele frequency because it leads to some members of the population reproducing more frequently than others.

   B.   Incorrect. Genetic drift refers to the random inheritance of traits.

   C.   Incorrect. Reproduction is the result of both random and nonrandom mating.

   D.   Incorrect. Migration is the movement of individuals from one population to another.

19) Which of the following two mechanisms leads to a change of allele frequency within a population?

   A.   gene flow and migration

   B.   genetic drift and gene flow

   C.   nonrandom mating and genetic drift

   D.   migration and distribution

   Answers:

   A.   Incorrect. Migration can lead to gene flow and can lead to changes in allele frequency between populations, rather than within a population.

   B.   Incorrect. Genetic drift happens within a population; gene flow happens between two populations.

   C.   **Correct.** These are the two main mechanisms that lead to allele frequency changes within a population.

   D.   Incorrect. Migration is a movement of organisms to a new population; distribution is a general term that applies to changes in allele frequency both within and between populations.

HARDY–WEINBERG EQUILIBRIUM

The **Hardy-Weinberg equilibrium** states that the allele and genotype frequencies of a population will not change over time if there are no outside evolutionary forces. These frequencies can be calculated using a mathematical formula. The Hardy-Weinberg equilibrium is based on five conditions, or assumptions, of the population being studied. The five conditions are listed below:

1. The population must be large in size and have no genetic drift.
2. The population must be isolated, with no **immigration** of native population members to another population or **emigration** of individuals from outside the population.
3. There are no genetic mutations within the population.
4. Mating is random, with no sexual selection.
5. There is no natural selection.

Evolutionary forces, such as genetic drift, nonrandom mating, and gene flow can alter the allele frequencies within a population and are therefore not incorporated into the equilibrium.

The Hardy-Weinberg equation is the mathematical expression of the equilibrium principle. The equation for a genotype is written as follows: $p^2 + 2pq + q^2 = 1$. The p represents the frequency of the dominant allele in the equation; q represents the frequency of the recessive allele. Therefore, p^2 represents the frequency of a homozygous dominant genotype, while q^2 is the frequency of the homozygous recessive genotype. The figure $2pq$ represents the frequency of the heterozygous genotype. The sum of p and q must always equal 1, or 100 percent of the population. The equation $p + q = 1$ is the equation for the allele frequency in a population.

To use the equation, imagine a population of pea plants with a sample population size of 100. Of these 100, 60 pea plants are homozygous for yellow flowers (YY), 20 are heterozygous for yellow flowers (Yy), and 20 are homozygous for green flowers (yy). The genotype frequency can be determined by dividing each of the above genotypes by the total population, as seen below:

▸ YY = 60/100 = 0.6
▸ Yy = 20/100 = 0.2
▸ yy = 20/100 = 0.2

Once the frequency is determined for the genotype, then the allele frequency can be determined. To do this, each allele must be accounted for within each genotype. Each YY plant has two Y alleles, which is a total of 120. Each The Yy plant has one Y allele, which is a total of 20. This brings the total number of Y alleles to 140. The same process is repeated for the y allele: each Yy plant has one y allele, which is a total of 20, and each yy has two y alleles, which is a total of 40. This brings the total number of y alleles to 60.

These individual totals are each divided by the total number of alleles in the population, which is 200. The resulting number is the allele frequency, which is represented in the Hardy-Weinberg equation as the *p* variable for the dominant Y allele and the *q* variable for the recessive y allele.

- ▸ $p = 140/200 = 0.7$
- ▸ $q = 60/200 = 0.3$

These numbers are plugged back into the Hardy-Weinberg equation for allele frequency: $0.7 + 0.3 = 1$.

Although there are few to zero examples of populations that meet all five conditions in the real world, the Hardy-Weinberg equation is still used as a model to help make predictions about a population. Population geneticists and other scientists can use the data determined from this equation and compare it to the data gathered from real-world populations. If the allele frequencies differ, then this means that the allele frequency is changing, and hypotheses can be made to determine why this is occurring.

SAMPLE QUESTIONS

20) **What does the *p* variable refer to in the Hardy-Weinberg equilibrium equation?**

   A.   the frequency of the recessive allele
   B.   the frequency of the homozygous genotype
   C.   the frequency of the heterozygous genotype
   D.   the frequency of the dominant allele

   Answers:

   A.   Incorrect. The recessive allele is represented as *q*.
   B.   Incorrect. The two homozygous genotypes are represented as p^2 and q^2.
   C.   Incorrect. The heterozygous genotype is represented as $2pq$.
   D.   Correct. The dominant allele is represented as *p*.

21) **Which of the following equations determines allele frequency?**

   A. $p + q = 1$
   B. $p^2 + 2pq + q^2 = 1$
   C. $p^2 + q^2 = 100$
   D. $p + q = 100$

   Answers:

   A.   Correct. The sum of the allele frequencies always equals 1.

MECHANISMS OF EVOLUTION

The simple definition of **evolution** is the gradual genetic change in species over time. Upon closer look, however, the process is quite complex. Multiple mechanisms of change are at play during this process. These mechanisms include natural and artificial selection, genetic drift, coevolution, and adaptive radiation. These mechanisms alter the variation and frequency of certain alleles and phenotypes within a population. This increased variation and frequency leads to varying reproductive success, in which individuals with certain traits survive over others. Combined, these mechanisms lead to a gradual change to individual populations of animals which, over time, can result in the creation of new species.

NATURAL AND ARTIFICIAL SELECTION

Natural selection is a process in which only the members of a population best adapted to their environment tend to survive and reproduce, which ensures that their favorable traits will be passed on in future generations of the species. There are four basic conditions that must be met in order for natural selection to occur, as seen below:

1. inherited variation
2. overproduction of offspring
3. fitness to environment
4. differential reproduction

Depending on which traits their parents passed on and individual DNA mutations, the offspring of a population will have inherited a wide variety of traits. Mutation and genetic recombination increase genetic variation by creating even more potential traits that occur among offspring. These various offspring have different combinations of traits that cause them to interact with their environment in different ways.

Overproduction of offspring happens when a population of a species produces more offspring than can possibly survive to reproductive age. Producing more offspring also means that there is more competition for resources such as food and water—in other words, a greater struggle to survive occurs. These offspring all vary in appearance and behavior; some will have inherited traits that give an individual an advantage in this competition for resources.

The offspring with inherited variations best suited for their environment will be more likely to survive than others and are therefore more likely to pass on their successful genes to future populations through reproduction. This is referred to as **fitness**. An organism that is considered biologically "fit" will be more successful passing on its genes through reproduction compared to other members of the population. The frequency of certain alleles in a gene pool will change as a result. The mechanism by which biologically fit animals alter the gene pool of a population is called **differential reproduction**. Simply put, differential reproduction is the idea that not all members of a population will reproduce at equal rates.

One factor that leads to differential reproduction within a population is sexual selection. As previously discussed, sexual selection occurs when individuals are actively choosing their mate based on certain advantageous characteristics. This, however, does not always mean that the most efficient, advantageous traits are being selected. **Intersexual selection** is a type of sexual selection in which one mate, usually the female, actively selects a mate based on many visual cues. The selection of male peacocks by peahens is a classic example of intersexual selection. Although there are no biological benefits to large, colorful feathers, the peahens consistently select mates with these characteristics. The bright feathers have become a visual cue to the peahens that the male peacock has advantageous traits to pass on to offspring.

Artificial selection occurs in a species when humans get involved in the reproductive process. Over the course of time, humans have intentionally bred together organisms with the same desirable traits in a process called **selective breeding**. This has led to the evolution of many common crops and farm animals that are bred specifically for human consumption, as well as among domesticated animals, such as horses or dogs. Although the mechanisms of evolution are different, the end result is the same as natural selection: the change in a population over time.

SAMPLE QUESTIONS

22) **Which of the following is NOT a condition of natural selection?**

A. differential reproduction

B. variation of inherited traits

C. selective breeding

D. overproduction of offspring

Answer:

C.   **Correct.** Selective breeding is an action that results in artificial selection, not natural selection. The other choices are conditions of natural selection.

23) **A female peahen selecting a mate based on the peacock's bright, showy feathers is an example of what kind of natural selection?**

A. artificial selection

B. differential reproduction

C. intersexual selection

D. selective breeding

Answers:

A.   Incorrect. Artificial selection is controlled by humans, rather than by nature.

B.   Incorrect. Differential reproduction occurs when all members of a population do not reproduce at equal rates.

C.   **Correct.** This is an example of one gender of a species selecting a mate based on desired characteristics, which is the definition of intersexual selection.

D.   Incorrect. Selective breeding leads to artificial selection and is the act of humans intentionally breeding two organisms with the same desirable traits.

GENETIC DRIFT

Natural selection is just one mechanism that leads to evolutionary change within a population or within a species. Genetic drift is another major driving force in this process. As previously discussed, genetic drift is a mechanism of evolution that does not involve "survival of the fittest." Rather, it results from random chance. Like natural selection, genetic drift alters the alleles and traits in a gene pool; unlike natural selection, it arises from random occurrences, such as natural disasters, disease, or human-caused incidents.

The effects of genetic drift is much stronger in smaller populations than larger ones. For example, an oil spill could wipe out half of a population of jellyfish in a certain geographic area. The animals that die as a result do not perish as a result of a non-advantageous gene or trait; their survival is random. The remaining gene pool has much less genetic diversity as a result, which alters the traits of the population. This phenomenon is known as the **bottleneck effect**. The jellyfish that survive and reproduce are all descendants of the same small population and are genetically very similar.

The **founder effect** is another example of genetic drift. In this situation, a small population of organisms becomes isolated from the large population through migration. The small population has much less genetic diversity. The genes that came with the founding population are passed on from generation to generation, especially if the population breeds among itself with few to no outside individuals immigrating to the group.

SAMPLE QUESTION

24)   **Which of the following mechanisms of evolution can lead to a loss of genetic diversity?**

A.   genetic drift

B.   natural selection

C.   adaptive radiation

D.   survival of the fittest

Answers:

A.   **Correct.** Random events lead to loss of population, which leads to loss of diversity in the gene pool.

B.   Incorrect. Natural selection requires a great variety of traits in a gene pool.

C.   Incorrect. Adaptive radiation leads to greater genetic diversity.

D.   Incorrect. This is not a mechanism of evolution.

COEVOLUTION

Coevolution is a mechanism of evolution in which the evolution of one organism affects the evolution of another organism. This most typically occurs among species of organisms that have a close, interdependent ecological relationship. A classic example of coevolution occurs between flower-producing plants and the insects that pollinate them. In order to successfully reproduce, flowering plants often depend on insects to transfer pollen from one plant to another. As flowers evolve to include characteristics that attract insects—such as flower color or sweet-tasting nectar—the insects respond by evolving to include characteristics that help them reach the flower, such as long mouthparts.

Organisms that have a **predator-prey** relationship are likely to coevolve. Predation occurs when one organism consumes another organism. The appearance and behavior of both predator and prey are strongly influenced by this relationship. Predators evolve strategies to help them be successful in capturing and consuming specific prey. This includes, for example, immunity to a particular prey's poison, or heightened senses to stalk prey in its environment. Similarly, prey evolve defense features in response. These can include increased camouflage or physical barriers, such as thorns or burrs.

Competition between species in an environment can also be a driving force of evolution. This occurs when two species within the same **ecological niche**, (the ecological space and role an organism plays in that space), compete for the same, limited resource. According to the **competitive exclusion principle**, one of these species will always become extinct in this scenario. Therefore, in order to survive, species must differentiate through evolution. Coevolution due to competition is frequently inferred among bird species, which differentiate bill shape and dietary requirements in their environment in response to species competing for the same food resources.

Mutualism is a relationship in which both species gain a mutual benefit from one another. For example, certain species

HELPFUL HINT

The phenomenon of predators and prey evolving increasingly stronger attack and defense mechanisms is commonly known as the coevolutionary arms race. For example, mollusks in the ocean may evolve stronger shells to avoid predation, but their predators may evolve increasingly stronger jaws or claws in response.

of algae and fungi coexist in a mutually-beneficial structure called a lichen. The algae photosynthesizes and provides a food source; the fungi provides a suitable habitat for algae. The two different species coevolved in response to one another—a change in one species prompted a change in another, which provides benefits to both organisms in the relationship and resulted in two species that have a dependent relationship upon one another.

SAMPLE QUESTION

25) Which of the following is NOT an example of relationships between organisms acting as a driving force of coevolution?

    A.   mutualism

    B.   competition

    C.   predator/prey

    D.   founder effect

Answers:

    A.   Incorrect. Both species in a mutualistic relationship evolved in response to one another to the benefit of both.

    B.   Incorrect. Competition can drive species to differentiate in order to survive.

    C.   Incorrect. Predators and prey evolve mechanisms to help them survive in this relationship.

    D.   **Correct.** The founder effect is not a relationship between two species of organisms.

ADAPTIVE RADIATION

A prime example of one of the driving mechanisms of evolution was initially observed by Charles Darwin during his study of the species of finches, a type of bird found throughout the Galápagos Islands. Natural selection in different habitats on the various Galápagos Islands led to differential reproductive success among finches with different traits—and eventually led to thirteen different species found throughout the islands. This phenomenon is known as **adaptive radiation**. Adaptive radiation is the rapid diversification of the gene pool when the species is introduced to new environments. This event usually leads to the development of many species originating from the original population of organisms.

Each of the newly formed populations of species are distinguished from the founding population by different **adaptations** to the environment. An adaptation is an inherited feature or behavior that has become common among the individuals of a species due to natural selection. Adaptations will provide a species with an advantage in their environment and will arise through natural selection when the need for a particular function is present. This is seen again with the adaptive radiation of the Galápagos finch species. Each of the thirteen species has slight morphological differences that make each group uniquely fit for its particular environment. After generations of inbreeding with individuals with similar adaptive traits, these groups have become distinct species.

SAMPLE QUESTION

26) **The rapid speciation of thirteen species of Galápagos finches stemming from one original species is an example of which of the following mechanisms of evolution?**

    A.   adaptation

    B.   morphological difference

    C.   adaptive radiation

    D.   artificial selection

Answers:

    A.   Incorrect. An adaptation is a result of natural selection but is not a mechanism of evolution.

    B.   Incorrect. Adaptive radiation can lead to morphological differences, but the differences are not mechanisms of evolution.

    C.   **Correct.** Adaptive radiation is the rapid change in a gene pool of a species.

    D.   Incorrect. Artificial selection is an evolutionary mechanism created by humans through selective breeding.

CONVERGENT AND DIVERGENT EVOLUTION

When two unrelated species face similar types of environments, they may evolve a similar trait or behavior in response to the environmental pressure. This process is called **convergent evolution**. The resulting similar traits are called **analogous structures**. These structures are very similar in appearance and function but evolved from distinct lineages. An example of this are the wings of bats compared to the wings of birds. In both cases, wings evolved in response to the environmental pressure to fly. However, a closer look at the genetics and morphology of these two sets of wings reveal that they are genetically distinct. Although the groups of species may have shared a **common ancestor** at some point in their lineage, wings were not a shared structure with the common ancestor; instead, bird wings and bat wings evolved independently of one another.

When two or more species descend from a common ancestor but evolve dissimilar traits, this is seen as an example of **divergent evolution**. Divergent evolution is essentially the opposite of convergent evolution, as it results in genetically similar species with very dissimilar structures and functions. Compare the wing of a bat with the arm of a human. These two structures are very different in terms of appearance and function. However, a close-up examination of their morphology shows that these limbs are similar in structure.

As different populations of the same species face different kinds of environments and environmental pressures, they begin to acquire different adaptations in response. The divergence of two populations can result in **speciation**—the division of a single species into two or more distinct species. This is seen again in the divergence of the Galápagos finches, as previously discussed. Adaptive radiation among the founding species led to populations of finches with distinct adaptations that evolved in response to different environmental pressures in their respective geographic areas. Generations of nature selecting for these divergent traits led to the genetic separation of this common ancestor into thirteen different species.

> **QUICK REVIEW**
>
> What are some examples of environmental pressures that could cause convergent evolution? Divergent evolution?

SAMPLE QUESTIONS

27) **Divergent evolution can lead to which of the following among two or more populations?**

   A.   common ancestors

   B.   speciation

   C.   analogous structures

   D.   natural selection

Answers:

   A.   Incorrect. Common ancestry is a prerequisite of divergent evolution.

   B.   Correct. Populations that diverge from one another can become a distinct species over time.

   C.   Incorrect. Analogous structures result from convergent evolution.

   D.   Incorrect. Natural selection is the greater evolutionary mechanism that can lead to divergent evolution; thus speciation.

28) **Which of the following types of evolution leads to analogous structures between two genetically distinct species?**

   A.   convergent evolution

   B.   coevolution

   C.   adaptive radiation

   D.   divergent evolution

Answers:

   A.   Correct. This is the correct definition of convergent evolution.

B.   Incorrect. Coevolution occurs as the result of an ecological relationship between two or more populations.

C.   Incorrect. Adaptive radiation is a type of evolution that stems from a common ancestor.

D.   Incorrect. Divergent evolution leads to differentiation or speciation between populations with a common ancestor.

THE RATE OF EVOLUTION

There is debate within the scientific community regarding the **rate** or speed at which evolution and speciation occurs. The two primary models of evolutionary rates are **gradualism** and **punctuated equilibrium**. Gradualism—one of Charles Darwin's early ideas regarding evolution—is the theory that evolution occurs as the result of small changes that are accumulated over a long period of time. This theory is backed up by geological findings and evidence in the fossil record. Fossils that support this theory are called **transitional fossils**. These fossils, also considered "missing link" fossils, exhibit traits found in both ancestral groups and their descendants. One primary example of a transitional fossil is the archaeopteryx, which exhibits traits of both feathered dinosaurs and their direct descendants, the birds. Many examples of transitional fossils exist among the geologic fossil record.

Although many transitional fossils exist, not enough have been found to account for all of the speciation and evolutionary diversity that exists on Earth. Comparatively, there are many more examples of species remaining unchanged for long periods of time. **Punctuated equilibrium** is the theory that species tend to remain in **stasis**—a long period of inactive equilibrium—and only experience significant evolution and speciation in short bursts of time. This theory originated in 1972 after the discovery of a series of trilobite fossils. These fossils showed rapid change in trilobites in the *Phacos* genus in a short period of time after a long period of stasis.

These competing models of evolutionary rates are both considered viable in the scientific community, although much debate exists regarding which model is the most plausible and is supported by the most evidence. It is probable that speciation through evolution happens both gradually and in punctuated bursts, although more evidence is needed to make a final determination.

SAMPLE QUESTION

29) **Which of the following are considered "missing links" between ancestral organisms and their descendants?**

A.   inherited traits

B.   common ancestors

C.   analogous structures

D.   transitional fossils

Answers:

A.   Incorrect. Inherited traits may be found in the "missing link," but the transitional fossil is considered the "missing link" itself.

B.   Incorrect. Common ancestors are not examples of "missing links."

C.   Incorrect. This refers to structures that share similar features and functions.

D.   **Correct.** Transitional fossils exhibit traits found in both ancestors and descendants.

SPECIATION

Species are the smallest taxonomic rank, consisting of a group of organisms with similar characteristics that breed together in nature, creating fertile offspring in the process. All individuals within a species can inherit genes from the same gene pool. Generally, these groups of organisms cannot interbreed with other species, although there are some exceptions to this rule. **Speciation** is the process of a population of organism becoming genetically distinct from its parent species. Speciation can occur as the result of reproductive isolation or the reduction of gene flow within a species. This section will examine the mechanisms of gene isolation in depth as well as compare and contrast different types of speciation.

The concept of species varies widely between the different domains of life. The standard definition of species applies most fittingly to sexually reproducing Eukaryotic organisms. Prokaryotic organisms, which include bacteria, do not follow the same rules and have a different species concept. As a result, proper classification of prokaryotes is a controversial subject in the field of biology.

REPRODUCTIVE ISOLATION

The concept of reproductive isolation is central to speciation. The isolation of a population alone will not result in speciation. Once they are isolated, however, there is no longer gene flow between populations. The isolated populations may undergo structural or behavioral changes that will differentiate them enough from the other populations so that inbreeding is no longer possible. There are several different mechanisms that cause this isolation to occur.

Pre-zygotic isolation describes types of isolation that occur before gametes are formed through fertilization. This group of mechanisms encompasses the different types of isolation that prevent two parent individuals from copulating and creating any offspring. Pre-zygotic isolation mechanisms are far more common than post-zygotic isolation, which will be discussed shortly. Types of pre-zygotic isolation include habitat, temporal, behavioral, mechanical, and gamete isolation.

Habitat isolation keeps two populations separated from one another because their needs are met in different geographic areas, thereby greatly reducing the possibility that the two groups of individuals will meet. This can include simple geographic barriers, such as impassable mountain ranges or bodies of water, as well as different types of habitats. For example, different bear species have their needs fulfilled in different types of areas. Polar bears and certain subspecies of grizzly bears live in the same general geographic area in the Arctic Circle. Since their specific needs are met by different habitats, however, they rarely meet and interbreed in the wild, despite their genetic similarities.

Behavioral isolation is a mechanism that results from the tendencies of certain species to select a mate for interbreeding. This choice usually involves mating rituals and displays that are specific to that particular species. These rituals can be as simple as a call or pheromone released, or they can be quite complex. The blue-footed booby, a large seabird found in warm-water areas of the Pacific, is renowned for an elaborate mating dance performed by males in order to attract a female. Even if other similar species of boobies were in the area, they would not select a blue-footed booby as a mate because their species has evolved a different set of behaviors for mate selection.

A type of isolation that commonly occurs among plant species is **temporal isolation**. This is isolation that occurs because the organisms are only able to reproduce within a short window of time. If another population reproduces at a different time, they are unlikely to mate and produce offspring. This can be seen among flowering plant species, which flower and release pollen for fertilization during very short windows of time. When these flowering windows do not overlap, the populations become isolated.

The previous forms of isolation prevent copulation from happening to begin with. Other forms of isolation prevent the formation of gametes even if two individuals from two species attempt to mate. **Mechanical isolation** results in structural changes to the reproductive organs of two populations that prevent male and female structures from coming together. The two groups are not physically compatible, and therefore cannot mate. **Gamete isolation** prevents an egg and a sperm from coming together, even if the reproductive structures are physically compatible and the two individuals are able to copulate. This can occur among groups of species that practice external fertilization—sperm and egg cells are released at similar times and can potentially meet but are not capable of fusing during fertilization.

Post-zygotic isolation, as previously mentioned, is isolation that occurs after members of two species have successfully mated and reproduced, resulting in an offspring that carries genetic information from both parents. These resulting offspring, known as **hybrids**, are unlikely to survive and reproduce. Since their genetic information comes from two different species, they often do not have a full set of chromosomes that are compatible with one another. Many examples of hybrid species are miscarried or self-aborted before development is complete. Others that make it to term are often malformed or weak and are unlikely to thrive in their environment. If the hybrid does make it to adulthood, it often experiences **hybrid infertility** and will be unable to successfully pass on its genes to offspring.

Mules, which are hybrid offspring of horses and donkeys, are a classic example of organisms that experience hybrid infertility.

SAMPLE QUESTIONS

30) Which of the following is an example of post-zygotic isolation?

    A.   mechanical isolation

    B.   hybrid infertility isolation

    C.   gamete isolation

    D.   temporal isolation

Answers:

    A.   Incorrect. This is an example of pre-zygotic isolation.

    B.   **Correct.** This type of isolation occurs after individuals from two species mate and form a zygote.

    C.   Incorrect. Gamete isolation is an example of pre-zygotic isolation.

    D.   Incorrect. Temporal isolation is an example of pre-zygotic isolation.

31) Which of the following mechanisms of reproductive isolation is caused by structural changes to the reproductive structures of two different species?

    A.   mechanical

    B.   temporal

    C.   pre-zygotic

    D.   post-zygotic

Answers:

    A.   **Correct.** Species that are separated by mechanical isolation do not have compatible reproductive organs.

    B.   Incorrect. Temporal isolation is caused by species that reproduce during different times of the year.

    C.   Incorrect. The answer does describe an example of pre-zygotic isolation; however, there is a better, more specific answer.

    D.   Incorrect. This occurs after two species with compatible reproductive systems mate and form a gamete.

TYPES OF SPECIATION

The reproductive isolation mechanisms discussed above are all factors that prevent inbreeding among populations or species. Once inbreeding has slowed or ceased, and there is no longer a gene flow between different populations of the same species, then the allele frequency of each population's gene pool will change. This can lead to alterations in structure and behavior, which can cause further differentiation between the groups until they are no longer capable of interbreeding. This is called speciation, and there are several types of speciation that can occur as a result of these reproductive isolation mechanisms.

The most common of these is **allopatric speciation**, which is speciation that occurs as a result of geographic isolation. Allopatric literally means "other places." In this type of speciation, populations become isolated due to physical barriers that prevent movement and migration. This includes separation due to natural events, such as rivers changing course, as well as species migrating further and further away from one another, becoming separated by physical barriers along the way. When physical barriers isolate two populations of the same species, they are no longer moving freely back and forth to continue gene flow between the two populations.

Peripatric speciation is a specific kind of allopatric speciation that occurs when one of the separated populations is very small in number. In small populations, the effects of genetic drift can occur much more prominently and rapidly than in larger populations. If one or more individuals of the new, small population possess a rare trait or mutation, it is much more likely to be passed down through offspring and alter the gene pool of that population. As a result, small populations that are physically isolated from the greater population can rapidly become a new, incompatible species.

Another type of speciation that occurs as the result of isolation between populations is **parapatric speciation**. Unlike allopatric and peripatric speciation, parapatric speciation does not occur due to a physical barrier separating the two groups. Instead, parapatric speciation results from two groups in the same habitat that become isolated because they only mate and reproduce with the individuals in the immediate area. Factors such as soil contamination, habitat change, or difficulty moving to new locations can all lead to parapatric speciation. This can happen between populations that occupy different niches of the same habitat.

Sympatric speciation is speciation that occurs with no isolation between populations. Like parapatric speciation, there are no physical barriers separating species; unlike parapatric speciation, there are no habitat isolation mechanisms that occur. Instead, sympatric speciation is likely to occur as the result of other reproductive isolation mechanisms, such as behavioral, temporal, or mechanical mechanisms. Populations in the same habitat niche may reproduce at slightly different times of the year or only respond to certain mating behaviors, which reduces gene flow between populations and eventually leads to speciation in the same area.

SAMPLE QUESTIONS

32) **Which of the following evolution mechanisms plays a pivotal role in peripatric speciation?**

A.   natural selection

B.   coevolution

C.   genetic drift

D.   convergent evolution

Answers:

A.   Incorrect. This mechanism does occur but is not the pivotal mechanism that drives peripatric evolution.

B.   Incorrect. This describes two or more species that evolve in response to one another.

C.   **Correct.** Genetic drift plays a pivotal role in the rapid speciation of small populations of geographically isolated species, which is the definition of peripatric speciation.

D.   Incorrect. This describes two unrelated species evolving similar traits due to similar environmental pressures.

33) **Which of the following is the distinguishing feature that separates parapatric speciation from allopatric speciation?**

A.   lack of gene flow

B.   genetic mutation

C.   lack of physical barrier

D.   reproductive isolation

Answers:

A.   Incorrect. Gene flow slows or stops in both cases of speciation.

B.   Incorrect. This could lead to differences in species but is not a distinguishing factor between these two kinds of speciation.

C.   **Correct.** Allopatric speciation occurs when there is a physical barrier preventing inbreeding between populations; parapatric speciation occurs when there is a non-physical barrier.

D.   Incorrect. Reproductive isolation is a mechanism that occurs in both cases of speciation.

THE EVIDENCE FOR EVOLUTION

A scientific theory is a collection of principles and facts that provide a thorough explanation of natural phenomena and is substantiated by observations and evidence. Evolution is an example of a scientific theory. This theory has been repeatedly confirmed through multiple lines of evidence from a wide variety of scientific disciplines, including biochemistry, genetics, paleontology, and developmental biology. Even more importantly, these different lines of evidence all agree with one another. This section will examine the different lines of evidence that confirm evolution, as well as highlight major evolutionary trends.

MOLECULAR EVIDENCE

Evidence for evolution can be gleaned from biochemistry—the study of chemical reactions within living things. These biochemical reactions happen at the molecular level of organisms.

Examples of biochemical compounds include carbohydrates, proteins, lipids, and the nucleic acids of DNA and **RNA**. RNA (ribonucleic acid) is a molecule that is similar in structure to DNA but differs in function. RNA is responsible for translating genetic instructions embedded in DNA to synthesize proteins. Proteins are the workhorses of the body, bearing responsibility for many of an organism's life functions performed by the cells. These life functions include transporting molecules, providing structure and support for the cell, and carrying out chemical reactions.

The DNA, RNA, and proteins found at the molecular level are profoundly similar across groups of living organisms. This structural similarity is known as a **homology** and indicates that the organisms that share these features also share common ancestry. All living organisms—from archaebacteria all the way to human beings—share a near-identical genetic code, which is considered a homology that connects all living things and provides evidence that all life evolved from a common ancestor. The relationships and processes that occur between DNA, RNA, and proteins are also nearly identical in all living things.

> **HELPFUL HINT**
>
> All species of organisms experience some sort of genetic mutation throughout their lineage. These mutations can alter the base DNA sequences found in the double helix structure. Their constant rate allows these mutations to act as **molecular clocks**; they can be used to estimate when species diverged from one another.

If the universal genetic code is the set of genetic instructions that all living things follow, then a DNA sequence is the way in which genetic information is organized as a result. Although the genetic code remains the same for all organisms, the structures of DNA sequences vary from species to species. The more similar the species, the more similar the DNA sequences will be. For example, a human and a chimpanzee share 98.8 percent of their DNA, indicating that they have a very close evolutionary relationship. Humans also share about 70 percent of their DNA with various worm species. This indicates that humans and worms share a common ancestor, despite strong differences in appearance, behavior, and functions.

SAMPLE QUESTION

34) **Which of the following is an example of molecular evidence that all life evolved from a single common ancestor?**

   A.   the DNA code shared by all living things

   B.   humans and roundworms sharing 70 percent of their DNA

   C.   the dissimilarity of DNA sequences between humans and chimpanzees

   D.   two types of mammals having homologous limbs

Answers:

   A.   **Correct.** This is a major indicator that life stems from a common ancestor.

   B.   Incorrect. This only indicates that humans and roundworms share a common ancestor.

   C.   Incorrect. The opposite of this is true, as humans and chimpanzees share the majority of their DNA.

   D.   Incorrect. This is an example of structural evidence.

STRUCTURAL AND DEVELOPMENTAL EVIDENCE

Evidence for evolutionary relationships between species can also be seen in side-by-side comparisons of structural anatomy and the developmental processes of organisms. Just as in molecular evidence, homology of structural and developmental features also indicates that the two species share common ancestry at some point in their respective lineages.

Comparative anatomy is the study of the similarities and differences that exist in the anatomy of different organisms. In some cases, the similarities of structures between organisms are obvious: cats and tigers, for example, share similar limb structures. Other similarities become evident upon further investigation, such as a fossil study or dissection. Structures on two different organisms are considered homologous if they meet the following criteria: they share the same basic structure, they are connected to the skeleton or other parts of the body in similar ways, and if they develop in the embryonic stage in a similar manner.

The forelimb structure of most vertebrate species is a classic example of a homology that is revealed through comparative anatomy. **Tetrapods** are any four-limbed vertebrate species. They include amphibians, reptiles, birds, and mammals. Although divergent evolution over the years has led to a great variety of adaptations and superficial differences between the limbs of these animals, comparative anatomy reveals that these limbs are homologous to one another. This is a source of evidence that all four-limbed vertebrates share a common ancestor in their evolutionary history.

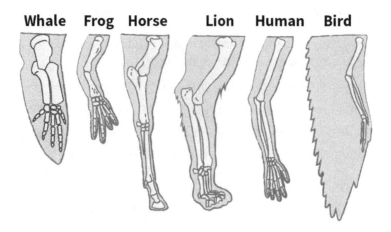

Figure 2.8. Homologous Structures

Another comparison study that provides more evidence for evolution comes from **embryology**—the study of embryo development from fertilization through birth. Comparative embryology, therefore, is the study of the similarities and differences in animals during all stages of embryonic and fetal development. If organisms share a structure—such as gill slits or a notochord—in one of their embryonic stages, then this offers another piece of evidence that these groups of organisms share a common ancestor at some point in their lineage.

> QUICK REVIEW
>
> Boa constrictors have **vestigial** limb structures on their skeleton. These limbs are effectively useless but exist in the same location with the same basic structure as limbs in other Tetrapods. Is this an example of a homology? Why or why not?

This evidence is further confirmed if it supports evidence found in other studies. For example, the tetrapods not only share homologous limb structures, but also form limbs in the same manner during their embryonic development.

SAMPLE QUESTION

35) Which of the following is NOT considered a criterion of a homologous structure between two species?

A. They share the same basic structure.

B. They are attached to the body in the same way.

C. They perform the same function.

D. They develop in the same way during embryonic development.

Answers:

A. Incorrect. This indicates the structures are homologous.

B. Incorrect. This indicates the structures are homologous.

C. **Correct.** Homologous structures can be adapted to perform different functions as a result of divergent evolution.

D. Incorrect. This indicates the structures are homologies.

FOSSIL RECORD

The fossil record serves as a preeminent source of evidence for change, evolution, and speciation over a long period of time. A **fossil** is the remnant or impression of an early life form that has been preserved in rock. Fossils can form through **permineralization** (minerals forming a cast by filling in space in the body tissue), or through the casting and/or molding process, as the body leaves an impression that is filled in by rock. The act of fossilization is a rare occurrence. As a result, it provides very important information but does not paint a complete picture of the history of life on Earth. Instead, it is used in conjunction with other previously discussed branches of science, such as molecular biology and comparative anatomy, to trace evolution.

Fossils form primarily in **sedimentary rock**, as this type of rock is formed by layers of sediment depositing on top of one another. As time goes by and more layers of sediment form on top, the lower layers experience pressure and eventually turn into rock. As a result, layers of sedimentary rock act as a marker for **geologic time**. The act of studying layers, or **strata**, of rock in this manner is called **stratigraphy**. Stratigraphy is governed by the law of superposition, which states that younger rock strata sit on top of older rock strata. This information has been used by scientists to develop the geologic time scale, which is a chronological history of Earth and divides life into periods, eras, and epochs.

Earth's geology is dynamic, meaning that various geological events such as plate movement, volcanic eruptions, and earthquakes have moved layers of rock over time. The law of superposition, therefore, cannot always be applied. Another method of age detection in rocks is **radiometric dating**, which determines the age of certain kinds of rocks by measuring the rate of the decay of any radioactive elements found in the rock.

The law of superposition also applies to fossils found within sedimentary rock—the older the fossil is, the lower it will be located in the rock strata. This law is consistent with the evidence collected for the theory of evolution. In general, fossils of simpler organism have been found in the lower layers of Earth's strata; the complexity of these organisms grows as scientists move up to newer strata. Long-extinct, prehistoric organisms are found in lower rock strata and do not occur in the same fossil beds as their descendants.

Once the age of fossils has been determined, scientists can look for similarities among fossils to help determine common ancestry and evolutionary relationships. For example, the fossil record has revealed many structural homologies that exist between modern birds and a group of prehistoric dinosaurs called **theropods**, suggesting that these two groups of organisms share an evolutionary lineage. A study of the fossil record can also provide clues about prehistoric organisms. When fossils of one species are found with other fossilized remains, it can be inferred that these two species lived in the same time period and interacted in some way. Structural features of these organisms can also be studied, giving scientists a better idea of how and why some adaptations evolved.

SAMPLE QUESTION

36) **Which of the following acts as a marker for geologic time, which helps to accurately date fossils?**

A. permineralized fossils

B. common ancestors

C. law of superposition

D. sedimentary rock strata

Answers:

A. Incorrect. This is something that can be found in sedimentary rock strata but is not the marker of time.

B. Incorrect. Common ancestry can be determined by studying fossils that are dated according to their location in sedimentary rock strata.

C. Incorrect. This is a method used to interpret findings from different rock strata; however, this is a law, not a marker itself.

D. **Correct.** The layers, or strata, of sedimentary rock serve as indicators of geologic time.

ENDOSYMBIOSIS

The first organisms that appeared on Earth were prokaryotic; eukaryotic cells, descended from these early prokaryotes, did not appear until much later. The theory of **endosymbiosis** is a concept that was thought to be outlandish by the scientific community several decades ago but is now accepted as a modern explanation of the evolution of eukaryotic cells. Endosymbiotic theory states that the mitochondria and chloroplasts—organelles found in eukaryotic organisms—originated as free-living bacteria over a billion years ago.

The theory suggests that these bacteria took up residence inside other bacteria. Each form of bacteria benefited from this symbiotic relationship: the would-be mitochondria used the oxygen absorbed by the host cell, while the host itself benefited from the energy produced by the mitochondria. Over time, the genetic information intertwined and the two distinct species became one. The primary pieces of evidence that support endosymbiotic theory are the homologies that exist between mitochondria and bacteria. Both lack a cell membrane, both reproduce through binary fission rather than mitosis, and both have circular genomes.

What does this have to do with evolution? Before the emergency of eukaryotic cells, all life on Earth consisted of single-celled prokaryotic organisms. Prokaryotes are simple organisms that are small in size and function with no nucleus and few organelles. Once the mitochondria became introduced, however, much more complex, multiple-celled eukaryotic organisms began to appear and evolve. The mitochondria are considered the powerhouses of the eukaryotic cell—these organelles are responsible for cellular respiration and the production of energy that keeps the organism alive.

Endosymbiotic theory also applies to the appearance of chloroplasts in the plant kingdom, which provides another piece of evidence about its evolutionary relationship with the other kingdoms. Animals, fungi, and plants are all mitochondria-containing eukaryotes that descend from a common ancestor. The lineage that would eventually evolve into plants experienced endosymbiosis with another form of bacteria which would eventually become the chloroplasts. Chloroplasts are organelles that are responsible for converting sunlight energy into a form of food energy for the plants. Similar to mitochondria, chloroplasts contain bacteria-like DNA and perform chemical reactions vital to the cells' survival; like mitochondria, they are thought to have evolved from bacteria. The animal and fungi kingdoms, which lack chloroplasts, form another branch of evolutionary lineage.

SAMPLE QUESTION

37) **Which of the following is NOT a kingdom of organisms that contain the mitochondria organelle?**

A. bacteria

B. fungi

C. animal

D. plant

Answers:

A. **Correct.** Mitochondria descended from bacteria, but the current form is not found within bacterial cells.

B. Incorrect. Fungi are eukaryotic organisms that contain mitochondria within their cells.

C. Incorrect. Animals are eukaryotic organisms that contain mitochondria within their cells.

D. Incorrect. Plants are eukaryotic organisms that contain mitochondria and chloroplasts within their cells.

MAJOR EVOLUTIONARY TRENDS

An evolutionary trend is a change to a trait or structure that occurs in one lineage or across the lineages of several groups of organisms. Trait changes in evolutionary trends are directional, meaning that they consistently appear in greater frequency throughout the lineage. These trends differ from random fluctuations of changes to structures or behavior because evolutionary trends are persistent and result in significant change over time. Evolutionary trends can impact the evolutionary development of one particular species and their relatives, or they can be widespread and account for major evolutionary shifts among higher taxa of organisms.

One major trend that differentiates the fungi, plant, and animal kingdoms from the protist, bacteria, and archaebacteria kingdoms is the trend of **multicellularity**. Archaebacteria, bacteria, and most protists are considered **unicellular**, performing all of their life functions in the confines of a single cell. Unicellular organisms are considered less advanced than multicellular organisms; as organisms developed more and more cells, more and more opportunities for diversification and specialization arose. Multicellularity leads to great diversity among organisms, and the advent of multicellular organisms evolving from unicellular relatives is considered one of the most significant trends to impact life on Earth. Evidence suggests that multicellularity arose multiple times throughout Earth's life history.

The formation of heads among animals is considered another major evolutionary trend that led to great diversification of animal life. Head formation begins with the advent of multicellular **nervous tissue**—tissue that consists primarily of specialized cells called neurons that help direct communication throughout the body. **Cephalization** is the tendency of nervous tissue to become concentrated at the anterior end of an organism during embryonic development. This concentration of tissue eventually forms into the head. These heads can contain a brain or centralized group of nerve cells that directs the activity of other nervous tissue in the body, sensory tissue or organs, and mouth structures for feeding.

Not all animals that have undergone cephalization will exhibit all of these traits, as there is a range of cephalization that can occur among different groups of organisms. Cephalization occurs among organisms that display **bilateral symmetry** (having two identical sides with a distinct head and tail end). As a general rule, the larger the mass of nervous tissue is that is found in the head, then the more advanced the group of organisms is. For example, planarians are flatworms that display cephalization but have rudimentary sensory tissue and no true brain. In contrast, an octopus has a much larger brain with much greater control over movement and is considered a much more highly advanced organism than a planarian.

SAMPLE QUESTION

38) **Animals with bilateral symmetry tend to undergo which evolutionary trend as part of this process?**

   A.   multicellularity

   B.   neuron development

   C.   cephalization

   D.   unicellularity

Answers:

A.   Incorrect. These organisms have already developed multicellularity.

B.   Incorrect. Neuron development is a prerequisite of the cephalization trend among bilateral animals.

C.   Correct. Animals with bilateral symmetry tend to form two identical halves with a head end, which is the end result of cephalization.

D.   Incorrect. Bilateral organisms have more than one cell.

The Origin of Life

Scientific hypotheses are testable explanations of natural phenomena and processes. Unlike scientific theory, they are not supported by multiple lines of evidence and are not generally accepted as truth. Instead, hypotheses are a starting point for scientific inquiry and investigation. The explanations for the origin of life on Earth are examples of hypotheses. They serve as a solid foundation for further scientific investigation, but much more evidence will need to be collected over a longer period of time for these ideas to become theory. It is likely that there is not one clear-cut answer from one hypothesis or discipline as to how life originated on Earth. The more likely answer is that life arose from a complex web of various conditions that were influenced by both Earth's early environment, the appearance of organic compounds, and the processes of these compounds.

Panspermia

Panspermia is the explanation that life on Earth was "seeded" by organic compounds and microscopic life found in outer space. According to this hypothesis, these compounds and organisms arrived on Earth via meteors that pummeled the planet during its early stages of formation. Since Earth's atmosphere was very thin during these early days, it did not offer much protection from meteors, asteroids, or other space debris. This explanation is also known as *asteroid seeding*. The hypothesis argues that any potential life forms that may have emerged before this bombardment period would have been wiped out and eventually replaced by materials that originated on these extraterrestrial objects.

Some proponents of the panspermia theory believe that organic matter that serves as a building block for life arrived during these meteor impacts. Organic matter includes any material that contains the carbon molecule. Examples of organic matter that may have originated in this way include carbohydrates, lipids, and amino acids. This hypothesis is corroborated by the frequent appearance of amino acids that arrive during modern-day meteor strikes. However, evidence of more complex organic material on meteors has not been found.

Other panspermia proponents suggest that microscopic life itself arrived on Earth via meteors, rather than the compounds that serve as the building blocks of life. If this explanation is true, then the most likely scenario would be that life arrived in the form of dormant bacteria spores from meteors derived from the solar system or from comets that travel between star systems. These bacteria would have had to have been able to survive in the absence of nutrients during long periods of interplanetary or interstellar travel; simulation experiments have shown that some bacteria species are able to remain dormant in extreme conditions for long periods of time.

SAMPLE QUESTION

39) According to the panspermia hypothesis, which of the following is a building block of life that could have originated from meteor impacts?

   A.   diploid cells

   B.   mitochondria

   C.   amino acids

   D.   alleles

Answers:

   A.   Incorrect. Diploid cells occur in advanced forms of life and are not considered part of the panspermia theory.

   B.   Incorrect. Mitochondria is an organelle found in eukaryotic cells and is not considered part of the panspermia theory.

   C.   Correct. Amino acids are organic molecules that are considered to be a building block of life and have been found on meteors that strike the earth.

   D.   Incorrect. Alleles are part of life, not a compound that leads to the development of life.

SYNTHESIS OF ORGANIC COMPOUNDS

In 1953, chemists Stanley Miller and Harold Urey performed what is now referred to as the **Miller-Urey experiment**. This experiment was based off of a theoretical model of chemical evolution developed in the 1920s, which hypothesizes that the organic molecules of life formed from inorganic compounds during a time of atmospheric reduction on early Earth, which resulted in an atmosphere with a limited amount of oxygen. The Miller-Urey experiment was built upon this model to develop a simulation of early Earth's atmosphere. Their simulation, which was a gas mixture that was exposed to heat and electricity, gave rise to organic amino acid compounds. This provided evidence that it was possible for organic compounds to rise **abiotically** (from non-living sources).

Miller and Urey used a mixture of various gases that were believed at the time to have been present in Earth's primordial atmosphere nearly 4 billion years ago. This mixture includes water, methane, ammonia, and hydrogen. More recent evidence has suggested that due to the large amount of volcanic activity during this period of Earth's history, there were more inorganic compounds—such as carbon dioxide and nitrogen—present in the atmosphere. This, combined with more modern technology, has led to experiments that resulted in the creation of even more amino acids, simple carbohydrates, and other organic compounds necessary for life.

> **HELPFUL HINT**
>
> After Miller's death, the vials containing the results from the original 1953 experiment were examined using modern detection technology. This revealed that the Miller-Urey experiment yielded many more amino acid compounds than previously thought at the time of the first experiment.

The discovery of organic compounds rising from inorganic compounds gives credence to the hypothesis of **abiogenesis**, which is the explanation that life evolved from non-living substances. However, the creation of organic materials from non-living matter has not led to a discovery of how these building blocks of life actually came together and formed life.

SAMPLE QUESTION

40) **The Miller-Urey experiment proved which of the following?**

    A.   organic compounds could arise from inorganic compounds

    B.   life evolved from abiotic material

    C.   amino acids are the only organic compounds necessary for life

    D.   inorganic compounds are the building blocks of life

Answers:

    A.   **Correct.** Miller and Urey's experiments created amino acids from a combination of inorganic material.

    B.   Incorrect. This experiment did not make the link between life and inorganic compounds.

    C.   Incorrect. Amino acids are one of many types of organic compounds that are required for life.

    D.   Incorrect. Organic compounds, including proteins and nucleic acid, are the building blocks of life.

BIOLOGICAL INFLUENCES ON THE ATMOSPHERE

The first primitive forms of life that emerged on Earth approximately 4 billion years ago arose in an atmosphere very different from the atmosphere that exists today. As previously mentioned, Earth was undergoing a period of extreme volcanism, releasing large amounts of carbon dioxide, sulfur dioxide, and nitrogen. Life during this time existed primarily of microbes, such as bacteria, which can withstand extreme environmental elements. Approximately 2.5 billion years ago, the first photosynthetic organisms began to appear. The earliest of these to appear in the fossil record are a type of blue-green algae.

Once these organisms appeared, both the trajectory of evolution and the composition of the atmosphere began to change at a quicker pace. The photosynthetic organisms took in carbon dioxide from the atmosphere and released oxygen as a byproduct. This process of change was still relatively slow, as it took nearly another billion years for oxygen to emerge as a major component of Earth's atmosphere.

Once oxygen was built up in the atmosphere around 1.8 billion years ago, the evolution of life began to occur even more rapidly. More primitive life forms that had evolved in the oxygen-poor environment began to die off and disappear and were replaced by more oxygen-tolerant species. As more photosynthetic organisms appeared, more oxygen was released into the atmosphere which, in turn, encouraged the growth and development of even more photosynthetic organisms.

The appearance of greater amounts of oxygen is believed to have been the driving force of the evolution of organisms growing larger and more complex, as positive correlations exist between the amount of oxygen in the atmosphere and the evolution of greater body size. Many other factors—such as multicellularity and Earth's climate—also played a major role. However, this correlation does lend support to the idea that life flourishes and evolves into more complex forms when there are greater amounts of oxygen in the atmosphere.

SAMPLE QUESTION

41) Which of the following atmospheric gases is correlated to the rapid increase in body size among organisms?

A.   carbon dioxide

B.   methane

C.   oxygen

D.   nitrogen

Answers:

A.   Incorrect. Carbon dioxide was found in larger proportions when life first evolved but is now only found in trace amounts. It is not correlated with the body size of organisms.

B.   Incorrect. Methane is found in trace amounts in the atmosphere but is not correlated with the body size of organisms.

C.   **Correct.** Oxygen was not present in the atmosphere when life first evolved, but it now makes up over 20 percent of the atmosphere's composition.

D.   Incorrect. Nitrogen was found in large amounts both then and now and is not correlated with body size.

DEVELOPMENT OF SELF-REPLICATION

The development of the ability to **self-replicate** is considered by many scientists to have been a vital step in the origin of life on Earth. Without this ability, there is no way to produce offspring by replicating and passing on genetic information from generation to generation. Scientists initially believed that proteins were the molecules that first evolved self-replication, as proteins are responsible for creating chemical reactions that drive most life processes. Proteins, however, cannot be made without the instructions embedded within DNA. Likewise, DNA cannot replicate its genetic information without proteins, leaving researchers with a classic chicken-or-the-egg scenario: which came first—DNA or proteins? The most likely answer to this question is neither. RNA, once regarded as a simple messenger substance, is now believed to potentially be a precursor to all life on Earth.

RNA is unique from proteins and DNA because it can carry out functions of both of these compounds. Like DNA, it can store genetic information; like proteins, it acts as a catalyst for chemical reactions. As a result, it is an example of a molecule that can potentially self-replicate without the influence of another outside compound. This has led to the development of the idea of the **RNA world**. According to the RNA-world hypothesis, RNA was the preeminent nucleic acid that existed among early life. Instead of proteins, it was RNA that was causing chemical reactions to drive photosynthesis, respiration, metabolism, or other life functions. Instead of DNA, it was RNA that was storing and replicating genetic information. Over time, proteins and DNA evolved to take over and specialize in these functions. The hypothesis argues that it was these molecules that were capable of self-replication without an outside influence and were responsible for beginning this evolutionary process.

SAMPLE QUESTION

42) Which of the following organic compounds is capable of both replicating genetic information and catalyzing chemical reactions?

    A. DNA

    B. RNA

    C. proteins

    D. amino acids

Answers:

    A. Incorrect. DNA is a replicating molecule but does not catalyze chemical reactions.

    B. **Correct.** RNA is capable of both of these functions.

    C. Incorrect. Proteins catalyze most of the chemical reactions responsible for life.

    D. Incorrect. Amino acids are the building blocks of proteins.

EXTINCTION

When a species of organism dies out, this event is known as **extinction**. It is difficult to determine exactly when a species has become extinct. Most scientists agree that a species is not considered extinct until it has not been seen in the wild for at least fifty years, or that there is no reasonable doubt that the last individual has died. Species can become functionally extinct before the last of the species die out if their population is no longer viable and will be unable to sustain itself long-term.

While human activity accounts for a large amount of environmental change that leads to extinction, it is important to note that extinction events are a natural part of the evolution of organisms on Earth. In fact, it is estimated that over 99 percent of the species that ever lived on Earth are now extinct. The background **extinction rate** is a measurement of how often species become extinct over a given period of time. These rates have not been constant throughout Earth's history; they are variable depending on the factors affecting Earth at a given time, including climate change and the presence of humans.

Extinction can be caused by one or a combination of several different factors. A lack of **genetic diversity** among a species of organism is one such factor that leads to a sharp decline in numbers. Genetic diversity is the amount of variation of genes within a population. Without genetic diversity, a population or species is less likely to adapt to outside influences, such as habitat change or disease. A small gene pool can also lead to genetic inbreeding among population or species members. Inbreeding can result in an increased amount of less-desirable or harmful genes in a gene pool, which has a negative impact on species fertility and fitness for their environment.

There are multiple **environmental factors** that can lead to population decline, loss of genetic diversity, and eventual extinction. One of these factors is **habitat change**—the change in the environmental conditions in which a particular population or species lives. Natural factors, such as fire, drought, or flood, can lead to localized or regional change. Organisms must either travel to a more suitable habitat or adapt to the changes in order to survive. Severe habitat change can lead to **habitat destruction**—the complete loss of biological functions that a species depends on. When this occurs, populations of species can become fragmented and unable to reproduce with one another, which lowers the genetic diversity of the gene pool of the species and leaves the remaining population even more vulnerable to environmental change.

Climate change is another environmental factor that can lead to species loss or extinction. Mass climate change accounts for most of Earth's major extinction events in which the majority of species were eliminated during the same short span of time. Several of these mass extinctions coincided with mass cooling events, which not only leads to colder temperatures throughout the planet but also creates mass glacial and freezing events that can destroy existing habitats as they develop.

Global warming has a similar effect, causing habitat loss in cold climates as ice melts, altering vegetation patterns, and flooding near shore areas.

Today, many of the world's species that face extinction are being negatively impacted by human activity. Agriculture and food production have led to massive amounts of habitat loss and fragmentation throughout Earth as the world's need for food grows along with the population. The growing human population also leads to habitat loss and fragmentation in urbanized, industrial areas. As more people populate Earth, more natural resources are needed; overharvesting of plant and animal species is a result of this need. And, as the world becomes more industrialized, more environmental degradation occurs as fossil fuels are extracted from the earth and pollutants contaminate air, water, and land. Habitat degradation, fragmentation, and destruction all lead to population declines among species.

Human-caused climate change has also impacted the risk of extinction of species in a global context. Carbon dioxide emissions stemming from the burning of fossil fuels have increased the impact of the greenhouse effect, which is a natural phenomenon that causes heat retention in Earth's atmosphere. Since the amount of carbon dioxide released has sharply increased, this natural phenomenon has been amplified and is causing Earth's temperatures to rise as more heat is retained. The rising temperatures alter the climate of various kinds of habitats and put many species at risk of extinction.

When humans move to new areas, they usually bring new species of organisms with them. When non-native species are introduced to new areas, they can often wreak havoc within their introduced ecosystem. In many cases, these new species are competing with native species in the same habitat. This phenomenon is known as **interspecific competition**. If the non-native species is more successful than the other, then the native species can decline in population and eventually become extinct.

QUICK REVIEW

Interspecific competition does not always have to lead to extinction of one species in an environment. In fact, local extinction is relatively rare, especially among species that are both native to the habitat. How can interspecific competition lead to differentiation or evolution?

SAMPLE QUESTIONS

43) **Which of the following is NOT an example of an environmental pressure that can lead to species extinction?**

   A.   lack of genetic diversity in a small population of fish

   B.   destruction of a mountaintop due to volcanic eruption

   C.   historic glaciation leading to destruction of tundra habitat

   D.   habitat fragmentation due to wildfire

Answers:

A.   **Correct.** This is a species-specific factor that can lead to extinction, not an environmental pressure.

B.   Incorrect. This is an example of habitat destruction, which is an environmental pressure.

C.   Incorrect. This is an example of historic climate change, which is an environmental pressure.

D.   Incorrect. Habitat fragmentation is an example of an environmental pressure.

44)   **A loss of biological function in a given area is an example of which of the following?**

A.   mass extinction

B.   interspecific competition

C.   climate change

D.   habitat loss

Answers:

A.   Incorrect. Mass extinctions are marked by a sharp decline in the total number of species across Earth during a short span of time.

B.   Incorrect. Interspecific competition is a competition for resources between species in the same habitat.

C.   Incorrect. Climate change is a slow, global process that does not necessarily lead to loss of biological function.

D.   **Correct.** Habitat loss occurs when so many of the resources in a habitat are destroyed that a species can no longer function in that location.

3

Biological Classification

Biology is defined as the study of life. Scientists have many different ideas regarding the exact definition of life, but there are a few basic shared characteristics that most scientists agree upon. This chapter will identify these defining characteristics of all living things, then discuss specifics of one complex defining feature: the hierarchy of organization that exists within all multicellular organisms. This includes how these organisms are divided into cells, tissues, organs, and organ systems.

Just as all living things share certain key characteristics in common, there are many variations of these characteristics that separate them into distinct groups. This process of grouping and naming living organisms is known as classification. Characteristics that scientists look at to divide living things into distinct groups include structure, organization, modes of nutrition, and reproduction. This chapter will delve into the different ranks of classification and how the domains and kingdoms, including the plant and animal kingdoms, differ from one another based on these characteristics.

CHARACTERISTICS OF LIVING THINGS

There are six basic characteristics that all living things must do to be considered alive. All living things:

1. are made of cells
2. can reproduce and pass traits to offspring
3. maintain homeostasis
4. perform metabolic activities
5. respond to stimuli
6. grow

The first major characteristic of living things is the appearance of organized cells, which are the smallest functional unit of life. Many organisms, such as bacteria and protists, consist of only a single cell, but this single cell still carries out all of the processes required for life. Other organisms are multicellular and display a hierarchy of organization among their cells, which will be discussed later in the chapter.

All living things grow and reproduce through cell enlargement and cell division. Single-celled organisms can grow due to cell enlargement (the expansion of volume within the cell). They reproduce through cell division, which results in two distinct single-celled organisms. Multicellular organisms experience a period of cell enlargement that is usually followed by the process of mitosis, which divides the enlarged parent cell into two daughter cells. This increases the cell number and the size of the organism. When cells divide through meiosis, gametes are formed and reproduction can occur. These processes of cell division also account for how organisms pass on their genetic information to offspring.

All living things respond to the environment and have regulatory mechanisms that are used to maintain homeostasis. These mechanisms respond to different stimuli within the environment, which allow the organism to adjust its internal functions or behavior to the change in the environment. This is seen even among the simplest of organisms.

HELPFUL HINT

Are viruses living or non-living? This is a question that has plagued scientists since their discovery in the nineteenth century. Viruses contain nucleic acid and genetic material, but lack the ability to reproduce without the aid of a host cell. They do not grow and are not organized into cells, but they do use energy obtained from a host cell and respond and adapt to their environment. Viruses are officially classified as non-living things, but there is more research that needs to be done to determine this one way or the other.

Organisms all have a way of obtaining energy from their environment and using this energy to maintain life processes in cells. This process of breaking down energy to maintain a cell is known as metabolism. There are multiple metabolic processes that can occur within an organism: for example, photosynthesis is the process of converting light energy into glucose for energy production, and cellular respiration is the process of absorbing oxygen and producing ATP energy.

SAMPLE QUESTION

1) Which of the following characteristics is NOT considered necessary for life?

    A. reproduction

    B. mobility

    C. growth

    D. regulation

Answers:

A.   Incorrect. The ability to reproduce and pass genes on to offspring is a major characteristic of life.

B.   Correct. Not all organisms have the ability to move.

C.   Incorrect. All organisms grow through cell enlargement and cell division.

D.   Incorrect. Living things regulate their cellular processes and behavior in response to their environment.

CLASSIFYING ORGANISMS

All living things are placed into different groups based on their biological similarities and relationships in a process known as **classification**. There are eight different hierarchal categories of groups in modern-day classification: domain, kingdom, phylum, class, order, family, genus, and species, with species constituting the smallest groups and domains encompassing the largest groups. Each distinct group of organisms within each category is known as a **taxon**. Therefore, the science of classifying organisms into their respective eight taxa is known as **taxonomy**.

The classification system that has been historically used by scientists is the **kingdom system**. This system is based on the classification system first developed by Carolus Linnaeus in the eighteenth century, which initially placed all living things into two kingdoms: animals and plants. The modern kingdom system, initially proposed in 1969, expanded this system to five distinct kingdoms: Monera, Protista, Fungi, Plantae, and Animalia. These divisions were based on observable characteristics that differentiated these groups from one another.

Over time, more molecular research and data revealed previously unseen evolutionary relationships between groups of animals, and a new system of classification was proposed. The **domain system**, first proposed by Carl Woese in 1977, added domain as a classification level that supersedes kingdom. Under this system, all living things are broken down into Bacteria, Archaea, and Eukaryota. The remaining taxa remain in the same order, but are rooted in molecular and evolutionary relationships rather than biological similarities only.

KINGDOM SYSTEM

The traditional kingdom system of classification divided living things into one of five kingdoms: Monera, Protista, Fungi, Plantae, and Animalia. More recent evidence has led scientists to divide the traditional Monera kingdom into two smaller kingdoms: Bacteria and Archaea.

Classification systems can change as more information is learned about the molecular, genetic, and evolutionary makeup of different groups of organisms. In several cases, scientists may not agree on where a group of organisms should be placed. For example, the placement of algae is contested among scientists. Some scientists place all algae in the Plantae kingdom, while others place some groups in Plantae and others in Protista. Still others place some groups of algae in Bacteria or a proposed additional kingdom, Chromista.

The organisms in the traditional **Monera** kingdom were initially grouped together because they are all single-celled organisms that lack a nucleus or highly organized genetic information. These organisms are considered the simplest, most primitive organisms. These microorganisms were the first forms of life to emerge on Earth, and there are many groups today that can still live in extreme environments. As mentioned previously, most scientists separate this kingdom into two distinct groups, Bacteria and Archaea, which will be further elaborated upon in the next section.

The **Protista** kingdom is also composed primarily of single-celled organisms, but unlike the monerans, their cells contain a true, membrane-bound nucleus. Most have one cell, but there are several multicellular groups of protists that are small in size and simple in organization. There is a great diversity of characteristics that exist within this kingdom; in fact, there are so many differences that a number of scientists believe they should be separated into distinct kingdoms.

The vast majority of organisms in the **Fungi** kingdom are multicellular. This group includes mold, yeast, and mushrooms. They differ from other groups due to their cell walls, ability to absorb nutrients from their environment, and their unique structures and modes of reproduction. Unlike plants, they do not contain chloroplasts or undergo photosynthesis. These two features are the defining characteristics of organisms in the **Plantae** kingdom. Likewise, the kingdom **Animalia** is also distinguished from fungi and plants due to its organisms' modes of nutrition, differing cell structure, and ability to move.

SAMPLE QUESTIONS

2) **Which of the following two groups of organisms are found within the traditional Monera kingdom?**

   A.   archaea and bacteria

   B.   protists and bacteria

   C.   protists and fungi

   D.   fungi and archaea

Answers:

   A.   Correct. The traditional Monera kingdom is subdivided into two distinct kingdoms: Bacteria and Archaea.

   B.   Incorrect. Bacteria were found in the traditional Monera kingdom; protists were not.

C.   Incorrect. Neither protists nor fungi are considered monerans.

D.   Incorrect. Archaea were found in the traditional Monera kingdom; fungi were not.

3)   Which of the following is a difference between fungi and plants?

A.   Plants photosynthesize; fungi do not.

B.   Plants have a cell wall; fungi do not.

C.   Fungi have chloroplasts; plants do not.

D.   Fungi are mobile; plants are not.

Answers:

A.   **Correct.** This is an accurate description of the modes of nutrition among these two kingdoms.

B.   Incorrect. Both plant and fungi cells contain a cell wall.

C.   Incorrect. Plants contain chloroplasts, while fungi do not.

D.   Incorrect. Neither of these groups is mobile.

DOMAIN SYSTEM

The three-domain system of classification arose to replace the traditional five-kingdom system throughout the last part of the twentieth century, eventually becoming the preferred classification method in the scientific community. This new classification system is rooted in the molecular biology of organisms. One of the primary dividing factors between domains is the **ribosomal RNA** (rRNA) that is unique to each domain of organisms. Under this system, all living things are placed into one of three categories: Archaea, Bacteria, and Eukaryota. This not only reclassifies organisms, but also represents a drastic rethinking of the evolutionary tree of life.

Archaea and bacteria are both **prokaryotic** organisms, meaning that they are unicellular and lack a nucleus. These are the two characteristics that led scientists to initially group them together in the Monera kingdom. However, there are differences between these two groups of prokaryotes. The Archaea domain consists primarily of **archaebacteria**. Although on the surface these organisms appear structurally similar to bacteria, they differ drastically in their biochemistry and have a unique rRNA type. Some archaebacteria are examples of **extremophiles**—organisms that thrive in environments that are unsuitable for most forms of life due to factors such as high temperatures, high acidity, or lack of oxygen. Many others live in more moderate environments all over Earth. The organisms in the Bacteria domain are also found nearly everywhere on Earth, although they are less likely to be extremophiles. Their genetic composition suggests that they are more primitive than the archaebacteria. In fact, the sequences of rRNA are as distinct from one another in these two domains as they are both distinct from the rRNA sequences of the Eukaryota domain.

The remaining four traditional kingdoms—Protista, Fungi, Plantae, and Animalia—are placed into a third domain, Eukaryota. All organisms in this domain are **eukaryotes** (organisms whose cells contain a membrane-bound nucleus). These organisms undergo a more complex process of cell division and reproduction and also contain organelles and cell components—including mitochondria and chromosomes—that are not found among either domain of prokaryotes.

SAMPLE QUESTIONS

4) Which of the following is NOT true about the domain system of classification?

   A.   All life is classified into one of three domains.

   B.   The domain system is based on the structure and sequence of rRNA.

   C.   The domain system was first proposed by Carolus Linnaeus in the seventeenth century.

   D.   The domain system represents a shift in the understanding of evolutionary relationships among living things.

Answers:

   A.   Incorrect. All life falls into the Archaea, Bacteria, or Eukaryota domains.

   B.   Incorrect. The domain system is based on the molecular structure of organisms.

   C.   Correct. Linnaeus originated the kingdom system of classification during this time period.

   D.   Incorrect. The domain system also incorporated a reconfiguration of the tree of life.

5) Which of the following kingdoms does NOT fall under the Eukaryota domain?

   A.   Fungi

   B.   Bacteria

   C.   Animalia

   D.   Plantae

Answers:

   A.   Incorrect. Fungi is one of the three kingdoms found in the Eukaryota domain.

   B.   Correct. Bacteria are found in the Bacteria domain.

   C.   Incorrect. Animalia is one of the three kingdoms found in the Eukaryota domain.

   D.   Incorrect. Plantae is one of the three kingdoms found in the Eukaryota domain.

CLASSIFICATION CHARACTERISTICS

As previously discussed, living things share certain characteristics: cellular organization, continual growth and development, and the ability to reproduce, self-regulate, use energy, and maintain homeostasis. The methods of maintaining these different characteristics, however, vary between the major divisions of classified life. This portion of the chapter will closely compare and contrast characteristics such as structure, organization, modes of nutrition, reproduction, and replication between the major kingdoms of life: Bacteria, Protista, Fungi, Plantae, and Animalia. Viruses, which have many life-like characteristics, will also be included in this detailed examination.

STRUCTURE

All living things contain genetic information within their cells. However, there is wide variation in the structures of this material when the bodies of viruses, prokaryotes, and eukaryotes are compared. Viruses—the microscopic particles that meet some, but not all, of the requirements for life—contain genetic material as well. These cell-like particles each have a central core that contains nucleic acid. Different types of viruses are classified depending on what kind of core they contain: a **DNA core** or an **RNA core**. They are also classified by the type of **capsid** they have. A capsid (protein coat) is the protein structure that encompasses the genetic material of a virus. The primary functions of a capsid are to protect the DNA and RNA strands within the virus and to provide the virus with mechanisms for attaching to a host cell. Viral structures are not considered cells because they do not contain organelles in order to reproduce or perform other cell functions.

As previously discussed, the structure of prokaryotic cells is distinguished from eukaryotic cells due to the lack of a membrane-bound nucleus. These cells also lack membrane-bound organelles, which are specialized structures that carry out many cell processes. Their genetic material, which is composed of DNA, is confined to a single chromosome that is usually circular in shape. Both archaea and bacteria cells are filled with cytoplasm, contain non-membrane-bound ribosomes, and are surrounded by a cell wall. Although these two groups of prokaryotic organisms share this cell wall structure, the components of the cell wall differ. Archaea cell walls lack peptidoglycan, which is a molecule found in bacteria that serves to strengthen and reinforce the cell wall while still allowing essential nutrients and materials to pass through.

Eukaryotic cells are distinguished by the appearance of a nuclear membrane. Also called nuclear envelopes, these structures contain two layers composed of an arrangement of **phospholipids**. These membrane layers are designed to protect the nucleus as well as regulate materials that enter and exit the area. Other membrane-bound organelles found almost exclusively in eukaryotes include mitochondria, Golgi apparatus, the endoplasmic reticulum, and lysosomes.

Fungi cells contain all of the above membrane-bound organelles as well as a cell wall. Some fungi have DNA that is more bacteria-like in structure, but most have a distinct nucleus enclosed by a membrane. Plant cells also have a cell wall but are distinguished from fungi and animal cells due to the appearance of membrane-bound chloroplasts. Their cell walls differ from the walls of fungi: fungi cell walls are supported and strengthened by **chitin**, while plant cell walls contain **cellulose**. In contrast, animal cells lack both chloroplasts and cell walls, but contain all of the previously mentioned eukaryotic organelles.

Protist cells, unlike the other groups of eukaryotes, can vary drastically in the types of organelles they contain. Some animal-like protists are surrounded only by a cell membrane, while other, plant-like protists are surrounded by cell walls and contain chloroplasts. Still others are surrounded by a **pellicle**—a layer that coats the outer cell membrane of a protist cell.

SAMPLE QUESTIONS

6) **Which of the following groups of organisms have cell walls supported by chitin?**

   A. bacteria

   B. animals

   C. plants

   D. fungi

   Answers:

   A. Incorrect. Bacteria cell walls do not contain chitin.

   B. Incorrect. Animal cells do not have cell walls.

   C. Incorrect. Plant cell walls are supported and strengthened by cellulose.

   D. Correct. Fungal cell walls are supported and strengthened by chitin.

7) **Which of the organelles distinguishes plant cells from animal and fungi cells?**

   A. mitochondria

   B. cellulose

   C. chloroplasts

   D. cell wall

   Answers:

   A. Incorrect. All eukaryotic cells contain mitochondria.

   B. Incorrect. Cellulose is not an organelle.

   C. Correct. Plants and some protists are the only organisms that contain chloroplasts.

   D. Incorrect. Fungi have a cell wall, while animals do not.

8) **Which of the following is a protein shell that protects the genetic information of a virus?**

    A.   nucleus

    B.   cell wall

    C.   capsid

    D.   cytoplasm

Answers:

    A.   Incorrect. Viruses do not contain nuclei.

    B.   Incorrect. Viruses do not contain cell walls.

    C.   **Correct.** Viruses are often classified by the shape of their protective protein coat, or capsid.

    D.   Incorrect. Many viruses do not contain cytoplasm, and this is not a protein layer protecting a virus.

ORGANIZATION

All living things are composed of cells. However, the different domains and kingdoms of organisms differ in terms of cellular organization. Prokaryotes, which include the bacteria and archaea, are unicellular organisms that do not contain membrane-bound organelles. Eukaryotes, which include the rest of the kingdoms of life, are unicellular or multicellular organisms that do contain membrane-bound organelles.

All bacteria and archaea, many protists, and some fungi are unicellular organisms. Both prokaryotic and eukaryotic unicellular organisms must perform all functions of life within the confines of a single cell and its organelles. These cells are often microscopic, although some species are visible to the naked eye. Some species of unicellular organisms live together in **colonies**. A colony is an aggregation of many single-celled organisms living together in a symbiotic, mutually-beneficial relationship. This is distinguished from multicellularity, however, because each cell can live independently of one another and does not specialize. Both prokaryotic and eukaryotic organisms can live in colonies.

True multicellularity arises only among eukaryotes. Examples of multicellular eukaryotes include some protists, such as algae; most fungi, excluding single-celled yeast; and all plant and animal species. In a multicellular organism, cells specialize to perform different essential life functions. These cells are all integrated and dependent upon one another for survival.

> **HELPFUL HINT**
>
> All multicellular organisms begin life as a unicellular gamete or haploid clone of the parent cell.

SAMPLE QUESTIONS

9) **Which of the following distinguishes a colony from a multicellular organism?**

A. Cells in a colony can live independently of one another, while cells in multicellular organisms cannot.

B. Colonies can only reproduce asexually, while multicellular organisms reproduce sexually.

C. Only eukaryotic organisms can live in colonies.

D. Only prokaryotic organisms can be multicellular.

Answers:

A. **Correct.** Cells in a multicellular organism can divide and replicate but cannot perform all life functions for an organism.

B. Incorrect. Mode of reproduction is not a distinguishing factor.

C. Incorrect. Both prokaryotes and eukaryotes can live in colonies.

D. Incorrect. The opposite is true; only eukaryotes can be multicellular.

10) **True multicellularity arises only among which of the following groups?**

A. archaea

B. prokaryotes

C. eukaryotes

D. bacteria

Answers:

A. Incorrect. Archaea are unicellular prokaryotes.

B. Incorrect. Prokaryotes can only be unicellular, although they can live in aggregate colonies.

C. **Correct.** Although some are unicellular, true multicellularity can only exist among eukaryotes.

D. Incorrect. Bacteria are unicellular prokaryotes.

MODES OF NUTRITION

The different groups of living things can be distinguished by their mode of nutrition, which is the method they use to obtain energy from the outside environment. Organisms tend to fall into one of two categories in this regard: **autotrophs**, or self-nourishing organisms, and **heterotrophs**, organisms that obtain nutrients from other sources.

Autotrophic organisms are able to produce their own food using internal cellular processes. In order to accomplish this, the organism must be able to obtain a source of carbon from outside its environment, as well as a source of energy to drive the food production process. Once these resources are obtained, the organism's cells can begin to break down the carbon-containing molecule into a usable form of energy.

There are two basic kinds of autotrophy: **photosynthetic** and **chemosynthetic**. Photosynthetic organisms include plants, plant-like protists, and some forms of bacteria. Photosynthetic organisms obtain carbon from carbon dioxide in the atmosphere and surrounding area. The energy that drives the photosynthetic process is derived from sun and light energy. Chemosynthetic organisms, which include some bacteria and archaea, also derive carbon from surrounding carbon dioxide, but the energy that drives their nutrient production is derived from inorganic chemicals, such as sulfur or ammonia. Chemosynthetic organisms typically live in areas where there is not a lot of sunlight, such as in hydrothermal vents in the deep ocean.

Unlike autotrophs, heterotrophs do not produce their own energy through the right inputs and cellular processes. Instead, heterotrophs obtain energy by consuming organic matter. They lack the cell structures and functions that enable autotrophs to produce energy from carbon. Therefore, heterotrophs rely on autotrophs to convert carbon into usable organic material, which is then consumed by the heterotroph and used to drive further cell processes. Organic material derived from autotrophs can be consumed by heterotrophs through several different methods, including ingestion and absorption. Animals, fungi, most bacteria, and animal-like protists all fall into this category.

SAMPLE QUESTIONS

11) **Which of the following modes of nutrition is found among animals, fungi, some protists, and most bacteria?**

   A.   chemosynthesis

   B.   heterotrophy

   C.   autotrophy

   D.   photosynthesis

   Answers:

   A.   Incorrect. Chemosynthesis applies to a small group of bacteria and archaea.

   B.   Correct. These organisms depend on food made by autotrophs.

   C.   Incorrect. Animals and fungi cannot make their own food and are therefore not autotrophs.

   D.   Incorrect. Photosynthesis applies to plants and some forms of cyanobacteria.

12) **Which of the following describes the relationship between autotrophs and heterotrophs?**

 A. Heterotrophs depend on food made by autotrophs.

 B. Autotrophs decompose waste left by heterotrophs.

 C. Heterotrophs and autotrophs compete for the same energy sources.

 D. Heterotrophs evolved from autotrophs.

Answers:

 A. **Correct.** Heterotrophs are unable to create organic matter from inorganic matter.

 B. Incorrect. This describes the relationship between decomposing heterotrophs and other forms of life.

 C. Incorrect. Autotrophs derive their energy from the sun; heterotrophs consume autotrophs for energy.

 D. Incorrect. This does not describe their evolutionary relationship.

REPRODUCTION AND REPLICATION

The reproductive process of viruses differs drastically from the reproductive processes of classified life, which further distinguishes this group as particles that straddle the line between living and non-living material. **Viral replication** is a multiple-step process in which a virus binds to a living cell and injects its genetic material into the host cell. The viral genetic material then uses the host cell's mechanisms and enzymes to replicate and assemble into clones of the parent virus. This results in hundreds, if not thousands, of viral clones residing inside the host cell.

Viral replication follows the **lytic cycle**, during which the host cell is broken apart and killed as the viral clones are released. This process is known as **lysis** and is triggered by a lytic enzyme that is produced to cause rupture within the host cell's membranes. Lysis occurs immediately after viral cloning and assembly for many types of viruses. Other viruses follow the **lysogenic cycle**. In this cycle, the viral genetic material integrates with the genome of the host cell and replicates each time the host cell divides. Lysis occurs when the conditions within the host cell begin to deteriorate and the virus ends its dormancy, releasing lytic enzymes in order to burst forth and release its clones.

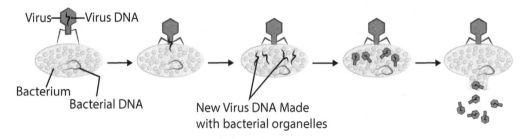

Figure 3.1. Viral Replication

Unlike viruses, the reproductive cycles of living things do not involve parasitizing a host or producing a vast number of genetic clones. All living things reproduce through the duplication of genetic material and cell division. As previously discussed, all DNA in a bacteria cell exists on one singular chromosome, which is usually circular. This is in direct contrast with higher kingdoms of organisms, which generally have pairs of chromosomes that are inherited from each parent. As a result, the bacteria cells are considered haploid and do not undergo meiosis during reproduction. Instead, bacteria reproduce via **binary fission**, a form of asexual cell division. During this process, a parent cell duplicates its genetic material and swells to twice its normal size before dividing into two equal daughter cells. Archaea cells also undergo binary fission in order to reproduce.

Protists can reproduce in many different ways. Like bacteria, most single-celled protists reproduce through binary fission. However, other organisms reproduce through both sexual and other asexual means. One of these forms of asexual reproduction—**budding**—occurs when an offspring is produced from a specialized generative site found on the parent body. Budding is not a process that is limited to the Protista kingdom; many forms of yeast fungi, plants, and lower animal phyla also reproduce asexually in this manner.

Fungi are also capable of reproducing both sexually and asexually. Examples of asexual reproduction among fungi include budding, **fragmentation**—which occurs when the parent divides into multiple pieces that each mature into adult forms—and asexual **sporulation**, during which parent cells undergo mitosis to create genetic clones which are then released into the environment. Sexual fungi reproduction occurs when parent fungi undergo meiosis to produce gametes to be released for fusion with a gamete of the opposite sex. Many species of plants and some species of animals also reproduce through budding, fragmentation, or sporulation; a more thorough discussion of the reproductive modes of these two kingdoms is found in later chapters.

SAMPLE QUESTIONS

13) **During which of the following processes does a virus release an enzyme that causes the host cell to rupture and release viral clones?**

  A. binary fission

  B. viral replication

  C. lytic cycle

  D. lysogenic cycle

Answers:

  A. Incorrect. This is the process of asexual reproduction among living things.

  B. Incorrect. This is just one part of the viral replication process.

C. **Correct.** The lytic cycle results in a virus releasing lytic enzymes to cause host cell membranes to rupture, killing the host cell in the process.

D. Incorrect. The lysogenic cycle is a part of the lytic cycle during which some viruses lay dormant and reproduce in a host cell.

14) **Which of the following is a form of reproduction in which parent cells undergo mitosis to create genetic clones which are then released into the environment?**

A. sporulation

B. fragmentation

C. binary fission

D. budding

Answers:

A. **Correct.** Sporulation is a form of asexual reproduction in which genetically identical spores are released by the parent fungi.

B. Incorrect. Fragmentation occurs when a parent divides into multiple pieces that each mature into adult forms.

C. Incorrect. Binary fission occurs when one parent cell splits into two equal copies.

D. Incorrect. Budding occurs when an offspring generates from a specialized site on the body of the parent.

BIOLOGICAL ORGANIZATION

Multicellular organisms display high levels of structure and organization. They are organized in a hierarchical manner that flows from small, relatively simple cells, to increasingly complex tissues, organs, and organ systems.

Even though the cell is the smallest functional unit of multicellular organisms, there is a level of organization of the material that is found within the cells themselves. Organic macromolecules, such as DNA, combine together within a cell to form cellular organelles, which are specialized to perform specific functions. In unicellular organisms, all life functions are performed within a single cell. In multicellular organisms, cells specialize to perform different essential functions. Examples of specialized cells include neurons—which are nerve cells that transmit information from a stimulus from one cell to another—or red blood cells, which function to transport oxygen to other cells found in a body.

A group of specialized cells that work together to perform a similar function are known as **tissues**. Plants contain specialized phloem cells, which are porous and allow for the easy transport of sugar between cells. A collection of phloem cells is known as phloem tissue, which functions to transport sugar from the site of production to other cells in the plant's body.

Organs are composed of tissues that perform a similar function. They are not composed of identical tissues and specialized cells. Instead, they are composed of several different kinds of tissues that work together in order to perform a more complex function. The heart, for example, is composed of muscle tissue, connective tissue, and nervous tissue. These different specialized tissues and cells work together to pump blood to the rest of the body.

QUICK REVIEW

Humans are complex organisms that display all levels of biological organization—cells, tissues, organs, and organ systems. Do all multicellular organisms display all levels of biological organization? If not, what are some examples?

Multiple organs that function together form a greater **organ system**. The heart is just one organ that is part of the circulatory system, just as the lungs are part of the respiratory system, and the brain is part of the nervous system. A collection of organ systems working together to perform all functions required for life is known as an **organism**.

SAMPLE QUESTION

15) **Which of the following is a group of specialized cells that work together to perform a similar function?**

   A.   organelles

   B.   tissues

   C.   organism

   D.   system

Answers:

   A.   Incorrect. Organelles are specialized units within a cell.

   B.   **Correct.** Tissues are a group of specialized cells that work together to perform a similar function.

   C.   Incorrect. An organism is the unit that performs all necessary functions for life.

   D.   Incorrect. *System* is a generalized term; an organ system is a group of functionally similar organs working together.

4

Animals

ANIMAL PHYLA

CHARACTERISTICS OF ANIMALS

The kingdom Animalia contains thirty-five different phyla, which are distinguished by characteristics such as body plans, body cavities, modes of reproduction, and modes of temperature. Of these thirty-five phyla, only one phylum (Chordata) incorporates vertebrates, or animals with a backbone. The remaining thirty-four phyla represent invertebrates—animals without a backbone.

Body plan, or the shape of an animal's body, is used to distinguish several animal phyla. This is often expressed in terms of symmetry—the distribution of body parts on the opposing sides of an imaginary line dividing the body. Animals with radial symmetry have body parts that are arranged circularly around a central point. The animals in the phylum Cnidaria, which includes jellyfish and coral, and the phylum Echinodermata, which includes sea stars and sea cucumbers, often display radial symmetry. The animals of the phylum Porifera, which includes the

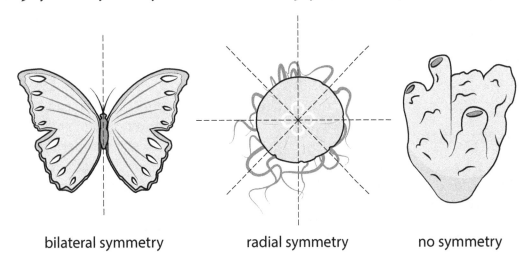

bilateral symmetry   radial symmetry   no symmetry

Figure 4.1. The Three Body Plans

sponges, display asymmetry in their body plans: their shapes are irregular and have no predictable pattern around the line of symmetry. Most animal phyla display bilateral symmetry. These animals are easily divided into right and left sides, with a distinguished head end and tail end. Several groups of animals, including the phyla Chordata, Arthropoda, and Annelida, have segmented bodies that consist of a series of repeated parts or compartments. Each segment tends to repeat a set of bodily structures, such as pairs of legs, and are grouped into larger segments in the body.

The type of body cavity also plays a distinguishing role between various animal phyla. **Coelomates** are animals with a true, fluid-filled body cavity with a **mesoderm** lining. A mesoderm is an embryonic layer that gives rise to bones, cartilage, blood, and other body tissue. The mesoderm-lined cavity, called a coelom, usually surrounds the digestive tract and provides protection and space for highly organized, efficient body systems, as seen in the phyla Chordata and Echinodermata. Animals with a functional body cavity that is not lined with mesoderm are known as **pseudocoelomates**. This includes the phyla Nemotoda and Rotifera. **Acoelomates** are animals that lack any sort of bodily cavity. Acoelomates are limited to just three major animal phyla: Porifera, Cnidaria, and Plathyhelminthes.

Animals can be classified by their various modes of reproduction. Reproduction modes are first classified as either asexual or sexual. Asexual reproduction results in offspring produced from a single parent. There are multiple modes of asexual reproduction. **Parthenogenesis**, the development of an embryo from an unfertilized female gamete, is common with some groups within the Arthropoda phylum, including ants and wasps. Total **regeneration**, the process of forming a new individual from a part of the parent, has been observed as a mode of reproduction in the Echinodermata phylum. Other forms include budding, in which offspring grow out of the body of a parent, and fragmentation, in which parent bodies break into separate, distinct pieces and become offspring.

In contrast, sexual reproduction results in offspring produced from the fusion of gametes between two parents. Animals in some phyla, such as Platyhelminthes, are **hermaphrodites,** each possessing both male and female reproductive systems. Hermaphroditic animals can reproduce sexually by copulating with another individual organism or self-fertilizing.

Modes of temperature regulation are used to classify a select number of animal groups. The vast majority of animal phyla are **ectotherms**, which means their internal body temperature is regulated by the temperature of their environment. Ectotherms tend to only live in environments where there is little temperature variation or have mechanisms that allow them to slow body processes when the temperature becomes too cool. The

HELPFUL HINT

Parthenogenesis is a common mode of reproduction of several groups of insects in the Arthropoda phylum, including honeybees. Fertilized honeybee eggs become female bees, while unfertilized eggs become male bees.

only **endotherms**—animals who self-regulate their internal body temperature—are found in the phylum Chordata: mammals and birds. Endotherms can live in extreme temperatures due to their relatively stable internal temperatures, but also require copious amounts of food to provide this energy.

SAMPLE QUESTIONS

1) **Which of the following groups of organisms contains a fluid-filled body cavity that has a mesoderm lining?**

   A.   acoelomate

   B.   coelomate

   C.   procoelomate

   D.   pseudocoelomate

   Answers:

   A.   Incorrect. Acoelomates lack any body cavity.

   B.   Correct. Coelomates have a body cavity that surrounds the digestive system and is lined with a mesoderm, giving rise to other bodily tissues.

   C.   Incorrect. Procoelomate is not a scientific term.

   D.   Incorrect. Pseudocoelomates have a body cavity, but it is partial and not lined with a mesoderm.

2) **Which of the following is NOT a form of asexual reproduction?**

   A.   parthenogenesis

   B.   regeneration

   C.   fragmentation

   D.   hermaphroditism

   Answers:

   A.   Incorrect. Parthenogenesis is a form of asexual reproduction in which an embryo develops from an unfertilized egg.

   B.   Incorrect. Regeneration is a form of asexual reproduction in which offspring are produced from a part of a parent.

   C.   Incorrect. Fragmentation is a form of asexual reproduction in which offspring are produced from a parent body that has fragmented into distinct pieces.

   D.   Correct. Hermaphroditism is the appearance of both male and female sexual organs in an individual and is not a form of sexual reproduction.

PORIFERA

The phylum Porifera contains sponges, which are some of the simplest organisms that exist in the animal kingdom. They are asymmetrical, ectothermic **sessile** organisms, meaning they live attached to one spot and do not move freely. Since they cannot move, they rely primarily on filtering to obtain both food and oxygen as water flows into the sponge body. The sponge body lacks a body cavity, as well as specific organs and tissues. Instead, the sponge relies on specialized cells that fulfill different functions. These cells are arranged into an outer layer, which contains pores along the body wall that allow water both in and out of the sponge. Some contain spicules—hard structures covering the outer body—or collagen to give the outer body structure and maintain open pores. The pores themselves contain specialized cells with **flagella** to facilitate water movement. The inner layer contains cells that specialize in digesting food particles and cells that specialize in filtering out oxygen. Sponges can reproduce both asexually by budding, and sexually by releasing gametes into the water.

SAMPLE QUESTION

3) Which of the following is NOT a descriptive term for a member of the Porifera phylum?

    A. asymmetrical
    B. sessile
    C. endotherm
    D. acoelomate

Answers:

    A. Incorrect. The body plan of a sponge does not display any predictable pattern.
    B. Incorrect. Sponges spend the majority of their lives fixed in one spot.
    C. Correct. Only certain members of the phylum Chordata have displayed the ability to be endothermic; sponges are ectotherms.
    D. Incorrect. Sponges lack a body cavity, which is the definition of an acoelomate.

CNIDARIA

Cnidarians are a phylum of simple animals that contains jellyfish, corals, and hydrozoans. Cnidarians display radial symmetry, with a single opening surrounded by a series of tentacles. The tentacles, which contain specialized stinging cells, immobilize prey and bring food into the opening where it is digested internally in a simple cavity. This **gastrovascular** cavity also plays a role in circulation as well as digestion. Food waste is then expelled through the same central opening. Cnidarians do not have any true organs; instead they have layers or simple tissues and specialized cells that give the organisms a primitive nervous system and muscle system. These specialized muscle cells contract to produce a swimming movement among some cnidarians, such as adult jellyfish.

Most cnidarians have a two-stage life cycle. During the **polyp** stage, a free-swimming larva settles in one location and becomes sessile. In this stage, the animal produces buds that are eventually released as motile **medusas**, in which they swim freely through the water. This is a form of asexual reproduction known as budding; however, many cnidarians can also reproduce sexually as male and female medusa release gametes into the water for fertilization.

SAMPLE QUESTION

4) **Which of the following is a true statement about animals in the Cnidaria phylum?**

    A.   They display radial symmetry.

    B.   They have true organ systems.

    C.   They only reproduce asexually.

    D.   They have two distinct openings.

Answers:

    A.   **Correct.** The body plans of cnidarians are all the same: tentacles surrounding a center opening.

    B.   Incorrect. Cnidarians have specialized cells and tissues that function similarly to organs, but lack true organ systems.

    C.   Incorrect. Both asexual and sexual reproduction is found within this phylum.

    D.   Incorrect. Cnidarians have a single opening that brings food in and expels waste.

PLATYHELMINTHES

The phylum Platyhelminthes—flatworms—display bilateral symmetry, with distinct left and right sides. These animals also have organized, albeit primitive, organ systems, including nervous, digestive, and reproductive systems. Despite this complexity, platyhelminths are still simple organisms in many ways. They are acoelomates, which limits their flexibility. They lack a circulatory system, which means they must absorb oxygen from their environment through the skin; oxygen is then processed in the digestive system. These organisms can also absorb nutrients through the skin;

QUICK REVIEW

Parasitism is a form of symbiosis, a relationship between two organisms. In parasitic symbiosis, one organism benefits while the other is harmed. What negative effects could a platyhelminth parasite, such as a tapeworm, have on its host?

as a result, a majority of platyhelminths are **parasitic**, meaning they live on and feed off of other organisms. Platyhelminths are also hermaphroditic and can reproduce both sexually—as two parents fertilize each other during copulation—as well as asexually through fragmentation.

SAMPLE QUESTION

5) **Which of the following describes how platyhelminths obtain and process oxygen?**

A. They absorb oxygen from the environment and process it in the digestive system.

B. They absorb oxygen from the environment and process it in the circulatory system.

C. They take oxygen from their host and process it in the circulatory system.

D. They take oxygen from their host and process it in the nervous system.

Answers:

A. **Correct.** Platyhelminths obtain oxygen from water or air diffusion, then distribute it throughout the body via the digestive system.

B. Incorrect. Platyhelminths do obtain oxygen from their environment, but they lack a circulatory system.

C. Incorrect. Platyhelminths obtain oxygen from air or water, not the host; they also lack a circulatory system.

D. Incorrect. Platyhelminths obtain oxygen from air or water, not the host; oxygen is then distributed via the digestive system.

NEMATODA

Animals in the phylum Nematoda—the roundworms, live in vast numbers in nearly every environment on the planet, fulfilling many important ecological roles. Many nematodes are parasitic and affect both plant and animal hosts. They also play a critical role in decomposition. Nematodes are invertebrates with bilateral symmetry. They are **pseudoecoels**, with a simple central body cavity, and have more complex organ systems than animals of the Platyhelminthes phylum. Their **complete digestive system** contains an anus and a mouth, rather than one opening used for both obtaining nutrients and expelling waste. Nematode reproduction is exclusively sexual, and the individuals are single sex, rather than hermaphroditic.

SAMPLE QUESTION

6) **Which of the following is NOT a distinguishing feature of the Nematoda phylum?**

A. They have complete digestive systems.

B. They reproduce sexually.

C. They are pseudocoelates.

D. They have a segmented body plan.

Answers:

A. Incorrect. Nematodes have a complete digestive system with both an anus and a mouth.

B. Incorrect. Nematodes exclusively reproduce in a sexual manner.

C. Incorrect. Nematodes have a prototypical body cavity that is not lined with a mesoderm, as a true coelom is.

D. Correct. Nematodes display bilateral symmetry but are not considered segmented like other animal phyla.

ANNELIDA

The annelids (phylum Annelida) consist of three major classes: sandworms (class Polychaeta), earthworms (class Oligochaeta), and leeches (class Hirudinea). They have bilateral symmetry and can reproduce both sexually and asexually. Hermaphrodites are common in this phylum, but annelids can also be one sex. Annelids are ectothermic and depend on their environment for both body temperature as well as absorption of water and oxygen.

Annelids are distinct from the other worm-like phyla due to their body segmentation, true coelom, and **closed circulatory system**. Body segmentation is widespread among more complex phyla of animals and gives such animals greater flexibility without sacrificing strength and greater mobility, as well as a greater ability for different body parts to specialize in different functions. The true coelom of annelids allows for the development of more complex organ systems by separating internal organs from the body wall. This includes a closed circulatory system in which blood is contained in vessels and pumped through the body by series of hearts. Annelids also have multiple layers of muscle tissue, digestive organs connected to an excretory system, and a nervous system with a brain, nerve cord, and sensory organs.

SAMPLE QUESTION

7) **Which of the following is NOT an advantage of body segmentation in annelids?**

A. mobility

B. respiration

C. differentiation

D. flexibility

Answers:

A.   Incorrect. Individual segments can contract and release independently of one another, giving the animal greater control over mobility.

B.   Correct. Annelids absorb oxygen through their skin as part of the process of respiration, which is not related to their body segmentation.

C.   Incorrect. Separate segments can take on different functions independently of other segments.

D.   Incorrect. Segmentation provides flexibility in movement to annelids while still providing strength.

Mollusca

The phylum Mollusca is large, with thousands of species and a great amount of phylogenetic diversity. Major classes of mollusks include the gastropods (snails, slugs), bivalves (clams, oysters), and cephalopods (octopus, squid). Mollusks are soft-bodied invertebrates that have bilateral symmetry, but lack body segmentation. They are coelomates and most have highly organized organ systems, including muscular, digestive, nervous, respiratory, and circulatory systems. Most mollusks have highly developed **open circulatory systems**. Blood is pumped through a two-chambered heart that pumps oxygenated blood through vessels and out into body spaces. Mollusks also have **gills**—specialized organs that allow the animal to take in oxygen from a centralized point. Most species also have single-sex reproductive organs, although some gastropods and bivalves can be hermaphroditic, and reproduce sexually both through internal and external fertilization.

The most distinguishing feature of all mollusks is the appearance of a **mantle**. A mantle is a flat, folded layer of tissue that covers and protects the soft mollusk body. In many mollusk species, this mantle produces material to create a hard shell. The cavity between the mantle and the body is the site of the gills. The body of most mollusks also functions as a **head-foot**, a muscular mass on the bottom side of the body that can contract to move the mollusk. This feature takes on a wide variety of functions depending on the class and species of the mollusk.

SAMPLE QUESTION

8)   **Which of the following is NOT a true statement about a mantle in the phylum Mollusca?**

A.   Mantles offer protection for the soft bodies of mollusks.

B.   Mantles can secrete material for a hard shell in most species.

C.   Mantles are not found in all species of mollusks.

D.   Mantles provide a cavity near the body for gill formation.

Answers:

A.   Incorrect. The skin-like tissue protects the internal organs of mollusks.

B. Incorrect. Many mollusks develop a hard protective shell that originates in the mantle.

C. **Correct.** Mantles are found in all species in the phylum Mollusca.

D. Incorrect. The mantle cavity is the site of gill formation in this phylum.

ARTHROPODA

The arthropods are by far the largest group of animals, constituting more than 75 percent of all species classified by scientists. All arthropods are invertebrates with a true coelom and a bilateral, segmented body plan. Most arthropods have three body segments: head, thorax, and abdomen. Arthropods are distinguished by their **exoskeleton**—a strong layer of chitin that provides protection and support. The exoskeleton is punctuated by joints along the three body segments and joints that allow arms and legs to move. Exoskeletons do not grow with the animal and must be **molted** periodically as the animal grows. This combination of exoskeleton and flexible joints gives arthropods great mobility and the ability to live in many different environments. The exoskeleton also plays a critical role in protecting the complex organ systems. Organ systems include an open circulatory system, a digestive system with a stomach, a nervous system with a brain and sensory organs, and male or female reproductive systems. All arthropods reproduce sexually, and there is no hermaphroditism in this phylum.

There is a great amount of diversity within this phylum, which can be further subdivided into three subphyla: Chelicerata (spiders, tics, mites); Crustacea (crab, shrimp, barnacles); and Unirama (insects, centipedes). Chelicerates are so named due to their paired **chelicerae**, or pincers, and many have four pairs of legs and two body segments. Crustaceans, which live primarily in the water, typically have three pairs of legs and two sets of antennae. Uniramians, which include the insects, have three body segments, six jointed legs, one pair of antennae, and go through metamorphosis. The insects are the largest and most diverse group of arthropods.

There are nearly thirty different orders of insects, and most can be found in one of seven orders. There is great diversity among these orders. Insects in the order Hemiptera, such as stink bugs and water scorpions, are considered the true bugs, with piercing mouthparts, four wings, and no **cerci**—a pair of sensory appendages found at the rear of the abdomen. The order Coleoptera encompasses all species of beetles, which is the most numerous group of insects. Common features of this order include four wings (usually hardened), a chewing mouthpart, and no cerci. Moths and butterflies are found in the order Lepidoptera. Moths can be distinguished by their **filiform** antennae (slender and thread-like), while butterflies are distinguished by knobbed antennae. Ants, bees, and wasps are the primary members of the Hymenoptera order. These animals all have four wings, with smaller hind wings. Females have an ovipositor, which is sometimes modified into a stinger in some groups. The order Diptera, which includes flies and mosquitoes, are notable for their two wings, small antennae, and diverse array of mouthparts. Insects in the order Odonata, including dragonflies and damselflies, have four large, membranous wings, large compound eyes, and long, slender abdomens. Grasshoppers and crickets are found in the order Orthoptera, which all have filiform antennae, short cerci, and hind legs adapted for jumping.

SAMPLE QUESTION

9)   **Which of the following is NOT an organ system found in the phylum Arthropoda?**

   A.   digestive system

   B.   male reproductive system

   C.   nervous system

   D.   closed circulatory system

Answers:

   A.   Incorrect. All arthropods have a digestive system that includes a stomach.

   B.   Incorrect. Arthropods are single sex and have either a male reproductive system or a female reproductive system.

   C.   Incorrect. Arthropods have a complex nervous system with a brain and sensory organs.

   D.   **Correct.** Arthropods have an open circulatory system.

ECHINODERMATA

Echinoderms are spiny-skinned animals that live primarily in the ocean. Animals within this phylum include sea stars (commonly known as starfish), sea cucumbers, and sea urchins. All echinoderms have radial symmetry, with a series of five segments radiating around a central mouth. Despite their radial symmetry, all larval forms have bilateral symmetry. This indicates that the echinoderm evolved this body plan from bilateral symmetry. They are invertebrates, meaning they do not have any bone structures, but they do have an internal skeleton consisting of calcium carbonate plates.

Echinoderms are coelomates and have some complex organ systems, such as a digestive tract, but are lacking several other major organ systems. They have no brain or head, no excretory system, and no respiratory system. They do, however, have some unique adaptations, such as a **water vascular system** that transports water collected from a series of **tube feet** that radiate around a center point. These tube feet can also be used for motion and can potentially hunt and capture prey if the species is not a filter feeder. Echinoderms are generally either male or female and reproduce sexually, although in some cases, such as in some sea stars, asexual reproduction is possible.

SAMPLE QUESTION

10) Which of the following organ systems is NOT found in the Echinodermata phylum?

   A.   excretory system

   B.   water vascular system

   C.   digestive system

   D.   nervous system

Answers:

   A.   Incorrect. Echinoderms lack an anus and an excretory system and instead excrete waste through the same opening in which they ingest food.

   B.   Correct. The water vascular system is a water transport system unique to echinoderms.

   C.   Incorrect. Echinoderms have a functioning digestive system.

   D.   Incorrect. Echinoderms lack a brain but do have a primitive nervous system that includes sensory organs, such as eye spots.

CHORDATA

The phylum Chordata encompasses all of the major groups of vertebrates—fish, amphibians, reptiles, birds, and mammals—as well as any other invertebrate that has a **notochord** at some stage of its life cycle. A notochord is a rod-shaped skeletal structure that extends from the head to the tail of the animal and is distinct from the backbone. Examples of invertebrates with a notochord are tunicates—a sessile, filter-feeding water animal that loses its notochord after the larval stage, and lancelets—a small, fish-like animal with no backbone but a well-developed notochord. Other characteristics of chordates include bilateral symmetry, a true coelom, the pretense of pharyngeal gill slits, dorsal nerve cord, and post-anal tail. Many of these last three features only exist in the larval stage.

The most numerous and familiar members of this phylum are the members of the subphylum Vertebrata. All members of this group have a true backbone composed of individual **vertebrae**. These structures, composed of either bone or cartilage, serve to protect the spinal cord, which is a primary component of a central nervous system. The vertebrae are just one part of an internal support system known as an **endoskeleton**, which distinguishes this group of animals from the invertebrates and gives these animals greater flexibility and mobility.

Vertebrates can be classified into five major groups of classes. The first group, the fish, are composed of three major classes: class Agnatha—the jawless lampreys and hagfish; class Chondrichthyes—the cartilaginous sharks and rays; and class Actinopterygii—the bony, ray-finned fish that make up over 97 percent of all fish species on Earth.

Fish in the Agnatha class, or the jawless fish, are the most primitive vertebrates. They do not have jaws, which are a more advanced animal adaptation, and they also lack other typical fish characteristics, such as fins and scales. They are long, tube-shaped animals with an oral disc for a mouth, which is used in conjunction with its teeth and a rasping tongue to latch on to prey or host animals.

Fish in the Chondrichthyes class are more advanced, with a jaw, paired fins, and gill slits. Their endoskeleton is primarily composed of flexible **cartilage** rather than hard bone, and the **placoid scales** that cover their body are made of the same material as their teeth. Sharks, one of the predominant groups of Chondrichthyes, have notable sensory organs including the **lateral line**, which is a pressure receptor located along the side of the animal that is used to help detect movement in the water. Unlike their bony fish relatives, members of Chondrichthyes lack a **swim bladder** that aids in buoyancy and instead depend on a large, oily liver to stay buoyant in the water. Reproduction is sexual and internal, with males attaching to females using **claspers**.

The Actinopterygii are by far the most populous group of fish, with at least 20,000 species worldwide. These species vary widely in size and function, but share several important characteristics. They are known as bony fish due to their skeletons which are composed of hard bone. They are also known as *ray-finned* fish due the ray-like structures that support their dorsal fins. Their bodies are covered with **cycloid** (smooth) and **ctenoid** (rough) scales that overlap to provide protection. Their gill arches are covered and protected by a bony plate called an **operculum**, and they stay buoyant by inflating or releasing air from an internal swim bladder organ. Bony fish also have a well-developed lateral line. Reproduction is sexual and fertilization is primarily external.

Animals in the Amphibian class are the first evolutionary group of vertebrates to be **terrestrial**, or live on land. However, most amphibians still depend on a water environment for at least one stage of their life. The term *amphibian* actually means *double life* and refers to the terrestrial and aquatic life stages of these animals, which include salamanders, frogs, toads, and caecilians. They all depend on the water as a place to lay eggs. Most spend their larval stage in an aquatic environment. Larval amphibians (tadpoles), have fish-like characteristics such as gills and a tail that disappear as they go through **metamorphosis**—the change to adult form. The adult amphibians develop terrestrial body structures, such as lungs and legs, but still live primarily near moist environments in order to continue absorbing water through their skin and be near a location to breed and lay eggs. Reproduction is sexual and fertilization is external, with a female laying soft eggs in the water and males fertilizing them, leaving the eggs to develop and hatch without parental involvement.

Reptiles and birds were traditionally separated into two distinct classes: Reptilia and Aves. More recent evolutionary research has prompted the scientific community to place both of these groups of animals in the class Reptilia due to their shared ancestry. These two groups of animals share many characteristics. All animals in the class Reptilia, which includes snakes, lizards, turtles, and crocodilians, in addition to birds, lay **amniotic eggs** that have protective membranes and a tough outer shell that allows the eggs to be laid on land without drying out. All reptilians reproduce sexually via internal fertilization. They have well-developed, efficient lungs that extract oxygen from the air. All have scales composed of keratin. On the traditional reptiles, this is evident in the dry, scaly skin covering their entire body. On birds, this is evident on their scaly legs and feet and in their feathers, which are elongated, modified scales.

The animals that have traditionally been classified as reptiles all share some important characteristics but are set apart by some notable features. The animals in the order Chelonia—the turtles and tortoises—are most distinguished by their modified skeleton that forms a shell. Chelonian shells are made out of keratin and have two parts: an upper **carapace** and a lower **plastron**. Turtles and tortoises have a beak, similar to the birds, and do not have any teeth. Lizards and snakes can both be found in the order Squamata. Lizards are distinguished from snakes by their movable eyelids and, in most cases, legs. Snakes, however, are legless and have eyes covered and protected by a transparent scale instead of eyelids. Animals in the order Crocodilia—which includes the crocodiles and alligators—are large reptiles that can be found either in fresh or saltwater.

There are several important characteristics that distinguish birds from the traditional reptiles. Snakes, lizards, turtles, and crocodilians are ectothermic, while birds are endothermic. Birds lack teeth and instead specialize feeding behaviors based on the size, shape, and function of their **beak**. Many of their other distinguishing features are directly related to flight, an adaptation that most birds share. Birds have lightweight, hollow bones supported by small, crisscrossing structures that provide strength while eliminating excess weight that would make it more difficult to attain flight. They have a highly efficient respiratory system composed of a series of lungs and air sacs in order to obtain as much oxygen as possible with every breath. Their wings are modified arm bones that are attached to a keeled sternum, which allow for greater muscle attachment to help generate flight. Finally, their wings are covered with **contour feathers**, which are specially shaped to create lift and generate gliding once the bird is in flight.

The last major group of vertebrate animals are the members of the class Mammalia, or the mammals. Mammals are distinguished by several important characteristics and are named after the presence of **mammary glands**, which are found in females and produce milk for the young of the species. All mammals are **endothermic**, which results in a near-constant body temperature that remains stable despite external temperatures. Hair, which is found on all mammals, plays an important role in keeping heat close to their bodies, as well as protecting them from extreme heat. Mammals also have teeth that are specialized for their particular feeding behavior: incisors (which tear food) canines (which bite food) and molars (which grind food).

There are three major groups of mammals in this class: the monotremes, the marsupials, and the placental mammals. The major differences between these subclasses stems from their reproductive habits and structures. The monotremes, which include the duck-billed platypus, lay eggs. The marsupials, such as kangaroos and opossums, develop their young in a shell within the mother. The shell disappears, leaving the young to finish developing in the mother's **marsupium**, or pouch. The placental mammals, which are the largest and most diverse group of mammals, are **viviparous**, meaning the young develop inside the mother rather than in an egg. The developing fetus is attached to and supported by a **placenta**, which provides nutrients and oxygen to the fetus while transporting waste to the mother.

HELPFUL HINT

Most evolutionary biologists agree that dinosaurs did not go extinct: birds, or avian dinosaurs, descended from a group of small, bipedal dinosaurs called therapods.

SAMPLE QUESTIONS

11) **Which of the following classes of chordates contain the monotremes?**

   A.   Mammalia

   B.   Reptilia

   C.   Chondrichthyes

   D.   Agnatha

   Answers:

   A.   Correct. Monotremes are egg-laying mammals in the class Mammalia.

   B.   Incorrect. Although the monotremes lay hard eggs, like the reptiles, the presence of fur and mammary glands places them in the Mammalia class.

   C.   Incorrect. Chondrichthyes is the class of vertebrates that contain cartilaginous fish, such as sharks.

   D.   Incorrect. The class Agnatha encompasses the jawless fish, such as lampreys.

12) **Which of the following is the function of a lateral line in the bony fishes?**

   A.   to cover and protect the gills

   B.   to detect pressure differences in the water

   C.   to make the fish more buoyant

   D.   to protect the spinal cord

   Answers:

   A.   Incorrect. This describes the function of the operculum.

B. **Correct.** The lateral line is a sensory organ found in bony fish and many species of cartilaginous fish.

C. Incorrect. This describes the function of the swim bladder.

D. Incorrect. This describes the function of the vertebrae in the backbone.

ANIMAL ANATOMY AND PHYSIOLOGY

Anatomy is the science of body structures among animals, while physiology is the study of the functions of anatomical structures. All animal bodies are composed of cells. Depending on the complexity of the animal, these cells may be specialized and organized first into tissues, which carry out a specialized function; then into organs, which are multiple tissues working together to carry out a function; and lastly into organ systems, which are a group of organs working together to carry out a function. Examples of major organ systems found in the animal kingdom include the cardiovascular, respiratory, reproductive, digestive, excretory, nervous, endocrine, and immune systems. These systems work together to create a living organism.

CARDIOVASCULAR SYSTEM

In most animals the cardiovascular system, also known as the circulatory system, is composed of a set of organs that work together to transport materials such as nutrients, wastes, and gases from one part of the body to the other. These materials are transported through **blood**, which delivers food and oxygen to body locations and removes waste from these areas for eventual excretion.

Different classifications of animals transport materials in a variety of different ways. Members of some primitive phyla, like the Porifera (sponges), do not have any sort of cardiovascular system and instead obtain necessary oxygen by absorbing it through their bodies. Others, such as the arthropods and mollusks, have an open circulatory system. In an open circulatory system, blood does not travel via blood vessels; instead, blood mixes with cells and surrounding fluid to deliver oxygen and remove waste.

Many groups, including the vertebrates, have a closed circulatory system. The primary organ of this system is the **heart**, a specialized organ composed of cardiac muscle that is designed to continually contract and relax. In a closed circulatory system, the **heart** actively pumps oxygenated blood to all regions of the body via **arteries**, which have strong walls in order to withstand the pressure of the pumping force coming from the heart. These arteries branch off into very small vessels, or **capillaries**, where oxygen, nutrients, and other materials are exchanged with the tissue at the site. Deoxygenated blood is then carried back to the heart through the **veins**.

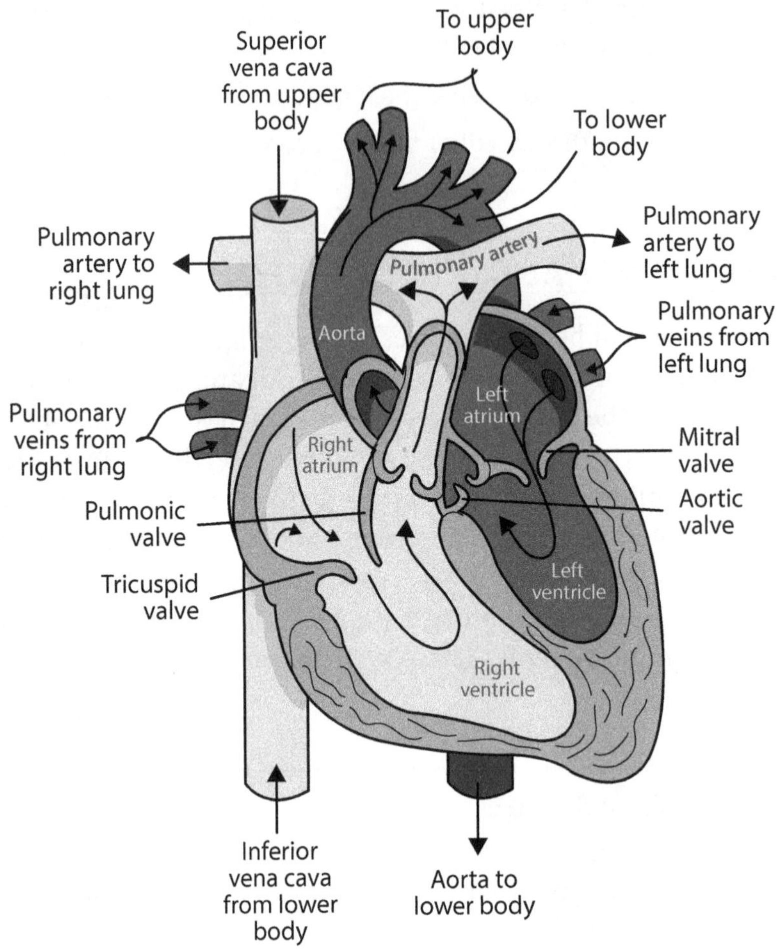

Figure 4.2. Four-Chambered Heart

Depending on the complexity of the animal, the heart can have anywhere from two to four chambers. Humans have a four-chambered heart that is composed of two **atria**, which receive the blood, and two **ventricles**, which pump the blood. Oxygen-poor blood from throughout the body is initially received in the right atrium. This atrium is separated from the right ventricle by the tricuspid **valve**. Valves function to prevent blood from flowing backwards from the ventricle to the atrium. As the heart beats, the valve opens and allows blood to flow into the right ventricle, which then pumps the blood from the heart to the lungs. Red blood cells absorb oxygen in the lungs, and then the blood is delivered back to the heart into the left atrium. The left atrium—separated from the left ventricle by the mitral (or bicuspid) valve—empties into the left ventricle in order to be pumped from the heart throughout the body.

QUICK REVIEW

Blood flows from the heart in one of two circuits: the pulmonary circuit, which moves blood from the lungs to the heart, and the systemic circuit, which moves blood from the heart to the rest of the body and vice versa. Which chambers of the heart are associated with these two different circuits?

As the heart pumps blood throughout the body, it exerts pressure on the vessels of the cardiovascular system. It is important that this **blood pressure** is maintained at a healthy level in order for oxygen to be efficiently and effectively delivered throughout the body. Blood pressure can be measured by first measuring the pressure at the **systole phase**, or period of ventricle contraction, and again at the **diastole phase**, or period of relaxation.

SAMPLE QUESTIONS

13) **Which of the following statements is true about the heart?**

    A.   All hearts contain four separate chambers.

    B.   Blood is received in the ventricle.

    C.   Heart chambers are separated by valves.

    D.   Blood exits the heart via veins.

    Answers:

    A.   Incorrect. Four-chambered hearts are only found in mammals and birds.

    B.   Incorrect. Blood is received in the atria and pumped from the ventricles.

    C.   Correct. Valves exist between the atria and ventricles of the heart in order to prevent backflow of blood.

    D.   Incorrect. Arteries are the vessels that carry blood away from the heart; veins carry blood to the heart.

14) **Which of the following is NOT transported by blood?**

    A.   impulses

    B.   oxygen

    C.   waste

    D.   nutrients

    Answers:

    A.   Correct. Nerve impulses are transported in the nervous system, not the cardiovascular system.

    B.   Incorrect. Oxygen, as well as other gases, are transported in the blood.

    C.   Incorrect. Blood carries waste from various parts of the body to other parts for eventual excretion.

    D.   Incorrect. Nutrients are one of many materials delivered to parts of the body by blood.

RESPIRATORY SYSTEM

All animals require oxygen intake in order to survive. Oxygen is an essential part of cellular respiration, which breaks down glucose to create energy. Without oxygen, animal cells cannot function. The byproduct of cellular respiration—carbon dioxide—must also be removed from the body as high levels of carbon dioxide can harm or kill cells. This process of exchanging gases between the atmosphere and animal cells is known as **respiration**.

There are different modes of respiration depending on the complexity of the animal. Small, simple animals whose majority of body cells are positioned close to the outside environment, such as the platyhelminthes and cnidarians, exchange oxygen and carbon dioxide through the process of **direct diffusion**. This allows these animals to absorb oxygen and eliminate carbon dioxide directly through their cells. Larger, more complex animals require more oxygen—and are more likely to have a complex respiratory system as a result. These respiratory systems work in conjunction with cardiovascular systems in order to efficiently transport oxygen and carbon dioxide throughout the body.

Animals that live in the water have respiratory systems that use specialized **gills** in order to obtain oxygen and eliminate carbon dioxide into their environment. Animals with gills include fish, amphibians in their larval stage, mollusks, and aquatic annelids and arthropods. Gills have many branches with specialized cells to exchange gases. These branches and their specialized cells primarily function to increase the surface area in order to maximize the amount of oxygen that can be obtained from the environment.

Gills are replaced by one of two different major respiratory organs among terrestrial animals. Simple land animals, such as insects, have a series of branching tubes called **tracheae** found throughout the body that directly diffuse and deliver gases to all parts of the body. Larger, more complex animals have a respiratory system that depends on a pair of **lungs** to breathe and exchange gases. In mammals, lungs are located near the heart in the **thoracic cavity**—a space in the body that is enclosed by the ribs, and the **diaphragm**—a large muscle that crosses the thoracic cavity and separates the lungs from organs in the abdomen.

Mammal respiration begins with **pulmonary ventilation**, or breathing. The first stage of breathing is inhalation. During this process, the thoracic cavity expands and the diaphragm contracts, which decreases pressure on the lungs and allows air to flow into the body, since atmospheric pressure is greater than lung pressure. Air is drawn in through the nose and mouth, then into the throat, where **cilia** and **mucus** filter out particles before the air enters the trachea.

Once it passes through the trachea, the air passes through either the left or right **bronchi**, which are divisions of the trachea that direct air into the left or right lung. These bronchi are further divided into smaller **bronchioles**, which branch throughout the lungs and become increasingly small. Air passes through these tubes, eventually entering **alveoli**—tiny air sacs located at the ends of the smallest bronchioles. The alveoli have very thin membranes, only one cell thick, and are the location of gas exchange with the blood: oxygen diffuses into the blood that has arrived from the right ventricle of the heart, while carbon dioxide is diffused from the blood into the alveoli. This process of gas exchange is known as **external respiration**. Carbon dioxide is then expelled from the lungs during the second stage of breathing—exhalation. During exhalation, the diaphragm relaxes and allows the lungs to return to their former state while air leaves the body, as the lung pressure is now greater than the surrounding atmospheric pressure.

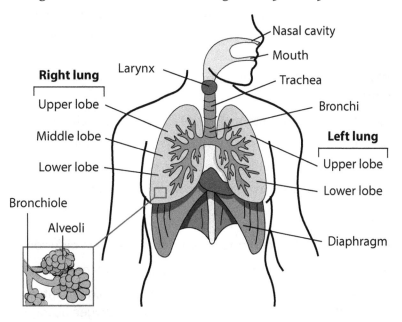

Figure 4.3. The Respiratory System

Respiration is not the only function of the respiratory system in humans. Air moving in during the inhalation process will move air over the vocal cords, located in the **larynx** at the top of the trachea. When air moves over these cords, the cords vibrate and produce sound, which can be manipulated to create speech. The respiratory system also allows the body to remove particles through coughs and sneezes, playing an important part in the immune system as well.

QUICK REVIEW

External respiration takes place in the lungs between the alveoli and blood. Internal respiration, or cellular respiration, is the exchange of gases at the cellular level to release energy from food.

SAMPLE QUESTIONS

15) **Which of the following structures are small air sacs that function as the site of external respiration and gas exchange in the lungs?**

   A.   capillaries

   B.   bronchi

   C.   alveoli

   D.   cilia

   Answers:

   A.   Incorrect. Capillaries are the smallest branches of blood vessels.

B.   Incorrect. The left and right bronchi are divisions of the trachea that direct gas in and out of the left and right lungs.

C.   **Correct.** The alveoli are sacs found at the terminal end of each bronchiole in the lungs and are the site of gas exchange with the blood.

D.   Incorrect. Cilia are small hairs that exist inside the nasal cavity to clean out particles from incoming air before it enters the respiratory system.

16) **Which of the following describes an advantage of gills over direct diffusion?**

A.   Gills allow for air to be directly absorbed by each cell.

B.   Gills allow animals to move between air and land.

C.   Gills provide more surface area to collect oxygen.

D.   Gills transport oxygen to all parts of the body.

Answers:

A.   Incorrect. This describes an advantage of direct diffusion.

B.   Incorrect. Gills are predominant in aquatic animals.

C.   **Correct.** Gills are highly branched, thereby significantly increasing the surface area of these tissues to maximize oxygen absorption.

D.   Incorrect. This is a function of an animal's cardiovascular system.

SKELETAL SYSTEM

The human skeletal system is the organ system that provides structure, protection, and support for body tissues. The skeletal system works in tandem with the muscular system to enable locomotion. The skeletal system also stores calcium and phosphate and produces blood and white blood cells within the bone marrow. In humans, the skeletal system is primarily composed of bone, with tendons connecting bone to muscle and ligaments connecting bone to bone, and small amounts of cartilage; some other chordates, such as sharks and rays, have skeletons made of cartilage.

Each of the human body's 206 bones is considered an individual organ. Bones are covered with a thin layer of vascular connective tissue called the **periosteum**, which serves as a point of muscle attachment and supplies blood to the bone that it covers. It also contains nerve endings. A connective tissue known as **osseous tissue** is the primary tissue that makes up bones. There are two types of osseous tissue: **cortical**, or compact, bone, and **cancellous**, or spongy, bone. Cortical bone is the dense, solid material that surrounds the bone and gives it hardness and strength. It is usually concentrated in the middle part of the bone. Cancellous bone is less dense, more porous, and softer. It is located at the ends of long bones, where it does not bear a structural load, but instead serves as a site of the bone's blood production and metabolic activity, as it stores both blood vessels and **bone marrow**.

Red bone marrow is responsible for producing red blood cells, platelets, and white blood cells. Yellow bone marrow is composed mostly of fat tissue and can be converted to red bone marrow in response to extreme blood loss in the body.

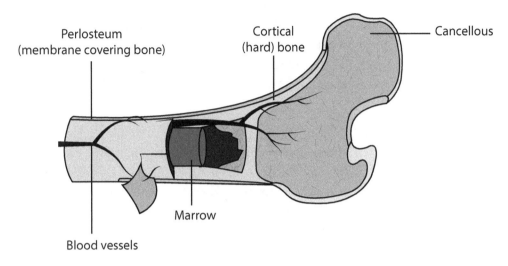

Figure 4.4. Structure of Bone

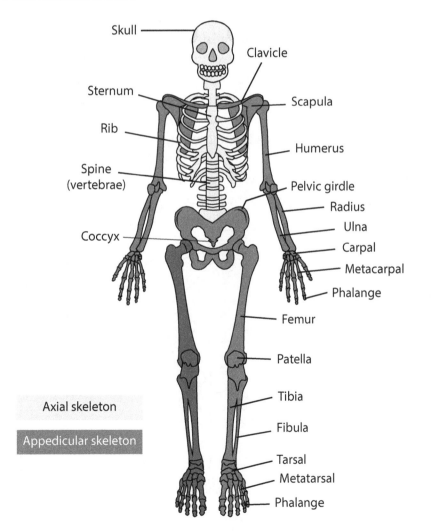

Figure 4.5. The Axial and Appendicular Skeletons

The human skeleton is divided into two distinct parts: the **axial skeleton** and the **appendicular skeleton**. The axial skeleton contains eighty bones and has three major subdivisions: the skull, which contains the cranium and facial bones; the thorax, which includes the sternum and twelve pairs of ribs; and the vertebral column, which contains the body's thirty-three vertebrae. These eighty bones function together to support and protect many of the body's vital organs, including the brain, lungs, heart, and spinal cord. The appendicular skeleton's 126 bones make up the body's appendages. The main function of the appendicular skeleton is locomotion.

The bones of the upper limbs, or the arms, are the humerus, ulna, and radius, as well as fifty-four carpals, metacarpals, and phalanges in the hand. The arms are attached to the rest of the body via the pectoral girdle, made up of the clavicle and scapula. The lower limbs, or legs, are composed of the femur, patella, tibia, and fibula, as well as fifty-two tarsals, metatarsals, and phalanges in the feet. The legs are attached to the rest of the body via the pelvic girdle, which consists of the left and right coxal bone.

The point at which a bone is attached to another bone is called a joint. There are three basic types of joints: immovable **fibrous joints**, like those found connecting the bones of the skull; **cartilaginous joints**, which connect bones together by cartilage and allow some limited movement; and highly moveable **synovial joints**. Bones in synovial joints are connected and supported by **ligaments**, or bands of flexible, fibrous connective tissue. Synovial joints allow for a greater range of motion than fibrous or cartilaginous joints, and they are covered by articular cartilage that protects the bones. Synovial joints include hinge joints, such as the joints at the knee and elbow; ball-and-socket joints, which rotate the shoulder and hip; and gliding joints, such as the joints between vertebrae, where bones move against each other. Other types of synovial joints include condyloid, pivot, and saddle.

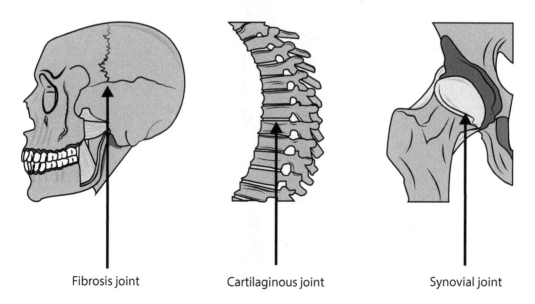

Fibrosis joint   Cartilaginous joint   Synovial joint

Figure 4.6. Types of Joints

SAMPLE QUESTIONS

17) **Which of the following types of bone tissue, also known as compact bone, gives bone its hardness and strength?**

    A.   osseous bone

    B.   cancellous bone

    C.   spongy bone

    D.   cortical bone

    Answers:

    A.   Incorrect. Compact, or cortical, bone is a type of osseous tissue.

    B.   Incorrect. Cancellous bone is softer and more porous than compact, or cortical, bone.

    C.   Incorrect. Spongy bone is another term for cancellous bone.

    D.   Correct. Cortical bone, also known as compact bone, is dense and solid and provides critical strength to the bone.

18) **Which of the following is NOT a primary function of the skeletal system?**

    A.   to protect vital organs and tissue

    B.   to store water for future use

    C.   to produce red and white blood cells

    D.   to provide structure and body shape

    Answers:

    A.   Incorrect. The skeletal system provides protection for the brain, spinal cord, abdominal organs, and other areas of soft tissue.

    B.   Correct. All cells in the body store water, so this is not a primary function unique to the skeletal system.

    C.   Incorrect. Bone marrow plays a vital role in producing blood cells.

    D.   Incorrect. Structure, shape, and support are all primary functions of the skeletal system.

MUSCULAR SYSTEM

The primary function of the muscular system is movement. Muscles contract and relax, resulting in motion. This includes both voluntary motion, such as walking, as well as involuntary motion that keeps the body systems, such as circulation, respiration, and digestion, running. Other functions of the muscular system include overall stability and protection of the spine as well as posture.

The main structural unit of a muscle is the **sarcomere**. Sarcomeres are composed of a series of **muscle fibers**, which are elongated individual cells that stretch from one end of the muscle to the other. Within each fiber are hundreds of **myofibrils**, long strands within the cells that contain alternating layers of thin filaments made of the protein **actin** and thick filaments made of the protein **myosin**. Each of these proteins plays a role in muscle contraction and relaxation.

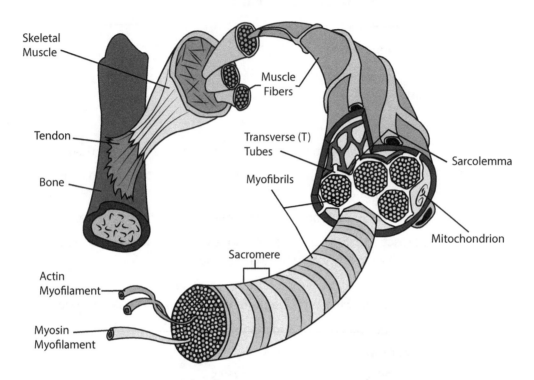

Figure 4.7. Structure of Skeletal Muscle

Muscle contraction is explained by the **sliding filament theory**. When the sarcomere is at rest, the thin filaments containing actin are found at both ends of the muscle, while the thick filaments containing myosin are found at the center. Myosin filaments contain "heads," which can attach and detach from actin filaments. The myosin attaches to actin and pulls the thin filaments to the center of the sarcomere, forcing the thin filaments to slide inward and causing the entire sarcomere to shorten, or contract, creating movement.

The muscular system consists of three types of muscle: cardiac, visceral, and skeletal. **Cardiac** muscle is only found in the heart. It is a **striated** muscle, with alternating segments of thick and thin filaments, that contracts involuntarily, creating the heartbeat and pumping blood through the heart's chambers and out through the rest of the body. **Visceral**, or smooth, muscle tissue is found in many of the body's essential organs, including the stomach and intestines. It slowly contracts and relaxes to move nutrients, blood, and other substances throughout the body. It is known as smooth muscle because, unlike cardiac and skeletal muscle, this tissue is not composed of sarcomeres with alternating thick and thin filaments. Visceral muscle movement is involuntary.

Skeletal muscle is responsible for voluntary movement, and, as the name suggests, is inextricably linked to the skeletal system. There are two basic types of skeletal muscles: **slow-twitch**, or type 1, which move more slowly but hold contractions for long periods of time and do not tire easily, and **fast-twitch**, or type II, muscles, which allow for powerful, quick motion for short periods of time. All skeletal muscles are attached to bones in the skeletal system by **tendons**, fibrous and elastic connective tissue that serves to not only anchor muscles to bones but also facilitates movement at the joints. As muscles contract, the tendon pulls the attached bone, causing the bone to move.

SAMPLE QUESTIONS

19) **Which of the following is considered the primary structural unit of muscle?**

   A.   sarcomere

   B.   fiber

   C.   cell

   D.   myosin

   Answers:

   A.   **Correct.** The sarcomere is the bundle of fibers responsible for muscle contraction.

   B.   Incorrect. Sarcomeres, the main unit of muscle, are composed of layers of fibers.

   C.   Incorrect. The cell is the basic structural unit of life.

   D.   Incorrect. Myosin is a protein comprising the thick filaments within a sarcomere.

20) **Which of the following type of muscle is responsible for voluntary movement in the body?**

   A.   cardiac

   B.   visceral

   C.   smooth

   D.   skeletal

   Answers:

   A.   Incorrect. Cardiac muscle produces involuntary muscle movement in the heart.

   B.   Incorrect. Visceral muscle produces involuntary movement within various organs and tissues.

   C.   Incorrect. Smooth muscle is another term for visceral muscle and produces involuntary movement.

   D.   **Correct.** Skeletal muscles are attached to the skeletal system and are controlled voluntarily.

DIGESTIVE AND EXCRETORY SYSTEMS

The primary goal of the digestive system in any animal is to slow the rate at which food moves through the body in order to maximize the amount of nutrients that can be absorbed. The process of taking in this food is called **ingestion**; the process of breaking food into nutrients is called **digestion**. The nutrients digested from the food are then diffused into the body for use in cellular respiration and energy production in the process of **absorption**. After absorption, excess waste is excreted from the body.

All animals direct food into a central cavity for digestion, as seen in animals as simple as the sponges. Sponges use cilia to move food particles from outside the body into the **gastrovascular cavity** for digestion by individual cells. Cnidarians, platyhelminthes, and echinoderms have an incomplete digestive system, with one central opening acting as the point of ingestion and excretion. Digestion for these animals with one opening is known as **intracellular digestion**. There is no digestive tract, so food items are instead digested in the cytoplasm of the cells that line the cavity.

More complex invertebrates, such as the annelids and arthropods, as well as the vertebrates, have a complete digestive system that ingests food at the mouth and excretes it at the anus. This digestion is known as **extracellular digestion**. Among animals with a complete digestive system, the **digestive tract**—the central tube through which food travels—varies in terms of size, function, organs, and parts. Digestive tracts move food through the body through **peristalsis**, or muscular contractions that produce waves to move food from one point to another. More complex digestive systems also incorporate **accessory organs**, such as a gall bladder and liver, that provide additional functions to aid in the digestion and absorption of nutrients.

As soon as food enters the digestive tract, the process of digestion begins. Digestion can be either **mechanical**—the physical breaking down of food, or **chemical**—the alteration of food into different substances. In humans, both mechanical and chemical digestion begins in the mouth, which is the primary site of ingestion. Teeth and jaws work together to mechanically tear and chew food into smaller pieces. **Secretions** such as mucus and saliva begin the process of chemical digestion, as enzymes secreted by these substances begin to break down carbohydrates.

After chewing, the process of swallowing begins as the muscles of the **pharynx**, or throat, contract to move food from the mouth to the **esophagus**. The esophagus is the primary organ that transports food from the throat all the way to the stomach for storage and further digestion.

In birds, there is one more digestive organ that food must travel to before it makes its way to the stomach. Many birds have a **crop** that is positioned between the esophagus and stomach that is used as temporary food storage before digestion continues in the stomach. For birds that practice maternal care and feed their young, food can be carried and stored in the crop for future regurgitation. Crops also allow birds to store food for later digestion, allowing small amounts of food in the stomach as needed.

Once food enters the stomach, strong stomach muscles begin to mix ingested food and further break it down through muscle contractions and the secretion of digestive juices. These juices, which contain hydrochloric acid and the protein-digesting enzyme **pepsin**, help break down macronutrients.

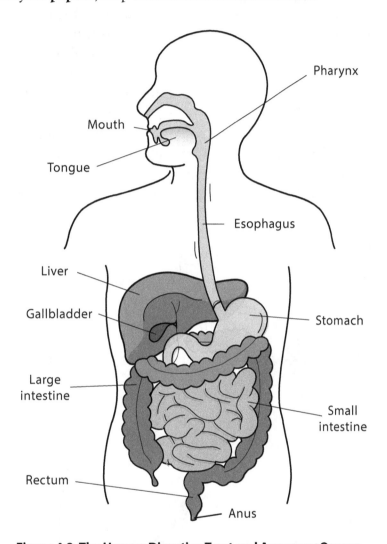

Figure 4.8. The Human Digestive Tract and Accessory Organs

Different groups of animals have a different number of stomach chambers that serve to break down and digest particular types of food. Birds have a two-chambered stomach, consisting of a **proventriculus** that secretes powerful acids that can break down and digest bone, and a **gizzard**, which provides powerful mechanical digestion to break down hard seeds and other tough food. Gizzards are also found among invertebrate species, such as arthropods.

Among the mammals, animals such as cows and sheep have a four-chambered stomach to help them process grasses and other tough vegetation. The first chamber, the **rumen**, contains bacteria and other microbes that ferment the food material that otherwise cannot be digested by the animal. This allows these animals, called the ruminants, to consume and digest the cellulose in this vegetative material.

HELPFUL HINT

Most nutrients can be classified as one of three macronutrients, each of which is essential for different body functions: fats, proteins, and carbohydrates. The digestive system breaks down food into nutrients, which are then transported by the cardiovascular system to all parts of the body.

The mixture of food and digestive juices, called **chyme**, moves from the stomach to the **small intestine** where the majority of digestion and absorption occurs. Chemicals produced by accessory organs, such as the pancreas and gall bladder, complete the chemical digestion of food. The small intestine contains **villi**—structures that contain multiple folds. This increases the surface area within the intestine and allows for maximum absorption of nutrients as food moves through the organ. After food moves through the small intestine, the remaining substances are moved to the **large intestine** for the final stage of digestion and preparation for excretion.

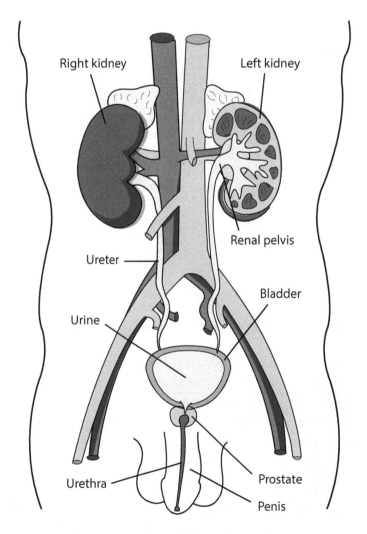

Figure 4.9. The Human Urinary System

The large intestine absorbs remaining water and nutrients, then compacts and stores remaining waste material until excretion. The chyme slowly moves through the **colon**—the longest part of the intestine—allowing for maximum reabsorption of water. Solid waste is then moved to the **rectum**, located at the end of the large intestine. Peristaltic movements will stretch the rectum wall and allow for **defecation**, which is the excretion of solid waste through the anus.

Wastes are excreted by other systems in the body. Excess fluids are processed and excreted by **kidneys** and their associated organs. Also known as the **urinary system**, this set of organs is responsible for filtering waste from blood and removing it from the body. The kidneys act as primary filters, receiving the blood and removing waste and then moving via long, thin **ureters** down to the bladder. **Urine** is stored in this organ until the body is ready to release the waste through the **urethra**. Excess fluid waste in mammals is also excreted through the **skin** via **sweat glands**, and gas waste is exhaled out by the lungs in the respiratory system.

> **HELPFUL HINT**
>
> Sweat is produced by mammals for multiple purposes, in addition to excreting excess fluids. Sweat helps protect internal organs from pathogens, produces odor for communication purposes, and reduces body temperature by cooling the skin through evaporation.

SAMPLE QUESTIONS

21) **Which of the following organs is an accessory organ and NOT a part of the digestive tract?**

   A. pharynx

   B. mouth

   C. small intestine

   D. liver

Answers:

   A. Incorrect. The pharynx is the throat, which connects the mouth to the esophagus.

   B. Incorrect. The mouth is the first part of the digestive tract.

   C. Incorrect. The small intestine is the largest organ in the digestive tract, where most digestion and nutrient absorption takes place.

   D. Correct. The liver is an accessory organ that detoxifies ingested toxins and produces bile for fat digestion.

22) Solid waste is stored and then excreted from the body in which of the following organs?

   A.   chyme

   B.   rectum

   C.   colon

   D.   large intestine

Answers:

   A.   Incorrect. Chyme is the partially digested food that leaves the stomach and enters the intestines.

   B.   **Correct.** The rectum is located at the end of the digestive tract and is the final storage space for wastes before they are defecated through the anus.

   C.   Incorrect. The colon is a large portion of the large intestine where water and nutrient absorption take place.

   D.   Incorrect. The large intestine compacts and stores waste material, but it is stored for final excretion at the rectum.

REPRODUCTIVE SYSTEM

All living things reproduce. Reproduction in animals can be either asexual or sexual, depending on the complexity of the animal. Many invertebrate species reproduce asexually—from one parent—through a variety of means. These offspring are clones of their one parent, inheriting one set of genes. Many invertebrate and vertebrate species reproduce sexually, with two parents each providing one set of genes. These specialized cells, known as **gametes**, from each parent, allow for the recombination of genes to produce genetically distinct offspring.

Gametes are produced in specialized reproductive organs, called **gonads**, in both males and females. Female gametes are called eggs; male gametes are called sperm. Each gamete is **haploid**, meaning that each has half of a full set of chromosomes. The development of these haploid gametes is collectively referred to as **gametogenesis**. During this process, cells go through **meiosis** and eventually specialize into a gamete.

Sperm are produced in the **testes**, a pair of organs found in the male reproductive system. Each testis contains small coiled tubes, which is the site of initial **spermatogenesis**, or sperm development. Cells called spermatogonia can develop into one of two different types of cells: another spermatogonia, or a **spermatocyte**, which will eventually become a sperm. The continuous production of more sperm-producing cells allows males to continue creating millions of sperm every day. As sperm mature, they move on to other organs for further development, storage, and ejaculation. In humans, this pathway first takes sperm to the **epididymis** for final development. This is where sperm finish developing their head, which is the location of the chromosomes, and flagellum, a whip-like tail that enables sperm movement. Sperm then travels through the **vas deferens**, a long tube that carries sperm to the urethra, mixing with nutrients and fluids from various glands along the way. This mixture of sperm and fluids is called **semen** and is ejaculated from the body at this site.

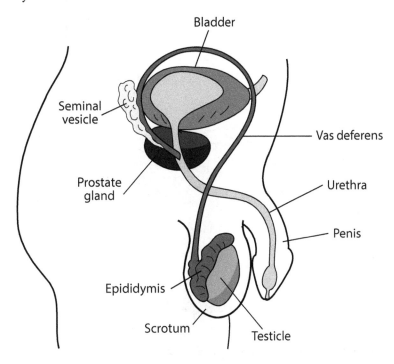

Bladder

Seminal vesicle

Vas deferens

Prostate gland

Urethra

Penis

Epididymis

Scrotum

Testicle

Figure 4.10. Human Male Reproductive System

Oogenesis is the production of female gametes, or eggs. This takes place in the outer layers of the **ovaries**. Here, primary cells called **oocytes** undergo one phase of meiosis, then lay in wait until adolescence, when they continue dividing and maturing in the **follicles** within the ovaries. Females are born with a finite number of follicles that could become eggs; unlike males, new oocytes are not formed. In human females, eggs mature and are released during **ovulation**, one of the stages of the monthly menstrual cycle. The eggs travel into the **fallopian tube** for potential fertilization from a sperm. If the egg is fertilized here by a sperm, then the egg will start to divide as it travels toward the **uterus** for potential implantation on the uterus lining. When human eggs are not fertilized after ovulation, the egg leaves the body and the uterine lining is shed as part of the **menstrual cycle**. Few other animals, including chimpanzees, go through a similar process. Other placental mammals undergo **estrous cycles**, in which the uterine lining is reabsorbed by the body.

Fertilization occurs when male and female gametes come together to form a **zygote** with a full **diploid** chromosome set. **External fertilization** occurs when each parent releases gametes outside of the body. This occurs in aquatic environments among fish and many invertebrates, such as crustaceans and mollusks. During this process, both male and females release their gametes in the same area near the same time in order to increase the chances that eggs will be fertilized. **Internal**

fertilization occurs in some aquatic species, such as sharks, but primarily occurs among terrestrial animals. This transfer of sperm to a female can happen through direct intercourse, with the male sex organ entering the female, or a simple transfer of sperm to the outside of the female **cloaca**.

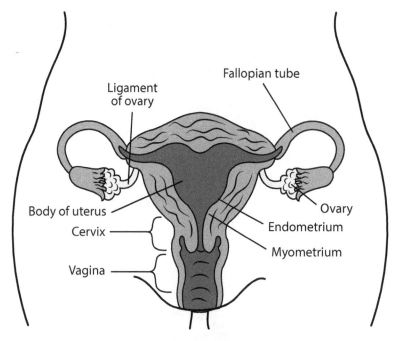

Figure 4.11. Human Female Reproductive System

When fertilization occurs, then **embryogenesis**, or embryo development begins to take place. The first stage of embryogenesis is called **cleavage**. During this stage, the zygote divides repeatedly while the resulting cells get progressively smaller, as the cells do not undergo growth at this stage. This results in a tight, solid ball of cells called a **morula**. Cells located at the center of the morula rearrange and reattach at the wall of the embryo, creating an interior cavity. This zygote formation is known as a **blastula**.

The wall of the blastula will quickly start to move inward, forming a horse-shoe-shaped structure of cells known as the **gastrula**. This is the second stage of embryogenesis known as **gastrulation**. During gastrulation, separate **germ layers** of cells begin to form. These layers will eventually differentiate into different specialized cells, tissues and organs as the embryo grows. Sponges will only develop one germ layer; cnidarians will only develop two. All other animals develop three distinct germ layers that will develop different functions.

The ectoderm is the outermost layer and will eventually develop into the nervous system, the skin, and sensory organs. The **mesoderm**, which is the middle layer, gives rise to the musculoskeletal system, the cardiovascular system and blood, male and female reproductive system organs, and the kidneys. The innermost layer is the **endoderm**, which will develop the respiratory system, the liver and pancreas, multiple glands, and the lining of the digestive tract, lungs and bladder.

After gastrulation and germ layer development, **organogenesis**, or organ development, begins. During this process, the three germ layers begin to develop specialized tissue. The notochord, a temporary structural organ, develops during this stage among the chordates. The notochord provides support to the embryo as well as stimulates the development of the **neural tube**, which serves as the initial development of the brain and spinal cord. In vertebrates, **neural crest** cells will separate from the neural tubes, which further differentiate into specialized organs. After germ layer formation and differentiation, the zygote is now considered an embryo and will continue to grow and develop, establishing the organ system and features specific to its species.

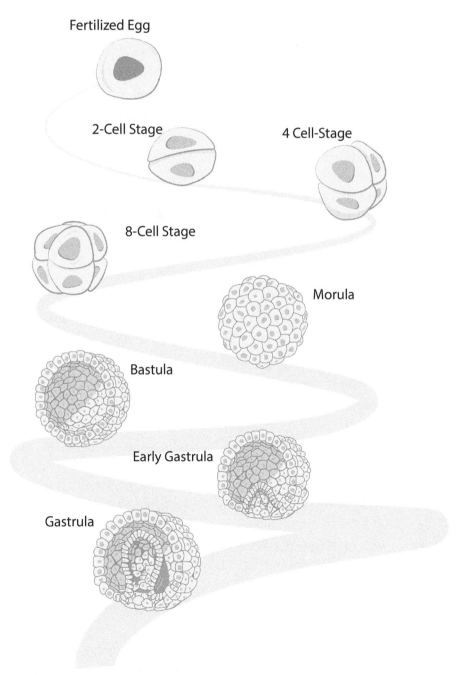

Figure 4.12. Stages of Embryogenesis

These three major stages—fertilization, embryogenesis, and organogenesis—are virtually identical among all members of the animal kingdom. Invertebrates are generally **oviparous**, laying eggs outside the female for further development. Invertebrate embryos hatch out of the eggs as **larva**—an incomplete version of the adult—and must often undergo metamorphosis in order to reach full maturity. Most vertebrate groups, such as fish and amphibians, are also oviparous and supply the developing young with nutrients via an attached yolk sac. Reptiles and birds lay amniotic eggs, which prevent the developing embryo from drying out. A few groups of animals, including some species of invertebrates, fish, and reptiles, are **ovoviviparous**. These embryos develop in eggs inside the mother and are supported by the yolk until they hatch.

> **QUICK REVIEW**
>
> What are some advantages to external fertilization for aquatic animals? What are some advantages to internal fertilization for terrestrial animals?

Most mammals are **viviparous**, with embryos developing inside the mother and directly receiving nutrients, rather than receiving nutrients through a yolk. In placental mammals, embryos implant in the uterus and become attached to the uterus lining via an **umbilical cord**, which transports blood to and from the embryo. The umbilical cord connects the embryo to the placenta, an organ that allows diffusion of nutrients and oxygen to the embryo and diffusion of embryo waste to the mother.

SAMPLE QUESTIONS

23) **Which of the following is the germ layer that eventually produces the organs of the circulatory and reproductive systems?**

   A.   mesoderm

   B.   neuroderm

   C.   ectoderm

   D.   endoderm

Answers:

   A.   Correct. The mesoderm gives rise to the heart, blood vessels, and blood, as well as major organs of the male and female reproductive systems.

   B.   Incorrect. This is not a germ layer; the neural tube arises after the germ layers form and eventually become the brain and spinal cord of vertebrates.

   C.   Incorrect. The ectoderm—the outermost layer—develops into sensory and nervous organs as well as the skin.

   D.   Incorrect. The endoderm—the innermost layer—becomes the respiratory system, digestive tract, and other organs.

24) Which of the following organs is the site of the first stages of spermatogenesis?

A. vas deferens

B. testes

C. epididymis

D. gonad

Answers:

A. Incorrect. The vas deferens is the tube-shaped organ that transports sperm to the urethra.

B. Correct. Initial spermatogenesis occurs in tightly wound tubes found within the testes.

C. Incorrect. The epididymis is a site of final maturation and storage of sperm.

D. Incorrect. Gonad is a broader term that refers to the gamete-producing organs of both males and females.

NERVOUS SYSTEM

The purpose of a nervous system is to monitor the environment and respond to both internal and external changes in the environment. This is done through the nervous system transmitting **nerve impulses**, or electrical signals. **Neurons** are the basic cell units that transport these impulses through the various components of the nervous system. Each neuron consists of a cell body, which contains the nucleus; **dendrites**, which are extensions that receive incoming impulses; and an **axon**, a long extension that transmits signals from the cell body to stimulate another neuron. This site of neuron communication is called a **synapse** and serves to trigger the receiving neuron to receive and transmit the impulse to the next neuron.

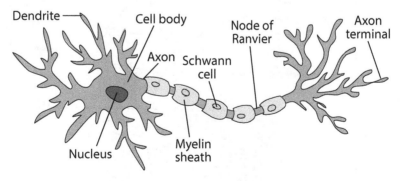

Figure 4.13. Neuron

Nervous systems are often accompanied by various specialized **sensory receptors** or organs among different groups of animals. This includes receptors that can receive information from an outside stimulus and send that information through the nervous system so that the animal can appropriately respond. Types of sensory receptors include vision, hearing, touch, balance, smell, taste, magnetism, and electric fields. The type, number, and complexity of these receptors and organs vary depending on the group of animal.

All animals have specialized nerve cells and some form of nerve-based monitoring and response system. Sponges lack a nervous system, but do exhibit responses to stimuli by contracting upon touch. Cnidarians, echinoderms, and other animals with radial symmetry have **nerve nets**. These are a series of interconnected neurons that sense stimuli and send messages throughout the body without the aid of a brain or central nervous system.

Most animals with bilateral symmetry have a distinct **central nervous system** and **peripheral nervous system**. Among invertebrates, this includes mollusks, arthropods, and annelids. The central nervous system is composed of a **brain** and centralized collections of neurons called **ganglia**. All central nervous systems are accompanied by a peripheral nervous system. Peripheral systems are created by extensions of nerve cells in invertebrates, which collect sensory information and deliver messages back and forth from the brain and centralized ganglia.

Brains are complex, centralized organs that are located adjacent to many sensory organs and are responsible for most bodily functions and animal behavior. Most bilateral invertebrate phyla have brains, with members of the arthropod and cephalopod phyla having especially well-developed brains with multiple lobes serving different functions. In vertebrates, the brain is the most important organ of the nervous system and is highly complex. All vertebrate brains contain the same major regions, although the size and development of these regions vary depending on the needs and environment of the particular animal species.

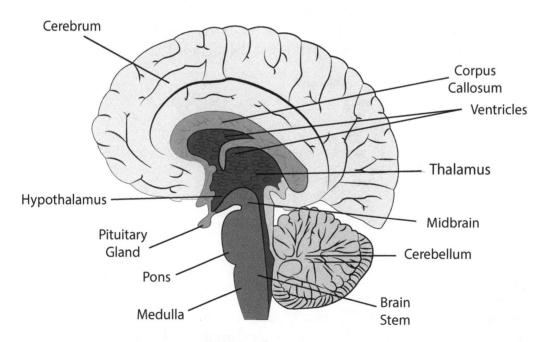

Figure 4.14. The Sections of the Human Brain

Vertebrate brains can be further divided into three main regions: the **forebrain**, **midbrain**, and **hindbrain**. The forebrain includes the **cerebrum**, which serves as the dominant portion of the brain and is responsible for conscious thoughts and movements, higher-order thinking, and memory storage. The **thalamus**, which processes sensory information, and **hypothalamus**, which regulates many involuntary body activities, are also part of the forebrain. The midbrain is responsible for receiving visual and auditory signals and sending sensory information to other parts of the brain. The hindbrain contains the **pons**, which bridges information from different parts of the brain; the **medulla oblongata**, which connects the **spinal cord** and the brain and regulates many automatic body activities; and the **cerebellum**, which helps the body maintain balance and equilibrium. The medulla oblongata, pons, and midbrain are also collectively known as the **brainstem**, controlling the messages as they move from brain to spinal cord and vice versa.

The central nervous system of vertebrate species also includes the spinal cord. The spinal cord is a long mass of nerve cells extending from the brain and serving as the main channel of impulse communication to and from the brain. In humans, information enters and exits the spinal cord through thirty-one spinal **nerves** that send messages to and from the left and right sides of the body. The spinal cord can also serve as the major communication center for **reflexes** in movement, and behavior occurs without transmitting the messages to the brain.

Information in the nervous system is carried from peripheral to central and back again through a series of nerves. Nerves are a collection of neurons that are bundled together in order to communicate information to different areas of the body. Different types of nerves can serve different types of functions. Nerves can be motor, transmitting information to muscles, or sensory, transmitting information from sensory organs to the central nervous system. These motor and sensory nerves are considered the **cranial nerves** and work in conjunction with the spinal nerves to comprise the **somatic nervous system**. The somatic nervous system is a subset of the peripheral nervous system. This is the part of the nervous system that animals have voluntary control over and includes the movement of muscle as well as reflexes.

Nerves can also connect and send messages from the central nervous system to major organs. These connecting and messaging nerves are part of the **autonomic nervous system**, which is the portion of the nervous system that controls unconscious, involuntary body functions such as the movement of cardiac muscle in the heart, the movement of smooth muscle in the digestive and circulatory systems, and the movement and function of glands in the endocrine system.

HELPFUL HINT

The movement of a nerve impulse across the entire neuron—from dendrites to body to axon—is known as the action potential. All action potentials are the same size, strength, and length. These impulses are known as "all or nothing," as the stimulated neuron carries the entire impulse or no impulse at all.

The autonomic system is further subdivided into two divisions. The **sympathetic nervous system** is primarily responsible for the *flight or fight* response of the body to outside stimuli and includes regulating functions such as metabolism and heart rate in response to emergency situations. More day-to-day automatic body functions are regulated by the **parasympathetic nervous system**, also known as the "rest and digest" system. The parasympathetic system offers alternate responses than the sympathetic system, such as slowing the heart beat and breathing rate in order to conserve energy in normal, non-emergency situations.

SAMPLE QUESTIONS

25) **Which of the following parts of the nervous system is responsible for reflexive movement in vertebrates?**

   A.   sensory receptors

   B.   spinal cord

   C.   neuron

   D.   axon

   Answers:

   A.   Incorrect. Sensory receptors receive outside stimuli and transmit the information via neurons to the body.

   B.   Correct. The spinal cord receives and responds to a stimulus without input from the brain.

   C.   Incorrect. Neurons describe all nerve cells that transmit nerve impulses through the body.

   D.   Incorrect. Axons are appendages of neurons that send impulses away from one neuron to another.

26) **Which of the following divisions of the nervous system is responsible for relaxing the body into a normal, non-emergency state?**

   A.   parasympathetic

   B.   sympathetic

   C.   autonomic

   D.   somatic

   Answers:

   A.   Correct. The parasympathetic system is responsible for the body's "rest and digest" state, in which the body relaxes and conserves energy as it performs non-emergency functions.

   B.   Incorrect. The sympathetic nervous system is responsible for the body's "fight or flight" state, enhancing alertness in order to respond to an emergency situation.

C.   Incorrect. The autonomic nervous system refers to all involuntary movement and functions of the body, which includes but is not limited to the parasympathetic responses.

D.   Incorrect. The somatic nervous system refers to all voluntary muscular movement of the body.

ENDOCRINE SYSTEM

The endocrine system is responsible for secreting **hormones**, or chemical messengers, directly into the bloodstream in order to regulate and control the body. These chemical hormones are responsible for affecting the activities of target cells and **target organs** throughout the body. They are produced in response to stimuli that occur both inside and outside the body and are responsible for maintaining many functions of the autonomic nervous system. These functions include metabolism, growth, and responding to external stimuli. Hormones transmit chemical messages by binding to receptor molecules extending from target cells. After binding, the hormones stimulate a change in the cell's activity by altering the production of enzymes, proteins, and other structures.

The earliest, most primitive forms of endocrine systems show up as a subset of the nervous system among different groups of invertebrate phyla. **Neurosecretory cells** are neurons that take signals from the nervous system and stimulate the

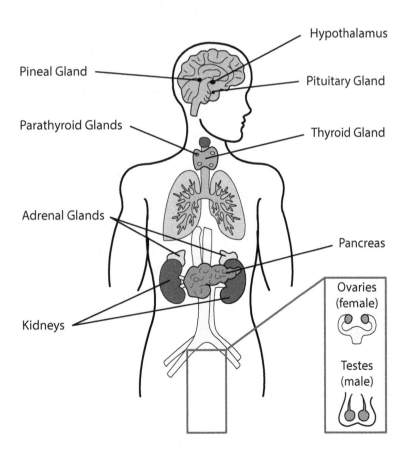

Figure 4.15. Endocrine Glands and Organs

production of **neurohormones** in response. This neurohormone production is found among many groups of invertebrates, including the mollusks, annelids, and arthropods. Insects, the biggest group of arthropods, use secretions from neurosecretory cells to regulate major body functions such as metamorphosis and molting. Other functions of neurohormones in invertebrate groups include sexual development, osmoregulation, and gamete maturity.

More advanced phyla of animals, such as the chordates, have a more complex endocrine system made up of a series of organs and ductless **endocrine glands**. Vertebrate species all have a similar arrangement of endocrine glands and hormones, although the location of these glands varies depending on the class of vertebrate. Major glands and organs of the endocrine system include the pituitary gland, the hypothalamus, the pineal glands, the thyroid and parathyroid glands, the thymus, the adrenal glands, the pancreas, and the gonads.

The hypothalamus region of the brain, located in the forebrain, is responsible for directing the activity of the pituitary gland. As the brain receives and interprets stimuli from sensory nerves throughout the body, the hypothalamus releases **neurosecretions** to the pituitary gland that stimulate it to produce and release hormones. Sensory stimuli include external sources of information collected by the body's sensory cells and organs, as well as internal sources such as levels of essential substances detected in the bloodstream.

In turn, the pituitary gland controls many of the functions performed by other endocrine glands and organs. This is accomplished through the release of **trophic hormones**—hormones that stimulate other glands to produce hormones. The pituitary gland has two major portions: the **posterior pituitary gland**, located in the back, and the **anterior pituitary gland**, located at the front. The posterior gland receives hormones from the hypothalamus and releases them as needed, while the anterior pituitary gland produces its own hormones and releases them as directed by the hypothalamus. Some of these hormones are sent directly to their target cells and organs to directly regulate change. The trophic hormones are sent to other glands and organs to stimulate functions such as sexual maturity and development, blood pressure regulation, production and secretion of gastric juices, and absorption of water and nutrients.

> **HELPFUL HINT**
>
> The hypothalamus serves as the control link between the nervous system and the endocrine system. In addition to regulating hormone production in the pituitary gland, the hypothalamus also secretes its own hormones, interprets sensory information, and maintains homeostasis within the body.

27) **Which of the following transmits chemical messages to target cells by binding to receptor molecules?**

    A.   glands

    B.   hormones

    C.   neurons

    D.   impulses

Answers:

    A.   Incorrect. Ductless glands produce many of the body's hormones but are not the messengers themselves.

    B.   **Correct.** Hormones are chemical messengers that bind to target cells to instigate change in response to a stimulus.

    C.   Incorrect. Neurons are nerve cells that transmit impulses to other neurons over a synapse.

    D.   Incorrect. Impulses are electrical messages that are transmitted by neurons.

28) **Which of the following glands of the endocrine system is responsible for producing a hormone that creates white blood cells?**

    A.   adrenal gland

    B.   pineal gland

    C.   thymus

    D.   thyroid

Answers:

    A.   Incorrect. The adrenal glands produce adrenaline, glucocorticoids, and mineralocorticoids.

    B.   Incorrect. The pineal gland is responsible for producing melatonin to regulate sleep cycles.

    C.   **Correct.** The thymus is a gland that produces white blood cells and other immunological activity.

    D.   Incorrect. The thyroid regulates metabolism and calcium levels in the blood.

IMMUNE SYSTEM

The immune system is primarily responsible for acting as a line of defense against **pathogens** that enter the body. Pathogens are any foreign substances that cause disease or infection. They include microbes such as viruses, bacteria, and fungi. Most microorganisms are harmless; however, there are still many that can cause disease by dissolving, blocking, or destroying cells of the animal in which they enter. Animal bodies have multiple strategies for both keeping pathogens out and destroying pathogens that do enter the body.

To keep pathogens out to begin with, animals rely on organs and characteristics of different organ systems. Animals with an integumentary system, including humans, rely on skin as a physical barrier to pathogens in the external environment. Animals with respiratory and digestive systems rely on hair-like cilia, tears, mucus, and saliva to trap, transport, or kill pathogens that enter the body via the mouth, eyes, or nose.

These physical barriers are all part of the body's **innate immune system**, which uses nonspecific defenses to prevent disease. Nonspecific defenses are thus named because they target any microorganism or injured cell that could pose a pathogenic threat to the body. One primary example of this is the **inflammation** response. When body tissue is injured or damaged, the localized tissue surrounding the damage releases **histamines** that raise the temperature and increase blood flow into the area in order to stimulate more **white blood cells** to enter the tissue for repair.

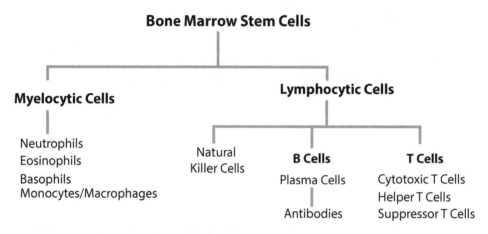

Figure 4.16. Types of White Blood Cells

Fever is another innate response to potential infection. This occurs when pathogens enter and affect the body in multiple locations, triggering the release of enough histamines to raise the overall body temperature in response. Low to moderate fevers are beneficial to the immune system, killing any pathogens that are negatively impacting the body.

Another nonspecific defense in the innate immune system is the production of **phagocytes**, which are specialized white blood cells that can engulf portions of or entire pathogens. The term phagocyte can be literally translated to mean *cell-eating*. These cells are capable of traveling throughout the body and are constantly present in every body tissue.

Not all immune responses are specific: some are *nonspecific responses*. The body also has an **adaptive immune system** that specifically targets pathogens and attacks them based on their specific properties. These properties are expressed by **antigens**—substances that exist on the surface of pathogenic cells that the immune system does not recognize. When antigens are detected on a foreign substance, the immune system is triggered to attack the cell. The series of events that occurs next is collectively referred to as the **immune response**.

Immune responses are performed by two distinct kinds of white blood cells called **lymphocytes**. The first type of lymphocyte that detects antigens are **T-cells**. After a phagocyte ingests a pathogen cell, T-cells are alerted to the presence of antigens that now exist in the phagocyte membrane. T-cells rapidly divide and form different kinds of T-cells that perform different functions. **Helper T-cells** are then activated to seek out and bind to the antigen. These helper T-cells are known as the coordinators of immune response due to their ability to stimulate one of two different kinds of immune responses.

Helper T-cells can stimulate **cytotoxic t-cells** to actively destroy the infected cells in a **cell-mediated response**. This response differs from a nonspecific response because the cytotoxic cells bind to the targeted cell's surface in order to kill it. Helper T-cells can also stimulate the production of **B-cells** in order to trigger an **antibody-mediated response**. Two kinds of B-cells arise in this response: **plasma cells** and **memory cells**. Rather than respond by killing the cell, the plasma produce **antibodies**, proteins that bind to the antigen to neutralize it and stimulate phagocytes to ingest the entire structure. The memory cells then store the information for producing the antibody and are quickly sprung into action if and when the same antigen appears in the body. This resistance to a now-known pathogen is known as **immunity**.

> **QUICK REVIEW**
>
> White blood cells are specialized cells that recognize and react to pathogens. There are many types of white blood cells that perform different functions throughout the body. In humans, white blood cells are produced by the endocrine system and are transported through the cardiovascular and lymphatic systems. In what other ways do many body organ systems work together to prevent disease?

SAMPLE QUESTIONS

29) **Which of the following is NOT considered a nonspecific defense of the innate immune system?**

   A. fever

   B. inflammation

   C. phagocyte production

   D. antibody production

Answers:

A. Incorrect. Fever is a nonspecific response that destroys pathogens by raising the internal body temperature.

B. Incorrect. Inflammation is a nonspecific response that triggers white blood cells to a damaged tissue area to remove cells and repair the tissue.

C. Incorrect. Phagocytes, or cell-eating cells, play an important role in both innate and adaptive immune systems.

D. **Correct.** Antibodies are produced by B-cells as part of an adaptive immunity response.

30) **Which of the following types of cells coordinate both cell-mediated and antibody-mediated responses?**

A. helper T-cells

B. memory cells

C. B-cells

D. phagocytes

Answers:

A. **Correct.** Helper T-cells are lymphocytes that attach to antigens and can trigger either cell-mediated or antibody-mediated responses.

B. Incorrect. Memory cells are a type of B-cell produced during an antibody-mediated response.

C. Incorrect. B-cells are lymphocytes that are produced during an antibody-mediated response.

D. Incorrect. Phagocytes are cells that ingest pathogens as part of either an innate or adaptive immune response.

HOMEOSTASIS

The external environment of animals is always fluctuating in some capacity. Temperatures rise and fall, levels of toxins and pollutants can increase, and food and water availability and intake can change. To counteract the external changes, the body uses several mechanisms to maintain stable internal conditions. This process of self-regulation is called **homeostasis**, and it allows the body to adapt its internal environment in response to the external environment. Animal bodies have three structural components that allow this process to occur: sensory **receptors**—organs to detect changes in the environment; a brain or **center of control** in the nervous system to interpret the change; and **effector** cells that will create an appropriate response or change. These structural components communicate to coordinate cells and organs to maintain homeostasis through **feedback mechanisms**, production of hormones, and alteration of behavior. These processes allow the body to monitor external changes and adapt by altering their body temperature, blood sugar, blood pressure, and other variables.

FEEDBACK MECHANISMS

Maintaining homeostasis requires the communication between multiple organ systems in the body. Feedback mechanisms are the primary forms of communication between these systems. The majority of these mechanisms consist of **negative feedback loops**. During a negative feedback loop, an external change occurs that elicits an internal response. The goal of this internal response is to return the body's state to normal. For example, the outside temperature may rise rapidly, which causes the internal body temperature to also rise. Receptors in the skin detect this change and relay the message to the hypothalamus, the center of control. The hypothalamus sends messages to the effectors, which in this case are sweat glands on the skin. This triggers the body to sweat, which cools the internal temperature to a normal range. The process of maintaining homeostasis of internal body temperature is known as **thermoregulation**.

The regulation of **blood sugar** within the body is also the result of a negative feedback loop. When food is consumed, the blood sugar levels within the body rise as a result of the influx of glucose. The negative feedback loop stimulates the pancreas to produce **insulin**, a hormone that allows sugar to be absorbed by the bloodstream to be processed for energy. Excess glucose is stored by insulin in the liver to keep blood sugar levels from staying too high, then released as needed when blood sugar levels begin to drop. This allows blood sugar levels to stay in a normal, healthy range.

> QUICK REVIEW
>
> When insulin production is insufficient and cannot maintain homeostasis, the increased blood sugar levels may cause type II diabetes to develop. How might other examples of failed homeostasis cause other diseases or dangerous issues to develop in the body?

Another example of a negative feedback loop is the regulation of blood pressure in the body. Various external factors, such as poor diet or stress, can cause blood pressure to rise. This increase is detected by sensory nerves, which communicate the change to the medulla oblongata and elicits **vasodilation** in response. Vasodilation widens the diameter of blood vessels, which increases the rate of blood flow and allows blood pressure to fall into a normal range. The opposite occurs when blood pressure becomes too low. The vessels constrict during **vasoconstriction**, which decreases the flow of blood and allows blood pressure to rise.

The above examples are considered negative feedback loops because the goal is to stop the initial negative response from the body to the external stimulus. Stopping the response to the stimulus causes homeostasis. **Positive feedback loops**, on the other hand, have the opposite effect. Rather than triggering a response to stop or reduce the initial response, a positive feedback loop exacerbates the initial response and does not maintain homeostasis. Positive feedback loops are rare, only occur in extreme circumstances, and only end once the extreme circumstance is over. One example of this is the release of **oxytocin** during childbirth. As the growing fetus pushes on the uterine lining, sensory receptors communicate the change to the brain, which triggers the release of oxytocin. Rather than try to reverse the stretching to bring the body back into homeostasis, oxytocin instead triggers more and more uterine stretching and muscle contractions, which is only stopped after the child is born.

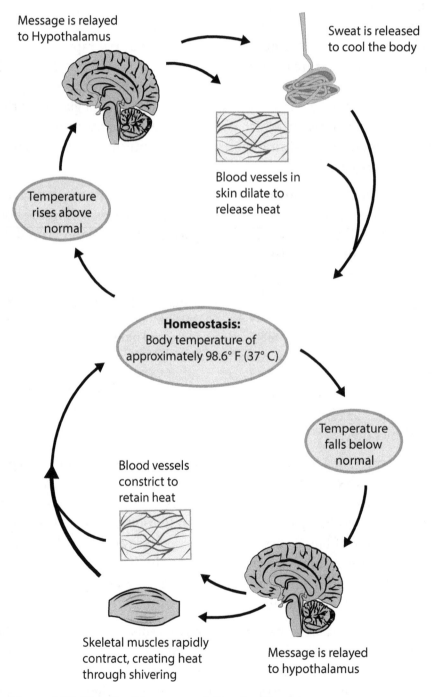

Figure 4.17. Negative Thermoregulation Feedback Loop

SAMPLE QUESTION

31) **Which of the following correctly describes the primary goal of a negative feedback loop?**

    A.   to reverse the change made by an external stimulus

    B.   to release hormones to the affected area of the body

    C.   to enhance the change made by an external stimulus

    D.   to alter behavior of the animal to avoid the external stimulus

Answers:

A.   **Correct.** A negative feedback loop seeks to return the body to homeostasis by stopping, slowing, or reversing the initial response to an external stimulus.

B.   Incorrect. This is one potential result of a negative feedback loop, but it is not always the primary goal.

C.   Incorrect. This is the primary goal of a positive feedback loop, which is rare and only used in extreme circumstances.

D.   Incorrect. This is one potential result of a negative feedback loop, but it is not always the primary goal.

MAINTAINING HOMEOSTASIS

All organ systems in the animal body play a role in maintaining homeostasis. Respiratory systems monitor and control breath intake, the digestive system regulates the body's blood sugar and takes action when it is too high or too low, and the cardiovascular system maintains normal blood pressure. However, of all the systems in the body, it is the nervous system and the endocrine system that exert the greatest amount of control over homeostasis.

The nervous system is responsible for detecting changes in the environment through sensory organs and sensory nerves. It is also responsible for relaying this information to the brain, where it is received, interpreted, and acted upon, depending on the nature of the stimulus.

One of these major brain regions acting upon sensory information is the hypothalamus. The hypothalamus has already been defined as the main control link between the nervous and endocrine systems. When the hypothalamus receives sensory stimuli, it interprets this information and secretes hormones or triggers the pituitary gland to produce hormones that will bring the body back to a normal state. Hormones—the driving force of the endocrine system—are sent to the target cells or organs that are directly affected by the stimulus and will transmit chemical messages across the cell membranes to perform an action that will stop or reduce the effects of the stimulus. Hormones, when secreted in the appropriate amounts at the appropriate times, help the body maintain internal stability.

One example of hormones being used to maintain internal stability is the production of **estrogen** and **progesterone**. Both of these hormones are produced by the ovaries and, in normal body state, are released in balance with one another during various stages of a female's reproductive life. If production of estrogen is reduced, as it is during the menopause process, then the imbalance of the two hormones can cause physical and emotional discomfort for the female. Progesterone is stimulated to increase production to counteract this imbalance, which returns a female's body to homeostasis at the conclusion of menopause.

Hormones are also produced to stimulate other hormones to act when there is an imbalance in the body. The pituitary gland produces **thyroid-stimulating hormones** (TSH) when the hypothalamus detects that thyroid levels are low—particularly in periods of rapid growth. The TSH released stimulates the thyroid gland to produce hormones that will encourage bone growth during this time. The release of TSH is also essential when regulating cell metabolism in the body. When the hypothalamus detects that metabolism has been altered due to aging, dietary changes, or stress, it then triggers the pituitary gland to produce an appropriate amount of **thyroxine** to bring the body back to homeostasis.

The nervous and the endocrine systems, as previously mentioned, are the main drivers of homeostasis in the body. Other structures in different organ systems, however, play a vital function in overall homeostasis. The **kidney** is one of these structures, due to its controlling function of maintaining fluid balance in the body, or **osmoregulation**. Osmoregulation prevents the fluids from becoming too concentrated or too diluted. Fluids controlled during this process include blood, urine, and sweat.

When blood pressure becomes too low, the posterior pituitary gland is stimulated to release **antidiuretic hormone** (ADH). This hormone, also known as vasopressin, controls how permeable the kidney duct cells are to water, thus impacting how much water the organ can conserve or release. During times of low blood pressure, this hormone can increase the amount of water in the body to increase blood pressure and return the body to homeostasis. Kidneys also rid the body of excess fluids, creating urine or sweat as products that are removed from the body via the excretory and integumentary systems.

In addition to altering internal body systems in response to a stimulus, animals are also capable of altering their behavior to maintain homeostasis. Behavior is defined as an animal's response to a stimulus, and can be triggered by hormones to maintain homeostasis in response to environmental changes. One such behavior is an animal's sleeping patterns. Animals that are active during the day but inactive at night are called **diurnal**; animals that are active at night but inactive during the day are known as **nocturnal**. Both of these sleeping pattern behaviors are instigated by the change of sunlight, which stimulates the melatonin hormone to increase or decrease. Melatonin is responsible for maintaining homeostasis of the animal's internal clock, ensuring the animal gets enough rest.

Another example of behavior that maintains homeostasis is **basking**. In order to maintain safe internal body temperatures, the body must respond to external changes through thermoregulation. In endothermic animals such as humans, this is controlled by the hypothalamus, which stimulates the body's internal heating and cooling processes. Ectothermic animals cannot internally alter their body temperature and must alter their behavior as a result. Falling temperatures stimulate animals such as reptiles to alter their location, positioning themselves to bask in the sun to absorb as much solar energy as possible. Rising temperatures can trigger the burrowing behavior, removing the animal from the heat source to cool down the body and return to homeostasis.

SAMPLE QUESTIONS

32) **Which two organ systems exert the most direct control over homeostasis in the body?**

    A.   nervous and urinary

    B.   integumentary and endocrine

    C.   endocrine and nervous

    D.   urinary and integumentary

Answers:

    A.   Incorrect. The nervous system receives stimuli and dictates responses and is considered a controlling organ system in homeostasis. The urinary system is vital in maintaining osmoregulatory homeostasis but is not considered an overall controlling system of homeostasis.

    B.   Incorrect. The integumentary system's organs, such as the skin, play an important role in both thermoregulation and osmoregulation, but they are not considered a controlling system like the endocrine system.

    C.   **Correct.** Most of the body's processes that maintain homeostasis are directly controlled by the endocrine and nervous systems.

    D.   Incorrect. Both the urinary and integumentary systems are essential to homeostasis but do not receive stimuli, direct responses, or trigger hormones like the nervous and endocrine systems.

33) **Which of the following hormones is responsible for the regulation of sleep/wake homeostasis and behavior?**

    A.   progesterone

    B.   ADH

    C.   melatonin

    D.   TSH

Answers:

A.   Incorrect. Progesterone is responsible for maintaining homeostasis in the reproductive system.

B.   Incorrect. ADH is responsible for maintaining homeostasis in osmoregulation.

C.   Correct. Melatonin is produced in response to sunlight to stimulate sleep/wake patterns in animals.

D.   Incorrect. TSH is produced by the hypothalamus to stimulate the thyroid into producing the hormones that dictate growth and metabolism.

5

Plants

PLANT ANATOMY AND PHYSIOLOGY

Organisms in the kingdom Plantae are multicellular, with specialized tissue and distinct organ systems. Undifferentiated cells in the **meristem** give rise to specialized tissues: **dermal** tissue, which covers the plant surface; **vascular** tissue, which transports water and nutrients throughout the plant; and **ground** tissue, which makes up the bulk of a plant's body. These tissues comprise the major organs found in plants, such as flowers, stems, leaves, and roots. These organs are divided into two organ systems: the root system, which contains all the organs found underground, and the shoot system, which contains the vegetative and reproductive systems of plants found above ground. Not all plants have all three tissues and all major organs and systems. Plant groups are classified based on which tissues, organs, and systems that occur throughout the group.

LEAVES AND STEMS

The shoot organ system of a plant is located above ground and is comprised of two major subsections: the reproductive section—which contains flowers and other reproductive organs, and the vegetative section—which contains the **stems** and **leaves** of the plant. The primary function of these organs is to capture energy from the sun and carbon dioxide from the atmosphere, and use this intake to drive **photosynthesis** and **transpiration**.

$$6CO_2 + 6H_2O \rightarrow C_6H_{12}O_6 + 6O_2$$

carbon dioxide   water   organic matter   oxygen

Figure 5.1. The Photosynthesis Reaction

Most leaves can be subdivided into two major parts: the **blade**—the broad part of a leaf, and the **petiole**—the piece that connects the leaf to the stem. The upper and lower sides of the blades play different roles to carry out important plant functions. The cells on the upper side have a high concentration of **chloroplasts**, which contain **chlorophyll** to absorb sunlight and initiate the process of photosynthesis. Plants require light energy, water, and carbon dioxide to undergo this process. The end product of photosynthesis is sugar (glucose). Sugar is moved through the petiole to the stems, which give the plant structure and also transport sugars to the rest of the plant.

The lower side of the leaf blade play an essential role during photosynthesis as well. During photosynthesis, the plant must take in carbon dioxide and expel oxygen as a byproduct. Both of these tasks are regulated by cells located on the underside of the leaf blade. Here, thousands of small pores called **stomata** regulate the exchange of gases that pass in and out of the plant. During the hours of sunlight, two **guard cells** that border the stomata swell and stretch open, allowing carbon dioxide to enter and oxygen to exit. As night falls, these guard cells collapse and close.

Stomata also play a critical role in the regulation of water in the plant. Water is an essential component of photosynthesis and is absorbed into the plant through all body surfaces, although the majority of water is absorbed through the root system. Plants do not directly use all of the water collected through the roots; much of it is lost through the open stomata during **transpiration**. Water loss through transpiration is normal and plays an important function in cooling off the plant. However, too much water loss can dry out the plant. Stomata are responsible for preventing excess water loss by closing when photosynthesis needs are met or conditions are too warm.

SAMPLE QUESTIONS

1) **Which of the following parts of the plant connect the leaf to other plant structures?**

   A. blade

   B. stomata

   C. petiole

   D. stem

   Answers:

   A. Incorrect. The blade is the broad part of the leaf where most photosynthesis and transpiration takes place.

   B. Incorrect. Stomata are openings on the underside of a leaf blade that allow the exchange of gases and regulation of water.

   C. Correct. The petiole is a thin stem that connects the leaf to the main stem.

   D. Incorrect. Stem is a broad term; the specific stem that connects the leaf to the rest of the plant is the petiole.

2) **Which of the following is NOT a required input for plants to perform photosynthesis?**

   A.   water

   B.   oxygen

   C.   sunlight

   D.   carbon dioxide

Answers:

   A.   Incorrect. Water is an essential component for photosynthesis

   B.   Correct. Oxygen, while required for other plant processes, is a byproduct rather than an input for photosynthesis.

   C.   Incorrect. Light energy from the sun is used to drive the photosynthesis process.

   D.   Incorrect. Carbon dioxide is collected through open stomata for use in photosynthesis.

FLOWERS

The vast majority of plants on Earth fall into a category known as **angiosperms**— the flowering plants. The flowers on these plants are their reproductive structures and comprise the remaining organs of the plant's shoot organ system. Flowers can vary widely in terms of size, mode of fertilization, and appearance.

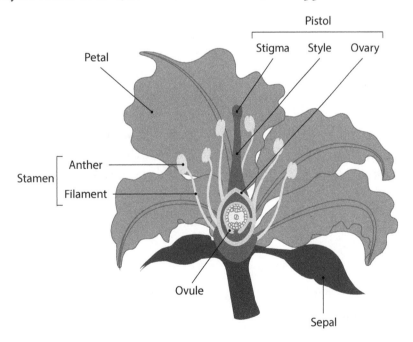

Figure 5.2. Flower with Male and Female Reproductive Structures

Flowers emerge at the tip of modified stems called **pedicels**. At the base of the pedicels rest a set of **sepals**—leaf-life structures that wrap around the flower bud before it opens, then form the base of the flower once it does open. The flower opens when conditions are right for reproduction. Many flowers have a layer of colorful **petals** at the base that function to attract potential animal **pollinators**, which play an essential role in reproduction for many plant species.

The male reproductive structure in a flower is called the **stamen**. Stamens have two main components: a **filament**—a long, stalk-like structure, and an **anther**, which produces sperm cells. These sperm cells are contained in structures called **pollen** grains. When the timing is right, the pollen is released and dispersed to flowers on other plants to potentially fertilize a female flower structure.

The basic female reproductive structure is known as a **pistil** and contains three distinct parts: the **stigma**—the pollen-receiving structure at the tip of the pistil; the **style**—a long slender tube that extends the stigma above the flower; and the **ovary**—the site of fertilization, egg maturation, and development. Each individual style–stigma–ovary structure is known as a **carpel**. Some plants have pistils that contain a single carpel; others have multiple carpels within the same pistil structure.

During plant fertilization, pollen grains are deposited at the stigma of a flower. Here, the pollen grain will germinate and form a **pollen tube** that begins to grow down the style toward the ovary. Fertilization occurs when the sperm within the pollen tube reaches the **ovule**—the egg—within the ovary.

As the wall of the ovary thickens after the ovule is fertilized, the entire ovary will mature into a **fruit**. The fertilized ovule itself is called a **seed**. Angiosperm fruits can contain one fertilized seed, or multiple fertilized seeds within its receptacle. Much like animal development, plant development from the fertilized egg begins with division into a zygote, then an embryo, before developing into a seed. During this development process, the seed is enclosed by an **endosperm** that provides nutrients to the developing plant embryo. The seed is eventually released and dispersed; it can then germinate in the soil and begin developing into an adult plant.

HELPFUL HINT

Many flowers contain both male and female reproductive structures, while a small number of angiosperms have distinct male and female members. Although some species of plants with male and female flower structures self-fertilize, the majority spread their genes by reproducing with other plants of the same species.

SAMPLE QUESTION

3) **Which of the following two structures comprise the stamen?**

   A.   stigma and filament

   B.   pollen and anther

   C.   stigma and style

   D.   anther and filament

Answers:

A.   Incorrect. The stigma is the tip of the carpel—the female reproductive structure; the filament is part of the stamen.

B.   Incorrect. The pollen is produced by the anther, but it is not a structure itself.

C.   Incorrect. The stigma and style are structures that comprise the female carpel.

D.   Correct. The anther contains sperm and produces pollen grains; the filament supports and extends the anther.

ROOTS

The root organ system of a plant exists primarily to absorb water and nutrients from the soil, then transport these materials to the rest of the plant. Water and nutrients are absorbed by a series of **root hairs**, which extend from the outer **epidermis** layer of root into the soil. The materials then pass through the **cortex**, a layer of cells located just under the epidermis in the root system. The cortex provides food and nutrient storage as well as structure for the root. The materials next pass through the **endodermis**—a compact series of cells that regulates the amount of materials that can be conducted into the vascular tissue at the core of the plant. The last root layer through which materials must pass before entering the vascular tissue is the **pericycle**. This tissue layer is responsible for growing branch roots that extend into the soil. Vascular tissue then transports the water and nutrients up to other parts of the plant body in an area known as the **vascular cylinder**.

Plants are stationary organisms, meaning that they cannot move to their required nutrients. Instead, the roots must continually grow in order to reach optimal water and nutrient resources in the soil. The growth of a root can be seen in four distinguishable zones. The root sections depicted in Figure 5.3 are all part of the **zone of maturation** within the root system. The zone of maturation is located at the upper end of the root tip. This is the site of cell differentiation within the root. Here, cells differentiate into specific vascular tissue cells with different functions, making transport possible.

Below the zone of maturation lies the **zone of elongation**. In this zone, newly formed cells lengthen, which stretches the overall length of the root and allows it to move closer to soil resources. The source of these new root cells is located just below in the **meristematic zone**. Also known as the zone of cell division, the meristematic zone is the site of cells rapidly undergoing mitosis to multiply in number.

QUICK REVIEW

Root systems are extensive, continually growing to reach new water supplies. Think about the relationship between the root system and the shoot system, with stomata that continually open up to let in carbon dioxide for photosynthesis. Why do plants need such an extensive root system? What are the advantages of absorbing as much water as possible from the soil?

These cells are undifferentiated and are the original source of the specialized cells that perform different functions in the plant. This layer of growth is protected by a thick layer of cells called the **root cap**.

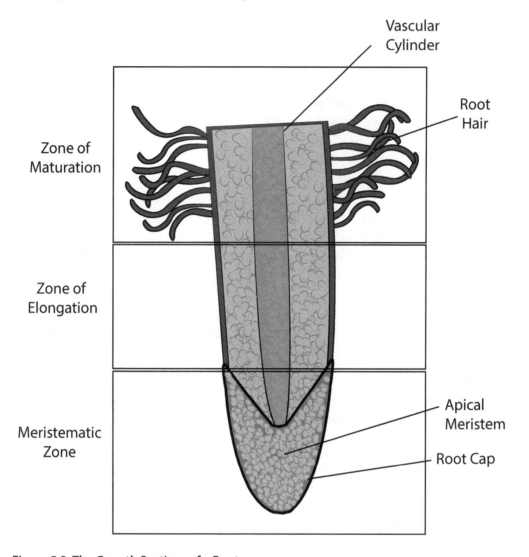

Figure 5.3. The Growth Sections of a Root

SAMPLE QUESTION

4) Which of the following sections of the root regulates the amount of water that enters the vascular tissue?

   A. root cap

   B. endodermis

   C. cortex

   D. meristem

Answers:

A. Incorrect. The root cap's function is to protect the growing tip of the root.

B.   **Correct.** The endodermis is an inner layer of root tissue that controls how much water and how much nutritional material can enter the vascular cylinder for transport.

C.   Incorrect. The cortex serves as a storage area for nutrients as they move from the root hairs into the interior of the root.

D.   Incorrect. The meristem is undifferentiated plant tissue.

DERMAL TISSUE

The tissue found on the surface of plants is known as dermal tissue. Much of the dermal tissue is **epidermis**—the outermost layer of plants. The epidermis consists of a single layer of tightly packed cells that cover and protect the plant from elements in the external environment. One of the primary functions of this tissue layer is to prevent water loss as well as defend against potential predators. Many parts of the epidermis are covered with a waxy **cuticle** coat to accomplish these functions. This waxy layer is impervious to water, which prevents excess water loss, and the thick wax also creates a barrier between the plant and potential bacteria, fungi, or other invaders.

The epidermis contains one of several specialized cells that help control the plant's interactions with the external environment. As previously mentioned, the stomata of leaves are surrounded by two guard cells that open and close the stomata as needed to regulate gas exchange while reducing water loss. Root hairs are another example of specialized epidermal cells located below the ground, increasing the plant's surface area in order to absorb as much water as possible from the roots.

The **periderm** is another example of dermal tissue. Periderm, also known as bark, is composed of several layers of cells and replaces the single-celled epidermis layer as plants age and grow thicker. One of the primary layers of this type of tissue is the **phellem**, or cork cells. Cork is made of nonliving cell tissue, with a waxy material called **suberin** found throughout the cell walls. The cork within the periderm exists to help insulate the plant as well as protect the plant from water loss and predators.

SAMPLE QUESTION

5)   **Which of the following is a difference between the epidermis and the periderm?**

A.   The epidermis is found in the shoot system; the periderm is found in the root system.

B.   The epidermis contains cork, while the periderm contains a cuticle.

C.   The epidermis protects against water loss, while the periderm only protects against predators.

D.   The epidermis has one layer of cells, while the periderm has multiple layers.

Answers:

A.   Incorrect. Both types of tissue are found in the shoot system of the plant.

B.   Incorrect. The periderm contains a layer of phellem—cork tissue—while the epidermis secretes a waxy cuticle layer.

C.   Incorrect. Both types of tissue protect against water loss and potential predators.

D.   Correct. The epidermis is only one cell layer in thickness, while the periderm has multiple cell layers that arise as the plant grows and ages.

VASCULAR TISSUE

Much like the cardiovascular tissue and blood vessels in animals, the **vascular tissue** in plants primarily transports material from one part of a plant to another. There are two major types of vascular tissue: **phloem** and **xylem**. The primary function of the phloem is to transport sugars produced by the leaves downward into the rest of the plant, while the xylem primarily transports water, minerals, and other nutrients absorbed by the root system upwards to other parts of the plant. Both types of tissue consist of long, tubular cells that allow materials to move up or down. These sets of tubes exist side by side in **vascular bundles**, supported by a stem as the tissues transport materials from leaf to root and back again.

Phloem tissue transports food from its production site in the leaves down through the stems and other parts of the plant using a series of **sieve elements**. These cells are long, hollow, living cells that are connected together to form a long tube running throughout the plant. Companion cells pack sugars into the tubular sieve element cells, which are then filled with water. This combined pressure, called **turgor pressure**, moves the sugars down the tube to other parts of the plant called **sugar sinks**. Sugar sinks are areas in the plant with low sugar. Sugar flows from the sources to the sinks through a process called pressure flow; once the sugar arrive, it is actively removed from the phloem into the sink. Excess sugar is stored at the plant roots, tubers, and bulbs. The sugar stays here until it is needed in other areas of the plant; it then moves up the phloem and breaks down into a form the plant cell can use.

Xylem tissue has the more difficult job of moving water, minerals, and other nutrients upward from the roots to the shoots and leaves. This tissue is composed of elongated, tube-like **tracheids** and **vessel elements**. Tracheids are found in many different groups of plants, but vessel elements are only found in angiosperms. Vessel elements are wider than tracheids and allow for faster, more efficient flow of water and nutrients. Both cells are made of nonliving material and conduct water from roots to leaves. This conduction happens in a process called **cohesion-tension.**

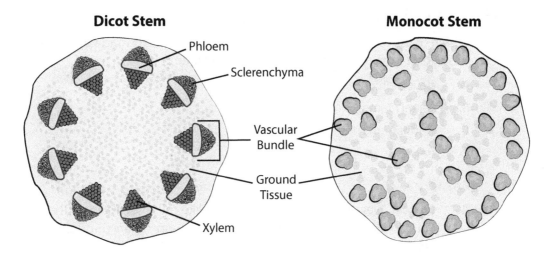

Figure 5.4. Vascular Bundles

Cohesion-tension is a complicated process that begins at the leaves, rather than at the roots. Here, plants experience a great amount of **transpiration** that causes water to exit and evaporate from the plant. This water loss causes a drop in pressure, and this pressure change creates a tension force that pushes water upwards from the roots. As this happens, water molecules in the xylem undergo cohesion, sticking together as they pull up the plant. When the stomata close and the pressure drops, water **adheres** to the cells within the plant. This action, along with transpiration, causes water to draw upwards through both cohesion and adhesion.

When transpiration is low, the plant still requires water. During these occasions, the roots absorb more water from the soil to ensure a continuous water flow. This process occurs due to **root pressure**. Roots generally have higher concentrations of minerals than the surrounding soil. Water moves into the areas of higher concentration areas during **osmosis**, which increases pressure in the roots and forces water up the xylem.

Both xylem and phloem are located within the stems of a plant. As noted earlier, stems grow thicker and tougher as they age and develop meristem tissue, or bark. The cork layer is located in the outer layers of the periderm and is made of rapidly dividing cells just under the outer layer of the plant. The **vascular cambium** is another source of growth within the bark. Here, cells divide in the vascular tissue area and become either xylem or phloem, based on their location. As the plant ages, more and more xylem and phloem tissue will develop in this layer, widening the stem of the plant.

SAMPLE QUESTION

6) Which of the following cells are elongated, tubular cells made out of living tissue that transport sugars throughout the plant?

 A. sieve elements

 B. vessel elements

 C. companion cells

 D. tracheids

Answers:

 A. **Correct.** Sieve elements are living tube-like cells that make up the bulk of the phloem and serve as a vessel to transport sugars throughout the plant.

 B. Incorrect. Vessel elements are nonliving tubular cells that are found in the xylem of angiosperms.

 C. Incorrect. Companion cells are living cells found in the phloem, but assist the movement rather than facilitating the movement of sugars themselves.

 D. Incorrect. Tracheids are nonliving cells found in the xylem that play a major role in transporting water from the roots through the rest of the plant.

GROUND TISSUE

The majority of tissue in a plant body is classified as ground tissue. Ground tissue is composed of three primary types of cells, each of which serves a different function and can work together in different combinations to perform a wide variety of functions within the plant. These three types of cells are the parenchyma cells, the sclerenchyma cells, and the collenchyma cells.

Parenchyma cells are the most abundant and versatile cells of the ground tissue. They are thin-walled, undifferentiated cells that can divide and regenerate quickly and adapt to many different situations. These cells are found all throughout the plant, including in leaves, stems, bark, and roots. They play a critical role in plant metabolism, photosynthesis, structure, and growth.

Some work in conjunction with cells in the vascular tissue to help transport food and water materials throughout the plant, offering support and structure as they surround the vascular bundles. Others compose the fleshy material surrounding the mature ovary in a plant's fruit. Since they are alive at maturity and undifferentiated, parenchyma cells can repair damage to plants and regenerate new plant tissue. Parenchyma cells are also found in the interior of leaf tissue, making up the **mesophyll** layer. The mesophyll tissue is sandwiched between the upper and lower epidermal layers of the leaf and is the major site of photosynthesis in the leaves. The **cortex**—the outermost layer of a plant's root system—is also composed of parenchyma cells. As previously discussed, this cortex plays an important role in nutrient storage in the root system, holding complex carbohydrates for later use. **Pith** tissue within the root is also composed of parenchyma cells, providing additional storage space for both carbohydrates and water in the interior of roots and stems.

Parenchyma cells can be differentiated into the other types of ground tissue: sclerenchyma cells and collenchyma cells. **Sclerenchyma cells**, unlike parenchyma cells, are nonliving at their mature state. They are very rigid, with a combination of cellulose and **lignin** found throughout their thick secondary cell walls. These agents act to harden and reinforce these cells, enabling them to withstand large amounts of weight and pressure. These cells are integral to plant shape and structure in the oldest parts of the plant. Sclerenchyma cells are generally produced in the vascular cambium, allowing the oldest stems of the plant to thicken and provide support at the base as the plant grows wider and taller. There are two types of sclerenchyma cells: **fibers**, elongated and interlocking cells, and **sclereids**, more versatile cells that can also specialize in forming the hard coat and/or shells surrounding seeds.

Collenchyma cells also play an important role in plant growth and structure. These cells support younger plants as they reinforce new lateral and vertical growth. Unlike sclerenchyma cells, these cells are living at maturity and do not have a hardening agent, making them flexible. Their cell walls, reinforced with cellulose and **pectin**, can thicken as needed to provide support to new plant growth and to help the plant withstand unstable external elements, such as high winds or rain. They are often found at the sites of rapid growth, such as new leaves or shoots arising from the ground.

SAMPLE QUESTIONS

7) Which of the following two substances act as hardening and thickening agents in sclerenchyma cell walls?

   A. pectin and fibers

   B. pectin and lignin

   C. cellulose and lignin

   D. cellulose and pectin

   Answers:

   A. Incorrect. Pectin lends flexible support and structure to collenchyma cells; fibers are a type of sclerenchyma cell.

   B. Incorrect. Pectin is found in collenchyma cells; lignin is one of the two hardening and thickening agents in sclerenchyma cells.

   C. Correct. Cellulose and lignin are the two agents working to harden and thicken sclerenchyma cells, making up the bulk of their secondary cell walls.

   D. Incorrect. While cellulose is a hardening agent in sclerenchyma cells, the combination of cellulose and pectin strengthens the collenchyma cells while giving them flexibility.

8) **Which of the following is NOT a function of parenchyma cells?**

A. to repair plant tissue damage

B. to provide storage in the root system

C. to support vascular bundles within the stems

D. to harden and strengthen the base of a plant

Answers:

A. Incorrect. Parenchyma cells can quickly divide and differentiate to repair tissue damage and regenerate growth.

B. Incorrect. Parenchyma cells can differentiate and store food and water in both cortex and pith tissue in the root system.

C. Incorrect. Parenchyma cells are found within vascular tissue and lend structure and support inside the stem.

D. **Correct.** This describes the primary function of the sclerenchyma cells.

MERISTEMS

Parenchyma, sclerenchyma, and collenchyma cells and tissues all arise from the same type of cell: **meristematic cells**. Meristems are a tissue of undifferentiated cells that give rise to the wide variety of differentiated cells, tissues, and organs in plants. These cells are located at the places where new plant growth can occur: at the ends of roots and shoots throughout the plant. Plant growth is distinct from animal growth because the meristem tissue allows the plant to continually grow throughout its life. As meristematic cells divide, they differentiate into the type of cells and tissues required by the plant and add to the overall length and width of the plant.

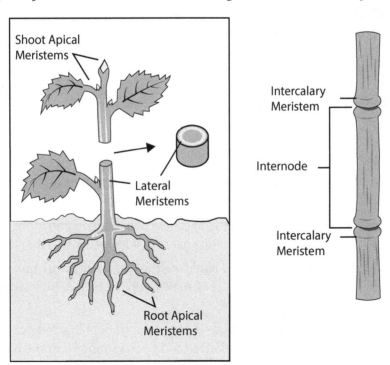

Figure 5.5. The Shoot, Root, and Intercalary Meristems

There are two different types of meristem tissue: **apical**, which allows for primary growth and lengthening, and **lateral**, which allows for secondary growth and thickening. Apical meristems are found in the roots of the plants as well as the shoots. The root apical meristem is located just under the root cap at the tip of each root in the meristematic zone. The shoot apical meristem is found at the tip of individual stems, which allows for continued growth of the stem. This meristem tissue is also found near the juncture between the leaf and stem, an area called the **node**. At this location, new flower structures such as flowers, leaves, or new stems can rise from a **bud**—a compact bundle of undifferentiated meristem. **Intercalary** meristem is also located at the nodes of some kinds of plants, such as the grasses. Rather than growing primary tissue and lengthening at the tip, these plants grow from each individual node.

Lateral meristem is found among the woody plants, which include **perennial** trees and shrubs that continue to grow and reproduce year after year. The vascular cambium, located between the xylem and phloem, contains meristematic tissue that gives rise to secondary xylem and secondary phloem (wood). The **cork cambium**, located within this secondary wood tissue, is another type of meristematic tissue that produces phellem cells, a previously discussed type of dermal tissue that thickens, insulates, and protects the plant.

HELPFUL HINT

Growth in plant length is called **primary growth**. This is the growth that occurs at the roots and shoots of the plant and allows the plant to grow taller and to extend its roots further into the soil. Growth in plant width is called **secondary growth**. Not all plants experience secondary growth. Secondary growth is the widening that occurs in plants that eventually develop wood and bark as they age.

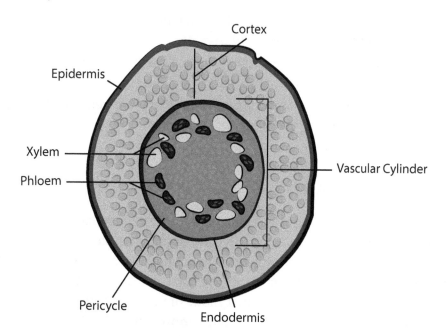

Figure 5.6. Cambium in a Woody Stem

SAMPLE QUESTIONS

9) **Which of the following types of meristem allows plants to increase the length of their roots?**

   A. apical meristem

   B. lateral meristem

   C. intercalary meristem

   D. secondary meristem

   Answers:

   A. **Correct.** Apical meristem is responsible for primary growth at the roots and shoots.

   B. Incorrect. Lateral meristem, located in the vascular cambium and cork cambium, provides secondary growth for woody plants.

   C. Incorrect. Intercalary meristem is a type of apical meristem which gives rise to primary growth at the nodes in shoots.

   D. Incorrect. Secondary meristem is another term for lateral meristem.

10) **Which of the following is NOT true about lateral meristem?**

   A. Lateral meristem produces thickening of the plant base.

   B. Lateral meristem is only found in woody plants.

   C. Lateral meristem is found in buds and gives rise to new structures.

   D. Lateral meristem can differentiate into phellem.

   Answers:

   A. Incorrect. Lateral meristem allows the plant to widen, or grow laterally.

   B. Incorrect. Herbaceous plants do not undergo secondary growth through a lateral meristem.

   C. **Correct.** This is a description of apical meristem found at the nodes of the shoot system.

   D. Incorrect. Phellem is one type of cell that is differentiated from lateral meristem.

CATEGORIZING PLANTS

Plants are classified into several distinct taxonomic groups based on a series of shared characteristics. The first major division of plants is based on whether they are vascular or **nonvascular**, meaning they do not have a transport system consisting of a xylem or phloem. Vascular plants are further divided into a nonflowering group or a flowering group based on their mode of reproduction. Flowering plants are once more divided into two distinct groups: **monocot** or **dicot**. This last division compares various structures of the plants, including seed and leaf structure.

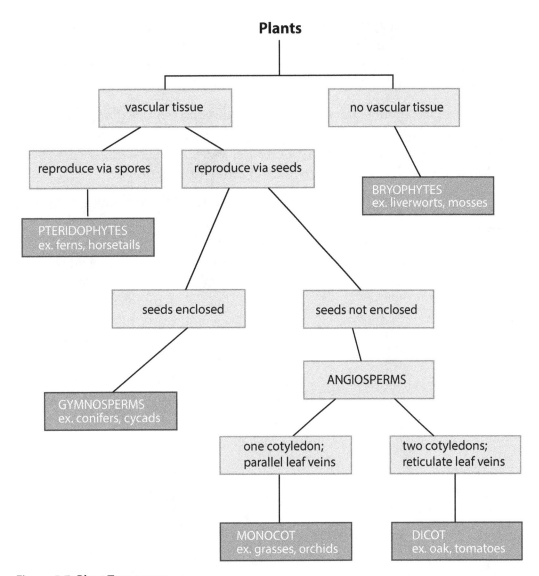

Figure 5.7. Plant Taxonomy

VASCULAR VERSUS NONVASCULAR PLANTS

The earliest-appearing plants in Earth's history were simple organisms that lacked a vascular system to transport water and nutrients throughout the plant body. They tended to be unicellular or have a simple, flat, multicellular body that lacked specialized cells or tissues. These plants were very similar to **algae**, a simple group of plant and plant-like organisms. These organisms primarily live in water and lack many of the structures that are familiar among other plants, such as leaves, stems, flowers, or seeds. They do, however, undergo photosynthesis and some forms of sexual reproduction.

Most non-vascular plant species fall into the **bryophyte** classification. Bryophytes are land plants and include **mosses**, liverworts, and hornworts. These organisms are multicellular and more complex than algae but still lack many of the specialized tissues and organs found in higher orders of plants. Bryophytes have no distinct root and shoot system, but many do have appendages called **rhizoids** that absorb water from the surrounding soil. They lack a vascular system but are small enough in size to transport water and nutrients by passing the materials from cell to cell. Mosses and their relatives reproduce by releasing **spores**.

The rest of the higher-order plants can be classified as vascular plants due to the appearance of specialized xylem and phloem tissue. This evolutionary development allowed these land plants to grow taller, wider, and heavier, as well as begin to develop more specialized tissue to take on different functions.

HELPFUL HINT

Plants with vascular tissue can transport food, water, and nutrients much more quickly and efficiently than plants without vascular tissue. What are the advantages of such a transport system? How does this lend itself to plant growth?

The simplest of these plants are the **ferns** and **fern allies**, a group classified together as the **pteridophytes**. The presence of vascular tissue allows these plants to grow much larger than the bryophytes. Pteridophytes also have more specialized plant structures such as stems, leaves, and roots that provide many advantages, including the ability to anchor into the soil and obtain more sunlight energy for photosynthesis. Like the mosses, the ferns and fern allies also reproduce sexually by releasing spores.

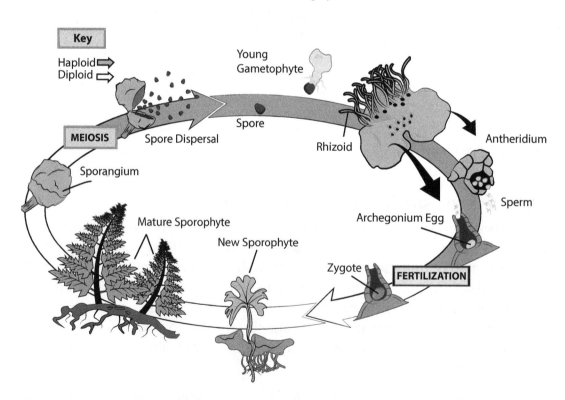

Figure 5.8. Reproduction in Ferns

SAMPLE QUESTIONS

11) **Which of the following characteristics do bryophytes and pteridophytes have in common?**

   A.   They reproduce with spores.

   B.   They lack a vascular system.

   C.   They have true root systems.

   D.   They have phloem cells.

   Answers:

   A.   **Correct.** Neither group of plants produces flowers or seeds; instead, they reproduce sexually by releasing spores.

   B.   Incorrect. Pteridophytes have a vascular system, while bryophytes do not.

   C.   Incorrect. Some bryophytes have root-like rhizoids, but only pteridophytes have a true root system.

   D.   Incorrect. Only pteridophytes have phloem cells, an essential part of vascular tissue.

12) **Which of the following is NOT true about rhizoids?**

   A.   They are found on nonvascular plants.

   B.   They anchor mosses to the ground.

   C.   They absorb water from the soil.

   D.   They are roots.

   Answers:

   A.   Incorrect. Rhizoids are found on bryophytes, a nonvascular plant.

   B.   Incorrect. This is a primary function of rhizoids.

   C.   Incorrect. Rhizoids are important in water absorption for bryophytes.

   D.   **Correct.** Rhizoids are root-like, but are not considered true roots.

FLOWERING VERSUS NONFLOWERING PLANTS

The modes and structures of sexual reproduction are the distinguishing characteristics of the next two taxonomic plant divisions. Vascular plants are considered either **seedless plants** or **seed plants**. The pteridophytes—the ferns and their relatives—comprise the seedless plants group, as they reproduce via spore cells. These spores are released into the air and eventually settle into the water, developing gametes that are then released for fertilization. This fertilized spore matures into an adult plant. In contrast, the **seed plants** reproduce by fertilizing eggs directly on the plant, then releasing the resulting seed. The seed consists of the embryo, its nutritional source, and its hard coat; it is then dispersed by the parent for germination and maturation.

The seed plants are broken down into two major categories: the **gymnosperms**—the nonflowering plants, and the **angiosperms**—the flowering plants. The gymnosperms are an ancient, successful group of plants and include the conifers, cycads, gnetophytes, and ginkgos. This group of plants is distinguished by the fact that its seeds are released without the protective covering of a mature ovary (fruit); in fact, the very name "gymnosperm" is Greek for "naked seed." There is also no flower structure comprising the reproductive organs. Instead, many groups of gymnosperms have reproductive structures that are enclosed in distinct male and female **cones**. This is seen in such gymnosperms as the pines and other conifers. Gymnosperms are generally woody, perennial plants. Some species have thin, scaly leaves, as are evident in the pine trees, while other species have broader leaves.

At one point in ecological history, the gymnosperms were the dominant plant species on Earth. However, they have been eclipsed by the large, diverse, successful group of flowering angiosperms. Angiosperms make up the majority of the plant species on Earth. They include plants as diverse as grasses, cacti, and many kinds of trees. Angiosperms are distinguished from gymnosperms by their flowers and their fruits. These reproductive structures have held many evolutionary advantages for this group of plants, attracting animals to the plant to help increase plant fertilization and seed dispersal. Angiosperms can be woody or **herbaceous**, meaning they do not experience secondary growth. Many of these herbaceous angiosperms are annual, going through all of their life cycles over the span of one year, while many of the woody plants are perennial—growing for many years.

HELPFUL HINT

Cones are tough, scaly structures that are made of modified leaf or branch structures. Sexual reproduction does happen on the tree; however, unlike the angiosperms, gymnosperm pollen must be distributed by wind to reach gymnosperm eggs. The eggs are not fertilized in an ovary, but within the cone structure instead. The seeds develop within the female cone before being dropped from the tree for dispersal and germination.

SAMPLE QUESTIONS

13) **Which of the following plants are seed plants that lack a floral reproductive structure?**

   A.   angiosperms

   B.   gymnosperms

   C.   pteridophytes

   D.   bryophytes

Answers:

   A.   Incorrect. Angiosperms are the flowering seed plants.

   B.   Correct. Gymnosperms are plants that have seeds that are produced by cones, rather than flowers.

C. Incorrect. Pteridophytes are seedless, vascular plants.

D. Incorrect. Bryophytes reproduce via spores, not seeds.

14) **Which of the following is NOT a feature that distinguishes angiosperms from gymnosperms?**

A. Angiosperms produce pollen cells.

B. Angiosperms have flowers.

C. Angiosperms develop fruit.

D. Angiosperms can be herbaceous.

Answers:

A. **Correct.** The male reproductive structures of both groups produce pollen.

B. Incorrect. Angiosperms have flower structures that the gymnosperms lack.

C. Incorrect. Angiosperms have ovaries that mature around developing seed, while gymnosperms do not.

D. Incorrect. Gymnosperms are woody, while angiosperms can be woody or herbaceous.

MONOCOT VERSUS DICOT

The angiosperms can be further subdivided into two major classes based on the number of **cotyledons** the plant has in its embryonic seed state. Also known as a *seed leaf*, cotyledon is a structure found within the seed that stores nourishment for the developing embryo. This structure is one of the first parts of the plant that emerges from the seed after germination, becoming the first leaves of the seedling. Plants that contain one cotyledon are called **monocots**; plants that have two cotyledons are called **dicots**.

Monocots are generally small, herbaceous plants that experience only primary growth. A notable exception to this general rule are the palms, which can reach large sizes without true secondary growth. Dicots can vary in size and can experience secondary growth, allowing them to become tall, woody plants. Monocots make up about a quarter of modern flowering plants, while dicots make up the vast majority.

Monocots and dicots have multiple distinguishing structural characteristics. These two groups of plants vary in terms of leaf, root, stem, and flower structure. Monocot leaves are generally narrow and have **parallel leaf veins** that run side by side throughout the leaf. Dicot leaves are broader and have **reticulate leaf veins**—veins that are arranged in a branching, net-like pattern. Leaf veins serve as an extension of vascular tissue that deliver materials throughout the leaf, as well as give the leaf support and structure.

Monocot stems are also structured differently than dicot stems. The vascular bundles of monocots are scattered all throughout the various stem structures, while dicot vascular bundles are formed in a ring-like pattern. The stems of monocots lack collenchyma cells and vascular cambium, which limits their ability to experience lateral growth at the base. This distinguishes them from the dicots, which have many species that grow laterally and develop wood and bark.

The root system of monocots is **adventitious**, meaning that the roots are fibrous and descend from a stem. These fibrous roots occupy a shallow layer of soil, branching out widely from the plant but not anchoring deep into the soil. In contrast, dicots have a taproot system that allows the plant to anchor more deeply into the soil. This taproot develops from the **radicle**, which is the root structure that first emerges from the embryo as it emerges from the seed. The taproot serves as the prominent root of this organ system, with many smaller roots branching out from the taproot at the center.

A major difference between the monocots and dicots also occurs on a microscopic level when the two groups' **pollen structures** are compared. All angiosperm pollen structures are characterized by openings in the pollen wall that allow the grain to grow or shrink, depending on the amount of moisture in the grain. These openings are called **furrows** if they are elongated, or **pores** if they are circular. The pollen grains of monocots contain one single furrow or pore, while the dicot pollen grains contain three.

The flower parts and structure also differ between these two groups of plants. Monocot flowers are arranged in multiples of three. For example, a monocot may have three or six petals, stamens, or pistils. Dicot flowers, however, are arranged in multiples of four or five.

SAMPLE QUESTION

15) **Which of the following types of structures is found in dicots but not in monocots?**

   A.   furrows

   B.   cotyledon

   C.   xylem

   D.   vascular cambium

Answers:

   A.   Incorrect. Monocots have one furrow or pore on the wall of their pollen grains, while dicots have three such openings.

   B.   Incorrect. Monocots have one cotyledon in their embryonic state, while dicots have two.

   C.   Incorrect. Both monocots and dicots are vascular, meaning that they both have xylem and phloem tissue.

   D.   Correct. Dicots can have vascular cambium in their stems, giving rise to secondary growth, while monocots do not have this tissue.

PLANT REPRODUCTION

Plant reproduction has much in common with animal reproduction. Like animals, plants can reproduce asexually and sexually. Asexual reproduction is commonly achieved through fragmentation—when a piece of a plant that has fragmented from the parent plant germinates in a different area and grows into a new, genetically identical plant. However, just like in animals, sexual reproduction in plants is more successful and leads to more genetically diverse and widely dispersed plants.

Sexual reproduction in plants involves the same general process that occurs among animals: male and female gametes, called egg and sperm, are formed through meiosis. The egg and sperm meet during fertilization, resulting in a diploid cell that begins to divide and become an embryo, and eventually, a mature organism. In plants, however, the gamete formation stage is a bit more complex and involves the **alternation of generations**—alternating haploid and diploid life stages. Plant reproduction is also distinguished from animal reproduction by the **pollination** method of fertilization and **seed dispersal**, a process that moves seeds far from their parents. These processes and mechanisms among plants have led to reproductive success among this kingdom of organisms.

ALTERNATION OF GENERATIONS

The alternation of generations—**metagenesis**—is a life cycle unique to plants. In this process, the plant alternates between two genetically distinct generations: a diploid form, which then gives rise to a haploid form. Members of the diploid generation of plants are called **sporophytes**. Since these organisms are diploid—containing genetic material from two parents—they are able to undergo meiosis and produce two haploid cells. In animals, the haploid cells that result from meiosis develop into male and female gametes. In plants, these haploid cells, or **spores**, undergo mitosis and develop into a new plant. This haploid offspring is known as a **gametophyte**. The gametophyte generation produces both male and female gametes, or egg and sperm, by undergoing mitosis. When the gametes and their structures have fully developed, these gametes are released for fertilization. Upon fertilization, the male and female gametes fuse and develop into an embryo, which gives rise to a new diploid sporophyte generation.

The physical differences between these two generations of plants can be stark. Among mosses and other primitive bryophytes, the gametophyte generation is the dominant generation. These organisms spend most of their reproductive lives in this

---

HELPFUL HINT

The structures that produce the spores are known as **sporangia**. The sporangia of most plants form one of two kinds of spores through meiosis: **microspores**, which are small in size and produce a male gametophyte that creates sperm, and **megaspores**, which are larger than microspores and develop a female gametophyte that creates eggs. In angiosperms, microspores are produced within the pollen cells, while megaspores are developed in the ovary.

haploid state, which is much larger than the sporophyte generation. The opposite is true among more advanced plants. In pteridophytes, gymnosperms, and angiosperms, the sporophyte is the large, visible plant—for example, an oak tree. The gametophyte generation of an oak tree is microscopic, consisting of only a few cells.

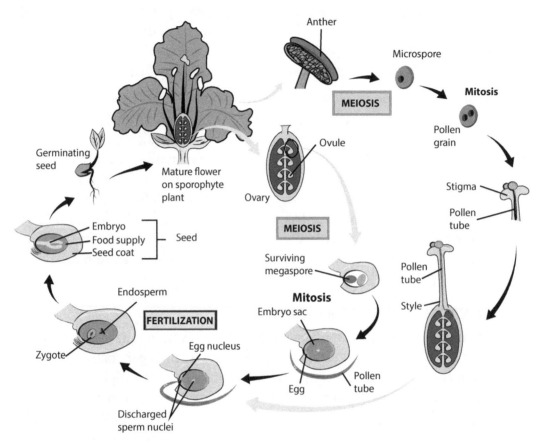

Figure 5.9. Reproduction in Angiosperms

SAMPLE QUESTIONS

16) **The gametophyte is the dominant plant generation in which of the following group of plants?**

A. dicots

B. bryophytes

C. angiosperms

D. pteridophytes

Answers:

A. Incorrect. Dicots, a type of angiosperm, have a dominant sporophyte generation.

B. **Correct.** The gametophyte of mosses and their relatives are much larger and longer lived than the sporophyte generation.

C. Incorrect. The gametophytes of angiosperms are microscopic.

D.   Incorrect. Ferns and fern allies have a dominant sporophyte generation.

17) **Which of the following is a correct description of the alteration of generations?**

A.   Sporophytes produce gametes, which then become gametophytes upon fertilization.

B.   Diploid gametophytes undergo meiosis to create a haploid sporophyte.

C.   A diploid sporophyte gives rise to a haploid gametophyte.

D.   Gametes undergo mitosis to create spores.

Answers:

A.   Incorrect. Gametophytes produce gametes, which eventually develop into sporophytes upon fertilization.

B.   Incorrect. Gametophytes are haploid and undergo mitosis to create gametes, which are then released for fertilization.

C.   **Correct.** Plant life cycles alternate between a diploid sporophyte generation and a haploid gametophyte generation.

D.   Incorrect. Gametophytes undergo mitosis to create gametes; sporophytes undergo meiosis to create spores.

POLLINATION AND SEED DISPERSAL

As stationary organisms, plants cannot rely on self-movement to conceive new plants or to widely disperse their offspring. Both of these components are essential to a successful spreading of genes, which helps ensure genetic diversity among the plant species. Gymnosperms and angiosperms have evolved mechanisms to help them reach both goals. **Pollination** occurs among the seed plants when the pollen grains of a male plant structure are transported and inserted into a female reproductive structure. Most plants rely on either wind or animals to move these pollen grains to the appropriate female structure. Successful **seed dispersal** also depends on wind and animals. Different species of seed plants use a variety of mechanisms to make the seeds more windborne or attractive to animals in order to disperse the seeds as widely from the parent as possible.

Wind pollination is the primary mechanism of pollination among the gymnosperms and is also a common occurrence among angiosperms. Pollen grains can have several different mechanisms to facilitate this. All of these pollen grains are very small and light. Gymnosperm pollen grains are released with a series of **air sacs**, making them even lighter in weight. The pollen grains of some gymnosperms, such as pines, are winged, enabling them to be picked up and moved by the wind. Vast quantities of pollen must be released in order for this pollination method to be successful. Similarly, some groups of water plants depend on water for pollination. Like the wind-pollinated species, these plants have pollen that is lightweight and buoyant in order to facilitate movement across the top of the water.

Wind pollination is common among many groups of angiosperms, including plants with small, inconspicuous flowers such as the grasses and oak trees. However, animal pollination is a much more common pollination mechanism among the angiosperms. Animal pollination is a more deliberate and successful reproductive approach than wind or water pollination. Flowers primarily attract animals to the flower using **nectar**, a sugary substance that is an essential food source for many insects and other animals. Other attractants include flower fragrance and bright petal colors. When the animal comes to the flower, pollen grains attach to the animal. As the animal moves to another plant or flower, this pollen is transferred to the new reproductive structure for potential fertilization and conception of a new plant.

Some plant seeds are not dispersed widely from the parent plant. Instead these plant seeds depend on gravity to drop the seed into the ground below for fertilization or ejection by the plant itself in a process called **explosive dehiscence**. Other plants depend on a secondary mechanism to disperse their seeds. Just like in pollination, these mechanisms depend on wind, water, and animals. This process is called **allochory**.

Seeds dispersed by allochory have a variety of characteristics and enable these different dispersal mechanisms. Some wind-dispersed seeds, like the seeds of maple trees, are winged; others, like dandelion seeds, are lightweight and feathery. Water-dispersed seeds are often covered with a waterproof coating and are buoyant, allowing them to float. Seeds that depend on animals are dispersed in one of two ways. Plants with dry fruits with burrs or barbs can attach themselves to animals passing by and are then dispersed when the animal removes the seed from its fur or skin. Plants with fleshy fruits are consumed by animals. After the fruit is digested, the seeds are excreted into the ground by the animal—complete with a fecal fertilizer to nourish the germinating seed.

SAMPLE QUESTIONS

18) **Which of the following is the process of a male pollen grain being transferred to a female reproductive structure?**

   A. fertilization

   B. germination

   C. pollination

   D. conception

Answers:

   A. Incorrect. Fertilization is a separate process that occurs after a male pollen grain has been transferred to a female reproductive structure.

   B. Incorrect. Germination refers to the process of the seed embryo growing into a seedling.

  C. **Correct.** Pollination is the physical movement of pollen to the female cone or pistil.

  D. Incorrect. Conception can only occur after pollination and fertilization have occurred.

19) **Which of the following is NOT a type of allochory dispersal?**

  A. dispersal by water
  B. dispersal by wind
  C. dispersal by gravity
  D. dispersal by animals

Answers:

  A. Incorrect. Water is a secondary agent acting to help disperse the seed.

  B. Incorrect. Wind is a secondary agent acting to help disperse the seed.

  C. **Correct.** Allochory mechanisms depend on a second agent to disperse the plant, such as wind, water, or animals.

  D. Incorrect. Animals are secondary agents acting to help disperse the seed.

6

Ecology

Ecology is the branch of science that studies the interactions and relationships between living things and their environment. The root word *eco* is derived from the Greek word *oikos*, which means *house*. In other words, ecology is the study of where things live.

Ecology is concerned with how organisms interact with each other and with their environment. It includes the study of many different systems, from small populations of organisms to the entire Earth system. Topics covered in ecology include interactions between living and non-living things, the flow of energy and nutrients within a system, and the effects of disturbances on the structure and biodiversity of ecological systems. This chapter will provide an overview of these basic ecological concepts; it will also describe in detail the subfields of population ecology, community ecology, and ecosystem ecology.

ECOLOGICAL HIERARCHY

Living organisms and the environment—the two components studied in ecology—are collectively known as the **biosphere**, which includes land, air, water, or any Earth system in which life is found. Within Earth's biosphere, there is a hierarchal organization of the groups of organisms that make up all living things. A **population** is the smallest level of ecological organization and consists of all the members of a species that live in a defined geological space. For many species, particularly plants and animals, members of the population are generally capable of **interbreeding** with one another, and the group itself is reproductively isolated from other populations of the same species.

The collection of populations of all the species within the same defined geographic space is known as a **community**. The various populations found within the community are dependent upon their interactions with one another. Populations within a community may interact through competition for food resources, predator and prey relationships, or mutually beneficial relationships.

The ecological community, combined with the surrounding physical environment, is known as an **ecosystem**. The ecosystem is the primary unit of study in the field of ecology. As the name suggests, an ecosystem is a system of separate, related parts that function together as a whole. Ecosystems are composed of **biotic** (living) material as well as **abiotic** (nonliving) material. Examples of biotic components in an environment are the populations of plants and animals that exist within a given community; abiotic components include air, water, rocks, and soil. The relationships between biotic and abiotic factors in an ecosystem (further detailed later in this chapter) are intricate and complex. These relationships are influenced by both internal factors, such as species competition or decomposition of nutrients, and by external factors, such as the introduction of an exotic species or climate.

The size of an ecosystem varies and is relative to the components found within its boundaries. An ecosystem can be found entirely in a single pond or on a rotting log in the forest. On the opposite extreme, an ecosystem can also comprise an entire country or continent. The largest ecosystems on Earth are known as **biomes**. Biomes are broad ecosystems characterized by a dominant form of plant life and the groups of animals that depend upon this flora. They have similar climates and the species found within them have shared characteristics.

SAMPLE QUESTION

1) Which of the following levels of organization is composed only of members of the same species?

   A. biosphere

   B. community

   C. ecosystem

   D. population

Answers:

   A. Incorrect. The biosphere includes all of the living things on Earth.

   B. Incorrect. Communities are composed of multiple populations.

   C. Incorrect. Ecosystems are composed of an environment and its community, which itself is composed of multiple populations.

   D. Correct. A population is all of the members of the same species in a given area.

BIOMES

Biomes are vast geographical areas with similar climates that share functionally similar ecosystems of flora and fauna. Even though lands within the same classified biome can be located far from one another, their similar environment and climate conditions have resulted in an ecosystem that is dominated by similar types of vegetation. For example, the tundra biomes found in Asia and in North America may not share the same species of vegetation, but the different species that inhabit these areas serve very similar ecological functions.

Biomes can be **aquatic biomes**, which are water based, or **terrestrial biomes**, which are found on land. The aquatic biome is by far the largest biome on Earth, with water composing approximately 75 percent of Earth's surface. The aquatic biome can be further subdivided into distinct saltwater biomes and freshwater biomes. Examples of **marine biomes** (saltwater biomes) include the oceans, coral reefs, and estuaries. Freshwater biomes include ponds, lakes, streams, and wetlands.

Covering 70 percent of Earth's surface, the ocean biomes encompass the greatest area and diversity of life. There are five major ocean biomes associated with Earth's major oceans: the Pacific, Atlantic, Indian, Arctic, and Southern Oceans. Each ocean biome environment is subdivided into three distinct vertical layers: the **benthic zone**, located on the ocean floor; the **pelagic zone**, (the open ocean); and the **photic zone** (the top layer closest to the sun). The photic layer is thus named because it is close enough to the surface to harbor life that undergoes photosynthesis. This layer is dominated by **phytoplankton**—floating, plant-like organisms, such as microalgae and photosynthetic bacteria. These photosynthesizing organisms are the dominant producers of the photic zone and serve as the base of the ocean biome food chain. The areas of the ocean biome that support the greatest number of organisms and diversity of life are areas located close to the coast as well as near Earth's North and South poles.

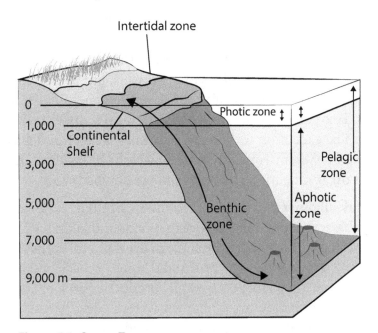

Figure 6.1. Ocean Zones

The **coral reef biome**, while located within the ocean, is distinct enough in structure and life diversity to constitute its own biome. Coral reefs are characterized by the buildup of countless generations of coral, a type of invertebrate that secretes calcium carbonate as its exoskeleton. This results in a coral reef that serves as the base of a complex ecosystem dominated by the youngest generation of coral polyps, protective microbial associates (such as bacteria and fungi), layers of algae that are anchored to the reef, and the countless invertebrates, fish, and other organisms that depend on the food produced on the reef.

The **estuary biome** is located where the ocean biomes meet freshwater habitats. There is a constant movement of water that occurs as rivers and streams flow into the ocean and ocean tides flow into the estuary, and this constant motion supports a great diversity of life. Phytoplankton from the ocean as well as nutrient-rich **detritus** that is stirred up by moving water results in a large amount of nutrients that becomes available for consumption by zooplankton and other animals. This matter attracts ocean organisms, migrating bird species, and other groups of organisms that depend on this productive ecosystem for food and survival.

Wetland biomes are another example of a productive aquatic biome. As the name suggests, these are terrestrial areas that are partially or wholly covered in water and able to support aquatic vegetation, which serves as the basis of the food chain in the ecosystem. Similar to estuaries, their food chain is rooted in nutrient-rich detritus and supports a great variety of life, including permanent residents, migratory species, ephemeral species, or transitional species. The majority of wetland biomes, such as bogs, swamps, and marshes, are dominated by freshwater and often fed by freshwater streams.

Stream biomes are freshwater biomes that flow in one direction from a headwater source—such as a lake—to the ocean. The conditions that support life change as the water flows. Toward the headwaters, there are generally higher levels of oxygen that support greater numbers of organisms, but by the time the stream reaches its end point, the amount of productive life generally decreases due to reduced light and oxygen resulting from the stirred-up sediment that flows along with the water. The exception to this are streams that end in deltas, which are highly productive ecosystems, or ecosystems in which the headwaters are nutrient poor and collect organic debris as the water moves downstream.

Pond and **lake biomes** can vary drastically in size but share certain similar structures and characteristics. Like the ocean, ponds and lakes have a photic zone that is found near the surface where the sun can drive photosynthesis in plant life. The area below the photic zone—the **profundal zone**—is dark and home to fewer forms of life as a result. The most ecologically productive area of lakes and ponds is the **littoral zone**, the shallow areas near the water's edge that support the most vegetation in the form of phytoplankton and rooted plants.

The ecosystems that compose Earth's major terrestrial biomes function in the same way. Not only do many share similar climates and environments, but in many cases, they also share latitude and geographic location. The biome in the northern- and southern-most regions of Earth, closest to the poles, is the **tundra**. This biome is characterized by flat, treeless land that is punctuated by small, simple forms of vegetation such as mosses, lichens, grasses, and shrubs. The ground tends to stay moist due to a layer of **permafrost** (permanent ice) that exists below the surface and prevents water drainage. Despite harsh, wet, cold, and windy conditions, there is still an abundance of animal life, including crane flies, lemmings, arctic hares, and caribou. The **alpine biome**, although geographically separated from the Arctic and Antarctic tundra environments, exhibits many similar characteristics due to its high altitude. The alpine biome is restricted to the world's mountains at altitudes of 10,000 feet or higher.

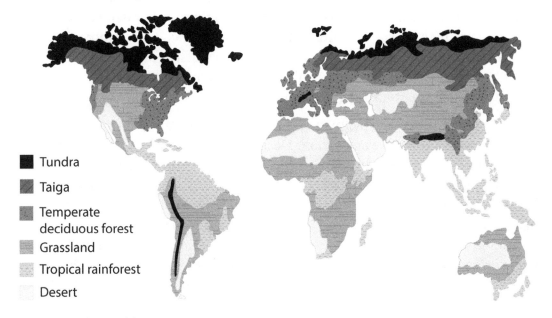

Tundra

Taiga

Temperate deciduous forest

Grassland

Tropical rainforest

Desert

Figure 6.2. The World's Biomes

The expanse of land located just south of the Arctic tundra is the northern boreal forest, or **taiga biome**. Taiga formations are found primarily in the northern hemisphere since the southern hemisphere does not contain extensive land masses in the equivalent latitudes. The vegetation in this biome is dominated by trees, par- ticularly conifer species such as spruces, firs, and pines. Many of the same groups of animals found in the taiga are also found in the tundra, such as arctic hare and caribou. Other animal life found in this biome include greater numbers of insects, small mammals such as squirrels and marmots, large mammals such as moose and wolves, and many species of migratory birds.

The **temperate deciduous forest**, which makes up much of the eastern United States, is dominated by trees that exhibit a pattern of leaf loss and regrowth that coincide with seasonal changes. These forests are often characterized by vertical stratification, with the tops of the tallest trees forming a canopy layer that shields a lower canopy, understory, shrub, and ground level. Forest stratification, richer soil, and less-harsh environmental conditions all contribute to a greater diversity of animal life, including amphibians and reptile species that do not survive in taiga or tundra ecosystems.

Sharing similar latitude with the temperate forests but exhibiting very different environmental conditions are the temperate **grassland biomes**. As the name suggests, the dominant vegetation in these areas are grass species that are well adapted to the light rainfall, periodic fires, and flat terrain. Grasslands are differentiated into prairie, steppe, pampas, and velds, depending on the part of the world in which they are found. These grasslands are subdivided into different types depending on the amount of precipitation received. There is a large diversity of invertebrate and vertebrate life that occupy this biome, including many species of large grazing animals and burrowing rodents. Grassland soil is some of the most fertile on Earth, which has led to a steep decline in natural grassland habitat as humans have instituted agriculture in many of these areas. The **savanna**, which is a type of tropical grassland, typically has soil that is much poorer in nutrients than its temperate grassland counterparts. The savanna biome is typically drier, warmer, and flatter than other types of grassland.

The **desert** is typically defined as an area with low rainfall—often under 10 inches a year—and high evaporation. Deserts can be found in temperate, cold-weather, or hot-weather climates. Although the species of vegetation depends on many factors, such as topography, moisture levels, and temperatures, most deserts are characterized by shrub-like and scattered plant life like succulents and sagebrush. Both plant and animal life in this biome are adapted to dry conditions, only flowering or exiting dormancy during the brief rainy seasons. The **chaparral** biome bridges the gap between the grassland and desert biomes, as they are characterized by dry summer seasons and wet winters. Also known as the shrubland biome, chaparrals are characterized by shrubs (small, woody plants) and complex animal life that depend on the different habitats offered by shrub stratification.

Closer to the equator, **tropical rain forests** are some of the most productive biomes in the world, accounting for over half of the world's identified plant and animal species while only occupying less than 10 percent of Earth's surface. Tropical rain forests are found in areas close to the equator that are below 1,000 meters in altitude and receive adequate precipitation. Like the temperate forests, the tropical rain forest is characterized by a complex series of stratified layers that create microclimates and support a vast number and wide variety of species. The soil in these areas often holds little nutritional value, due to the extreme efficiency of decomposers that consume and recycle nutrients before they get a chance to settle and form into soil.

HELPFUL HINT

In addition to supporting a productive food chain, estuaries offer a protective area of ocean water shielded from fast-moving ocean tides and currents. They are often called the "nurseries of the sea," as this combination of plentiful food and relative production drives many species of ocean organisms to spend at least some part of their early life cycles there.

SAMPLE QUESTIONS

2) Which of the following aquatic biomes are located where freshwater streams empty into the ocean?

    A.   wetlands

    B.   coral reef

    C.   estuaries

    D.   littoral

Answers:

    A.   Incorrect. Wetlands are terrestrial-based ecosystems that are covered by water for a significant portion of the year.

    B.   Incorrect. Coral reef biomes are found in the ocean.

    C.   **Correct.** Estuaries are found at the boundary of ocean and stream biomes and are very ecologically productive areas.

    D.   Incorrect. This is a zone found within a pond or lake biome.

3) Which of the following terrestrial biomes is considered the most ecologically productive?

    A.   grasslands

    B.   chaparral

    C.   temperate deciduous forest

    D.   tropical rain forest

Answers:

    A.   Incorrect. Although the soil of grasslands is some of the most fertile in the world, it is not considered the most ecologically productive biome.

    B.   Incorrect. The chaparral has a good diversity of life in its vegetated areas, but is not considered the most ecologically productive biome.

    C.   Incorrect. The temperate deciduous forest is much more productive than the tundra and taiga, but it is not considered the most ecologically productive biome.

    D.   **Correct.** The tropical rain forest produces a great abundance and diversity of life in a relatively small area of the earth's surface, making it the most ecologically productive biome on land.

POPULATION ECOLOGY

The study of populations (all members of a species in a defined geographic area) and how they interact with their environment is known as **population ecology**. Populations are studied through the lens of two defining characteristics: their **density** (the number of population members found per unit of space) and their **dispersion** (the pattern of spacing of individual organisms within the defined geographic area). The pattern of dispersion influences the density of a population in a given space, which in turn determines how environmental factors will impact size, growth, and reproductive rates of a given population. This section will focus on factors that impact population size, study models of population growth, and examine reproductive strategies and survival dynamics within individual populations.

POPULATION SIZE

The size of a population is heavily influenced by both biotic and abiotic components of the ecosystem in which the population is found. One of these factors is the availability of **resources** within an ecosystem. An ecological resource is an object or material that an organism requires in order to grow, develop, and thrive. In general, the fewer resources that are readily available, the smaller a population size will be—and if resources are consumed by another population member or a member of another species, then there will be less resource availability for others. Resources can be either biotic or abiotic. Examples of resources that directly affect population size include food, water, light, nutritious soil, and adequate structures or land for shelter and territory.

Abiotic environmental factors also influence population size. These factors are not considered resources because they are not consumed or used by organisms in such a way that reduces availability. Nonetheless, they play a direct role in the survival of individuals within a population. These include weather and climate factors, such as temperature and precipitation; soil conditions, such as pH or pollution; and natural events or disasters, such as fire or erosion.

The physical location where an organism lives is known as its **habitat**. Members of the same population generally inhabit the same or similar habitats that incorporate the same biotic and abiotic factors. An organism's role in that habitat is known as a **niche** and includes all of the biotic and abiotic factors that influence that organism. For example, the niche of a barnacle includes its specific location in ocean water, its specific behavior of living attached to a hard surface such as a conch shell or boat dock, and its specific feeding behavior of filter feeding plankton from the surrounding water.

SAMPLE QUESTION

4) Which of the following is an abiotic environmental factor that influences population size?

A. food availability

B. rate of precipitation

C. interspecific competition

D. resource partitioning

Answers:

A. Incorrect. Food availability is an example of a biotic factor.

B. Correct. Precipitation is a non-living (abiotic) factor that influences population size.

C. Incorrect. Interspecific competition refers to the competition between species of populations for the same resources.

D. Incorrect. Resource partitioning is a method of coexistence among species that occupy similar niches.

MODELS OF POPULATION GROWTH

The increase of the size of a population over a period of time is known as population growth. Ecologists measure population growth in order to gain a more accurate understanding of the environmental needs of a species, how different species interact in the same environment, and how external and internal changes cause change in the population over time. There are two models primarily used by ecologists in order to measure population growth: the exponential growth model and the logistic growth model.

The **exponential growth model** is based on a growth rate of a population that increases at a consistent pace. This rate of growth is proportional to the number of individuals in a population. As a result, even though the rate of growth remains constant, the total number in the population rises rapidly. Imagine a single cell bacterium that undergoes binary fission to divide into two. If binary fission takes place at least once per day, then the total number of bacteria will increase to four on the second day. On the third day, all four bacteria divide and increase the total number to eight. By the fourth day, the population doubles again to sixteen. This results in a J-shaped growth curve, which gets steeper with time.

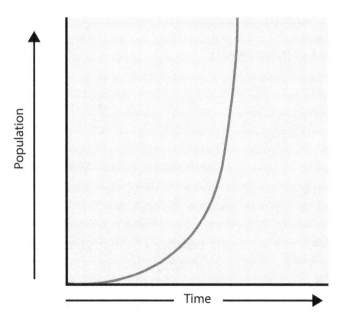

Figure 6.3. Exponential Growth

The exponential growth model assumes that the resources in an environment are constant and unlimited. In reality, species encounter **limiting factors** (biotic and abiotic ecosystem components) that restrict or reduce growth in a population. A more common population growth model that is seen among real-world populations is the logistic growth model.

Logistic growth is represented graphically as an S-shaped curve. A population will begin to grow at an exponential rate, which is expressed as the initial steep curve in a logistic growth graph. As limiting factors impact the population and resources become scarcer, then the population will start to grow at a slower rate or even decrease. At some point, the growth curve will level off and become stable. This point, which occurs when a population has reached the maximum size and density that a geographic area can support, is known as a population's **carrying capacity**.

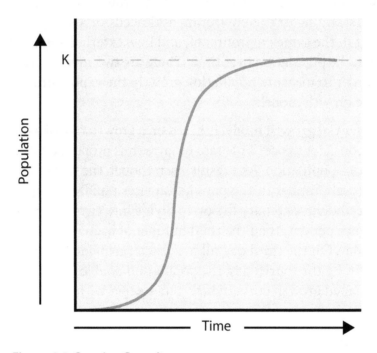

Figure 6.4. Carrying Capacity

QUICK REVIEW

Without any **limiting factors** to keep a check on a population's growth, the population's numbers continue to increase exponentially. What are some examples of resources that could be a limiting factor for a population of deer in a forest habitat?

Exponential and logistic growth models are useful tools for ecologists studying the population changes of a group of organisms, but real-world growth situations are rarely as simple as the above models suggest. Growth rates can be altered by several factors, such as a temporary increase in water or food resources, which could inflate the number of a population above the normal carrying capacity line. Alternatively, an abnormal event, such as a natural disaster, could cause the population size to plummet before it begins to grow toward carrying capacity once again.

SAMPLE QUESTION

5) **Which of the following scenarios is an example of exponential growth?**

A. bacteria cells rapidly reproducing then leveling off when their numbers have reached carrying capacity

B. houseflies steadily reproducing, then experiencing a sudden drop in numbers due to an environmental change

C. yeast cells undergoing mitosis and doubling their numbers with every division

D. mayfly populations steadily decreasing due to increased pollution in their habitat

Answers:

A. Incorrect. This is an example of logistic growth.

B. Incorrect. This is an example of a complex growth pattern, with elements of both exponential and logistic growth occurring.

C. Correct. This is an example of exponential growth, assuming that the numbers increase indefinitely.

D. Incorrect. This is not an example of population growth.

REPRODUCTIVE STRATEGIES

Different species of organisms exhibit a variety of **reproductive strategies**—adaptations that positively impact the number of fertile offspring produced by individuals. In turn, the successful nature of a species' reproductive strategy can either increase or decrease **mortality rates** (the number of deaths in a population over a defined period of time). Some reproductive strategies lead to a much higher mortality rate early in an organism's life span, while other strategies lead to higher mortality rates late in life. The success rate of different reproductive strategies always involves a series of trade-offs: the survival of some offspring is more likely if greater numbers of offspring are produced, but high levels of parental investment and favorable environmental conditions can increase survival of small numbers of offspring.

Reproduction can be divided into two main types, each with a variety of unique adaptations and strategies associated with it: **asexual reproduction**, in which offspring arise from a single parent, and **sexual reproduction**, in which offspring are produced through the fusion of gametes from two distinct parents.

Asexual reproduction is rapid, leading to a great number of offspring within a short period of time. This occurs because the organisms do not have to spend time finding a suitable, receptive mate or go through the process of copulation and fertilization. The rapid nature of asexual reproduction is advantageous when a population has an opportunity to quickly exploit new, favorable environmental conditions in order to colonize and populate new habitats or to quickly rebound from a sudden population loss. There are, however, major disadvantages to this reproductive strategy, primarily the loss of genetic variation that comes from having a single parent.

While less efficient than asexual reproduction, sexual reproduction compensates by ensuring greater genetic diversity among a group of organisms. Sexually reproducing organisms must balance the resources needed to produce and then raise offspring. For example, the common housefly reproduces sexually, but, like asexual organisms, produces a large number of offspring in a short period of time. However, it puts no resources into rearing offspring, so flies have a high mortality rate early in life. The housefly is an example of an **opportunist species**, which are small in size and have short life cycles in order to take advantage of new environmental conditions.

At the other end of the spectrum are **equilibrium species**, which tend to produce fewer offspring, provide great care for offspring, and have much longer life spans than opportunist species. Humans and elephants are examples of equilibrium species. Not all species fall into one of these two extreme categories, however. A great number of species, called **constant loss species**, produce a moderate amount of offspring and have a constant mortality rate throughout their life span.

The parental behaviors that a species exhibits also have a great impact on an offspring's chance of survival. **Parental investment** is the amount of time and energy a parent expends to support an offspring that has a negative impact on the parent's ability to invest in his or her own biological fitness. The amount of parental investment is inversely proportional to the number of offspring produced by a parent. Many opportunist species cannot afford the time and energy to invest in each of their many offspring, so these species have a low level of parental investment. Other species with very few young can expend much more energy and time on each individual. The degree and amount of care between groups of organisms varies. Few insect, fish, amphibian, and reptile species exhibit large amounts of parental investment. Bird and mammal species tend to make the greatest amount of parental investment in offspring, providing nurture, protection, and, in the case of mammals, lactation.

Just as previously seen with methods of reproduction, there are trade-offs for the amount of parental investment a species puts forth. This investment can be detrimental to the parent providing the care and can reduce a parent's **fecundity**—the ability to produce offspring. However, increased parental investment also boosts an offspring's chance for survival into adulthood to produce more viable offspring.

SAMPLE QUESTIONS

6) **Which of the following describes an ecological advantage of asexual reproduction over sexual reproduction?**

   A. Asexual reproduction produces greater genetic variation.

   B. Parental investment is higher in organisms that reproduce asexually.

   C. Offspring can be produced rapidly using asexual reproduction.

   D. Species that reproduce asexually tend to have a much longer life span.

Answers:

A. Incorrect. This is an advantage of sexual reproduction.

B. Incorrect. Parental investment is usually seen among organisms that reproduce sexually.

C. Correct. Asexual reproduction happens at a faster rate than sexual reproduction, which potentially allows more offspring to survive.

D. Incorrect. This is a characteristic of equilibrium species.

7) **Which of the following statements about parental investment is true?**

A. Parental investment is only seen among opportunistic species.

B. Parental investment is only seen among constant loss species.

C. The amount of parental investment is directly proportional to the number of offspring produced by a parent.

D. The amount of parental investment is inversely proportional to the number of offspring produced by a parent.

Answers:

A. Incorrect. Most species with high levels of parental investment are equilibrium species, but there are exceptions to this rule.

B. Incorrect. Constant loss species may or may not have high levels of parental investment.

C. Incorrect. The opposite of this statement is true.

D. Correct. Parents can invest greater time and energy into individual offspring when there are fewer offspring to provide for.

COMMUNITY ECOLOGY

Community ecology is the discipline of ecology that focuses on organization, functioning, and relationships among communities. Communities, as previously defined, are collections of populations of all the species within the same defined geographic space. This includes populations of all living things found in all domains and kingdoms of life. Together, communities interact with the environment and compose an ecosystem. The number of populations and the variety of species interacting within a community account for its **biodiversity**, an important measure of ecosystem health. This section will focus on the relationships among populations in a community, discuss how communities change over time, and trace the flow of energy as it moves through a community.

RELATIONSHIPS AMONG SPECIES

The populations found within an ecosystem develop intricate, complex relationships that shape the dynamics and health of an ecosystem as a whole. Species depend on one on another for a wide variety of reasons, but most reasons can be boiled down to the basic ideas of gaining access to reliable food, water, and shelter. In most of these relationships, at least one of the species or organisms involved gains a **benefit** from the interaction; in some cases, at least one of the organisms incurs **costs**. In all cases, these relationships shape the overall dynamics and determine the success of an ecosystem and all of its parts.

One major category of interspecies interactions is known as **symbiosis**. Symbiosis is a close, interdependent, long-term relationship between two usually dissimilar species. There are three major kinds of symbiotic relationships, each defined by how it harms or benefits the species involved in the relationship: **parasitism**, **commensalism**, and **mutualism**.

Parasitism involves two distinct species: a parasite and a host. In this relationship, the parasite benefits from its close proximity and interactions with the host to the detriment of the host's health and well-being. Parasitic organisms tend to be smaller than the host and quickly reproduce to take advantage of the relationship. They can be found both inside the host organism or attached to the outside. Parasites rely on host organisms for food resources or as part of their reproductive cycle—or sometimes both. It is not in the interest of most parasites to kill the host, as they depend on the host for their survival. However, a parasite can inflict a wide range of negative impacts on the host, from the annoying, itchy presence of fleas feeding on a dog's blood, to the more devastating impacts of a tapeworm that lays eggs within an animal's digestive tract.

Commensalism is another example of a symbiotic relationship between two species—a commensal and a host. Like parasites, the commensal species benefits from its close proximity to the host organism; unlike parasitism, there is little to no effect on the host organism as a result. An example of commensalism is the relationship between the cattle egret and cattle. The cattle egret, which gets its name from this interaction, follows the host cattle or other livestock and feeds on the insects that are stirred up from the ground as the larger host organisms move through a field of grass or other vegetation. The cattle egret benefits from a reliable food source, while the cattle remain unaffected by the presence of this population of birds.

Mutualism is a symbiotic relationship in which both species benefit from the presence of the other. In many cases, both species coevolved with one another, each adapting to changes and adaptations in the other and developing an interdependent bond through evolution. One of the most well-known examples of mutualism can be found in the relationship between clownfish and sea anemones. The clownfish provides for the anemone by chasing away predators, supplying the anemone with food through its waste, and preening parasites off of it. At the same time, the anemone offers the clownfish protection from predators as it conceals the fish with its venom-producing tentacles. In a case of coevolution, the clownfish evolved a thick, protective mucus layer that is immune to the venom produced by the anemone.

Another major category of relationships between species is **predation**—a mode of interaction in which one species, the **predator**, captures and feeds on the other organism, the **prey**. This is seen among predatory animals feeding upon other animals, such as a bald eagle diving for and eating fish, but this is also seen among animals consuming plant matter, such as a turtle feeding on algae in a pond. The dynamics between predator and prey relationships are complex. Not only is predation an essential relationship for energy transfer between organisms, but it also is an essential component of population numbers and growth. The population size of one species is dependent on the presence, abundance, or absence of the other. In general, predator numbers rise when there is an abundance of prey, while numbers of prey go down when there is an increase in predator abundance. Similarly, a decline in predator numbers would result in an increase in the abundance of prey when there is less predation to keep population numbers down. This results in a predator-prey cycle that influences the dynamics within an ecosystem.

When niches overlap in terms of food resources, similar habitats, or similar feeding behavior, then patterns of competition begin to emerge. This is known as **interspecific competition** (competition for food, water, or space resources between two different species). Competition for the exact same resource does not often persist over long periods of time. This is due to the **competitive exclusion principle**, which states that one population will outcompete another when vying for the same limited resource and result in the local extinction of the other population. However, coexistence in the same habitat has been observed in many instances due to **resource partitioning**. Resource partitioning occurs when two populations divide the resources required of their shared or similar niche by using resources in different ways, at different times, or different locations. For example, different species or populations of nectar-feeding organisms may consume nectar from different-sized flowers or select flowers on other parts of the same plant. Other forms of species competition and relationships, including predator-prey relationships, will be explored later in the chapter.

In some cases, competition for resources can lead to **territoriality** among some populations in a community. Territoriality is a behavior in which an organism actively defends a geographic space from rivals both within its own species and from other populations occupying the same habitat or niche. Defense mechanisms among organisms vary: they can range from songs or calls, marking a space with scents, intimidation displays, or chasing and attacking other organisms. There are great costs associated with territoriality, as the organism has to expend time and energy and divert its attention from other behaviors, such as mating or feeding. The trade-off for a territorial organism is increased access to resources to further promote reproduction and success among its population, while other organisms must relocate to other areas with fewer resources, which may have a negative impact on their population's success.

QUICK REVIEW

Does predation always have to result in the loss of life of the prey organism? Why or why not?

Some organisms in a community display **altruism**—a series of behaviors that benefit another organism at the cost of the organism that is displaying the behavior. Animals engage in altruistic behaviors in order to benefit the population as a whole. This is especially prevalent among species that have high levels of parental investment or in populations that have complex social behavior. Examples of **altruistic behaviors** include aiding weaker or injured members of the population, group defense mechanisms from intruders or other threats, and closely tending to and protecting offspring.

SAMPLE QUESTIONS

8) A barnacle is attached to the outside of the whale to collect and consume particulate matter as the whale moves through the ocean. The barnacle benefits, while the whale is unaffected.

The phenomenon described is an example of

A. predation

B. commensalism

C. mutualism

D. parasitism

Answers:

A. Incorrect. The barnacle is not feeding on the whale, or vice versa, so this is not an example of a predatory relationship.

B. Correct. In a commensal relationship, one species benefits with no impact on the other.

C. Incorrect. Mutualism occurs when both species benefit.

D. Incorrect. Parasitism harms the host in the relationship.

9) Which of the following is NOT an example of a territorial behavior?

A. aiding injured members of a population

B. projecting songs and calls

C. marking a territory with scent

D. baring teeth as a display of intimidation

Answers:

A. Correct. This is an example of an altruistic behavior.

B. Incorrect. Songs and calls are territorial; the organism is claiming a territory and communicating it to others.

C. Incorrect. Leaving scents is an example of marking territory and communicating it to others.

D. Incorrect. Intimidating behaviors are territorial.

10) **Which of the following describes the relationship in which one organism captures and feeds on another?**

   A.   territoriality

   B.   commensalism

   C.   predation

   D.   competition

Answers:

   A.   Incorrect. This is a series of behaviors in which an organism defends its chosen habitat from another organism or population.

   B.   Incorrect. This is a symbiotic relationship in which one organism benefits while the other has no effect.

   C.   Correct. Predation involves one organism consuming part of—or the whole of—another.

   D.   Incorrect. Competition exists between species that vie for the same resources.

ECOLOGICAL SUCCESSION

Ecosystems are not stable environments. Due to internal and external factors, ecosystems and the habitats within them are consistently evolving in a process called **ecological succession**. Ecological succession is the process of ecosystem change and development over time, which occurs as the number and types of species and their relationships and structures change. These changes can be incremental and happen slowly over a long period of time; they can also happen rapidly due to sudden major changes to one or more components of the ecosystem.

There are two major types of succession. The first type of is known as **primary succession**. Primary succession occurs on **substrates** (surfaces that support life) that have not been **colonized** or inhabited by life before. This includes places such as newly formed sand dunes or surfacing rock formations. These areas are characterized by soil that contains little to no nutritional value. The second type, **secondary succession**, occurs in areas that once had life but are starting anew after a major environmental disturbance such as fire, clear-cutting for human development, or farming. Like primary succession, there is little to no existing life at inception; unlike primary succession, there are more substantive nutrients due to the earlier presence of life that enriched the soil.

Regardless of the type of succession, ecosystems generally follow a similar set of successional changes over time. Each stage is marked by a major change to the nutritional value of the soil and the development of different dominant forms of vegetation that benefit from increased soil quality. As the vegetation changes, the diversity of other forms of life—including bacteria, fungi, and animal species—changes and increases as well. This results in the accumulation of **biomass** (total mass of organisms) and an increase in ecosystem **productivity**, which is the rate of production of biomass. With each major successional change, the ecosystem sees more productivity and biomass and becomes more stable over time.

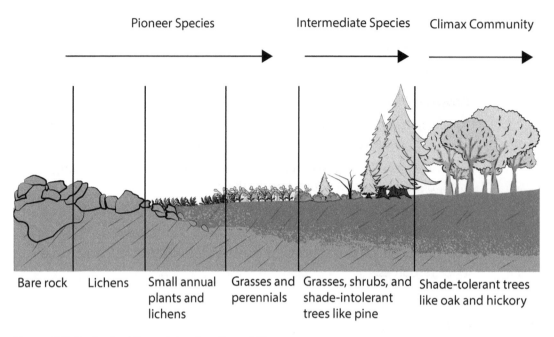

Figure 6.5. Ecological Succession in a Forest Biome

The first stage of ecological succession is the **pioneer plant** stage. This stage is marked by the appearance of pioneer species, which tend to be photosynthetic microbes—such as bacteria or lichen—or plants that are adapted to living in areas with little resources. They tend to be small, reproduce quickly, have long roots to reach out to sparse soil, and are adapted to live in areas with little water. Examples include simple plants and plant-like organisms such as lichens and algae, or hardy, resistant flowering plants such as grasses. Other pioneer organisms that feed on these producers, such as invertebrates, will soon follow.

As these organisms die and decompose, their decaying bodies provide additional nutrition to the soil, which in turn supports greater complexity and diversity of plant life. The pioneer plants are succeeded by **intermediate species**. These species, such as grasses and shrub-like plants, tend to be bigger, reproduce more slowly, and have longer life spans than the pioneer plants before them. The changes and complexity they bring to the ecosystem encourage more diversity and biomass to be produced in this area since organisms take advantage of new habitats provided by bigger plants and the resources they provide. As these organisms die and decompose, it further enriches the soil and encourages the growth of even bigger, more complex plants.

This cycle continues until the relatively stable **climax community** emerges. The climax community is characterized by mature plant growth that is dominated by a few species well suited to the habitat. These communities have the greatest amount of species diversity, biomass, and productivity. Although the communities exist in equilibrium, they are still susceptible to potential changes in the environment.

Natural or human-caused events such as drought, fire, or deforestation can cause major changes. In extreme cases, these changes result in an ecosystem starting over and a process of secondary succession beginning in the area.

SAMPLE QUESTIONS

11) Which of the following is NOT a difference between primary and secondary succession?

   A. Primary succession occurs where no life has existed before; secondary succession exists where life has previously existed.

   B. Primary succession is characterized by soil with little to no nutrients; secondary succession has soil that is more nutrient rich.

   C. Primary succession begins on newly formed or exposed surfaces; secondary succession begins on land that has existed for a period of time.

   D. Primary succession begins with pioneer species; secondary succession begins with intermediate species.

Answers:

   A. Incorrect. This is an accurate distinction between the two types of succession.

   B. Incorrect. The soil in a secondary succession area has been enriched by previous forms of life.

   C. Incorrect. This is an accurate distinction between the two types of succession.

   D. Correct. Both types of succession begin with pioneer species.

12) Which of the following species would most likely be an intermediate species?

   A. a shrub that reproduces once a year

   B. a slow-growing tree species

   C. an algae species that reproduces quickly

   D. a wind-pollinated grass species

Answers:

   A. Correct. Shrubs are an intermediate species that appear after pioneer species have established themselves.

   B. Incorrect. A slow-growing tree would appear in a climax community after intermediate species have established themselves.

   C. Incorrect. A quickly reproducing algae is most likely a pioneer species colonizing a barren landscape.

   D. Incorrect. Wind-pollinated grasses are also pioneer species.

ENERGY FLOW

Ecosystems cannot exist without energy; all organisms require some form of energy in order to perform basic cellular functions. Energy cannot be created or destroyed, as per the law of conservation of energy; therefore, in an ecosystem, energy must be transferred from one organism to another. All energy in an ecosystem originates with the sun, which provides abundant **solar energy** to the earth's surface, then flows from organism to organism through an ecosystem's **food web**. A food web is a complex chain of energy transfer in an ecosystem that is composed of multiple **food chains**, which in turn are a series of organisms, each dependent on the next in the series for its source of food.

In a food chain, solar energy is first transformed and utilized by a group of organisms called **producers**. Producers are a type of **autotroph** (organism that generates its own food) that convert solar energy into food energy through photosynthesis. Other forms of autotrophs produce food through chemosynthesis, in which carbon dioxide or methane are converted to food energy. Examples of producers include some forms of bacteria, algae, and other plantlike protists and plants themselves. These organisms constitute the first **trophic level** of an ecosystem. A trophic level is a class of organisms that share the same position in the food chain or food web in an ecosystem.

The second trophic level of an ecosystem consists of **primary consumers**—organisms that eat the producers. All consumers belong to a group of organisms

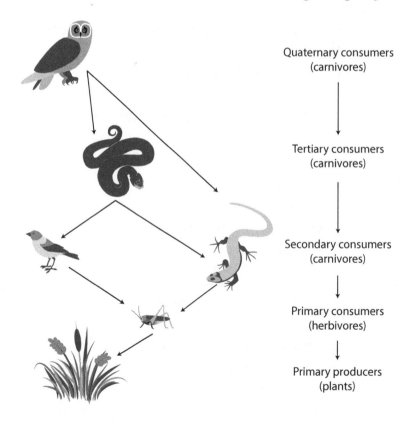

Figure 6.6. Food Web

called **heterotrophs**, which are organisms that cannot produce their own food and obtain energy by consuming organic matter. The primary consumers are generally **herbivores** (organisms that feed exclusively on plant matter) or **omnivores** (organisms that eat both plant and animal matter).

Secondary consumers (consumers that feed upon the primary consumers) compose the third trophic level in an ecosystem. These organisms tend to be either omnivores or **carnivores**, which are organisms that subsist primarily on other animals. Carnivores also make up the fourth trophic level, the **tertiary consumers**. These organisms feed upon the secondary consumers. Some communities may have higher level consumers that in turn feed on tertiary consumers.

Another type of consumer not represented by its own trophic level is the **decomposers**. A decomposer is an organism that primarily consumes dead, dying, or otherwise discarded matter called **detritus**. When consuming and excreting this material, decomposers are breaking down organic matter into its separate inorganic components. These organisms can be microscopic—such as bacteria—or macroscopic, such as earthworms, fly larvae, and other macroinvertebrates.

This chain of energy flow in an ecosystem is graphically represented by a **pyramid of energy**. As energy moves up the food chain, there is a net loss of energy from one stage to the next. As a result, the pyramid of energy narrows as it reaches the tertiary consumers at the apex of the diagram. These pyramids are created to show how the energy flows from the producers to the tertiary consumers in an ecosystem.

Similar in structure but differing slightly in function are **pyramids of biomass**. Like energy pyramids, these diagrams visually represent organisms in terms of trophic levels. Unlike energy pyramids, these diagrams are based on the total amount of biomass represented by each trophic level rather than the types or number of organisms. As the graphic suggests, producers are the trophic level with the greatest amounts of biomass, while the tertiary consumers at the top have the smallest amounts of biomass. This occurs because there is not as much energy in the ecosystem to support larger numbers.

Energy transfer is also visually represented through food webs, which, as previously mentioned, are diagrams encompassing all of the individual food chains and feeding relationships within an ecological community. Food webs and interdependent feeding relationships vary widely depending on the community. Some small, less complex

HELPFUL HINT

The amount of energy decreases by a magnitude of 10 every time it passes through a trophic level in the ecosystem. This energy is measured in kilocalories (kcal), which is a measure of heat. For example, if a plant produces 100 kcal of energy, only 10 kcal will be available to primary consumers that eat the plant. This reduction occurs because much energy is lost by an organism through cellular metabolism, which manifests as heat loss.

communities have similarly simple food webs; other, more complex communities have many possible paths through which energy could flow. For example, in a small ecosystem with few species of living things, such as a pond, the chain is relatively simple.

Figure 6.7. Biomass Pyramid

The bigger and more diverse the ecosystem, the more complex the food web becomes. Compare the relatively simple pond food web to one seen in a much larger aquatic environment, such as a lake. There are greater numbers and types of species, which creates many more paths for energy to follow.

SAMPLE QUESTIONS

13) **Which of the following groups of organisms are included in the third trophic level?**

A. tertiary consumers

B. secondary consumers

C. decomposers

D. primary consumers

Answers:

A. Incorrect. This is the fourth trophic level.

B. Correct. Secondary consumers make up the third level, after producers and primary consumers.

C. Incorrect. Decomposers do not constitute their own trophic level.

D. Incorrect. This is the second trophic level.

14) **Which of the following organisms generate their own food through photosynthesis and make up the first level of the energy pyramid?**

A. heterotrophs

B. autotrophs

C. producers

D. consumers

Answers:

A. Incorrect. Heterotrophs, which include consumers, are organisms that cannot generate their own food.

B. Incorrect. Producers are autotrophs; however, autotrophs also include organisms that produce food via means other than photosynthesis.

C. Correct. Producers are a kind of autotroph that are found on the energy pyramid and produce food via photosynthesis.

D. Incorrect. Consumers rely on eating organic material produced by other organisms as their source of nutrition.

ECOSYSTEM ECOLOGY

Ecosystem ecology is the discipline within the field of ecology that examines the individual components of an ecosystem and closely examines their interrelationships and interactions. As previously discussed, an ecosystem is composed of both the living community of organisms as well as the abiotic components of the surrounding environments. Ecosystems can be studied on a local scale, examining the dynamics of nutrient cycling or the impact of natural and human-caused disturbances; on a regional scale, studying the flow of material from one ecosystem to another; and on a global scale, understanding how nutrients cycle back into the atmosphere and how disturbances to these cycles can impact ecosystems worldwide. This section will examine the individual components of the cycles of nutrients and the disturbances that affect all ecosystems.

BIOGEOCHEMICAL CYCLES

An ecosystem is as dependent on its abiotic components as it is on its biotic components. Without abiotic resources such as water, carbon, nitrogen, and phosphorus, organisms are unable to undergo the cellular processes that maintain life. A **biogeochemical cycle** is a process in which chemicals essential to life, such as oxygen or carbon, move back and forth between biotic and abiotic pathways. Like all matter, these chemicals cannot be created or destroyed—they simply move back and forth between different components of the ecosystem.

One of the major biogeochemical cycles that impacts all life on Earth is the **hydrologic cycle**, also known as the water cycle. The hydrologic cycle is an example of a **closed system** because the amount of water on Earth does not change. Water can change states or locations, but no new water can be added to the system. Water in its liquid state makes up the vast majority of water on Earth. Approximately 97.5 percent of water on Earth is salt water found in the oceans, with the remaining 2.5 percent existing as freshwater in solid form in polar ice caps (1.7 percent) and in liquid form in groundwater, lakes, and rivers (1.7 percent). A scant 0.001 percent of freshwater is found as vapor in Earth's atmosphere.

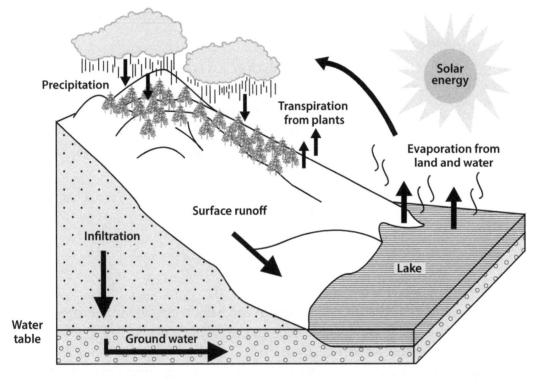

Figure 6.8. Water Cycle

Water moves from one state to another in the hydrologic cycle. Water changes from liquid to gas in one of two major ways. Liquid water on the earth's surface experiences a phase change from liquid to vapor in a process called **evaporation**. Water found in biotic matter, such as plants, also vaporizes and returns to the atmosphere in a process called **transpiration**, in which water moves from plant roots through the stems and transpires out through the leaves in gas form. Together, water vapor from these two sources rises up into the atmosphere, where it undergoes a process called **condensation**. As the vapor rises and meets cooler temperatures in the atmosphere, the molecules undergo a phase change and return to their liquid state in the form of atmospheric clouds. Clouds grow in size and eventually release the liquid water in one of several different forms of **precipitation**. These precipitates, including rain and snow, then return to Earth's surface.

When water reaches the surface, it can take multiple routes. The majority of precipitation falls over the ocean. Some water evaporates back into the atmosphere and begins the cycle anew. Other water seeps into groundwater or flows into rivers, lakes or streams, or remains in the soil. At this stage in the water cycle, the water that is accessible to life will begin following biotic pathways. Water standing in liquid form is consumed by animal life, while in the soil it is absorbed by plant life and other producers which are then eaten by consumers as they work their way through the food web. When organisms die and decompose, the body is broken down into its most basic components, which release the water molecules back into the ecosystem.

Carbon is the most essential element to life; it is an essential component of all the organic molecules that sustain life: proteins, lipids, carbohydrates, and nucleic acid. Similar to water, carbon also moves through abiotic and biotic pathways in the **carbon cycle**. Carbon is located in four distinct **carbon reservoirs**: the atmosphere, the oceans, the land biosphere, and in the earth's sediments and rocks. Carbon exists in different forms in these different reservoirs. In the atmosphere, carbon is found in gas form as carbon dioxide and methane, which only make up approximately 0.04 percent and 0.00017 percent, respectively, of the earth's atmospheric composition. The oceans contain far greater proportions of carbon than are found in the atmosphere, primarily in the form of dissolved carbon dioxide. Within the land biosphere, carbon is found both in living organisms, such as plants, as well as in the soil. The largest amounts of carbon are found in the sedimentary reservoir, which includes **carbonate** rocks, volcanic eruptions, and **fossil fuels**, such as coal or gas, that were formed millions of years ago from the remains of once-living organisms.

Carbon exits the abiotic components of the environment and enters the biotic pathway via plants and other photosynthetic organisms. Carbon dioxide is a required molecule for photosynthesis, and these organisms take in great quantities of the gas and convert it to sugars for food; the sugars are then stored in the plant. This carbon-containing plant matter can be consumed by animals and other consumers, and thus the carbon continues its biotic pathway. As organisms—including both plants and animals—undergo cellular respiration, some of this carbon is converted back into carbon dioxide and released into the atmosphere. The rest of the carbon, stored in organism structures, is only released once the organism dies and is decomposed. Some of this carbon makes its way to the atmosphere; some will eventually join the sedimentary reservoir in the form of fossil fuels. When fossil fuels are burned, carbon dioxide is released back into the atmosphere. It is this influx of carbon dioxide into the atmosphere that is contributing to the intensification of the greenhouse effect.

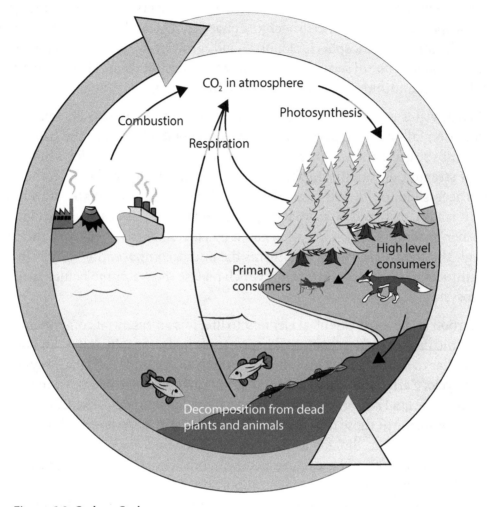

Figure 6.9. Carbon Cycle

Nitrogen is another element essential to life on Earth, playing a key role in the formation of amino acids, chlorophyll, and more. It is found in abundance in the atmosphere—in fact, it makes up 78 percent of the air that organisms breathe. However, organisms cannot access nitrogen in its pure gas form. Therefore, all living things depend on nitrogen that has gone through the **nitrogen fixation process**. In this process, nitrogen-fixing bacteria that live in the oceans and the soil break down nitrogen gas and convert it to ammonia during **ammonification**; ammonia is then converted by bacteria or archaea into usable compounds in a process called **nitrification**. Nitrification results in nitrate, which is then taken up and used by plants through **nitrogen assimilation**. Plants can also directly use ammonia that exists in the form of ammonium ions, which are formed by nitrogen-fixing bacteria in the soil that live in a mutualistic relationship with the plants. This nitrogen stays stored in plant and animal structures until the organisms die and decompose, returning the nitrate to the soil. Nitrate is then converted back into nitrogen gas by **denitrifying** bacteria and released back into the atmosphere.

However, nitrate can also leach from wet soils and enter the water cycle as it is introduced into waterways in the form of runoff.

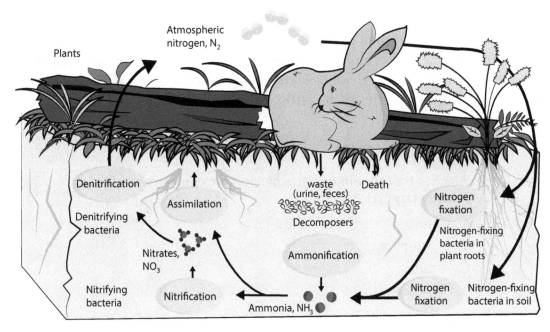

Figure 6.10. Nitrogen Cycle

Phosphorus is a mineral essential for life, providing components of DNA and cell membranes and making up the bulk of human bones and teeth. Unlike the water, carbon, and nitrogen cycles, which are all **gaseous cycles** that include the atmosphere, the **phosphorus cycle** is an example of a **sedimentary cycle**. Phosphorus does not exist within the atmosphere; its abiotic pathway takes place primarily in the earth's minerals and sedimentary rock. Reserves of phosphates found in rocks are released into the soil through **weathering**, as wind or water forces the breakdown of rock into smaller particles over long periods of time.

The phosphorus contained in the rock enters the soil as minerals, often in the form of salts. These salts can then be dissolved into water, enabling them to enter the biotic pathway as plants assimilate the mineral and convert it from inorganic phosphorus to organic phosphorus. Organic phosphorus is consumed and used by animals and other organisms. After organisms die and decompose, phosphorus is released back into the soil and cycles again through the food chain. When it reaches the bottom of the ocean or other body of water, phosphorus can also settle down and become stored in sedimentary rock, at which point it becomes lost to the phosphorus cycle supporting life. For this reason, phosphorus is a limited resource in the ecosystem.

Nitrogen and phosphorus are two nutrients that are added to fertilizers used to increase crop yields in agriculture. Nitrogen is even produced in such great quantities by industrial processes that human life on Earth in its current population could not be sustained without it. However, there are drawbacks to adding concentrated nitrogen and phosphorus to the ecosystem. Excessive nutrients exit agricultural areas via runoff and cause **eutrophication**, a dense growth of vegetative material in bodies of water that depletes oxygen and leads to overcrowding and death among plant and animal species. A sharp increase in nitrogen and phosphorus induces an algal bloom (a rapid growth of photosynthetic organisms in the water). As these blooms die off, the heterotrophic microbes consume the material, causing them to grow quickly and use up the available oxygen in the ecosystem. With less oxygen in the water, bigger animals, such as fish, will begin to die off.

SAMPLE QUESTIONS

15) Which of the following biogeochemical cycles is an example of a sedimentary cycle?

    A.   water

    B.   phosphorus

    C.   carbon

    D.   nitrogen

Answers:

    B.   **Correct.** Phosphorus does not have a gaseous state in the atmosphere and is restricted to sediments in its abiotic pathway. The other three choices are gaseous cycles.

16) Bacteria convert nitrate to nitrogen gas during which of the following processes?

    A.   ammonification

    B.   nitrification

    C.   denitrification

    D.   nitrogen assimilation

Answers:

    A.   Incorrect. During ammonification, nitrogen gas is converted to ammonia.

    B.   Incorrect. During nitrification, ammonia is converted to nitrate.

    C.   **Correct.** Denitrification is the process of converting nitrate to nitrogen gas.

    D.   Incorrect. Nitrogen assimilation is the process by which plants take up and use nitrate.

NATURAL DISTURBANCES

A **disturbance** is an event that disrupts an ecosystem by altering the physical space of an environment changing resource availability. Disturbances can be natural, including both biological disturbances (such as disease) and physical disturbances (such as fire or flooding), or man-made (such as logging or construction).

Disturbances can also be explained in terms of their **temporal** qualities (the time and frequency in which they occur) and their **spatial** qualities (the size and structure of the actual space in the ecosystem in which they occur). The range of these temporal and spatial disturbances varies greatly. The size of the space impacted by the disturbance varies, as well as the frequency of the event and the length of time in which it occurs. Some disturbances are small and frequent, such as the loss of a single tree or other habitat or food source. Others are large and frequent, such as seasonal wildfires in fire-dependent ecosystems like the longleaf pine forest. Other disturbances are much larger in scale and can happen at frequent intervals or at unpredictable times. Some can occur over long periods of geologic time while others cause large changes in a sudden manner. Glacial advances and climate change are examples of the former, causing gradual changes over long periods of time. Volcanic activity and earthquakes due to geologic faults are examples of sudden changes to an ecosystem, causing a tremendous amount of habitat alteration or destruction as well as population mortality in a relatively short period of time. Major disturbances can lead to deforestation or habitat destruction, which leads to population mortality or the relocation of species to different habitats.

Disturbances often lead to the **fragmentation** of a habitat. Fragmentation occurs when natural and anthropogenic disturbances break up a continuous habitat into smaller, isolated fragments of habitat. Fragmentation has several major negative impacts on the health of the ecosystem that is dependent on the habitat. Reduced habitat size leads to less resource availability for members of a population or community, which can lead to more competition and loss of population. Isolation from other reproducing populations of the same species leads to a decline in genetic variation, which can have negative consequences on the population and its ability to adapt to changing conditions.

Reduced space and increased **edge habitat** (disturbed habitat along the boundaries) can have a negative impact on species that require large amounts of space. These phenomena also increase the frequency of **invasive species** (non-native species) that encroach on the habitat and interfere with ecosystem dynamics through increased predation, the introduction of diseases, or the outcompeting of native species.

Ecosystem **recovery**—the speed and ability of an ecosystem to regain population numbers and species diversity after a disturbance—depends on several factors. The first major factor is the frequency of the disturbance. Frequent events, such as seasonal fires or floods, tend to result in a community of organisms that are not only adapted to change, but dependent upon it. For example,

QUICK REVIEW

Are all natural disturbances to an ecosystem detrimental to the overall health and survival of an ecosystem? Why or why not?

the longleaf pine species that dominates longleaf pine ecosystems depends upon seasonal fires as part of its reproductive cycle. The second major factor is the size of the disturbance. Small disturbances create opportunities for new life to develop and, in some cases, start the process of secondary succession—both of which contribute to higher species biodiversity. A third major factor is the size of and distance among fragmented habitats that emerge from the disturbance. Small patches that are close together are more likely to recover quickly, as are larger patches that have plentiful space and resources. A fourth major factor is the scale of the disturbance. If a disturbance is so detrimental that the original community cannot flourish in the new environmental conditions, then secondary succession will begin and a new type of community will emerge in the wake of the disturbance.

SAMPLE QUESTIONS

17) Which of the following is an example of a biological disturbance to a habitat?

   A.   earthquake

   B.   flood

   C.   mining

   D.   disease

Answers:

   A.   Incorrect. An earthquake is a natural, physical disturbance.

   B.   Incorrect. A flood is a natural, physical disturbance.

   C.   Incorrect. Mining is a man-made disturbance.

   D.   **Correct.** Disease is a natural, biological disturbance.

18) Fragmentation is best defined as which of the following?

   A.   the process of change in which a species becomes better fitted to survive in its environment

   B.   the emergence of new species as the result of the genetic isolation of populations

   C.   the gradual change of an environment over time

   D.   the breaking up of continuous habitats into smaller, isolated patches of habitat

Answers:

   A.   Incorrect. This defines adaptation.

   B.   Incorrect. This describes the process of speciation.

   C.   Incorrect. This is a definition of succession.

   D.   **Correct.** Fragmentation occurs when habitats become separated and isolated due to external disturbances.

HUMAN EFFECTS ON ECOSYSTEMS

Like any other species on Earth, humans have relied on resources from the ecosystem for their survival throughout the course of human history. However, as human populations have grown, and the demands on resources and the ability to access and use them has increased, humans have had a disproportionately larger impact on natural resource use throughout the world. Compared to other ecological impacts on a larger geographic time scale, humans have quickly and greatly affected ecological systems and biodiversity. These impacts have occurred through negative actions—such as pollution, habitat destruction, and the introduction of species—as well as through positive actions, such as remediation.

A **pollutant** is an artificial or natural contaminant that has a negative effect on the ecosystem into which it is introduced. As a result, resources in the ecosystem are often unsafe for use or consumption by the populations of species living there. Pollutants can enter the ecosystem in a number of different ways, often in the form of a byproduct. Water and soil ecosystems can become polluted by pesticides or chemical fertilizer runoff from gardens or farms, leaching into the soil or being carried by moving water into river and pond ecosystems. This can have many adverse effects, such as the contamination of drinking water or the contamination of a food chain through the process of **bioaccumulation**, during which an organism intakes the pollutant faster than it loses it through metabolization or excretion.

Air pollution often enters the ecosystem as a byproduct of industrial processes, transportation, and agriculture. Heavy machinery involved in these processes releases gases and particulate matter into the atmosphere, which can impact the chemical composition of the atmosphere itself or interact with other substances to create new pollutants. A primary negative impact of air pollution is the creation of **smog**. When the term *smog* was first coined, it referred to a combination of fog and smoke that created a haze in areas such as coal-burning plants, but the definition has been expanded to include **photochemical smog** that results from a reaction between sunlight, hydrocarbons, and nitrous oxide that creates smog that remains trapped close to the ground.

The temperature of the earth's atmosphere is impacted by the presence of certain gases that trap thermal energy emitted from the earth's surface, which in turn is radiating heat that is absorbed from the sun. This process is known as the **greenhouse effect** and results in atmospheric warming. Any gas in the atmosphere that contributes to the greenhouse effect is known as a **greenhouse gas**. Greenhouse gases include carbon dioxide, methane, and nitrous oxides, among others. Although these gases do occur naturally in the atmosphere, human activities are rapidly and disproportionately increasing the atmosphere's concentration of such greenhouse gases. Greenhouse gases are emitted as byproducts by many different human activities that are powered by fossil fuels, such as electricity, industrial power, transportation, and agriculture. It is estimated that human activities have doubled the natural amount of carbon dioxide—which makes up the largest proportion of greenhouse gases—in the atmosphere. Models produced and used by climate change scientists globally all reveal a pattern of atmospheric warming that occurs as a result of the overconcentration of greenhouse gases, with several predicting an increase in global temperature at the rate of 2 to 4 degrees Celsius by the end of the century. This change is drastic enough to disrupt ecosystems and food production, drastically alter weather patterns, and cause quick, high extremes in temperature in some areas of the globe.

Other greenhouse gases have negative impacts beyond global warming. **Chlorofluorocarbons** (CFCs) are human-produced gases that are composed of a combination of carbon, fluorine, and chlorine. They were originally produced as a refrigerator coolant and aerosol spray. When released into the atmosphere, CFCs break down into their organic components and react with other atmospheric gases. When chlorine interacts with ozone—a UV-absorbing gas found in the stratosphere—the resulting chemical reaction destroys the ozone and converts it to oxygen, which has a damaging impact on the atmosphere's ability to protect life on Earth from the harmful UV radiation caused by solar energy.

Acid precipitation, or acid rain, occurs when air pollutants such as sulfur dioxide and nitrogen oxide mix with water vapor in the Earth's atmosphere and form sulfuric and nitric acids that fall back to the surface through rain, snow, or other forms of precipitation. Acid precipitation most significantly impacts areas with poor soil. The acid added to already-acidic soil results in greater leaching of essential nutrients and reduces the soil's ability to support greater numbers of populations and biodiversity. Acid precipitation also has a negative impact on aquatic ecosystems, altering the chemistry of the water and leading to loss of life and biodiversity.

There are multiple human activities that have led to many different forms of habitat destruction, which has reduced biodiversity as populations of species are displaced or eliminated along with the habitat. **Deforestation** is one such example of habitat destruction. Deforestation is defined as the complete clear-cutting of forest land or similar habitat on a massive scale in order to make room for other land uses, such as **agriculture** or **urban sprawl**. Agriculture accounts for the majority of the human-caused deforestation around the globe, as an increasing human population requires more food resources. Urban sprawl also accounts for large amounts of deforestation or other habitat loss, as humans move from city centers and expand into car-dependent suburban and rural areas, occupying more land space.

There are negative impacts of deforestation beyond the immediate effects of habitat loss for the populations living in the area. The soil degradation and loss that occur as a result of deforestation and agricultural mismanagement of arid land can lead to **desertification**, the creation of new desert space that is inhospitable to many forms of life. With fewer forest habitats, fewer trees and other plants are available to absorb the rising levels of carbon dioxide in the atmosphere, amplifying the effects of global warming. Decreased biodiversity across the globe disrupts ecosystems, with fewer resources available for humans and other organisms. Ecosystems are also more vulnerable to both natural and human-caused disturbances and face greater challenges in recovering from them.

Loss of species biodiversity is also the result of the introduction of non-native species to an area. These species, also known as **introduced species** or exotic species, are brought to new areas either intentionally or accidentally as humans migrate and expand into previously uninhabited areas. Examples of introduced species include new plants brought in as ornamentals, animals for consumption or as pets, and the invertebrates and microorganisms that travel with larger organisms or plant products, such as wood.

Introduced species that have a negative impact on human or ecosystem health are known as **invasive species**. Invasive species are organisms that cause disruptions in the food chain by preying heavily upon native species or outcompeting them for resources, altering the ecosystem and making it unsuitable for the native species. Invasive species can also cause diseases that decimate local populations. They have devastating consequences for both the ecosystem and human interests. For example, the redbay ambrosia beetle—a non-native species that was introduced in the southeastern US—carries a fungus that causes laurel wilt disease, a deadly disease that impacts native redbay trees as well as important agricultural crops, such as avocado trees.

Species can also be introduced by humans with the intent to leave a positive impact upon the ecosystem. One example of this is the idea of **reintroduced species** (the release of once-common species into an ecosystem or species whose overall or local populations are declining). Individuals of the species are sometimes bred in captivity and released into the ecosystem or relocated from other areas in an attempt to restore their former numbers, introduce greater genetic variety, and obtain ecosystem balance.

Reintroducing species is just one example of different human efforts to restore disturbed ecological areas and return them to stability and health. **Remediation** is the process of removing or extracting contaminants from polluted areas, including air, water, and soil. For example, **oil spill remediation** is obtained through the use of technologies, such as booms, which are floating barriers designed to trap and contain water-based oil spills. Skimmers, which are boats designed to remove oil from the water's surface, are also used in oil spill remediation.

Habitat restoration—the restoration of land to usable states—is another example of a human effort to correct human effects on ecosystems. Restoration involves more than just reintroducing species or cleaning up pollutants; it requires the protection and management of a habitat as well. **Reforestation** describes deliberate efforts to plant new trees and other vegetation in forest areas that have been deforested or reduced in size. This requires not only the planting of new seeds or young plants, but also continued management in order to restore the ecosystem to full health. This also occurs in forest land that is continually harvested, allowing the ecosystem to remain intact while still providing resources for future harvesting.

Mine reclamation is an example of habitat restoration that occurs when an area has reached the end of its human use and is restored back to its natural state. Thanks to legislation like the Surface Mining Control and Reclamation Act of 1977, this process is started before a mine is used by humans in order to help mitigate its environmental impacts.

SAMPLE QUESTIONS

19) **Which of the following is NOT a greenhouse gas?**

    A.   methane

    B.   carbon dioxide

    C.   oxygen

    D.   chlorofluorocarbon

    Answers:

    A.   Incorrect. Methane makes up a large proportion of greenhouse gases.

    B.   Incorrect. Carbon dioxide composes the majority of greenhouse gases.

    C.   Correct. Oxygen does not play a role in the greenhouse effect to the extent that other gases do.

    D.   Incorrect. This is a human-produced greenhouse gas.

20) **Which of the following terms refers specifically to the process of removing contaminants from the air, water, and soil?**

    A.   reclamation

    B.   remediation

    C.   restoration

    D.   recalibration

    Answers:

    A.   Incorrect. Reclamation incorporates more than the remediation of contaminants from the environment.

    B.   Correct. Remediation specifically refers to the removal of hazardous chemicals.

    C.   Incorrect. Restoration refers to reestablishing lost habitats and populations of organisms.

    D.   Incorrect. Recalibration refers to instruments of measurement.

CONNECTIONS AMONG ECOSYSTEMS

Within any ecosystem, there is a movement and flow of organisms and materials, like energy and nutrients, from one place to another. Many examples of this movement and flow, such as biogeochemical cycling and energy flow, have already been discussed in great detail. Energy starts with the sun and flows through the food web. Nutrients like phosphorus, carbon, and nitrogen flow from abiotic to biotic sources and back again. This flow of energy and nutrients within a single ecosystem unit is known as **nutrient cycling**.

The movement and flow of materials and organisms takes place not just within ecosystems, but also between ecosystems. This is accomplished organically and by humans transporting materials among ecosystems. Although ecosystems are often studied as individual units, many ecosystems have, in reality, open borders that allow plants, animals, and other components to flow naturally from one place to the next. Natural flow of materials between ecosystems most commonly occurs between similar ecosystems that are located in close proximity to one another. This can be seen as seeds from plants are carried by wind, water, or animals to suitable habitats in nearby ecosystems. Another example is that of a wading bird transporting the small eggs of aquatic organisms within its feathers and depositing them in different bodies of water.

The more similar the different ecosystems are in structure and function, the greater the exchange of materials is likely to be. The less well-defined and distinct an ecosystem is, the greater the chance that its species will gain resource access in other areas.

Humans are also responsible for transporting materials from one location to another, providing an additional layer of ecosystem connection. Humans bring in materials to new environments for their own use. For instance, agricultural activity creates a new series of ecosystem dynamics as different species are introduced: native species are reduced or eliminated, or previously rare species begin to exist in greater numbers. Humans also play a major role in moving abiotic material from one ecosystem to another. Various human activities alter soil composition and chemistry, the availability of water resources, and access to substrate or other structures that serve as species habitats within an ecosystem.

Animal species also physically move themselves from one ecosystem to another in a process called **migration**. Migration falls into one of two major categories: **immigration** (movement *to* a new area) and **emigration** (movement *from* a habitat). Some degree of migration exists among nearly all groups of animal species. Migration occurs for various reasons: to adapt to changing or cyclical resource availability, to find new reproductive partners and increase genetic variation of a population, and to utilize particular resources required during different stages of life. For example, Pacific salmon migrate from the freshwater in which they were hatched to the ocean for much of their adult lives—and then back to their freshwater habitat to spawn. The

HELPFUL HINT

The study of the processes that connect similar ecosystems in the same geographic area is known as **landscape ecology**. In addition to understanding this interconnected nature of ecosystems, this field of study also aims to improve the relationships among ecosystems through ecosystem management.

two habitats provide the different resources the salmon need at the various stages of their life cycle. These animal migrations have a significant impact on the transport and exchange of materials among ecosystems and also spread genetic material and alter competition dynamics between species.

SAMPLE QUESTIONS

21) Which of the following describes the movement of an organism out of its natural habitat?

   A.   emigration

   B.   immigration

   C.   transport

   D.   exchange

   Answer:

   A.   **Correct.** Emigration is a form of migration in which animals leave a habitat.

22) Which of the following terms refers to the flow of all materials within an ecosystem?

   A.   biogeochemical cycling

   B.   nutrient cycling

   C.   food web

   D.   food chain

   Answers:

   A.   Incorrect. *Biogeochemical cycling* refers to the cycling of materials on a local and a global scale.

   B.   **Correct.** *Nutrient cycling* refers to how all biotic and abiotic materials flow in an ecosystem unit.

   C.   Incorrect. A food web is one example of material flow.

   D.   Incorrect. A food chain is an example of material flow.

7

The Nature of Science

Science is simply defined as the study of the natural world. Although there are many disciplines within science, all scientific understanding is reached using a systematic gathering of observations and evidence. The investigations that scientists use to gather this information vary and can be descriptive, comparative, or experimental in nature. Once scientists conduct investigations using a range of methods and technology, they can begin to form explanations about natural phenomena. Over time, these explanations are collected in the general body of scientific knowledge and are used to form laws, or generalizations of the natural world, and theories, or explanations of laws.

Scientific Inquiry

If science is defined as the study of the natural world, then **scientific inquiry** is defined as the myriad ways in which scientists conduct their studies and form explanations. There is no one set path that all scientists must follow in order to conduct scientific inquiry, but observations, hypotheses, variables, controls, drawing conclusions, using sources, and communicating findings all play major roles in the process.

Observations, or the receipt of knowledge of the natural world using senses or technology, are considered the core element of scientific inquiry. Observations can be quantitative or qualitative in nature. **Quantitative observations** are ones which can be measured, such as number, length, mass, or volume. Conversely, **qualitative observations** cannot be measured and are general qualities, such as color, shape, or texture.

Scientists observe the natural world in order to collect data of **natural phenomena**, or any state or process that occurs in nature. These observations are used to propose scientific **explanations** that describe how and why these phenomena occur. A proposed explanation of natural phenomena is also known as a **hypothesis**. Once a testable hypothesis is formed, then a scientific investigation can begin.

HELPFUL HINT

A hypothesis consists of more than an educated guess. Instead, a hypothesis is a testable proposition that scientists can use as the basis for an investigation. If it is not capable of being tested scientifically, it is not a hypothesis.

A scientific investigation contains an **experimental variable** that scientists can manipulate during the course of the investigation, as well as **experimental controls**, which are variables that are kept constant. Both are vital in the course of an investigation. The experimental variable is the element of the hypothesis that is being tested, but if any other variables are altered, then any observed changes that occur cannot be attributed to the experimental variable.

The results that stem from an investigation with experimental and control variables are collectively known as **scientific evidence**. The evidence is then analyzed and used to draw **conclusions** based on whether or not it **supports** or counters the original hypothesis. The conclusions are then communicated to the scientific community. Evidence is not known as scientific **proof**; unlike mathematical proofs, scientific conclusions and evidence are not accepted as final proven knowledge. The nature of science depends on other scientists conducting independent investigations that can further support or counter evidence, which strengthens the body of knowledge in the scientific community.

When communicating scientific **findings**, such as results, conclusions, and suggestions for future research, it is essential to maintain accuracy and clarity. Properly citing sources used over the course of the investigation not only avoids plagiarism by giving proper credit, but also lends validity to findings and provides the scientific community with the tools necessary to build upon the new findings—one of the hallmarks and defining features of the nature of science.

SAMPLE QUESTIONS

1) **Which of the following is NOT an example of a form of scientific investigation?**

   A.   experiments

   B.   observations

   C.   descriptive studies

   D.   comparative studies

   Answers:

   A.   Incorrect. Experiments are a form of scientific investigation.

   B.   **Correct.** Observations are pieces of knowledge that are accumulated throughout the course of a scientific investigation.

C.   Incorrect. Descriptive studies are a form of scientific investigation.

D.   Incorrect. Comparative studies are a form of scientific investigation.

2)   **Which of the following best defines a hypothesis?**

A.   an educated guess

B.   a study of the natural world

C.   an explanation of natural phenomena

D.   a testable proposed scientific explanation

Answers:

A.   Incorrect. Hypotheses are more than simple educated guesses; they must also be testable.

B.   Incorrect. This is the general definition of science.

C.   Incorrect. A hypothesis is a proposed explanation, but not the explanation itself.

D.   Correct. A hypothesis must be testable and propose an explanation of observed natural phenomena.

3)   **Which of the following is NOT a reason to cite sources throughout the investigation process?**

A.   to suggest potential further research

B.   to avoid plagiarism

C.   to lend validity to findings

D.   to provide information to future researchers

Answers:

A.   Correct. Suggestions for further research are found in the body of the scientific communication, not in cited work.

B.   Incorrect. Scientists avoid plagiarism and provide proper credit by correctly citing sources.

C.   Incorrect. Citing sources lends validity by showing readers that the research was done thoroughly and correctly.

D.   Incorrect. Citing sources gives future researchers the ability to track down information sources to aid them in their research endeavors.

INTERDISCIPLINARY SCIENCES

This book primarily covers biology, but it is important to include an understanding of how other disciplines, such as chemistry, mathematics, and physics, contribute to the body of knowledge surrounding the natural world.

Chemistry is the study of matter—or any physical substance that takes up space and has mass. All living things are made up of matter, and all matter is made up of atoms. Atoms make up elements, which are 103 different pure substances each made up of the same type of atom. Living organisms are primarily made of carbon, hydrogen, oxygen, nitrogen, phosphorus, and sulfur. Biochemistry studies exactly how these elements combine into biomolecules, or combinations of atoms in the living body. Biomolecules include carbohydrates, proteins, nucleic acids, and lipids. Molecular biology examines how these molecules control activity at a cellular level. The actions and reactions of these biomolecules at a molecular and cellular level drive system-wide living processes, such as photosynthesis, respiration, and digestion.

Mathematics plays a critical role in all stages of biological study and throughout all different disciplines. Mathematical **models** that simulate natural phenomena and predict their future are a core component of any biological study. Throughout an investigation, quantitative data must be collected that describes natural phenomena. At the conclusion of an investigation, biologists must utilize various methods of mathematical computation in order to analyze and present their data. Descriptive and inferential **statistics** are used to summarize and draw conclusions about data in biological experiments. The field of biology has expanded to include **mathematical biology**, which is rooted in multifaceted mathematical models inspired by complex biological processes, and **theoretical biology**, which develops and uses the data from these complex models to develop theoretical assessments of biological processes, as opposed to observations or experimental results.

Physical biology also plays a vital role in the understanding of natural processes. Physics—the study of matter, energy, and motion—has yielded a multitude of laws that describe consistent generalizations of the natural world. Examples of such laws include the laws of motion, the laws of thermodynamics, and the laws of conservation and symmetry. Living organisms are not exempt from the laws and principles that govern the physical world, and this is evident from the results stemming from the interdisciplinary field of **biophysics**. Biophysicists study physical laws and principles that describe and explain patterns in biological processes from the molecular to the systems level. For example, the first law of thermodynamics—which states that energy cannot be created or destroyed—governs the flow of energy in ecosystems as it moves through producers, consumers, and decomposers. It also governs the flow of energy at the molecular level in the cells of living organisms, as carbohydrate macromolecules convert energy from food sources into energy to maintain the organism.

SAMPLE QUESTIONS

4) **Which of the following describes the difference between mathematical and theoretical biology?**

   A.   Mathematical biology consists of complex models inspired by biology, while theoretical biology consists of complex models that explain biology.

   B.   Mathematical biology is rooted in statistics and probability, while theoretical biology is rooted in experimental results.

   C.   Mathematical biology studies system-wide biological processes, while theoretical biology studies molecular-level biological processes.

   D.   Mathematical biology involves mathematical models, while theoretical biology does not.

   Answers:

   A.   **Correct.** This describes the nuance that exists between these closely related fields.

   B.   Incorrect. Mathematical biology consists of many more fields of mathematical study, and theoretical biology is rooted in developing explanatory theories.

   C.   Incorrect. Both mathematical and theoretical biology are used to model and explain natural phenomena at all biological levels.

   D.   Incorrect. Both mathematical and theoretical biology use complex mathematical models to simulate natural phenomena.

5) **Which of the following correctly describes how the laws of thermodynamics govern energy movement in ecological systems?**

   A.   Energy is created when producers absorb sunlight and undergo photosynthesis.

   B.   Only consumers have to get their energy from a source other than themselves.

   C.   Decomposers destroy energy as they break down organic matter in an ecosystem.

   D.   Energy is transferred when a consumer eats a producer.

   Answers:

   A.   Incorrect. The first law of thermodynamics states that energy cannot be created or destroyed.

   B.   Incorrect. All components of ecological systems—producers, consumers, decomposers—obtain energy from another source in accordance with the first law of thermodynamics.

   C.   Incorrect. The first law of thermodynamics states that energy cannot be created or destroyed.

   D.   **Correct.** Energy being transferred from one organism to another follows the first law of thermodynamics.

FACTS, THEORIES, AND LAWS

Scientific facts, theories, and laws are terms with specific, distinct definitions. **Scientific facts** are objective observations that have been repeatedly confirmed by **data** collected by multiple scientific **investigations**. Facts are generally accepted as truth, but they are never considered final proof. Facts are the observations themselves, rather than the explanations for a natural phenomenon.

Explanations of natural phenomena are the realm of hypotheses and theories. Hypotheses, as earlier defined, are proposed testable explanations of natural phenomena. In order to be testable, a hypothesis must contain specific observations researchers could expect to see if the hypothesis were confirmed. Hypotheses that are tested and confirmed time and time again could eventually accumulate enough data to be considered a **theory**. A theory is a well-founded explanation that is supported by large amounts of data and incorporates multiple sources of evidence. Unlike the everyday definition of theory, which suggests just an idea, a scientific theory is widely accepted as a valid explanation of phenomena.

Scientific **laws**, unlike theories, are not explanations of phenomena but rather a generalized description of natural phenomena based on multiple observations over time. Laws are distinguished from facts by their durability—or ability to stay constant over time—and their predictive nature. If multiple investigations are run under the exact same conditions time and time again, the new observations will conform to the scientific law. If results are not as predicted, then the law can be modified and narrowed to incorporate the new information.

SAMPLE QUESTIONS

6) Which of the following correctly describes a scientific theory?

A.   a proposed explanation for an observation in nature

B.   an explanation for natural phenomena that has not been refuted despite multiple tests

C.   specific observations that have been documented by multiple sources

D.   a conjecture that is based on limited information

Answers:

A.   Incorrect. This is a correct description of a hypothesis.

B.   Correct. Scientific theories are explanatory in nature and are supported by a large accumulation of data in the scientific community.

C.   Incorrect. A theory goes beyond simply cataloging observations; it provides explanations for natural phenomena.

D.   Incorrect. This is an alternate definition of theory that is found in conversational speech but not in science.

7) Which of the following describes why scientific laws are held up over time?

- A. Scientific laws are explanatory.
- B. Scientific laws are objective.
- C. Scientific laws are durable.
- D. Scientific laws are proven.

Answers:

- A. Incorrect. Scientific laws are descriptive, rather than explanatory.
- B. Incorrect. Scientific laws are objective, but this applies to all scientific knowledge and does not make a special contribution to their durability.
- **C. Correct.** Scientific laws are defined by their durability, or ability to stay constant over time even after repeated tests. They may be modified and narrowed, but the core description stays constant.
- D. Incorrect. There is no such thing as a proven fact or law in science; although laws are durable, they are still subject to modification.

HISTORIC SCIENTIFIC MILESTONES

In all disciplines of scientific study, new evidence is discovered regularly. This may be due to new observations or emergent technologies, but it may also occur simply because a scientist is struck by an idea. The nature of science is dynamic—old ideas about how the natural world works are replaced by new ones in time. Many different men and women throughout history have made important contributions to the body of scientific knowledge that consistently challenged what the scientific community understood about the natural world.

CELL THEORY AND GERM THEORY

Cell theory states that all living things are made up of cells: Cell structures carry out the functions required to support life, and cells can only come from other living cells. Cell theory began to develop thanks to the initial contributions of **Robert Hooke**, who used a microscope to identify, describe, and name cells in the 1660s.

Germ theory reached a major turning point in the 1850s due to the work of **Louis Pasteur**. Pasteur discovered that microorganisms, or "germs," were found everywhere and caused both food spoilage and disease. Not only did Pasteur's work revolutionize germ theory, but it also confirmed cell theory by displaying that cells only come from other cells.

HEREDITY, EVOLUTION, AND ECOLOGY

A monk named **Gregor Mendel** pioneered the study of **heredity**—or how genes are passed through generations—in the 1860s. In his experiments, he observed variation in pea plants by cross-breeding the plants for specific traits. His work revealed a pattern that led him to conclude that plants receive one allele from each parent, and one of these alleles will be expressed as a trait. This finding became the basis of the modern study of genetics.

Charles Darwin is credited with laying the foundational work for the theory of **evolution**, or how species change over time. Darwin's observations of species variety provided him with the initial insight to identify the driving forces of evolution: descent with modification and natural selection. Both Darwin's work in evolution and Mendel's contributions to heredity play a major role in the study of **ecology**, or how living things interact with each other and their environment.

> QUICK REVIEW
>
> The study of ecology incorporates many other fields of study. How does our understanding of evolution and genetics impact ecology?

STRUCTURE OF GENETIC MATERIAL

The study of **genetics** closely examines the structure and function of how genetic material embedded in chromosomes is passed from one generation to the next. In 1952, **Alfred Hershey** and **Martha Chase** initially confirmed that **DNA**—deoxyribonucleic acid—comprises genetic material in cells. This work was further confirmed and expanded upon by **James Watson** and **Francis Crick**, whose 1953 investigation revealed that DNA is structured in a double-helix configuration. Watson and Crick's model was based heavily on the work of **Rosalind Franklin**, whose expertise in x-ray crystallography provided necessary data for the double helix model. The double helix model allowed future scientists to discover and understand replication, protein production, mutation, and other functions of genetic material.

CLASSIFICATION OF ORGANISMS

Biological classification is the process of grouping organisms based on their similarities. The practice of systematically classifying organisms is known as **taxonomy**. The modern classification system is based on the hierarchical system developed by **Carl Linnaeus**, which grouped species into seven levels: kingdom, phylum, class, order, family, genus, and species. This system was modified in the twentieth century by **Carl Woese**. Woese's discovery of a previously unknown group of organisms—Archaea—prompted

> HELPFUL HINT
>
> The modern taxonomic order, which incorporates domain, can be memorized using the following mnemonic device: **D**ear **K**ing **P**hillip **C**ame **O**ver **F**or **G**reat **S**paghetti.

him to redraw the taxonomic tree, adding the dimension of "domain" to the top of the taxonomic classification system.

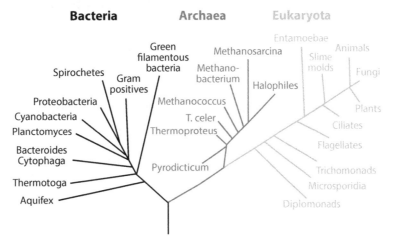

Figure 7.1. Phylogentic Tree with the Three Domains

SAMPLE QUESTIONS

8) **Which of the following is not a major concept of cell theory?**

   A. Cells arise from nonliving material.

   B. Every organism is made up of one or more cells.

   C. Cells arise from living material.

   D. Cell structures and functions support life.

   Answers:

   A. **Correct.** This describes the now-rejected idea of spontaneous generation.

   B. Incorrect. Cell theory states that all living things are made up of cells.

   C. Incorrect. Cell theory states that cells only come from other living cells.

   D. Incorrect. Cell theory states that cells structures carry out the functions required to support life.

9) **Which of the following is a major driving force of evolution that was initially proposed by Charles Darwin?**

   A. change in species over time

   B. the interaction of living things and their environment

   C. organisms receiving at least one allele from each parent for every trait

   D. descent with modification

   Answers:

   A. Incorrect. This is the definition of evolution, as opposed to a driving force.

B. Incorrect. This is the definition of ecology, in which evolution plays a major role.

C. Incorrect. This describes Mendel's conclusion from his experiments in heredity.

D. Correct. Descent with modification is a major principle at the core of the theory of evolution.

10) **Which of the following terms is the study of the passing of genetic information from one generation to the next?**

A. evolution

B. alleles

C. heredity

D. ecology

Answers:

A. Incorrect. Evolution is defined as the change in species over time, due in large part to the passing of genetic material between generations.

B. Incorrect. Alleles are the "factors" identified by Mendel that pass genetic material but are not considered the field of study themselves.

C. Correct. Heredity is the study of how genes are passed through generations.

D. Incorrect. Ecology is the study of how living things interact with each other and their environment.

11) **Which of the following scientists' work made an initial discovery of the components of genetic material, paving the way for further research and understanding of its structure and function?**

A. Hershey and Chase

B. Watson and Crick

C. Mendel and Franklin

D. Watson, Crick, and Franklin

Answers:

A. Correct. Hershey and Chase's initial discovery of the purpose of DNA laid the foundation for the work of Watson, Crick, and Franklin.

B. Incorrect. The work of Watson and Crick, which revealed the double helix nature of DNA, would not have been possible without Hershey and Chase's initial discovery.

C. Incorrect. Mendel and Franklin completed their work in different periods of time; Mendel's discoveries laid the groundwork for Hershey and Chase, while their work in turn laid the groundwork for Franklin.

D. Incorrect. Watson, Crick, and Franklin all based their work on Hershey's and Chase's initial discovery.

12) Which of the following is a model of the structure of genetic material?

   A.   DNA
   B.   double helix
   C.   mutation
   D.   replication

Answers:

   A.   Incorrect. DNA is the molecule that contains genetic material, but the double helix is the structure of DNA.
   B.   Correct. The double helix is a model that shows the configuration of how the components of DNA fit together.
   C.   Incorrect. A mutation is an alteration of DNA.
   D.   Incorrect. Replication is a process that DNA undergoes, not its structure.

13) Which of the following does NOT describe the relationship between the work of Linnaeus and the work of Woese?

   A.   Woese's work rejected the work of Linnaeus.
   B.   Woese's work refined the work of Linnaeus based on new evidence.
   C.   Linnaeus's work laid the foundation for the work of Woese.
   D.   Linnaeus and Woese represent two scientists whose work contributed to the development of classification and taxonomy.

Answers:

   A.   Correct. Woese's work did not disprove or reject the work of Linnaeus; instead, it improved upon it.
   B.   Incorrect. Woese's work incorporated new evidence about the tree of life and used it to refine Linnaeus's work.
   C.   Incorrect. Woese's contributions to taxonomy are rooted in Linnaeus's initial work.
   D.   Incorrect. Both Linnaeus and Woese had significant contributions to the continued development of the science of taxonomy.

MEASUREMENT

The scientific community depends on all scientists to take accurate, error-free **measurements** when both planning and implementing investigations. Collecting accurate **quantitative** data is essential in drawing reliable and valid scientific conclusions. In order to maintain standardization of data across all countries and disciplines, the scientific community universally uses the **SI system**, which is the modern form of the metric system.

PRECISION VERSUS ACCURACY

During an investigation, scientists make measurements multiple times to account for potential errors, and these values must be both precise and accurate. **Precision** refers to how close repeated values are to one another. **Accuracy** refers to how close a measured value is to the true value. Measurements must be both precise and accurate in order to draw sufficient conclusions about data.

METRIC AND SI UNITS

The **metric system** is a decimal measurement system based on a consistent set of **metric units**, indicated by a prefix paired with a base unit. The metric system, which originated in the 1700s, was expanded upon and standardized in 1960 as the International System of Units, or **SI units**. There are seven base SI units: meter (length), kilogram (mass), second (time), ampere (electric current), kelvin (temperature), candela (luminous intensity), and mole (amount of substance). SI units are used consistently across all disciplines in order to coordinate research efforts and reduce communication errors.

Conversion is the process of changing a metric or SI unit into another metric or SI unit by either multiplying or dividing by a power of 10. This power of 10 is known as a **conversion factor** and is indicated by the name of the prefix, as seen below.

Table 7.1. Metric Units and Prefixes

Prefix	Conversion Factor
Kilo	1000
Hecto	100
Deca	10
Deci	1/10
Centi	1/100
Milli	1/1000

The conversion factor is multiplied for converting to a smaller unit and divided for converting to a larger unit. For example, converting 500 grams into kilograms requires dividing 500 by 1000. Converting 500 grams into milligrams requires multiplying by 1000.

SI units are virtually identical to metric units and are measured and converted using the same methods; the major exception is the eliminated use of some outdated metric units, such as calorie (replaced by joule or kilojoule) and gamma (replaced by nanotesla).

Table 7.2. Units and Conversion Factors

Dimension	American	SI
length	inch/foot/yard/mile	meter
mass	ounce/pound/ton	kilogram
volume	cup/pint/quart/gallon	liter
force	pound-force	newton
pressure	pound-force per square inch	pascal
work and energy	cal/British thermal unit	joule
temperature	Fahrenheit	kelvin
charge	faraday	coulomb

UNIT CONVERSIONS

Unit conversion can also occur between SI units and US customary units. These units are commonly used in the United States, but are not accepted for use in the international scientific community. The figure shows the conversion factors between common SI measurements and their US customary unit counterparts.

Table 7.3. Converting between SI and US Customary Units

To Convert From	To	Multiply By
mile	kilometers (km)	1.609344
foot (ft.)	meter (m)	0.3048
inch (in.)	centimeter (cm)	2.54
	millimeter (mm)	25.4
square mile	square kilometer (km^2)	2.589988
square foot	square meter (m^2)	0.09290304
square inch	square centimeter (cm^2)	6.4516
	square millimeter (mm^2)	645.16
gallon	liter (L)	3.785412
quart	liter (L)	0.9463529
pint	liter (L)	0.4731765
fluid ounce	milliliter (mL)	29.57353
pound (lb.)	kilogram (kg)	0.45359237
ounce	gram (g)	28.3495

SCIENTIFIC NOTATION AND SIGNIFICANT FIGURES

Scientific notation is a shorthand method of writing very large or small numbers using a number between 1 and 10, then multiplied by a power of 10. This can be done by moving the decimal from the end to the first non-zero digit. For example: 652,000,000—in scientific notation—is 6.52×10^8, because the decimal is moved over 8 spaces to the 6. The non-zero numbers, the zeros between them, and the final zero in a measurement are known as **significant figures**. These are the numbers that signify accuracy and are read using the measuring devices. Precision in measurements can be identified by how many significant numbers are found within a given measurement: the more significant numbers that are found, the more precise the measurement will be.

LINEAR AND LOGARITHMIC SCALES

Scientific data can be expressed in one of two primary types of scales: a **linear scale** or a **logarithmic scale**. A linear scale shows equal values using equal divisions. Many standard tools of measurement, such as rulers, use linear scales. Linear scales used to explain direct relationships in science, such as waves or mechanical motion. A logarithmic scale is nonlinear, with units written in **orders of magnitude**, or powers of 10. It is used to make **ratio-based** comparisons for large amounts of numbers.

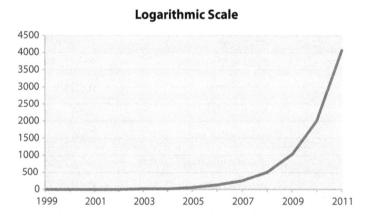

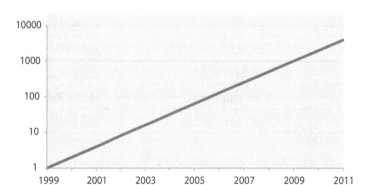

Figure 7.2. Types of Scales

Examples of logarithmic scales used in science include the Richter scale for measuring earthquakes, measurements of entropy, and the decibel unit used to measure sound.

SAMPLE QUESTIONS

14) **Examine the targets below for both precision and accuracy. Which of the following shows accuracy, but not precision?**

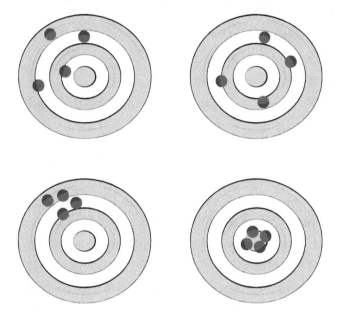

A.   top left

B.   bottom left

C.   top right

D.   bottom right

Answers:

A.   Incorrect. This displays measurements that are neither accurate nor precise.

B.   Incorrect. This displays measurements that are precise, but not accurate.

C.   Correct. This displays measurements that are accurate, but not precise.

D.   Incorrect. This displays measurements that are both accurate and precise.

15) **Which of the following is NOT a base SI unit?**

A.   meter

B.   gram

C.   second

D.   ampere

Answers:

A.   Incorrect. The meter is the base SI unit for length.

B.   Correct. The base SI unit for mass is the kilogram.

C.   Incorrect. The second is the base SI unit for time.

D.   Incorrect. The ampere is the base SI unit for electric current.

16) **Which of the following is NOT a reason why the international scientific community uses SI units?**

A.   to better communicate findings

B.   to create consistency across disciplines

C.   to coordinate research efforts

D.   to provide multiple ways for scientists to record their data

Answers:

A.   Incorrect. Communication is a primary reason why the SI system was standardized and adapted.

B.   Incorrect. Consistency across disciplines is a primary reason why the SI system was standardized and adapted.

C.   Incorrect. Using standardized units limits errors and facilitates the coordination of research efforts globally and across disciplines.

D.   Correct. Using the SI system streamlines the data collecting process, giving scientists one accepted method of recording data.

17) **In order to convert 0.75 liters to milliliters, 0.75 should be multiplied by which of the following numbers?**

A. $\frac{1}{1000}$

B. $\frac{1}{100}$

C.   100

D.   1000

Answers:

A.   Incorrect. Dividing by 1000 will convert the unit to kiloliters.

B.   Incorrect. Dividing by 100 will convert the unit to a hectoliter.

C.   Incorrect. Multiplying by 100 will convert the unit to centiliters.

D.   Correct. Multiplying by 100 will convert the unit to milliliters.

18) **Which of the following numbers represents the correct conversion of 67 pounds into kilograms?**

A.   1,899.45 kg

B.   147.4 kg

C.   30.15 kg

D.   2.345 kg

Answers:

A.   Incorrect. This is the correct answer when converting 67 pounds into grams using a conversion factor of 28.35.

B.   Incorrect. This is the correct answer when converting 67 kilograms into pounds using a conversion factor of 2.2.

C.   Correct. Multiplying by 0.45 will provide the answer of 30.15 kg.

D.   Incorrect. This is the correct answer when converting 67 kilograms into ounces using a conversion factor of 0.035.

19) **Which of the following is the correct scientific notation for 844,000?**

A. 84.4×10^4

B. 84.4×10^5

C. 8.44×10^6

D. 8.44×10^5

Answers:

A.   Incorrect. The decimal is moved to the second significant figure, instead of the first. The power of 10 is also off by one digit.

B.   Incorrect. The decimal is moved to the second significant figure, instead of the first.

C.   Incorrect. The decimal is moved over 5 spots to the first significant figure, not 6 like this answer suggests.

D.   Correct. The decimal is moved over 5 spots to the first significant figure.

20) **Which of the following are the significant figures found in the number 92,830,100?**

A.   9, 2, 8, 3, 0, 1, and the final zero

B.   9, 2, 9, 3, and 1

C.   9, 2, 8, and 3

D.   9, 2, 8, 3, and the final zero

Answers:

A.   Correct. All non-zero digits, the zeros between them, and the final zero are considered significant figures.

B.   Incorrect. This answer omits the zero between 3 and 1 as well as the final zero.

C.   Incorrect. This answer omits the 1 and the zero between 3 and 1 as well as the final zero.

D.   Incorrect. This answer omits the 1 and the zero between 3 and 1.

21) **Linear scales and logarithmic scales have which of the following features in common?**

    A.   Their units are divided equally.

    B.   Their units increase by a magnitude of 10.

    C.   They are used to explain the relationship between data.

    D.   The relationships shown are directly proportional.

Answers:

    A.   Incorrect. This is a feature of a linear scale only.

    B.   Incorrect. This is a feature of a logarithmic scale only.

    C.   Correct. Both linear and logarithmic scales are used to explain relationships; linear are used for more direct relationships with low quantities of data, while logarithmic are used to explain exponential relationships between vast amounts of data.

    D.   Incorrect. This is a feature of a linear scale only.

22) **Which of the following is an example of a linear scale used in science?**

    A.   the Richter scale

    B.   entropy in thermodynamics

    C.   wave propagation

    D.   decibel system

Answers:

    A.   Incorrect. This is an example of a logarithmic scale.

    B.   Incorrect. This is an example of a logarithmic scale.

    C.   Correct. Wave propagation is displayed using a linear scale.

    D.   Incorrect. This is an example of a logarithmic scale.

INTERPRETING DATA

Scientists read and interpret data in different visual forms in order to identify patterns and trends. **Data tables** are used to organize and record measurements and other numerical information, such as time or frequencies. **Graphs** and **charts** are both visual figures that show relationships among variables. Scientists **analyze** the data in these figures to draw conclusions from these trends and make **predictions** about future results. They use **statistics** to further analyze large amounts of data to describe and make inferences about populations.

IDENTIFYING PATTERNS AND TRENDS

Tables, graphs, and charts are all useful in identifying **patterns** of similar or repeated sequences of data and tracking **trends** as the data moves in a general direction over the course of its collection. Accurate data collection is essential in this process in order to correctly identify trends and conduct further analysis.

GRAPHS AND CHARTS

Various types of graphs and charts are used to interpret an assortment of data in different ways. **Line graphs** and **scatter plots** each show relationships between variables. Generally, both graphs record **quantitative data** as individual data points, expressing the **independent variable** on the *x*-axis, and the **dependent variable** on the *y*-axis. Scatter plot points remain unconnected and are used to visually determine trends; line graphs are used to determine larger trends as well as local trends as lines move from point to point.

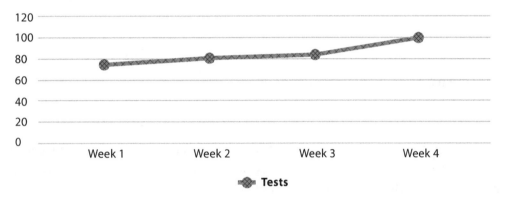

Figure 7.3. Line Graph

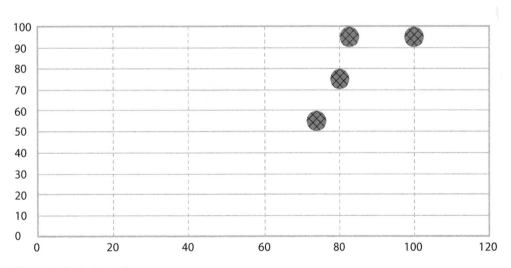

Figure 7.4. Scatter Plot

Bar graphs are best used to compare data that exist in different categories, especially if a set of data is qualitative. **Histograms** are similar in structure to bar graphs but represent data that can be expressed in ranges of numbers, rather than categories.

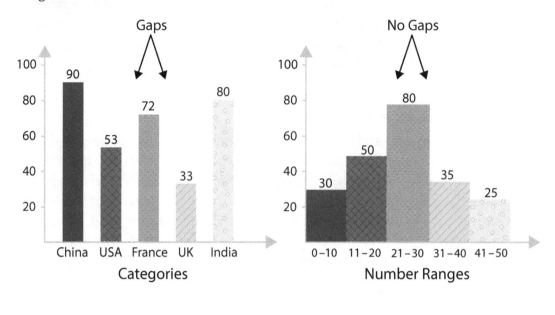

Bar Chart   **Histogram**

Figure 7.5. Bar Chart versus Histogram

Circle graphs—or **pie charts**—can be used to represent data when expressed as a proportion of a whole. These are best used when data needs to be interpreted in comparison with all the other data collected.

TESTS

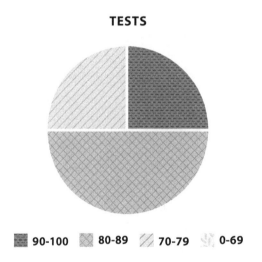

■ 90-100   ▨ 80-89   ▨ 70-79   ░ 0-69

Figure 7.6. Pie Chart

ERROR ANALYSIS

Error can occur in one of two ways in scientific investigations: Systematic errors stem from flaws in the data collection procedures and alter the accuracy of an investigation; random errors are caused by unpredictable changes, such as imprecise measurements, and can limit the precision of an investigation. Both are regular occurrences in investigations and must be accounted for in an **error analysis**. An error analysis calculates the percent error observed in the experiment, which is done by comparing the scientist's results to an established value.

A percent error of less than 10 percent is generally considered acceptable by the scientific community; however this is a general guideline that does not apply to every investigation. Any error should be incorporated into conclusions.

QUICK REVIEW

If an error analysis reveals a percent error of 1.05 percent, what are some ways to account for this in a conclusion?

SAMPLE QUESTIONS

23) **Which of the following is the primary difference between patterns and trends?**

   A. Patterns are only visible in tables; trends are only visible in graphs.

   B. Patterns show repetition of data; trends show the direction in which data moves.

   C. Patterns show data; trends show analysis.

   D. Patterns do not have to be accurate; trends must be accurate.

   Answers:

   A. Incorrect. Both tables and graphs can help scientists determine patterns and trends.

   B. **Correct.** Patterns are the similar data that emerge from a collection, and trends show in which direction this data moves over time.

   C. Incorrect. Data is used to determine patterns and trends; it is up to the scientist to provide an analysis of the patterns and trends observed.

   D. Incorrect. Both patterns and trends rely on accurate data collection in order to be meaningful.

24) **Which of the following types of graphs best shows the quantitative relationship and trends between an independent and dependent variable over time?**

   A. scatter plot

   B. histogram

   C. bar graph

   D. pie chart

Answers:

A.   **Correct.** Scatter plots show trends among quantitative independent and dependent variables.

B.   Incorrect. Histograms show data in ranges of numbers.

C.   Incorrect. Bar graphs show the relationship between categories of individual data, some of which may be qualitative.

D.   Incorrect. Pie charts are best suited for showing data as a percentage compared to the entire data set.

25)   **Which of the following is NOT a difference between a line graph and a bar graph?**

A.   Line graphs use quantitative data; bar graphs can use both quantitative and qualitative data.

B.   The *y*-axis of a bar graph shows scales; the *y*-axis of a line graph shows dependent variables.

C.   The *x*-axis of a bar graph shows independent variables; the *x*-axis of a line graph shows dependent variables.

D.   Line graphs show data points; bar graphs show data categories.

Answers:

A.   Incorrect. Although both may solely use quantitative data, bar graphs can represent qualitative data as well.

B.   Incorrect. This is an accurate description of the respective *y*-axes of bar and line graphs.

C.   **Correct.** The *x*-axis of a bar graph shows categories of data; the *x*-axis of a line graph shows independent variables.

D.   Incorrect. Line graphs show individual points, while bar graphs show numerical categories of data.

26)   **Which of the following types of errors can alter the precision of a scientific investigation?**

A.   procedural flaws

B.   systematic errors

C.   analyzed error

D.   random errors

Answers:

A.   Incorrect. A procedural flaw is a root cause of a systematic error, which can alter the accuracy of an investigation.

B.   Incorrect. Systematic errors impact the accuracy of an investigation, not the precision.

C.   Incorrect. All error is analyzed error; only the random error impacts the precision of an investigation.

D.   **Correct.** Random errors—or unpredictable changes—alter the precision of a measurement or how close measurements are to one another.

SCIENTIFIC MODELS

A model is a description or representation of a natural phenomenon that is used to help explain or understand the phenomenon or process. Different models are selected for different purposes of investigation.

TYPES OF MODELS

Physical models are physical copies of a phenomenon that are built to scale and are used to physically visualize processes and phenomena, such as solar system movement. **Conceptual models** are also used to provide a visual representation of abstract concepts while also describing behavior, such as the fluid mosaic model. Models can also be **mathematical** or **graphical**. Mathematical models are used to describe and predict behavior or phenomena, such as population growth, while graphical models are used in probability and statistics. Graphical models are also used prominently in disciplines such as genetics in order to analyze genetic links.

> **HELPFUL HINT**
>
> Many models are used in the process of simulation, or imitating a natural phenomenon or process. Simulations play a major role in both scientific investigations as well as engineering, which applies information learned from simulations to design real-world technology.

LIMITATIONS OF MODELS

Scientific models are representations of natural phenomena and processes, but cannot be exact replicas. In order to provide simple, useful explanations, scientists must make trade-offs regarding details, approximations, and accuracy of information. All models must be evaluated for their potential **limitations**. For example, the Bohr atomic model is limited by the fact that it is only useful for describing hydrogen atoms. To compensate for model limitations, scientists will often use multiple models in their investigations as well as modify existing models to explain new observations.

SAMPLE QUESTIONS

27) The Bohr model, which is an atomic model that describes the concept of how components of an atom behave, is an example of which of the following types of models?

   A.   physical model

   B.   graphical model

   C.   mathematical model

   D.   conceptual model

Answers:

   A.   Incorrect. Physical models are physical representations; the Bohr model is a conceptual diagram.

   B.   Incorrect. The Bohr model is a conceptual diagram and does not factor in probability or statistics like a graphical model does.

   C.   Incorrect. Mathematical models represent phenomena by using equations, while the Bohr model is a conceptual diagram.

   D.   **Correct.** The Bohr model is an example of a conceptual model that describes and explains the behavior of atoms.

28) Which of the following describes the difference between mathematical and conceptual models?

   A.   Mathematical models represent concepts using equations; conceptual models represent concepts using frameworks and diagrams.

   B.   Mathematical models graphically represent concepts; conceptual models physically represent concepts.

   C.   Conceptual models are a type of mathematical model

   D.   Mathematical concepts are only used in math—heavy disciplines, such as physics; conceptual models are only used in observation—heavy disciplines, like biology.

Answers:

   A.   **Correct.** This is an accurate distinction between mathematical and conceptual models.

   B.   Incorrect. This describes the distinction between graphical and physical models.

   C.   Incorrect. Mathematical models may be used to describe a concept, but conceptual models are not considered a type of mathematical model.

   D.   Incorrect. Both mathematical and conceptual models are used in all scientific disciplines.

29) **Which of the following is NOT an accurate statement about the limitations of scientific models?**

    A.   All scientific models have limitations.

    B.   Models with limitations are discarded in favor of newer, more comprehensive models.

    C.   Scientists use multiple models to account for model limitations.

    D.   Models are evaluated for limitations.

Answers:

    A.   Incorrect. This is an accurate description of scientific models.

    B.   **Correct.** This may happen in some cases, but, in many cases, scientists will modify existing models to account for new observations.

    C.   Incorrect. This is one of several tactics used by scientists to account for model limitations.

    D.   Incorrect. All models must be evaluated for their limitations, as this has an impact on the results of the investigation.

SAFETY AND EMERGENCY PROCEDURES

All scientific investigations taking place in a laboratory should follow standard lab safety and emergency procedures. This includes being aware of all information available, wearing protective gear appropriate to the investigation, and knowing the location and proper use of **lab safety equipment**.

USE OF MATERIAL SAFETY DATA SHEETS

Chemical compounds and solutions used in a laboratory all must come from the manufacturer with a **material safety data sheet**, or **MSDS**. An MSDS contains information on all potential health, fire, reactivity, and environmental hazards; instructions for the proper and safe preparation, use, storage, and handling of the material; and preventative and first aid measures. To ensure **chemical safety** when working in a laboratory, the MSDS for each chemical should be thoroughly read before the investigation begins, and the instructions for preparation, use, storage, and disposal should be followed.

USE OF PERSONAL SAFETY EQUIPMENT

Personal safety equipment in a science laboratory includes **personal protective equipment (PPE)**, or any protective garments and/or equipment that work to minimize hazard exposure and reduce risk of injury or illness. When using PPE, PPE programs need to be implemented that follow OSHA—Occupational Safety and Health Administration—guidelines. A PPE program needs to identify and address potential hazards, identify and select proper PPE for those hazards, train employees or people involved, and maintain and monitor the use of the PPE.

Lab aprons and **lab coats** are designed to protect the clothing from chemical spillage. The material used in these garments depends on the type of chemicals being used. Some materials, such as polyethylene, can be used for non-hazardous chemicals; other materials, such as nitrile, should be used when working with more aggressive or caustic chemicals. This material selection also applies to **gloves**, which are worn to protect the hands from absorbing or being exposed to chemicals through the skin. **Safety goggles**, such as chemical splash or impact goggles, are used to protect the eyes from exposure while offering full field of vision and ventilation.

Use of Laboratory Safety Equipment

Before beginning an investigation, anyone working in a laboratory must be made aware of, learn how to use, and visually inspect lab safety equipment. To prevent potential accidents, it is imperative to use safe **chemical storage** techniques and to avoid taking out or preparing materials that will not be used. It is important to keep a well-stocked **first aid kit** in the lab that meets OSHA requirements. Safety equipment should not be used for any other purposes.

Fire is a common potential hazard in many laboratory investigations. **Fire blankets** should be used to smother and put out grease or electric fires. **Fire extinguishers** should be used to put out other types of fires. Both should be inspected at least once a month to ensure they are not damaged or blocked.

When using glassware, it must be inspected first for damage. Glassware that is chipped cannot be used. If glass chips or breaks, proper **glass disposal** procedures must be followed by placing pieces in an appropriate bag or box as designated by your organization, sealing bag and/or box to cover all seams, and disposing with regular trash. This does not apply if glassware contains hazardous material; MSDS guidelines should be followed for those chemicals.

If skin and/or eyes are exposed to chemicals, the **eye wash station** and/or **emergency shower** should be used immediately in order to decontaminate and flush out the chemical. The affected areas should be flushed out for at least 15 minutes. If necessary, medical attention should be sought right away and MSDS emergency procedures for the chemicals involved must be followed.

SAMPLE QUESTIONS

30) **Which of the following pieces of information is NOT found on a material safety data sheet?**

    A.   reactivity data

    B.   alternative chemicals to use

    C.   hazardous ingredients

    D.   preventative measures

Answers:

A. Incorrect. An MSDS must identify all hazards, including data, on its reactivity.

B. Correct. The MSDS for a chemical is primarily focused on the manufactured chemical, not other compounds or solutions.

C. Incorrect. An MSDS must identify all hazards.

D. Incorrect. An MSDS includes measures to take to prevent safety or emergency situations.

31) **Which of the following correctly describes an effective PPE plan?**

A. identifies hazards, uses nitrile materials for all investigations, monitors the program

B. addresses potential hazards, selects proper PPEs, trains employees, monitors the program, and maintains the equipment

C. selects appropriate PPEs, maintains equipment, does not follow OSHA guidelines

D. addresses potential hazards, only uses PPEs when using caustic chemicals, trains employees, monitors the program

Answers:

A. Incorrect. Nitrile protective materials are not necessary for all investigations.

B. Correct. These are all important steps of a successful PPE program as dictated by OSHA.

C. Incorrect. PPE programs should all follow OSHA guidelines.

D. Incorrect. PPEs should still be used for non-caustic chemicals.

32) **Which of the following is NOT a purpose or function of safety goggles?**

A. protect eyes from chemical exposure

B. offer full field of vision

C. allow particles to pass through

D. provide ventilation

Answers:

A. Incorrect. Safety goggles should protect the eyes and the surrounding skin from exposure to chemicals of all types.

B. Incorrect. Safety goggles should not impair vision.

C. Correct. Protective safety goggles should protect eyes from all exposure, including chemical and physical particle sources.

D. Incorrect. Safety goggles should be safe and comfortable for the wearer to use.

33) **Which of the following describes a situation in which an emergency shower should be used?**

A. to rinse out beakers

B. to put out a grease fire

C. to rinse out eyes that have been exposed to chemicals

D. to flush out an arm that has been exposed to a caustic chemical

Answers:

A. Incorrect. Safety equipment should only be used for its intended purpose.

B. Incorrect. Grease fires should only be put out by fire blankets; safety equipment should only be used for its intended purpose.

C. Incorrect. The eye wash station should be used to flush out eyes.

D. **Correct.** Emergency wash stations should be used to flush out skin that has been exposed to a hazard.

34) **Which of the following is NOT a step included in proper glass disposal procedure for glassware that has not been exposed to hazardous material?**

A. Put out sealed box containing glass with regular trash.

B. Seal bag containing glass.

C. Close all seams of box containing glass.

D. Place small broken glass pieces in regular lab trash bin.

Answers:

A. Incorrect. Once the box is properly sealed, then it can be placed with regular trash.

B. Incorrect. The interior bag containing the glass should be taped or sealed shut.

C. Incorrect. The box containing the sealed bag of broken glass should be shut and have all seams sealed.

D. **Correct.** All broken glass should be initially disposed of in the designated container, not the regular trash.

FIELD AND LABORATORY SAFETY

It is important to follow proper lab safety procedures while conducting investigations in both the field and in the laboratory. This includes appropriate and safe preparation, storage, and use of all chemicals, biological specimens, and waste.

When preparing and using different concentrations of a **solution**, certain safety procedures must be followed. **Molarity** is the measure of a **solute**, or dissolved material found in a solution, and is used to express the **percent concentration** of that solution. Solutions can be **diluted** by adding more **solvent**—the substance in which the solute is dissolved.

Before beginning to create or dilute a solution, a thorough review of the material safety data sheet, or MSDS, must be conducted for each chemical. The concentration and amount of solution needed must then be determined before beginning the process. It is always imperative to wear appropriate gloves, goggles, and apron. Personal hygiene should be maintained at all times. It is important to maintain all equipment and to keep working area clean and free of extra materials. Awareness of all fire safety equipment in the laboratory is essential. To reduce safety hazards, only as much solution as is needed for the experiment or investigation should be prepared; calculations should be scaled down as necessary. Amounts must be measured using only the appropriate tools and then poured over a sink. Graduated cylinders should be used to measure liquids; balances should be used to measure solids. When finished, it is important to store and dispose of materials in accordance with the chemicals' MSDS sheet.

Preparing and using acid and base solutions requires additional safety procedures. Due to the **corrosive** nature of acids, aprons, nitrile rubber gloves and chemical splash goggles should be worn, the area must be properly ventilated, and materials such as eyewash stations and spill control materials must be readily available. When preparing and using, it is important to always add acid to water, and not vice versa. All acids must be stored in a dedicated corrosives cabinet. Bases may be stored in the same space but need to be physically separated from the acids. All prepared and stored solutions must be labeled with acid, concentration, hazard warning, and date prepared. It is necessary to review MSDS before disposal, remembering to always dilute and neutralize acids.

Some solutions may be **flammable** or **caustic**, or able to destroy organic material. These materials should be substituted for less hazardous materials whenever possible to reduce risk. When preparing, it is important to dispense materials carefully from one container at a time, closing tightly when finished. It is also necessary to avoid contaminating the air with dust or fumes, eliminate ignition sources, and maintain good ventilation. Corrosives should always be added slowly to cold water when mixing. When transferring flammable materials, any metal containers must be bonded and grounded. When storing flammable or caustic materials, it is necessary to inspect all containers for defects and ensure the container is made of approved materials and stored in a cool, dry, dedicated cabinet away from other materials. It is imperative to never return materials to their original container and not to reuse empty containers. Containers must be vented

QUICK REVIEW

Look up the OSHA and environmental regulations in your state. What specific disposal requirements does it have for laboratory materials? What do these requirements add to standard procedures?

periodically according to OSHA regulations to avoid rupture. Disposal must be in accordance with MSDS or manufacturer's instructions.

Biological specimens include blood samples, urine samples, organism tissue, and culture specimens. When handling and transporting, it is essential to use pipettes (see below), secondary leak-proof containers, and other safe transporting devices to contain potential **biohazards**. All containers should be inspected for damage prior to and during use. If working with infectious materials, disinfectants should be used when needed, contact lenses should not be worn in the lab, and potentially contaminated protective clothing must be safely removed before leaving. The use of syringes should be avoided when possible. Hazard warning signs must be posted at all entry points into the laboratory. Materials need to be contained according to standard microbiological procedures and appropriate materials for the specific procedure must be used. Materials must be stored in properly maintained biological safety cabinets. When disposing infectious **biological waste**, it must first be inactivated by autoclaving or bleach-treating within 24 hours. Syringes or sharps, including unused ones, must be properly disposed of. All inactivated and non-biological waste as well as sharps are to be placed in appropriate closed, leak-proof biowaste containers and transported out of the lab to area designated by the lab or in accordance with environmental regulations.

SAMPLE QUESTIONS

35) **When disposing of biological waste, you should follow these procedures EXCEPT for which of the following?**

    A.   Inactivate all infectious waste within 24 hours.

    B.   Dispose of all used and unused sharps and syringes.

    C.   Bleach all non-infectious specimens.

    D.   Transport waste from lab in approved leak-proof containers.

Answers:

    A.   Incorrect. All infectious waste must be autoclaved or bleached within 24 hours of use.

    B.   Incorrect. All sharps in the lab must be disposed of properly, even if they were unused.

    C.   **Correct.** Non-infectious waste does not need to be inactivated before disposal.

    D.   Incorrect. All materials must be transported to designated area in a safe container that is approved by OSHA and the organization.

36) **Which of the following extra precautions must take place when handling flammable materials?**

    A.   Store in a separate, designated space away from other materials.

    B.   Be aware of all fire safety equipment that is in laboratory.

    C.   Eliminate all ignition sources.

    D.   Only prepare as much material as is needed.

Answers:

    A.   Incorrect. This is true for both flammable and caustic materials.

    B.   Incorrect. Fire extinguishers and fire blankets should be visible and accessible for all scientific investigations.

    C.   **Correct.** This is specifically required for use of flammable materials.

    D.   Incorrect. This is true for all solutions and chemicals used in scientific investigations.

LABORATORY EQUIPMENT

Although the subject matter and focus of investigations vary widely, there are many common pieces of equipment used across all disciplines. All equipment must be appropriately and safely used and maintained in order to preserve a safe laboratory space and ensure the accuracy, precision, validity, and reliability of the investigations taking place. Before using any equipment, all components must be checked for potential damage and all manufacturer instructions must be read and followed. Equipment and its components should also be used and stored in cool, dry laboratory spaces. If working with potentially hazardous equipment, such as powerful industrial magnets, warning signs need to be posted in the work area. Equipment components should be regularly cleaned, maintained, and replaced according to the manufacturer's instructions.

OPTICAL EQUIPMENT

Optical lab equipment includes any equipment that disperses, concentrates, or redirects light using **lenses**, mirrors, or **prisms**. **Microscopes** and **telescopes** both commonly use an objective lens and eyepiece lens to magnify objects. Microscopes are used to magnify small objects at a short distance, while telescopes are used to magnify large objects from a great distance. Light Amplification by Stimulated Emission of Radiation, or **LASERs**, produce high-energy, narrow beams of concentrated, monochromatic light that can travel great distances and are used in a wide variety of applications, ranging from CD/DVD technology to anti-missile defense. **Spectrometers** are used to measure and record light properties and wave spectrums. Glass or plastic mirrors, prisms, and lenses used in any of these instruments must be cared for appropriately. Dust covers or lens caps should be placed over glass when the equipment is not in use, stored in a cool, dry area, and cleaned at appropriate intervals according to manufacturer instructions.

SEPARATION EQUIPMENT

Separation lab equipment is used to **separate** a mixture into its distinct, separate components. There are several methods commonly used to complete this task. **Mechanical separation** is the separation of components using physical machines. This includes **filtration** via **funnels**, sieves, and other equipment to remove large particles from liquid and a **centrifuge** to separate a mixture by spinning it at high speeds. Centrifuges can be used to separate organelles or to isolate nucleic acid. The individual tubes must be balanced when placing in the equipment to avoid a large force unbalance as it spins at high speeds.

Chemical separation relies on chemically removing compounds through procedures such as **distillation**, which purifies and separates liquids through a heating and cooling process using burners, tubing, and flasks; and **chromatography**, which separates mixtures by allowing a gas or liquid to flow over a material, which causes the various components to separate as they flow at different rates. Chromatography systems typically involve the use of columns, detectors, and pumps.

Magnetic separation occurs when magnetic devices are used to attract and remove magnetic components out of the non-magnetic substance in the mixture. Scientific applications of this technology include magnetic-activated cell sorting (MACS), in which magnetic nanoparticles are used to separate cells based on their surface antigens. This equipment is highly specialized and includes separators and columns.

Separation on the cellular level can also be conducted using **electric separation**. A primary example of this is gel electrophoresis, which uses electrical pulses to separate DNA, RNA, and/or proteins. This process requires the use of a power supply, a series of chambers, and tables, trays, and combs for the gel.

MEASUREMENT, MIXING, AND HEATING EQUIPMENT

Measurement lab equipment includes **meter sticks** to measure lengths in meters, **graduated cylinders** to measure volume, **balances** to measure mass, and **thermometers** to measure temperature in Celsius or Kelvin. All measurement instruments must use **the metric system** and be able to read SI units in accordance with worldwide scientific standards. The **pH** of a substance is measured according to the 14-point pH scale using pH meters, which use probes. These devices should be carefully cleaned and calibrated before use. Precise, traceable **timers**—including decimal stopwatches and clocks—are used to measure and record time elapsed.

Mixing lab equipment includes any of the individual pieces of equipment used to move materials and mix together. **Pipettes** are used to transport precise amounts of liquids from one container to another. Containers include beakers, flasks, and test tubes. **Stirrers** are used to physically mix substances. These can be as simple as glass or plastic rods in small investigational settings, or as advanced as mechanical overhead stirrers, magnetic stirrers, or shakers in order to mix components at high speeds and/or at controlled temperatures.

There are multiple varieties of **heating lab equipment** that are used depending on the type and size of the laboratory investigation. When using any heating device, great care should be taken to remove all flammable materials from the work area. Plastic, closed or narrow-necked containers, such as flasks or reagent bottles, should be avoided. When heating things at very high temperatures, **crucibles**, which are resistant to high temperatures, should be used. Protective clothing should be worn and protective equipment, such as tongs or hot pads, should be used when transporting.

Some heating equipment uses open flames. **Alcohol burners** produce low, open flames at relatively low temperatures. **Bunsen burners** are similar in nature but produce higher, hotter flames. Both are used for heating and sterilizing non-flammable materials. When using any open flame heating equipment, all loose clothing or hair should be secured. Flames should never be leaned over or left unattended. Other heating equipment does not use open flames. This includes **hot plates**, which are used when controlled temperatures are required for heating substances, and **ovens**, which are used to uniformly heat and dry materials.

STERILIZATION EQUIPMENT

Highly specialized **sterilization lab equipment** is used in laboratory settings to sterilize, effectively removing bacteria or any other microorganism that could present a hazard or manipulate the investigation. Quick, small scale sterilization can be completed by wiping materials with appropriate solvents or by heating in ovens or over burners. For larger scale sterilization, and in the case of potential biohazards, industrial **sterilizers** or **autoclaves** can be used. Autoclaves are strong vessels that use high pressure and temperatures, and autoclaving is considered the most reliable form of sterilization. Equipment and materials can be sterilized by placing in a high-pressure autoclave at a sustained temperature of 250 degrees for 15 minutes.

> **HELPFUL HINT**
>
> Autoclave machines have uses other than sterilization. The combination of pressure and heat applied appropriately can also inactivate potential biohazards, vulcanize rubber, and cure composites.

⟶
Go on

SAMPLE QUESTIONS

37) **Which of the following is an example of safe, appropriate use of a piece of optical equipment?**

A. leaving a spectrometer open and accessible for the next use

B. storing spectrometers in a humid storage space

C. cleaning glass lenses but not plastic lenses

D. placing a dust cover over a telescope after use is complete

Answers:

A. Incorrect. Optical equipment should be stored appropriately when not in use.

B. Incorrect. Optical equipment should be stored in a cool, dry place.

C. Incorrect. All lenses—both glass and plastic—must be cleaned at appropriate intervals.

D. **Correct.** Dust covers are an important piece of protective equipment that maintains the safety, cleanliness, and accuracy of the instrument.

38) **Which of the following is NOT an example of an optical equipment component that disperses, concentrates, or redirects light?**

A. eyepiece

B. lens

C. prism

D. mirror

Answers:

A. **Correct.** Eyepieces of microscopes and telescopes contain lenses, but are not the optical components themselves.

B. Incorrect. Lenses are a type of optical material that concentrate or disperse light.

C. Incorrect. Prisms are a type of optical material that alters the pattern light travels.

D. Incorrect. Mirrors are a type of optical material that reflect light.

39) **Columns, pumps, and detectors are examples of primary equipment commonly used for which of the following methods of separation?**

A. electric separation

B. chromatography

C. mechanical separation

D. filtration

Answers:

A. Incorrect. Electric separation also requires a power supply and separation chambers.

B. Correct. This is a basic list of equipment that is required to complete separation using chromatography.

C. Incorrect. Mechanical separation could use these components, but the primary definition of this type of equipment is that it relies on machines.

D. Incorrect. This is not the defining list of equipment for filtration methods, as it does not contain a sieve, mesh, or any filter.

40) **Which of the following methods of separation can be used to separate nucleic components of a cell using electrical impulses?**

A. gel electrophoresis

B. distillation

C. centrifuge

D. filtration

Answers:

A. Correct. Gel electrophoresis can separate DNA and RNA from the rest of a cell.

B. Incorrect. Distillation is used to separate components into liquids or gases.

C. Incorrect. Centrifuges use mechanical spinning to separate components.

D. Incorrect. Filtration is used to separate large components from a mixture.

41) **Which of the following extra care steps should be taken when using pH meters?**

A. Calibrate the probe before use.

B. Remove flammable material from work area.

C. Attend to pH meters constantly, never leaving them unattended.

D. Inspect all parts before use.

Answers:

A. Correct. Due to the sensitive nature of the probe, pH meter probes should be cleaned and calibrated before each use.

B. Incorrect. This is a step necessary when using heating equipment.

C. Incorrect. This is a step necessary when using heating equipment that uses an open flame.

D. Incorrect. This is a step that is taken when using any piece of laboratory equipment.

42) **Which of the following is an acceptable container for use when heating a substance?**

    A.   reagent bottle

    B.   flask

    C.   plastic beaker

    D.   crucible

Answers:

    A.   Incorrect. Reagent bottles have narrow necks. Heating substances in a narrow-necked container could lead to a buildup of pressure in the bottle and potentially cause an explosion.

    B.   Incorrect. Flasks have wide bodies and narrow necks. Heating substances in a narrow-necked container could lead to a buildup of pressure in the bottle and potentially cause an explosion.

    C.   Incorrect. Some plastics can be flammable, and their use should be avoided when heating substances. These should be replaced with a glass container.

    D.   **Correct.** Crucibles are wide-mouthed, open containers that are constructed with materials that are resistant to high temperatures.

43) **Which of the following correctly describes the definition of sterilization?**

    A.   eliminating hazards from equipment

    B.   removing microorganism from a surface

    C.   storing equipment at high pressures and temperatures

    D.   removing all sources of investigation manipulation

Answers:

    A.   Incorrect. Sterilization removes potential biohazards from equipment by removing microorganisms but does not eliminate all potential hazards.

    B.   **Correct.** Sterilization uses solvents and heat to denature and remove microorganisms.

    C.   Incorrect. This process can be used to sterilize but is not the definition of sterilization itself.

    D.   Incorrect. Sterilization removes potentially unintentional biological manipulations from equipment used in an investigation by removing microorganisms, but it does not eliminate sources of potential data manipulation.

8

Technology and Social Perspectives

O ne of the major differences between humans and other animal species is the ability to create and use technology to leave a positive impact on society. This technological drive not only affects the society it was created to serve, but also leaves a mark on the world's environments and natural phenomena. In turn, natural phenomena can influence society in both positive and negative ways—which leads to more technological innovation from humans to either reap the benefits or shield society from further negative harm. This chapter will examine the various relationships between science and technology, the environment and society, and discuss how each one of these forces impacts the other ones.

EFFECTS ON THE ENVIRONMENT

Human activities, such as agriculture, transportation infrastructure, and the development of urban areas can all have a negative impact on the environment. In order to conserve land and natural resources for continued human use and to maintain the ecological biodiversity and health of Earth's environments, humans have devised multiple methods of managing environmental resources. This section explores how science and technology have led to pollution that has a negative impact on the environment. It will also discuss management and mitigation efforts put forth by humans to mitigate damage, manage resources, and conserve and protect wildlife species and shared resources in the natural environment.

POLLUTION

Pollution is the introduction of harmful or poisonous substances, such as chemicals or particulate matter, into the environment. Some pollution on Earth is natural, stemming from events such as volcanic eruptions or fire, but many examples of pollution are caused by human-related science and technological advances.

There are multiple sources of human-caused pollution that impact the Earth's air, water, and land. Burning **fossil fuels**, such as oil and coal, will form byproducts during the combustion process that act as pollutants to the environments on Earth. Harmful gas byproducts of fossil fuel combustion include carbon monoxide, sulfur dioxide, and nitrogen oxide. These gases contribute to smog and rain and can also impact the health of plants and animals that breathe them in during respiration. **Pesticides**—chemicals such as insecticides and herbicides that are used to control invasive plant and animal populations in agricultural areas—are another major source of human-caused pollution. Excess chemicals, which can be either natural or synthetic, enter the waterways from the soil as runoff. Harmful chemicals found in the pesticides accumulate in plants and animals that consume the water, and high levels of pesticide exposure has been linked to birth defects and disease among both wildlife and human populations.

Technology and other human-led efforts are used to lessen the damage caused by pollution. Pollution **mitigation** activities are designed to reduce or offset negative impacts of pollution in the environment. One example of mitigation that uses technology to reduce pollution is **green building**. Green building is sustainable construction that is designed to be energy and water-efficient, have minimal impact on the surrounding area, and utilize sustainable wood, concrete, insulation, and other building materials. **Environmental cleanup** is an example of mitigation that uses technology to offset pollution. Remedial cleanup efforts physically remove contaminants from air, soil, and water using technologies such as incineration, chemical treatment, and air stripping.

HELPFUL HINT

Point source pollution can be directly linked to the place where waste is discharged, such as pipes or drains. Such sources are easily identified and managed. **Nonpoint source pollution** is harder to link to a specific output. These pollutants enter the environment over a wide area, often through runoff into waterways. Examples include lawn fertilizers, pesticides, urban storm drain water, and sediment from erosion-prone environments.

SAMPLE QUESTION

1) Fertilizers leaching from multiple suburban lawns and entering the waterway through runoff is an example of which of the following types of pollution?

   A.   point source pollution

   B.   pesticide pollution

   C.   byproduct pollution

   D.   nonpoint source pollution

   Answers:

   A.   Incorrect. Point source pollution originates from a single location, such as a drain.

B.   Incorrect. Fertilizers are not examples of pesticides.

C.   Incorrect. Byproduct pollution is not a recognized classification of pollution.

D.   Correct. Nonpoint source pollution enters the environment over a wide area, such as a series of lawns.

RESOURCE MANAGEMENT

Science and technological advances can manage environmental resources as well as the impact of human influences on the environment. Environmental and natural **resource management** strives to protect natural resources such as land, water, and wildlife for continued use by humans. The goal of many environmental resource management programs is to use Earth's natural resources in a sustainable and efficient manner. For sustainability, the use of natural resources must be able to continue indefinitely; for efficiency, natural resource use must result in minimal waste or pollution.

No matter how efficiently a natural resource is used by humans, there will always be some amount of waste produced as a byproduct. **Waste management** is the process of handling garbage, sewage, and other various waste products. The management process includes collecting waste as it is produced, transporting the waste to proper areas, and safely treating or disposing of it according to human health and environmental regulations. The process of recovering waste and converting to new products for additional reuse is known as **recycling**. The goal of recycling is to reduce overall waste and the consumption of fresh natural resources while also reducing the creation of harmful byproducts, such as pollution or greenhouse gas emissions that come from processing new materials.

SAMPLE QUESTION

2)   **Which of the following is the goal of natural resource management?**

A.   to transport waste to proper areas

B.   to use natural resources sustainably and efficiently

C.   to offset impacts of pollution

D.   to process fresh natural resources for human consumption

Answers:

A.   Incorrect. This is one of the goals of waste management.

B.   Correct. This is the primary goal of natural resource management.

C.   Incorrect. This is the primary goal of pollution mitigation.

D.   Incorrect. Resource management seeks to minimize the processing of new materials.

CONSERVATION

The act of saving or protecting natural resources, environments, and ecological communities is known as **conservation**. Conservation is achieved through several different management methods that use science to inform decision-making and technology to implement changes. Habitat conservation is a practice that conserves natural environments through both **habitat preservation** (the preservation of existing natural habitats) and **habitat restoration** (the act of returning a human-influenced habitat to its former state). Both habitat protection and restoration plans require a deep understanding of the ecological balance of the habitat in order for the plans to be successful. Habitat restoration also requires the use of technology to make physical changes to restore the environment. This includes altering the soil content to its former richness by adding fertilizers, using controlled fires and floods to bring fire- and flood-dependent ecosystems back into balance, and the removal of silt and other obstructions from areas that have seen a lot of erosion or other damage.

Multiple state, national, and international laws and agreements are in place to achieve **species protection** for wildlife that is in danger of extinction. Acts, such as the Migratory Bird Treaty Act of 1918, the Endangered Species Act of 1973, and the Convention on International Trade in Endangered Species of Wild Fauna and Flora (CITES), promote species protection through identifying and labeling animals threatened with extinction. These acts are also designed to protect the habitats in which these species live in the wild, and they place restrictions on the use or trade of protected species. Much like habitat conservation plans, in order to offer proper protection, species protection plans rely heavily on scientific understandings of a species' biology, niche, and relationship with the environment. For example, to provide proper protection for the bald eagle, which was once classified as an endangered species, management plans had to account for the protection of bald eagle habitats and food sources in order to support species growth.

SAMPLE QUESTION

3) Which of the following is the act of returning a habitat to its former state?

   A. preservation

   B. conservation

   C. restoration

   D. management

Answers:

   A. Incorrect. Preservation is the act of setting aside a habitat and restricting it from human use.

   B. Incorrect. Conservation is the overall act of protecting species and habitats while humans are using them and includes, but is not limited to, restoration.

C.   **Correct.** Habitat restoration is the physical act of restoring a habitat to its natural, non-human-influenced state.

D.   Incorrect. Restoration is one of many steps that can be taken when managing an environment.

EFFECTS ON SOCIETY

Human activity and natural phenomena can have large scale impacts on society, on both an economic scale and a socio-cultural scale. Humans use scientific knowledge and technological advances to satisfy their needs, such as food and water, and their wants, such as consumer products. The use of land and natural resources to accomplish these goals drives economic growth and impacts the environment while also satisfying societal needs. Similarly, natural phenomena—such as weather-related processes, disasters, and disease—can hamper the economic growth and societal needs of people. Such phenomena also require humans to develop scientific understanding and use technology to reduce their impact on society. This section examines specific impacts of humans on the environment and vice versa, as well as the technological tools used by humans in response.

DISASTER MANAGEMENT

Disaster management is the organization and control of the people and resources that deal directly with the preparation, response, and recovery efforts in order to minimize the humanitarian impact of disasters. Disasters are events that cause major disruption within a community and lead to human, environmental, and economic losses. Many disasters are classified as natural hazards, such as earthquakes or hurricanes, but can also include man-made disasters, such as oil or chemical spills, that cause major losses and requires the assistance of outside sources.

Science and technology play major roles in disaster management during the preparation stage. Weather forecasting tools, such as radars, surveillance aircraft, and satellite data, reveal changing weather patterns and give local governments ample time to respond to potential natural hazards. Likewise, seismic surveillance networks are used in earthquake-vulnerable areas to quickly determine the location and intensity of earthquakes and issue tsunami warnings for certain areas. The internet and mobile telephone technology has increased the speed of disaster warnings and information.

> **HELPFUL HINT**
>
> The internet and mobile technology allow the public the ability to assist with relief efforts, whether intentionally or unintentionally. Relief personnel are increasingly calling on the public to provide data on GEOINT systems or to check on social media to help them determine which areas need assistance first.

The response effort is also improved through the application of modern technology. **Hurricane relief** efforts, for example, are made more directed and efficient thanks to geospatial intelligence (GEOINT), which provides real-time maps of disaster-hit areas and gives hurricane relief personnel critical information about which areas need assistance first.

Post-disaster clean ups can be dangerous due to increased amounts of potentially harmful particles and substances, such as mold, bacteria, and chemicals. Technological tools are used to make the cleanup efforts faster, safer, and more efficient. Examples of tools helpful in **hurricane cleanup** include water pumps (to quickly move water) and dehumidifiers (to dry out areas and prevent mold from forming). **Oil spill cleanup** tools include physical barriers, such as booms. These help contain the oil and prevent the spread of dispersants, which are chemicals that are sprayed to move oil down the water column and minimize the impact of oil at the water's surface.

SAMPLE QUESTION

4) Which of the following is a physical barrier used to contain oil during a spill?

A. boom

B. dispersant

C. pump

D. levee

Answers:

A. **Correct.** A boom is a floating barrier that is deployed to temporarily contain oil spills from spreading.

B. Incorrect. Dispersants distribute oil throughout the water column to minimize its surface impact.

C. Incorrect. Pumps are used to remove substances.

D. Incorrect. Levees are banks that are designed to prevent flooding along waterways and coasts.

GLOBAL WARMING

Increased concentrations of greenhouse gases, such as carbon dioxide and methane, are being continually emitted into the atmosphere through human activity. These gases contribute to the greenhouse effect, trapping heat energy radiating from the Earth's surface. The rapid increase of greenhouse gases has caused the global temperature to rise at a rate of 2 degrees a year in a process called **global warming**. **Climate change** is a term that is often used interchangeably with global warming but actually refers to any long-term shift in the earth's climate, such as changes in precipitation, wind, and variations in temperature. Alterations to the climate—

long-term atmospheric conditions—lead to changes and volatility in weather, which are the day-to-day conditions of the atmosphere. As such, climate change has led to higher numbers of storms, droughts, floods, and other weather-related disasters.

Rising **sea levels** are a direct consequence of climate change. One of the factors leading to this is **thermal expansion**. Water expands as it warms up, which leads to the same amount of water taking up more volume on the earth's surface. Rising temperatures have also led to loss of ice in glaciers and polar regions, which hold approximately 70 percent of the earth's freshwater in their frozen state. Higher temperatures have led to greater melting in these regions, and changes to seasonal precipitation patterns have led to smaller amounts of snowfall. Warmer seawater also moves below the ice sheets at the poles and increases the pace at which these melt and break off into the sea. All of these factors contribute to rising sea levels, which have risen 4 inches during the last century at an increasingly accelerated rate and are estimated to rise several more feet by the end of this century. Higher sea levels lead to devastating effects on coastal and low-lying areas, causing damage to life, property, and natural habitats.

SAMPLE QUESTION

5) **Which of the following terms describes the long-term changes in atmospheric conditions on Earth, including temperature, wind, and precipitation?**

    A.   greenhouse effect

    B.   global warming

    C.   weather pattern

    D.   climate change

Answers:

    A.   Incorrect. The greenhouse effect is the tendency for atmospheric gases to trap thermal energy rising from Earth's surface.

    B.   Incorrect. Global warming is one of multiple types of climate change.

    C.   Incorrect. Shifts in weather patterns can arise from climate change, but here the term *weather* describes short-term changes.

    D.   **Correct.** Climate change is the alteration of Earth's atmospheric conditions over long periods of time.

EPIDEMIOLOGY

Epidemiology is the study of the causes, effects, and control of diseases and other health-related issues. This branch of medicine pays particular attention to the incidences and prevalence of infectious diseases in areas of large populations, determining the source of disease epidemics that are rapidly spread across the population in a given period of time. Examples of major diseases that spread rapidly through populations are **malaria**, a blood disease transmitted by parasites in infected mosquitoes; **influenza**, a seasonal respiratory viral infection; and **Ebola**, a deadly viral infection spread through direct contact.

Epidemiology is the branch of science that informs policy decisions regarding **public health**, which is the practice of protecting the health of people in their communities. Public health agencies, such as the Centers for Disease Control (CDC), determine and implement effective prevention and control strategies, such as vaccinations, antibiotics and antiviral medications. Such agencies also educate the public about risk factors for disease and recommend policies to promote health, like tobacco control or influenza vaccination plans.

SAMPLE QUESTION

6) Which of the following is the practice of protecting the health of people in their communities?

    A.   public health

    B.   medicine

    C.   epidemiology

    D.   disease control

Answers:

    A.   **Correct.** Public health promotes the health of entire populations by using research from epidemiology and medicine to inform decisions and initiatives.

    B.   Incorrect. Medicine is one of the many branches of science that inform public health decisions.

    C.   Incorrect. Epidemiology is the study of the causes, effects, and control of diseases.

    D.   Incorrect. Disease control is one of the many goals of public health initiatives.

AGRICULTURE AND SOIL EROSION

Erosion is the process of land, rock, or soil being worn away by Earth's forces—such as wind and water—over time. Erosion is a natural process that occurs continually and on every land surface on Earth. However, human agricultural activities, such as **tillage** (the plowing and preparation of soil for agricultural use) and the **overgrazing** of vegetation by agricultural animals, act as additional agents of erosion and either speed up the process or cause erosion to occur at faster rates. Tillage and overgrazing both reduce the amount of **vegetative cover** on the land. Vegetation protects soil from erosion by acting as a shield against water and wind; the less vegetation found in the soil, the higher the rates of erosion will be. Agricultural methods, such as **crop rotation** (the cultivation of different crops in different seasons on the same field), or **conservation tillage** (which leaves the residue of previous crops on the land before the next growing season), ensure vegetation will be present to reduce erosion year-round.

When soil erosion occurs at an accelerated rate, the negative impacts on soil quality can be severe. The first layer of soil to be stripped away by wind and water forces is the rich layer of **topsoil** located closest to the surface. The loss of this soil is detrimental to the agricultural operation, as it contains high concentrations of organic matter and nutrients. When water exits agricultural land that has little vegetative cover, it carries off eroded soil particles as **sediment**. This sediment-laden water either drains back into the ground or flows downhill as **runoff**, carrying excess sediment into streams and lakes and potentially degrading the water quality of those bodies of water by introducing materials such as silt, excess nutrients, pesticides, and agricultural waste.

SAMPLE QUESTION

7) **Which of the following is NOT an agent of erosion?**

A. wind

B. runoff

C. tillage

D. water

Answers:

A. Incorrect. Wind forces wear down land over time.

B. Correct. Runoff is the water that carries away sediment after erosion takes place.

C. Incorrect. Tillage reduces vegetative cover, which increases erosion rates.

D. Incorrect. Water forces wear down land over time.

ESTUARY AND WETLAND DEGRADATION

Wetlands, which include marshes, bogs, and swamps, are any land mass that is covered with water either part or all of the time. In coastal areas, wetlands are frequently found around the edges of **estuaries**—areas where rivers empty out into the sea. Wetlands are very productive ecosystems due to their fertile soil and constantly moving water, which leads to biological diversity and a suitable habitat for aquatic animals to spawn and for migrating animals to stop and feed. Extensive **buffer zones** of vegetation around their borders also provide critical habitat for many terrestrial species and help protect wetland areas from erosion. Wetlands serve as natural filters since the soil traps pollution and sediment as they flow through the area. Wetlands also play a vital role in **flood protection**, storing influxes of water during storm events or tidal surges.

Human activities, such as wetland draining, the dredging of boat and shipping channels, the construction of levees, and stream diversion have all led to the degradation of both estuaries and wetlands. These activities alter the water flow, add increased sediment to wetland areas, and lead to decreased soil fertility, loss of biological diversity, and overall degradation of ecosystems. This results in decreased water quality and flood protection, which have a negative impact on human life and property. Conservation efforts to restore both wetland and estuary habitats include protecting land, mitigation projects to restore ecosystem help, and curbing further human development through laws and regulations.

SAMPLE QUESTION

8) Wetland degradation can lead directly to which of the following negative impacts on human life and property?

   A.   decreased agricultural production

   B.   increased wildlife diversity

   C.   decreased water pollution

   D.   increased potential for flooding

   Answers:

   A.   Incorrect. This could be an indirect impact but is not a direct impact.

   B.   Incorrect. Wildlife diversity decreases with wetland degradation.

   C.   Incorrect. The potential for water pollution increases with wetland degradation.

   D.   Correct. Wetlands play a major role in flood protection.

WATER MANAGEMENT

Water management is the act of planning for water storage and use, distributing water in a fair and efficient manner, and conserving water resources for human purposes. Water resources are obtained from surface water, such as rivers or irrigation ditches, groundwater, and locally collected rainwater. Nearly 70 percent of the world's water usage is reserved for agriculture, which primarily uses water for crop irrigation. Another 20 percent is used for industrial purposes, primarily during the production process, and the remaining 10 percent is used in domestic settings for activities such as drinking, bathing, and cleaning.

Water management does not only involve planning and allocating water resources in an appropriate and efficient manner, but it also incorporates **water treatment** techniques to enhance water quality and make it useable for its intended purpose. This includes using chlorination to prevent biological growths in the water, filtration to remove suspended particles in the water, and disinfection to remove pathogens.

Water that has been used by humans for any agricultural, industrial, or domestic use is known as **wastewater**. Wastewater that is not lost as runoff or evaporation can be collected as **sewage** and treated at wastewater treatment plants. Here, water undergoes mechanical, biological, and chemical treatments and is reused for a wide variety of agricultural, industrial, and domestic purposes.

SAMPLE QUESTION

9) **Which of the following is NOT an example of a water treatment technique?**

    A.   extraction

    B.   filtration

    C.   chlorination

    D.   disinfection

Answers:

    A.   **Correct.** Extraction is not the name of any of the major water treatment techniques.

    B.   Incorrect. Filtration is one of the stages of water treatment.

    C.   Incorrect. Chlorination is an early stage of water treatment.

    D.   Incorrect. Disinfection is one of the last stages of water treatment.

CONSUMER PRODUCTS

Consumer products are any material goods that are produced and purchased by a person for private (nonbusiness-related) use. Whether they are made of wood, glass, metal, or other materials, all consumer products undergo a similar **product life cycle**. Commodities known as **raw materials** are the substances that are used in the production and manufacturing stage of products; the term refers to substances in their unprocessed state, such as crude oil or lumber. These raw materials are processed into usable materials such as **plastics**, which are synthetic, moldable materials that are derived from chemicals found in petroleum. Finished products are distributed to stores, products are used by consumers; then products are disposed either through recycling or into **landfills.**

Each stage of this cycle is accompanied by some form of environmental impact. Obtaining raw materials requires removing resources from the environment, such as harvesting a forest, extracting oil from the ground, or collecting sand for glassmaking. The processing stage usually occurs in industrial plants, which require the use of energy and water, the use of chemicals, such as resins or dyes, and the release of byproducts

QUICK REVIEW

Bacteria, fungi, and other decomposers do not break down petroleum-based plastics like they break down other materials, such as wood or biomass-based products. Why? What problems does this pose for the environment?

into the surrounding environment. Product distribution requires the heavy use of fossil fuels as products are transported worldwide. After use, products are either recycled, which requires energy; disposed into landfills, which, while often well maintained, can lead to groundwater contamination or methane production; or discarded as litter, which can cause problems for wildlife and environmental health at a local level.

SAMPLE QUESTION

10) Which of the following is NOT an example of a raw material used in a consumer product?

    A.   lumber

    B.   plastic

    C.   cotton

    D.   metal

Answers:

    A.   Incorrect. Lumber is the raw material processed to make several wood and paper products.

    B.   **Correct.** Plastic is made from the raw material of petroleum.

    C.   Incorrect. Cotton is a raw material that is processed to create material for several products.

    D.   Incorrect. Metals are extracted from the earth and further processed to make consumer products.

MANAGEMENT OF NATURAL RESOURCES

Humans rely heavily on natural resources in nearly all aspects of everyday life. From the oil that is converted to gasoline to power most modes of transportation, to the wood pulp used to make the paper of this book, and the copper found in the inner parts of cell phones. Natural resources also include the food products obtained through agriculture as well as resources used for recreation, such as woods for hiking and wildlife hunted as game. To ensure these resources are profitable and usable for a long period of time without degrading the environment or wildlife species, many organizations and government entities work toward managing natural resources for the greater good of both the environment and human society.

HABITAT PRESERVATION

Habitat preservation is distinct from habitat conservation. While the goal of habitat conservation is to promote sustainable use and management of natural resources and habitats for continued human use, the goal of preservation is to maintain habitats in their natural, unaltered state without further human influence.

Public policy plays a major role in efforts to preserve habitats. Habitat preservation is often achieved through restricting or eliminating human development in natural areas through the establishment of public lands, such as national forests, national wildlife refuges, and **national parks**. The **Endangered Species Act of 1973** authorizes the acquisition of land by the federal government in order to protect critical habitat areas of species included on the list. Preservation can also be achieved on privately-owned land through incentives, such as conservation easements, which are voluntary agreements between the government and landowners that prevent future land development. The **National Environmental Policy Act (NEPA)** requires federal, state, and local government agencies to undertake environmental impact studies before implementing any new project, which helps ensure that new roads, bridges, buildings, and other human activities are balanced with the goals of habitat preservation and conservation.

SAMPLE QUESTION

11) **Which of the following describes the distinction between preservation and conservation?**

   A. Preservation applies to species; conservation applies to habitats.

   B. Preservation promotes the use of renewable resources; conservation promotes the reduction of human consumption.

   C. Preservation uses reclamation to restore habitats; conservation leaves habitats to self-restore.

   D. Preservation maintains habitats in an unaltered state; conservation promotes sustainable human use of natural resources.

Answers:

   A. Incorrect. Both preservation and conservation apply to all biotic and abiotic factors in an environment, including both species and habitats.

   B. Incorrect. Renewable resources and reduction of consumption are both important concepts behind conservation.

   C. Incorrect. Habitat restoration is an important part of both preservation and conservation.

   D. **Correct.** Conservation is tied to the human use of resources, while preservation aims to leave habitats out of the reach of human use.

EXTRACTION OF RESOURCES

Much of the mineral and energy resources that humans depend on are extracted from the earth. Mineral resources, which include iron, aluminum, and copper, are usually extracted from mineral-dense areas known as **mineral deposits** found in the ground. Similarly, energy resources, such as oil and coal are found in **reserves** below the earth's surface. These resources are commodities that generally benefit human life, society, and technology. Mineral and energy extraction also have significant economic impacts in modern civilization, providing jobs for many individuals across the globe and making up a large portion of the gross domestic product of many countries.

There are several different technologies used to extract both mineral and energy resources from the earth. **Mining** is the process of extracting minerals and other resources. Mines are created by drilling holes into the rock or other surface covering the deposit, then using explosives in the holes to break the rock apart and extract the minerals, coal, or other resources. There are several major environmental impacts associated with mining. Breaking apart rocks can expose dust particles and carcinogens to the atmosphere, extraction can displace local wildlife, and runoff from the site can contaminate local waterways.

A form of mining that extracts resources, such as oil or gas, from deeper within the earth's surface is known as **drilling**. During this process, a hole is bored into a resource reserve and is extracted through a series of pipes by using a pump. Environmental impacts of drilling include increased erosion damage, wildlife habitat at the surface, increased air and noise pollution around the well site, and contamination of soil and water resources due to oil spills and splashes.

As the demand for non-renewable oil resources increases, humans have begun to extract resources from deeper in the earth's surface through a process called hydraulic fracturing, or **fracking**. Fracking is the process of injecting high-pressure liquid deep within the earth's surface to break apart rock and extract oil or gas. Fracking is a controversial process due to its environmental and health impacts. Like mining and drilling, fracking can lead to increased water contamination, air pollution, and exposure to toxic chemicals and carcinogens; it also has the added risk of altering seismic activity and inducing earthquakes.

SAMPLE QUESTION

12) **Which of the following forms of natural resource removal from the earth causes an increased frequency of earthquake activity?**

  A. mining
  B. extracting
  C. fracking
  D. injecting

Answers:

  A. Incorrect. Mining is generally not correlated with seismic activity to the same degree that fracking is.
  B. Incorrect. Extracting refers to all forms of resource removal from the earth.
  C. **Correct.** Fracking, which breaks apart rock at subterranean levels, has been known to cause increases in seismic activity at the site.

D.   Incorrect. Injection is a part of the fracking process but is not a form of extraction.

MANAGING AGRICULTURE AND WILDLIFE

Land and water environments that provide essential food sources and other natural resources must be carefully managed by people to ensure long-term sustainability of the resources. Scientists, technicians, and managers are employed in the agriculture, forestry, wildlife, and fisheries industries to accomplish this goal. For each of these industries, professionals must maintain a delicate balance between the needs of the people and the needs of the environment. Sustainable techniques used across these industries can help maximize production while also protecting environmental health and providing economic incentives to all involved.

Sustainable **agriculture management** involves utilizing various techniques to control invasive plant and animal pests, reduce or eliminate disease, and increase soil quality while minimizing erosion. Sustainable management techniques include covering crops during the growing off-seasons and using biological pest management practices, such as incorporating natural pest predators instead of resorting to the use of chemical pesticides.

Sustainable **forestry** requires a carefully controlled system of replacing harvested trees with seedlings that will eventually grow into mature trees for harvesting. This system allows for maximum productivity without sacrificing long-term renewability of resources and business growth. Many sectors of society benefit from sustainable forest management; local residents gain employment opportunities, and tourists enjoy recreational activities in the area.

Overfishing and unsustainable fishing practices have led to steep declines in the numbers and diversity of fish and other water-based wildlife. Sustainable **fisheries management** involves using techniques such as fishing quotas, establishing protected areas, cycling between different species of fish, and curbing illegal fishing practices.

Wildlife management aims to protect ecosystem balance while still accommodating human use of lands and wildlife. This includes the management of game species and hunting seasons, the control of invasive species that cause damage to both ecosystems and human development, and the preservation and restoration of habitats to achieve wildlife conservation.

Go on →

SAMPLE QUESTION

13) Which of the following is NOT an example of a shared goal of sustainable agricultural, forestry, wildlife, and fisheries management?

A. decreasing profits

B. encouraging production

C. economic incentives

D. protecting environmental health

Answers:

A. **Correct.** Sustainable practices balance economic profits with resource renewability and longevity for maximum gain over time.

B. Incorrect. The production of natural resource commodities is a shared goal.

C. Incorrect. Providing economic incentives for all people involved in the management process is a shared goal.

D. Incorrect. Protecting the health of the environment that produces the resource ensures that the resource will be available and profitable for longer periods of time.

RENEWABLE AND SUSTAINABLE RESOURCES

Environmental resources can be classified several different ways depending on their sustainability and potential for renewal. **Sustainable resources** are natural resources that are used and harvested without resource **depletion** (exhausting the supply of the resource) or causing harm to the environment. These resources, when harvested and managed in a sustainable manner, can provide subsistence for human populations indefinitely. Examples of sustainable resources include agriculture, which can provide both food and biomass for energy consumption, and solar energy. Solar energy can also be categorized as a form of a **renewable resource**, which is any resource that can be replenished or replaced in time. Other examples of renewable resources include wood, water, and wind energy. Unlike renewable resources, **non-renewable resources**, such as fossil fuels and minerals, are finite and cannot renew themselves within human lifetimes.

QUICK REVIEW

Solar energy is an example of a renewable resource that is also sustainable—the sun constantly supplies a source of energy, so the resource can never be depleted. Are all renewable resources always sustainable? Name examples of resources that meet one definition, but not necessarily the other.

SAMPLE QUESTION

14) **Which of the following is an example of a non-renewable resource?**

A. wind energy

B. solar energy

C. natural gas energy

D. biomass energy

Answers:

A. Incorrect. Wind energy is an example of a renewable resource.

B. Incorrect. Solar energy is an example of a renewable resource.

C. **Correct.** Natural gas is an example of a fossil fuel, which is non-renewable because it cannot be replenished on a human timescale.

D. Incorrect. Biomass energy is derived from agriculture, which is a renewable source.

ETHICAL ISSUES

Ethics are a set of moral principles that act as a guide regarding human behavior, including scientific research and the applications of technology. With every new research method, scientific discovery, or technological revolution comes a new set of ethical questions and concerns about how the use of new science and technology could adversely impact society at large. This section discusses contemporary societal concerns and ethical issues that arise due to scientific research and technology.

RESEARCH

Stem cells are unspecialized cells that can differentiate into different cell types as they divide. Adult stem cells can only differentiate into certain kinds of cells, while embryonic stem cells can develop into virtually any type of human cell. Researchers have an unparalleled ability to study human development, research causes of genetic diseases, and develop new drugs and treatments. The source of most of the stem cells is donated embryos left over after in vitro fertilization (IVF) procedures; however, their use in research is controversial because the embryos are destroyed in the process. **Animal research** is also controversial due to potential harm to test subjects. Animals, such as mice and rats, are often used in studying human disease and disease treatment, but this leads to harm and potential death of these animals and raises the question of whether animals have the same moral status and innate rights as humans.

Chemical research also comes with its own set of ethical debates. When new chemical substances are synthesized, researchers must not overlook the potential **toxicity**, or harmful potential to biological life, of the new substance. When dealing with toxic chemicals, researchers must account for risk and practice responsibility to ensure their proper development, use, and disposal. These steps are sometimes overlooked, with highly detrimental effects to humans and other forms of life. This was seen in the case of the development of dichlorodiphenyltrichloroethane (DDT), a synthetic insecticide that was later classified as a probable carcinogen and led to the decimation of multiple ecosystems and species.

SAMPLE QUESTION

15) Which of the following terms describes a chemical substance that has an ability to harm biological life?

    A.   detrimental

    B.   venomous

    C.   pollutive

    D.   toxic

Answers:

    A.   Incorrect. Toxic chemicals are detrimental, but *detrimental* is a generic term, and *toxic* is the specific term this phrase describes.

    B.   Incorrect. Venom is a specific toxin that is found in some animal species.

    C.   Incorrect. Pollutants are toxic, but not all toxins are pollutants.

    D.   **Correct.** Toxins are poisonous substances.

USE OF TECHNOLOGY

Genetically modified organisms (GMOs) are created when genetic material is altered to create more desirable traits in a living thing. Many common food items, such as soy and corn, have been genetically modified to produce traits that are disease resistant and increase crop yield. As this technology is in its early stages, the long-term effects on the environment and human health are yet to be determined. Potential detrimental effects, such as herbicide and antibiotic resistance, the decimation of untargeted species, and the spread of allergies among consumers are still being researched.

Artificial **cloning** techniques use technology to make identical copies of genetic material. Gene cloning is used to produce copies of specific genes or DNA segments in order to study the genetic sequence of the DNA material, which can then be manipulated and transferred to a new organism for genetic

> ### HELPFUL HINT
>
> Plants and animals have been genetically modified by humans for centuries through breeding practices, such as artificial selection, which have resulted in the multiple domesticated crops and animal species consumed by humans. GMO technology, however, allows for faster, more precise changes to specific genes.

modification. Other forms of cloning use a similar technique to produce embryos that are genetically identical to the donor organism. This is done either to create a new organism, as in reproductive cloning, or to produce embryonic stem cells for research and disease treatment, as is the case with therapeutic cloning. Gene cloning is a routine procedure that is generally accepted by society and the scientific community; reproductive and therapeutic cloning, however, are newer technologies that attract a great deal of ethical controversy. This includes the moral and religious implications of cloning entire organisms and the ethical questions of creating and destroying cloned embryos to obtain stem cells.

SAMPLE QUESTION

16) **The DNA of a common tomato subspecies has been altered to make the skin tougher and less penetrable by insects and other pests. This is an example of which of the following?**

    A.   stem cell therapy

    B.   artificial selection

    C.   a genetically modified organism

    D.   reproductive cloning

Answers:

    A.   Incorrect. This process does not involve the use of stem cell technology.

    B.   Incorrect. Artificial selection is a breeding technique.

    C.   **Correct.** This is an example of a precise gene modification that results in a genetically modified organism.

    D.   Incorrect. This did not result in an organism cloned from the donor organism, so it is not reproductive cloning.

SOCIETAL CONCERNS

The **security of genetic information** is a prevalent concern in society as the scientific and medical communities have been able to accumulate individual-specific genetic information, such as **genetic markers**, or easily identifiable DNA sequences with a known physical location of a chromosome. This includes the use of technology, such as DNA fingerprinting, to identify humans or predict genetic diseases. Ethical issues arise from the safe and secure storage of this personal genetic information, which is also stored as an electronic health record. Policies that restrict access to files and encrypt the data are used to protect individual privacy and reduce the chance of misuse of information. The advent of genetic data and electronic health records have also led to societal concerns regarding **equal access to medical treatment**, especially if positive disease results from genetic test information lead to denial of health insurance.

SAMPLE QUESTION

17) An easily identifiable DNA sequence with a known physical location on a chromosome is known as which of the following?

A.   genetic marker

B.   DNA fingerprinting

C.   genetic information

D.   genomic sequencing

Answers:

A.   **Correct.** A genetic marker is a gene or DNA sequence that can be used to identify an individual.

B.   Incorrect. DNA fingerprinting is a specific laboratory technique that matches genetic information with an individual.

C.   Incorrect. A genetic marker is just one form of genetic information.

D.   Incorrect. Genomic sequencing is a laboratory technique that determines a complete DNA sequence of an organism.

Practice Test

1

Sugars are built using which of the following monomers?

A. monosaccharides

B. nucleotides

C. amino acids

D. fatty acids

2

During which of the following phases of cellular respiration is the most ATP generated?

A. glycolysis

B. fermentation

C. the Krebs cycle

D. electron transport

3

Which of the following mutations turns a codon for an amino acid into a stop codon?

A. missense mutation

B. silent mutation

C. nonsense mutation

D. insertion mutation

4

Which of the following kingdoms contain organisms that are primarily multicellular?

A. Bacteria

B. Monera

C. Fungi

D. Protista

5

When the guard cells swell around a stomate, which of the following happens to the opening?

A. The stomate opens as the swelling causes the guard cells to stretch outward.

B. The stomate opens as the swelling causes more water to rush in.

C. The stomate closes as the swelling seals the pore.

D. The stomate closes as the swelling causes the pore opening to collapse.

6

Which of the following occurs when individuals with extreme or unusual traits are eliminated from a population, leaving the most common traits in the majority of the population?

A.   stabilizing selection

B.   directional selection

C.   disruptive selection

D.   sexual selection

7

Which of the given environments below would contain the largest number of K-selected organisms?

A.   the sand dune communities in a beach ecosystem

B.   the coast of Florida after a hurricane

C.   the Great Barrier Reef off the coast of Australia

D.   a recently abandoned farmland in Indiana

8

Which of the following is NOT an accurate statement about a gamete's genetic material during meiosis?

A.   The alleles of different gametes contain identical information.

B.   The genes will separate into distinct alleles.

C.   Each genetic combination has an equal chance of occurring.

D.   The gamete will contain one half of a cell's genetic information.

9

Which of the following phyla includes animals that regulate their body own temperature?

A.   Echinodermata

B.   Chordata

C.   Arthropoda

D.   Annelida

10

Which of the following is the layer of leaf tissue found between the epidermal layers that is primarily responsible for photosynthesis?

A.   parenchyma

B.   cuticle

C.   mesophyll

D.   cortex

11

Which of the following kingdoms of organisms does NOT contain a membrane-bound nucleus in the cell?

A.   Monera

B.   Protista

C.   Fungi

D.   Animalia

12

In a molecule of methane (CH_4), carbon shares four electrons with four atoms of hydrogen. Which of the following bonds is formed between the carbon and four hydrogen atoms?

A.   metallic

B.   ionic

C.   covalent

D.   hydrogen

13

The following reaction describes cellular respiration: $C_6H_{12}O_6 + 6O_2 \rightarrow 6CO_2 + 6H_2O$. Which molecule is reduced in this reaction?

A. $C_6H_{12}O_6$

B. O_2

C. CO_2

D. H_2O

14

Which of the following is a repressor that binds to an enzyme, but not at the active site, during feedback inhibition?

A. enhancer

B. inhibitor

C. competitive inhibitor

D. noncompetitive inhibitor

15

Which of the following pairs of organelles perform similar functions?

A. the nucleus and ribosomes

B. vacuoles and mitochondria

C. chloroplasts and mitochondria

D. ribosomes and chloroplasts

16

Which kind of DNA sequence can exert its effects on the expression of a gene from a distance?

A. promoter

B. operator

C. operon

D. enhancer

17

Which of the following describes an impact Louis Pasteur's work had on cell theory?

A. Pasteur found evidence to support spontaneous generation.

B. Pasteur confirmed that cells arise from other living cells.

C. Pasteur developed pasteurization in order to use heat to kill bacteria.

D. Pasteur used microscopes to study bacteria.

18

A female who carries the recessive color blindness gene mates with a color-blind male, resulting in a male child. Which of the following numbers represents the likelihood the offspring will also be color blind?

A. 25 percent

B. 50 percent

C. 100 percent

D. 0 percent

19

The small intestine has a pH higher than 7. Predict what would happen to the activity of gastric protease when it enters the small intestine.

A. activity will increase gradually

B. activity will remain the same

C. activity will increase initially, then decrease

D. activity will decrease

20

Which of the following hierarchical levels of ecological organization is composed of a community and its environment?

A. ecosystem

B. habitat

C. biosphere

D. population

Use the figure below to answer question 21.

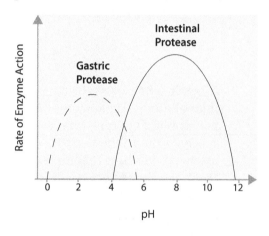

21

What is the optimal pH level for intestinal protease?

A. 3

B. 4

C. 8

D. 10

E. 11

22

Which of the following does NOT pass through open stomata?

A. carbon dioxide

B. sunlight

C. water

D. oxygen

23

Why is RNA thought to have played an important role in the evolution of life?

I. RNA can function as an enzyme in some cases, catalyzing cellular reactions.

II. RNA uses a complementary chain of nitrogenous bases to self-replicate.

III. RNA is the most stable form for storing genetic information.

A. II only

B. III only

C. I and II only

D. I, II, and III

24

Which of the following is the most accurate term to associate with the development of an embryo from a single female gamete, with no gametes from a male?

A. sexual

B. regeneration

C. asexual

D. parthenogenesis

25

Which of the following is true about the Eukaryota domain?

A. This domain consists solely of the Plantae and Animalia kingdoms.

B. Organisms in this domain have cells with a nucleus and organelles.

C. All eukaryotes are multicellular.

D. They reproduce primarily through binary fission.

26

Which of the following is NOT an example of organelle inheritance?

A. chromosome segregation

B. biparental inheritance

C. vegetative segregation

D. uniparental inheritance

27

Which of the following explains why phototropism is beneficial to plants?

A. Phototropism encourages a deep root system, anchoring the plant to the ground.

B. Phototropism enables the plants to grow toward the sunlight, helping the plant to get the highest amount of sunlight possible.

C. Phototropism provides structural support for plants to grow tall and straight.

D. Phototropism allows the root systems of a plant to branch off and reach nutrients and water deep in the soil.

28

Mitochondria are thought to be descendant from endosymbiotic bacteria-like cells. Which statement below best supports this theory?

A. Neither mitochondria nor bacteria have chloroplasts.

B. Both mitochondria and bacteria perform glycolysis.

C. Mitochondria and bacteria possess similar ribosomes and DNA.

D. Mitochondria and bacteria have similar nuclear structures.

29

The diagram below shows a chloroplast. In which area of the chloroplast would the light-dependent reactions occur?

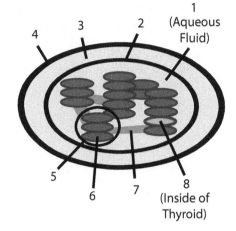

A. 2

B. 3

C. 4

D. 6

30

In translation, which molecule adds a new amino acid to a growing polypeptide chain?

A. mRNA

B. rRNA

C. tRNA

D. RNA polymerase

31

Genes are transferred from one chromatid to another during the prophase I stage of meiosis in which of the following processes?

A. recombination

B. genetic linking

C. fertilization

D. genetic crossing

32

Which of the following describes a distinction between flatworms (Platyhelminthes) and roundworms (Nematoda)?

A. Flatworms reproduce sexually and asexually; roundworms only reproduce sexually.

B. Flatworms are asymmetrical; roundworms have bilateral symmetry.

C. Flatworms have a coelom; roundworms do not.

D. Flatworms are parasitic; roundworms are not.

33

Which of the following systems is responsible for detecting changes in the external environment and transmitting these messages to a center of control?

A. endocrine system

B. integumentary system

C. nervous system

D. cardiovascular system

34

Which of the following describes a difference between tundra and taiga?

A. Taiga is dominated by coniferous trees; tundra is dominated by small mosses and shrubs.

B. Taiga is found further north than tundra in the Northern Hemisphere.

C. Tundra hosts a greater variety of animal life than taiga.

D. Taiga is a terrestrial biome; tundra is an aquatic biome.

35

Which of the following is a symbiotic relationship in which both species benefit from the presence of the other?

A. altruism

B. opportunism

C. mutualism

D. commensalism

36

Which stage of ecological succession has the greatest amount of diversity, biomass, and productivity?

A. climax community

B. pioneer plant

C. intermediate species

D. inception stage

37

Which statement accurately describes a density-dependent limiting factor?

A. A deer population is drastically reduced during a forest fire.

B. A huge surge in a rabbit population in a certain meadow creates more competition for natural resources.

C. A volcanic eruption on a small island damages or kills several species of plant life.

D. An unusually dry summer causes many different species in a specific environment to struggle to survive.

38

Which of the following is an example of pollution mitigation that is designed to reduce environmental impact before it occurs?

A. waste incineration

B. green buildings

C. chemical treatment

D. air stripping

39

Which of the following is an example of convergent evolution?

A. similar bone structures in the forelimbs of both horses and bats

B. similar amino acid sequences in the hemoglobin of both humans and chimpanzees

C. similar plant species found on both an island nation and the closest mainland continent

D. differing flight structures in both bats and insects

Use the following information for questions 40 and 41.

The group of questions below consists of four lettered headings followed by a list of phrases or sentences. For each sentence, select the one heading that is most closely related to it. One heading may be used once, more than once, or not at all.

A. bottleneck

B. allotropic speciation

C. directional selection

D. sympatric speciation

40

Due to human predation, the variation and population size of most elephant species are declining very rapidly. The result has been a rapidly shrinking pool of genetic information within elephant populations.

41

Along the Western half of North America, two distinct species of spotted owl exist, separated by a substantial geographic distance.

42

In a eukaryotic cell, DNA is transcribed in the

A. cytoplasm.

B. ribosome.

C. Golgi body.

D. nucleus.

43

Which of the following statements is true about modifier genes?

A. Modifier genes enhance, diminish, or mask traits derived from other genes.

B. Modifier genes always mask traits expressed by other genes.

C. All pigmentation genes are influenced by modifier genes.

D. Modifier genes are always recessive.

44

Which of the following is a process that leads to a mutation of the chromosome number within a cell?

A. recombination

B. variation

C. transformation

D. nondisjunction

45

Which of the following root growth zones is the site of cell differentiation?

A. root cap

B. meristematic zone

C. zone of elongation

D. zone of maturation

46

Which of the following types of cells are the most abundant and versatile cells found in the plant?

A. ground cells

B. parenchyma

C. vascular cells

D. collenchyma

47

Glucagon is an example of which of the following types of proteins?

A. transport proteins

B. signaling proteins

C. motor proteins

D. regulatory proteins

48

Which of the following statements describes the differences the plants and fungi?

A. Plants have cell walls, but fungi do not.

B. Plants are autotrophs; fungi are heterotrophs.

C. Plants are decomposers, while fungi are primary producers.

D. Plants are multicellular eukaryotes; fungi are not.

49

One similarity between cell division in prokaryotic and eukaryotic cells is

A. how chromosomes are packaged.

B. that DNA is copied, and the cell divides by binary fission.

C. that genetically identical daughter cells are produced.

D. that cell division in both cell types requires microtubules.

50

Consider a prokaryotic organism that typically lives in a 10 percent saline concentration environment. Which of the following environments would cause the organism to lose mass at the greatest rate due to osmosis?

A. a solution of pure water

B. a solution of 3 percent saline concentration

C. a solution of 10 percent saline concentration

D. a solution of 20 percent saline concentration

51

The information stored in DNA is used to make which of the following molecules?

A. amino acids

B. proteins

C. fatty acids

D. monosaccharides

52

Embryos develop in eggs inside the mother while receiving nutrients from a yolk sac in which of the following modes of reproduction?

A. oviparity

B. viviovoparity

C. viviparity

D. ovoviviparity

53

Which of the following organisms lacks a membrane-bound nucleus?

A. protist

B. bacterium

C. mold

D. moss

54

Adding fertilizer to nutrient-poor soil in an agricultural area that used to be forest is an example of using technology to achieve which of the following?

A. habitat restoration

B. waste management

C. species protection

D. conservation easement

55

Which of the following is NOT an example of sustainable agricultural management?

A. continual grazing of vegetation year-round

B. growing cover crops during the growing off-season

C. biological pest control

D. conservation tillage

56

Which of the following techniques is used to produce copies of specific genes or DNA segments?

A. gene cloning

B. reproductive cloning

C. genetic modification

D. DNA fingerprinting

57

Which of the following is a form of support for the idea of abiogenesis?

A. amino acids arising from inorganic compounds

B. genetic diversity among organisms

C. increase of oxygen in Earth's early atmosphere

D. replication of DNA

58

Which of the following is the tendency of nervous tissue to become concentrated at the anterior end of an organism during embryonic development?

A. endosymbiosis

B. cephalization

C. embryology

D. multicellularity

59

Which of the following is true of cellular respiration?

A. Two molecules of ATP are produced during electron transport.

B. Thirty-four molecules of ATP are produced during glycolysis.

C. Thirty-four molecules of ATP are produced during the Krebs cycle.

D. Thirty-eight molecules of ATP are produced during the entire process of cellular respiration.

60

A distinct difference between a plant cell and an animal cell is the presence of

A. ribosomes.

B. mitochondria.

C. a cell wall.

D. a nucleus.

63

Which of the following is a difference between the Archaea and Bacteria domains?

A. Bacteria are unicellular; archaea are multicellular.

B. Archaea cells have a different rRNA sequence than bacteria.

C. Archaea cells photosynthesize; bacteria cells do not.

D. Bacteria and archaea are not found in the same environments.

64

A scientist believes that a particular species of algae, *S. sponferus*, is able to grow even when living deep underwater. However, he hypothesizes that this species may grow more slowly than algae in other environments due to the lack of sunlight at this depth. Which of the following findings would not support the scientist's hypothesis?

A. Many other species of algae are able to live at depths of 1000 meters under the surface of the water.

B. Laboratory experiments show that *S. sponferus* grows equally well under a wide range of light conditions.

C. *S. sponferus* is found growing in abundance on the ocean's surface.

D. Some species of algae are discovered that do not need much light to grow.

65

Which of the following life characteristics are found across all kingdoms of life, including viruses?

A. chromosome pairs

B. cell wall

C. DNA

D. nucleic acid

66

Which of the following components of the endocrine system is located in the abdomen and secretes insulin to regulate blood sugar?

A.   parathyroid

B.   pancreas

C.   testes

D.   thymus

67

Which of the following terms refers to the stage of the human menstrual cycle in which female eggs are released for potential fertilization?

A.   follicular

B.   menstruation

C.   estrous

D.   ovulation

68

Which of the following terrestrial biomes is tropical, dominated by grasses, and has poor soil?

A.   taiga

B.   estuary

C.   chaparral

D.   savanna

69

Which plant hormone is responsible for the ripening of fruit?

A.   gibberellins

B.   citric acid

C.   cytokinins

D.   ethylene

70

Mature red blood cells are adapted to not contain a nucleus. This allows them to carry more hemoglobin. As a result of this adaptation, red blood cells

A.   cannot undergo mitosis.

B.   have large energy reserves.

C.   have extensive repairing capabilities.

D.   never die.

71

Which type(s) of RNA is essential for transferring amino acids during protein synthesis?

I.   mRNA

II.   tRNA

III.   rRNA

A.   I only

B.   II only

C.   III only

D.   I and II only

72

At the G_2 checkpoint, damaged DNA that cannot be fixed will initiate a cellular, self-destruct process called

A.   gene expression.

B.   feedback inhibition.

C.   apoptosis.

D.   negative feedback.

73

The mitotic spindle forms during which phase of mitosis?

A.   prophase

B.   metaphase

C.   anaphase

D.   telophase

74

If a plant that is homozygous dominant (T) for a trait is crossed with a plant that is homozygous recessive (t) for the same trait, what will be the phenotype of the offspring if the trait follows Mendelian patterns of inheritance?

A. All offspring will show the dominant phenotype.

B. All offspring will show the recessive phenotype.

C. Half the offspring will show the dominant trait, and the other half will show the recessive phenotype.

D. All the offspring will show a mix of the dominant and recessive phenotypes.

75

In all living organisms, RNA acts as the chemical messenger between DNA and proteins. This similarity is considered which of the following?

A. analogous process

B. convergent evolution

C. divergent evolution

D. homologous process

76

Transitional fossils provide the bulk of the evidence supporting which of the following models of evolutionary rate?

A. allopatric speciation

B. punctuated equilibrium

C. gradualism

D. adaptation

77

Which of the following is NOT one of the five conditions of the Hardy-Weinberg equilibrium?

A. large population

B. nonrandom mating

C. no natural selection

D. no mutations

78

A box turtle is an omnivore, subsisting primarily on vegetation as well as macroinvertebrates. When a box turtle is consuming mealworms, which of the following trophic levels is it occupying?

A. producer

B. autotroph

C. heterotroph

D. secondary consumer

79

Which of the following is NOT a common characteristic of pioneer plants?

A. long life spans

B. long root systems

C. quick reproduction

D. They easily obtain and store water.

80

Herbivores are found in which of the following trophic levels?

A. producers

B. secondary consumers

C. primary consumers

D. tertiary consumers

81

Which of the following is the complementary strand for the DNA sequence below?

ATT CCA TGC GTA

A. ATT CCA TGC GTA
B. CGG AAC GTA TGC
C. TAA GGT ACG CAT
D. ATT GGT TGC CAT

Use the description and data below to answer questions 82 – 83.

An experiment was conducted to study the effect of temperature on the survival rate of a group of 100 algae organisms. The study used five different temperatures, kept constant, for a total of ten days. A record of how many organisms survived out of the starting 100 was taken.

Temperature	Number of Surviving Individuals		
	Day 1	Day 5	Day 10
15°C	100	91	80
20°C	100	96	94
25°C	100	88	73
30°C	100	84	58
35°C	100	72	41

82

Using the information from the table above, what temperature is best for the organism's long-term survival?

A. 20°C
B. 25°C
C. 30°C
D. 35°C

83

What would happen to the organism's survival rate if the temperature was increased to 40°C?

A. The organism would experience an increased survival rate.
B. The organism's survival rate would be the lowest on the table.
C. The survival rate would most likely plateau at the 30°C rate.
D. The organism's survival rate would be higher than at 15°C.

84

Which of the following is NOT true about the dynamics between predator and prey?

A. The population of predators depends on the number of prey available.
B. Predators depend on prey for food resources.
C. Prey population numbers tend to go down when there is an increase in predator numbers.
D. As the number of predators increases, prey numbers go up exponentially.

85

Which of the following enzymes joins the segments of DNA complementary to the lagging strand during DNA replication?

A. DNA polymerase
B. DNA ligase
C. RNA polymerase
D. helicase

86

The result of meiosis and cytokinesis is

A.   two haploid (1n) cells.

B.   four haploid (1n) cells.

C.   two diploid (2n) cells.

D.   four diploid (2n) cells.

87

Which of the following is NOT a source of genetic variation?

A.   mutation

B.   sexual reproduction

C.   codominance

D.   crossing-over

88

Which of the following disorders arises as a result of an extra chromosome within a fertilized egg?

A.   Down syndrome

B.   Turner syndrome

C.   sickle-cell anemia

D.   cystic fibrosis

89

Which of the following is the movement of alleles from one population to another?

A.   migration

B.   genetic drift

C.   gene flow

D.   evolutionary force

90

Which of the following groups of organisms includes both autotrophic and heterotrophic groups?

A.   plants

B.   fungi

C.   protists

D.   animals

91

Which of the following describes the difference between classification and taxonomy?

A.   Classification is the process of grouping organisms; taxonomy is the process of naming the organisms in these groups.

B.   Classification is the process of naming organisms; taxonomy is the process of creating groups into which organisms can be classified.

C.   Classification refers to all organisms; taxonomy refers to animals only.

D.   Classification was developed by Carl Linneaus; taxonomy was developed by Carl Woese.

92

Which of the following is a form of asexual reproduction in which an offspring generates from a specialized site on the body of the parent?

A.   budding

B.   fragmentation

C.   sporulation

D.   binary fission

93

Which of the following is an evolutionary advantage of the angiosperms, giving them the competitive edge over other groups of plants?

A.   broad leaves that absorb more sunlight for photosynthesis

B.   the ability to be perennial, living and growing year after year

C.   fruit that nourishes the developing seed

D.   flowers that attract pollinators, ensuring more successful plant fertilization

94

Seeds that are contained in a dry fruit that has a barb-like appendage are most likely to be dispersed by which method?

A.   attracting animals to consume the fruit

B.   flinging from the plant via fruit disintegration

C.   attaching to animal fur to be brushed off in a new location

D.   blowing through the wind via wind dispersal

95

Organic molecules and inorganic molecules differ in many ways. Organic molecules, for instance, always contain which of the following?

A.   carbon

B.   carbon and hydrogen

C.   carbon, hydrogen, and oxygen

D.   carbon, hydrogen, oxygen, and nitrogen

96

Which of the following would be the most likely electron donor in a chemosynthetic reaction?

A. NH_3

B. O_2

C. $C_6H_{12}O_6$

D. CO_2

97

Which of the following is considered the simplest phyla in the animal kingdom?

A.   Cnidaria

B.   Porifera

C.   Nematoda

D.   Arthropoda

98

Which of the following is NOT a characteristic shared by all reptiles, including the birds?

A.   amniotic egg

B.   scales

C.   hollow bones

D.   lungs

100

The majority of the DNA found in eukaryotic genomes is noncoding, meaning it does not carry the genetic code needed for protein synthesis. This noncoding DNA would be found in all of the following locations EXCEPT

A.   the small gaps between genes.

B.   in the centromeres.

C.   in the telomeres.

D.   in exons.

101

Which of the following would contain the code for making a protein?

A. mRNA

B. tRNA

C. rRNA

D. DNA polymerase

102

Which of the following produce fewer offspring but can provide great care and lower mortality rates early in their offspring's lifespan as a result?

A. equilibrium species

B. constant loss species

C. fecund species

D. opportunistic species

61

Actin is the key component in which protein fibers of the cytoskeleton?

A. intermediate filaments

B. microtubules

C. microfilaments

D. flagella

62

What is an energy-consuming process that brings molecules into the cell called?

A. facilitated diffusion

B. simple diffusion

C. exocytosis

D. endocytosis

103

Which of the following is a series of behaviors in which one organism completes an action that benefits one species at the cost of its own biological fitness?

A. parasitism

B. mutualism

C. territorialism

D. altruism

104

Lilies are small flowering plants with vascular tissue and a thin, fibrous root system that does not reach deep into the soil. Which of the following groups does this plant belong to?

A. gymnosperm

B. monocot

C. bryophyte

D. pteridophyte

105

Which of the following is NOT an example of the end result of a negative feedback loop?

A. release of oxytocin during childbirth

B. vasoconstriction during an incident of low blood pressure

C. stimulus of sweat glands in thermoregulation

D. insulin production and storage of glucose during digestion

106

Which of the following is NOT a function of the pituitary gland?

A. receive and interpret internal and external stimuli from sensory nerves

B. release trophic hormones to trigger other glands to produce hormones

C. store hormones from the hypothalamus and release as needed

D. produce hormones and send to target cells via the bloodstream

107

In which of the following stages of zygote formation do cells migrate to the walls to create a cavity?

A. gastrula

B. embryo

C. blastula

D. morula

108

Which of the following groups contain no unicellular organisms?

A. fungi

B. plants

C. protists

D. archaea

109

A neuron is an example of which of the following levels of biological organization?

A. cell

B. tissue

C. organ

D. organ system

110

Which of the following is an example of an environmental impact resulting from the disposal portion of a consumer product's life cycle?

A. contamination of groundwater from a landfill

B. the use of chemicals, such as resins or dyes

C. extracting oil from the ground

D. the release of byproducts in industrial plants

111

The enzyme-substrate complex forms when a substrate binds to the _____ of an enzyme.

A. promoter

B. operator

C. start codon

D. active site

112

The 5' end of a nucleotide is a

A. nitrogenous base.

B. 5-carbon sugar molecule.

C. phosphate group.

D. all of the above

113

Gel electrophoresis separates proteins or fragments of DNA and RNA based on

A. G – C content.

B. the total number of amino acids.

C. size.

D. all of the above

114

Which of the following contains a full set of genetic material in a given individual?

A.   gene

B.   genotype

C.   allele

D.   chromosome

115

Which of the following forms of prokaryotic genetic exchange results in plasmids moving from one bacteria cell to another via a connecting bridge?

A.   transformation

B.   transduction

C.   connection

D.   conjugation

116

The first step in gene expression is

A.   transcription of DNA into a molecule of mRNA.

B.   translation of DNA into a molecule of mRNA.

C.   transcription of mRNA into protein.

D.   translation of mRNA into protein.

117

Which of the following is not true of active transport?

A.   Molecules are transported against their concentration gradient.

B.   ATP is oxidized in the process.

C.   ATP is reduced in the process.

D.   Energy is required to transport molecules into or out of the cell.

118

The chromosomes of a eukaryotic organism would be found in the

A.   chloroplast.

B.   nucleus.

C.   ribosome.

D.   cytoplasm.

119

Which of the following populations would be the most likely to exhibit uniform dispersion?

A.   a group of nesting penguins

B.   a field full of dandelions

C.   a herd of African elephants

D.   a forest of oak trees

120

What role does the electron transport chain play in cellular respiration?

A.   The electron transport chain excites electrons while they are attached to their carriers so they can excite more carbon atoms.

B.   The electron transport chain breaks down the phosphate bonds in ATP to release the energy required to produce glucose molecules for glycolysis.

C.   The electron transport chain facilitates the transport of pyruvic acid from the Krebs cycle, which in turn provides the raw materials needed to create useable energy.

D.   The electron transport chain gradually removes electrons from carriers during a step-by-step process, providing the energy needed to change ADP into ATP.

121

Which of the following is most similar to glucose in its structural formula?

A. fructose

B. lactose

C. sucrose

D. cellulose

122

Which of the following terms describes an ecosystem found on land but partially or completely submerged in water?

A. floodplain

B. estuary

C. wetland

D. lagoon

123

Which of the following distinguishes a scientific fact from a scientific law?

A. Scientific facts are observations; scientific laws are explanations for those observations.

B. Scientific facts are proposed explanations; scientific laws confirm or refute those proposed explanations.

C. Scientific facts are confirmed observations; scientific laws are generalized descriptions that predict future behavior.

D. Scientific facts explain natural phenomena; scientific laws do not.

124

Which of the following is an anion?

A. Br⁻

B. K⁺

C. Na

D. all of the above

125

Which protein is an important component of the nucleosome?

A. methionine

B. centromere

C. DNA polymerase

D. histone

126

A mutation that occurs in the DNA of a nonreproductive cell is called a

A. germ-line mutation.

B. somatic mutation.

C. point mutation.

D. frame-shift mutation.

127

Which of the following is NOT an accurate statement about sickle-cell anemia?

A. It causes distortion of the shape of red blood cells.

B. It is caused by the presence of an excess chromosome.

C. It is a recessive genetic disorder.

D. It can lead to a low blood cell count.

128

Which of the following best describes the order of events in photosynthesis?

A. photosystem I → photosystem II → electron transport → ATP production

B. photosystem I → electron transport → ATP production → photosystem II

C. photosystem II → electron transport → ATP production → photosystem I

D. photosystem II → photosystem I → ATP production → electron transport

129

Which of the following groups of organisms serves as the base of the ocean food chain in the photic zone?

A. coral

B. detritus

C. phytoplankton

D. zooplankton

130

Which of the following is the correct definition of a habitat?

A. the preferred physical location where an organism lives

B. the geographic area where a population is found

C. an organism's role within a specified area

D. the combination of all biotic and abiotic factors in an environment

131

Enzymes function by

A. giving strength to a cell, tissue, or organ.

B. helping cells communicate.

C. storing nutrients.

D. lowering the activation energy of a chemical reaction.

132

Actin filaments play a key role in which phase of mitosis?

A. metaphase

B. anaphase

C. telophase

D. cytokinesis

133

Which of the following is the correct definition of biological fitness?

A. Individuals with adaptations best suited for their environment will be more likely to survive and pass on their successful genes to future populations through reproduction.

B. Individuals are selected by mates for their advantageous traits.

C. It is an inherited trait that gives an individual an advantage in this competition for resources.

D. It is the rule that all species do not reproduce in equal rates.

134

Which of the following changes to chromosomal structure is most likely to lead to the miscarriage of a zygote?

A.   transformation

B.   deletion

C.   nondisjunction

D.   mutation

135

Which of the following is the distinguishing feature between the kingdom classification system and the domain classification system?

A.   The domain system eliminates the kingdom level from the classification hierarchy.

B.   The kingdom system places domain on a lower level in the classification hierarchy.

C.   The domain system adds an eighth classification level based on molecular evidence.

D.   The kingdom system adds an eighth classification category based on biological evidence.

136

Which of the following is true about all unicellular organisms?

A.   They depend on symbiotic relationships with other unicellular organisms.

B.   They must reproduce via binary fission.

C.   They must perform all functions of life within the confines of a single cell.

D.   They must be specialized cells.

137

All organisms in this phylum are carnivores that use specialized stinging cells to capture their prey and also display radial symmetry.

A.   Echinodermata

B.   Chordata

C.   Mollusca

D.   Cnidaria

138

Which statement accurately describes the relationship between genes and alleles?

A.   Genes are the physical manifestations (observable) of the allele combinations present.

B.   Alleles represent the variety of forms a specific gene can take.

C.   Two alleles are necessary for proper gene expression.

D.   Recessive alleles are the less advantageous forms of a gene.

139

Which of the following structures is a mature, ripened ovary of a flowering plant?

A.   flower

B.   fruit

C.   seed

D.   ovule

140

Which of the following describes the difference between apical and lateral meristem?

A. Apical meristem is located in the roots; lateral meristem is located in the shoots.

B. Apical meristem produces vertical growth; lateral meristem produces thickening growth.

C. Apical meristem is found in the vascular cambium; lateral meristem is found in the cork cambium.

D. Apical meristem produces new flowers; lateral meristem produces new stems.

141

Which of the following is the variable in a scientific investigation that is manipulated by the researcher in order to test the hypothesis?

A. control

B. experimental

C. dependent

D. hypothetical

142

Which technique uses the amount of light absorbed by a molecule or microbe to determine the concentration of that molecule/microbe?

A. gel electrophoresis

B. microscopy

C. spectrophotometry

D. DNA sequencing

143

Which of the following is NOT a distinguishing feature found in all members of the Mollusca phylum?

A. mantle

B. heart

C. gills

D. shell

144

A species of mouse has two alleles for fur color. The allele for brown fur (B) is dominant, and the allele for white fur (b) is recessive. Which of the following genotypes will result in a mouse with white fur?

I. bb

II. Bb

III. BB

A. I only

B. III only

C. II and III only

D. I, II, and III

145

Two pea plants are cross bred to determine the resulting flower color and flower position in the offspring. If the two plants are heterozygous for flower color and position, what type of experiment is this?

A. parental cross

B. filial cross

C. dihybrid cross

D. monohybrid cross

146

A restriction enzyme cuts DNA at specific sites that include symmetrical sequences of DNA. Which of the following is an example of a site that could be cut by a restriction enzyme?

A. 5' GATTAG 3'

B. 5' GACGAC 3'

C. 5' GGTTCC 3'

D. 5' GAATTC 3'

147

Population models, which are models that predict change in population growth over time using logistic growth or species-area equations, are an example of which of the following?

A. conceptual models

B. graphical models

C. physical models

D. mathematical models

148

Which of the following is an enzyme that is found in the stomach and aids in digestion?

A. trypsin

B. gastrin

C. secretin

D. pepsin

99

Which of the following is NOT a function of the liver?

A. digestive juice production

B. bile production

C. detoxification

D. blood preparation

149

Which of the following statements about monocot plants is NOT true?

A. Monocots have a fibrous root system.

B. Monocots have leaves with parallel veins.

C. Monocots have one cotyledon.

D. Monocots have vascular bundles in a ring formation.

150

A dihybrid cross is done between mice for two traits: white fur (Ww) and short fur (Ss). Each parent is heterozygous for both traits. The offspring are most likely to have which of the following genotypes for these traits?

A. wwss

B. WWSS

C. WwSs

D. WWSs

Answer Key

1)

A. **Correct.** Sugars are built from monosaccharides like glucose.

B. Incorrect. Nucleic acids are built from nucleotides.

C. Incorrect. Proteins are built from amino acids.

D. Incorrect. Lipids are built from fatty acids and glycerol.

2)

A. Incorrect. Two molecules of ATP are produced during glycolysis.

B. Incorrect. Fermentation usually occurs under anaerobic conditions.

C. Incorrect. Two molecules of ATP are produced during the Krebs cycle.

D. **Correct.** Thirty-four molecules of ATP are usually produced during electron transport.

3)

A. Incorrect. A missense mutation leads to the substitution of one amino acid for a different amino acid in the polypeptide chain that is synthesized during translation.

B. Incorrect. A mutation that causes no change in the translation of a piece of mRNA is a silent mutation.

C. **Correct.** A stop codon is produced by a nonsense mutation.

D. Incorrect. The number of bases in a DNA sequence increases with an insertion mutation.

4)

A. Incorrect. All bacteria are single-celled organisms.

B. Incorrect. All monerans, which include bacteria and archaea, are single-celled organisms.

C. **Correct.** Some fungi—such as yeast—are single-celled, but most are multicellular.

D. Incorrect. Although some protists are multicellular, the majority are unicellular.

5)

A. **Correct.** Water fills the guard cells, which causes them to bend apart and let the stomate open.

B. Incorrect. Water vapor exits through the stomate but does not enter.

C. Incorrect. Swelling causes the stomate to open, not close.

D. Incorrect. The guard cells collapse when water is released from the cell, causing stomate closure.

6)

A.   **Correct.** Stabilizing selection eliminates extreme/unusual traits (e.g., extremely low or high human height) so that the most common traits are the best adapted for survival.

B.   Incorrect. Directional selection favors traits that are at one extreme, whereas the other extreme is selected against.

C.   Incorrect. Disruptive selection occurs because the environment favors extreme traits, causing selection against common traits.

D.   Incorrect. Sexual selection is the result of males seeking to increase their fitness by increasing the quantity of their offspring and females choosing to increase the quality of their offspring by choosing the best mate.

7)

A.   Incorrect. Sand dune communities are inhabited by r-selected organisms due to constant exposure to harsh storms and winds.

B.   Incorrect. Often after a natural disaster destroys an environment, only r-selected organisms will return for some time.

C.   **Correct.** K-selected species are found in relatively stable conditions that reproduce few offspring but often spend considerable time raising offspring to maturation. Along the Great Barrier Reef, there are several examples of K-selected organisms, such as sea turtles and sharks.

D.   Incorrect. Old farmlands are mostly inhabited by r-selected species, such as mice and grasses.

8)

A.   **Correct.** The law of independent assortment states that alleles divide randomly and independently of one another, meaning it is virtually impossible for different gametes to contain identical genetic information.

B.   Incorrect. This is true according to the law of segregation.

C.   Incorrect. This is true according to the law of independent assortment.

D.   Incorrect. This is true of all cells undergoing meiosis.

9)

A.   Incorrect. Echinoderms are ectotherms—dependent on outside temperature to regulate their body temperature.

B.   **Correct.** Two classes of the chordate phyla—mammals and birds—display endothermy.

C.   Incorrect. Arthropods are ectotherms—dependent on outside temperature to regulate their body temperature.

D.   Incorrect. Annelids are ectotherms—dependent on outside temperature to regulate their body temperature.

10)

A.   Incorrect. The parenchyma cells differentiate and give rise to the mesophyll, which performs the bulk of photosynthesis.

B.   Incorrect. The cuticle is the waxy layer secreted by the epidermis that covers and protects the leaf.

C.   **Correct.** The mesophyll is found within the interior of a leaf and contains a vast number of chloroplasts, which carry out photosynthesis.

D.   Incorrect. The cortex is a collection of parenchyma cells that stores starches and other materials for future plant use.

11)

A. **Correct.** Neither bacteria nor archaea cells contain a membrane-bound nucleus.

B. Incorrect. All protists have membrane-bound nuclei in their cells.

C. Incorrect. All fungi have membrane-bound nuclei in their cells.

D. Incorrect. All animals have membrane-bound nuclei in their cells.

12)

A. Incorrect. Metallic bonds are formed when valence electrons are shared within a lattice of cations.

B. Incorrect. In an ionic bond, one atom donates an electron to another atom.

C. **Correct.** In a covalent bond, two atoms share a pair of electrons.

D. Incorrect. When the hydrogen atom of one molecule is attracted to the electronegative atom—like O_2—of another molecule, a hydrogen bond joins the two molecules.

13)

A. Incorrect. Glucose is the electron donor, so it is oxidized in the reaction.

B. **Correct.** Oxygen is the final electron acceptor in cellular respiration and is reduced to water.

C. Incorrect. Carbon dioxide is a product of the reaction.

D. Incorrect. Water is also a product of cellular respiration.

14)

A. Incorrect. Transcription factors can bind enhancers to regulate gene expression.

B. Incorrect. A repressor does inhibit the action of an enzyme, but the best answer to this question is answer choice D.

C. Incorrect. Competitive inhibitors bind the active site of an enzyme; hence, they compete with the substrate for this site.

D. **Correct.** Noncompetitive inhibitors induce a conformational change in an enzyme that prevents substrate binding, but the inhibitor does not bind the active site directly.

15)

A. Incorrect. The nucleus stores DNA, while ribosomes are sites of protein synthesis.

B. Incorrect. Vacuoles store waste; mitochondria are sites of ATP production.

C. **Correct.** These two organelles use an ATP synthase to generate ATP.

D. Incorrect. Protein synthesis is catalyzed by ribosomes, while chloroplasts are plant organelles that house the machinery for photosynthesis.

16)

A. Incorrect. RNA polymerase binds a promoter to initiate transcription.

B. Incorrect. A repressor can bind an operator, which is situated near a promoter, to prevent RNA polymerase from initiating transcription.

C. Incorrect. An operon is a cluster of genes transcribed in sequence.

D. **Correct.** An enhancer is often situated far from a gene but can be bound by a transcription factor that regulates the expression of that gene.

17)

A. Incorrect. Pasteur's work did not support the concept of spontaneous generation, which states that cells arise from non-living material.

B. **Correct.** Pasteur's experiment provided evidence that airborne bacteria regenerate to create more bacteria, which supported the concept of cell theory that states that cells arise from living cells.

C.   Incorrect. Pasteurization is an important scientific contribution that Pasteur made but does not contribute to cell theory.

D.   Incorrect. Pasteur did use microscopes in his work, but this does not contribute to cell theory.

18)

A.   Incorrect. The child has a 50 percent chance of receiving the recessive color-blind allele from his mother.

B.   Correct. The offspring has a 50 percent chance of inheriting the dominant allele and a 50 percent chance of inheriting the recessive allele from his mother.

C.   Incorrect. The male offspring does not receive an X chromosome from his father; therefore, the father's colorblind gene is not passed on to the offspring.

D.   Incorrect. The child has a 50 percent chance of receiving the recessive color-blind allele from his mother.

19)

D.   Correct. From the graph, it is clear that the activity of gastric protease drops off completely at a pH just below 6. Entering the small intestine with a pH greater than 7 would cause the enzyme reactivity to decrease drastically. It would most likely not be reactive at all.

20)

A.   Correct. An ecosystem contains all biotic and abiotic components in a given area.

B.   Incorrect. A habitat is the environment in which a population of species lives.

C.   Incorrect. The biosphere encompasses all the spaces living things occupy on Earth.

D.   Incorrect. A population is all of the members of the same species in a given area.

21)

C.   Correct. The highest point on the graph for intestinal protease is its optimal pH level because that is where it is the most reactive. According to this graph, that level is pH 8.

22)

A.   Incorrect. The stomata are the major site of gas exchange for plants, including the intake of carbon dioxide.

B.   Correct. Sunlight is absorbed by chlorophyll in the leaf, not the stomata.

C.   Incorrect. Water exits an open stoma during the process of transpiration.

D.   Incorrect. The stomata are the major site of gas exchange for plants, including the release of oxygen.

23)

C.   Correct. I and II are true.

I.   True. RNA enzymes such as riboenzymes and RNA polymerase play an important role in protein synthesis and replication.

II.   True. RNA is also able to self-replicate and make other RNA molecules.

III.   False. DNA is more stable than RNA.

24)

A.   Incorrect. Sexual reproduction requires the fusion of gametes from two parents.

B.   Incorrect. Regeneration is a form of asexual reproduction in which a new offspring arises from a piece of the parent that was removed from the original body.

C.   Incorrect. This is a form of asexual reproduction, but there are many forms of asexual reproduction that do not involve offspring forming from an unfertilized egg.

D.   **Correct.** Parthenogenesis is a form of reproduction that occurs without fertilization of the female egg.

25)

A.   Incorrect. Protists and fungi are also included in this domain.

B.   **Correct.** Eukaryotic cells contain a membrane-bound nucleus as well as other organelles.

C.   Incorrect. Most protists and some fungi are unicellular.

D.   Incorrect. This is a reproductive method of bacteria and archaebacteria.

26)

A.   **Correct.** Chromosome segregation occurs within the nucleus and is not considered a type of organelle inheritance, which occurs outside the nucleus.

B.   Incorrect. Biparental inheritance occurs when both parents contribute to organelle inheritance.

C.   Incorrect. Vegetative segregation is a form of organelle inheritance that occurs among organisms with asexual reproduction.

D.   Incorrect. Uniparental inheritance occurs when one parent—usually the mother—contributes to organelle inheritance.

27)

A.   Incorrect. Geotropism encourages a deep root system, as root tips display positive geotropism to grow toward the pull of gravity. This allows the plant to find moisture and nutrients within the soil.

B.   **Correct.** Phototropism is a type of physical response in plants to grow toward light (positive tropism) or away from light (negative tropism). Most plants need light to perform photosynthesis, and their stems will grow toward a light source.

C.   Incorrect. Phototropism is related to a light source and does not impact the structural system support of the plant.

D.   Incorrect. Root growth is more positively affected by geotropism.

28)

A.   Incorrect. Although this is a true statement, it does not support the endosymbiotic theory that explains the origins of mitochondria.

B.   Incorrect. Mitochondria are often called the "powerhouse of the cell" because they extract energy through cellular respiration and glycolysis (in the absence of oxygen). Bacteria also perform glycolysis for energy, but this does not support the theory from the question.

C.   **Correct.** Mitochondria are double-membrane organelles found within eukaryotic cells. Although they are considered organelles, they resemble some primitive prokaryotic cells and contain circular DNA and ribosomes like bacteria do.

D.   Incorrect. Neither bacteria nor mitochondria have a true nucleus.

29)

A.   Incorrect. This is the inner membrane of the chloroplast; it is less permeable than the outer membrane and has transport proteins embedded throughout.

B.   Incorrect. This part of the chloroplast is the intermembrane space where oxidative phosphorylation occurs.

C.   Incorrect. This part of the chloroplast is the outer membrane; it is permeable to small organic molecules.

D.   **Correct.** The light dependent reactions take place in the thylakoid membranes of the chloroplast, correctly labeled as F.

30)

A.   Incorrect. The ribosome binds the mRNA transcript and provides a site for tRNA molecules to interact with a codon.

B.   Incorrect. rRNA plays a key role in the binding of mRNA and the ribosome.

C.   **Correct.** tRNA molecules carry specific amino acids to the ribosome, bind a complementary codon, and play an important role in the growth of a polypeptide chain.

D.   Incorrect. The main function of RNA polymerase is in transcription.

31)

A.   **Correct.** Recombination occurs when the chromatids of duplicated chromosomes intertwine and swap genetic information during meiosis.

B.   Incorrect. This refers for the tendency of pairs of genes to be inherited together.

C.   Incorrect. This refers to the fusion of male and female gametes.

D.   Incorrect. This refers to the selective breeding that occurs as part of a genetic study.

32)

A.   **Correct.** Flatworms can reproduce through both fertilization and fragmentation; roundworms do not reproduce asexually.

B.   Incorrect. Members of both phyla display bilateral symmetry.

C.   Incorrect. Neither flatworms nor roundworms have a true coelom; flatworms are acoelomates while roundworms are pseudocoelomates.

D.   Incorrect. Both phyla of animals have parasitic and non-parasitic groups.

33)

A.   Incorrect. The endocrine system stimulates hormone production in response to stimuli but does not detect the stimuli.

B.   Incorrect. Organs in the integumentary system act as effectors but do not act as messengers.

C.   **Correct.** Sensory organs and sensory nerves throughout the body receive messages indicating a change due to a stimulus and send nerve impulses to the brain to communicate the changes.

D.   Incorrect. The cardiovascular system delivers hormonal messages as produced by the endocrine system but does not detect changes in the external environment.

34)

A.   **Correct.** These two biomes are dominated by different types of vegetation.

B.   Incorrect. Tundra is the northernmost biome.

C.   Incorrect. Both of these biomes harbor an abundance of life, but taiga is more ecologically diverse than tundra.

D.   Incorrect. Both tundra and taiga are terrestrial biomes.

35)

A.   Incorrect. Altruism is a type of behavior that benefits other organisms to the detriment of the organism that initiates the behavior.

B.   Incorrect. Opportunism is not a type of symbiotic relationship.

C. **Correct.** Mutualism occurs when both species benefit.

D. Incorrect. Commensalism occurs when one species benefits with no impact on the other.

36)

A. **Correct.** The climax community is the oldest, most mature stage that has the greatest amount of diversity, biomass, and productivity.

B. Incorrect. The pioneer plant stage has the lowest amount of diversity, biomass, and productivity.

C. Incorrect. The intermediate species stage has a moderate amount of diversity, biomass, and productivity.

D. Incorrect. There is no life and little to no soil at the inception of ecological succession.

37)

A. Incorrect. Natural disasters impact a population regardless of the size of the population (its density). A forest fire is an example of a natural disaster. The deer population would be impacted regardless of its size during a forest fire.

B. **Correct.** Density-dependent factors are those that relate directly to the number of individuals within a population. In this scenario, the increased numbers of rabbits means that fewer resources are available for survival.

C. Incorrect. A volcanic eruption will impact all surrounding species regardless of their population.

D. Incorrect. Drought is an example of a natural disaster that is not related to the density of a population.

38)

A. Incorrect. Waste incineration is an example of environmental cleanup that occurs after the pollutant has entered the environment.

B. **Correct.** Green buildings are areas of construction that strive to reduce environmental impacts through various means.

C. Incorrect. Chemical treatment is a form of environmental cleanup that occurs after the pollutant has entered the environment.

D. Incorrect. Air stripping is an example of environmental cleanup that occurs after the pollutant has entered the environment.

39)

A. Incorrect. A similar bone structure in the forearms of both horses and bats is an example of a homologous structure. Although the organisms have the same basic types of bones, the bones have been modified for different functions.

B. Incorrect. Similar amino acid structures in the hemoglobin of two organisms suggest a common ancestor.

C. Incorrect. Similar plant species found in two different areas suggest that at one time these two populations were close in proximity to each other but were most likely separated due to some barrier.

D. **Correct.** Convergent evolution is a trait of evolution in which species that are not of similar recent origin acquire the same trait due to natural selection.

40)

A. **Correct.** A bottleneck occurs when a population size starts to decline rapidly, leaving a shallow pool of genetic traits from the surviving individuals. A bottleneck can occur due to extreme events or over-predation.

41)

B. **Correct.** Allotropic speciation occurs when a population is prevented from reproducing due to some physical, geographic barrier. The two populations on either side of the barrier can become two separate species. In this case the geographic barrier is the distance between the two species of spotted owl.

42)

A. Incorrect. Transcription occurs in the cytoplasm of prokaryotic cells.

B. Incorrect. Protein synthesis is the function of a ribosome.

C. Incorrect. The Golgi body packages proteins.

D. **Correct.** Transcription occurs in the nucleus while translation occurs in the cytoplasm.

43)

A. **Correct.** Modifier genes can have multiple kinds of influences on the genes they are modifying.

B. Incorrect. This is only true of genes involved in epistasis.

C. Incorrect. This is true in many—but not all—cases of pigmentation.

D. Incorrect. Dominant modifier genes influence the traits expressed by other genes.

44)

A. Incorrect. Recombination occurs in all cells and is not considered a mutation.

B. Incorrect. Genetic variation is a result of a chromosomal mutation, but it is not a mutation itself.

C. Incorrect. Transformation is a form of genetic exchange among prokaryotes.

D. **Correct.** Nondisjunction results in cells with abnormal chromosome numbers being produced.

45)

A. Incorrect. The root cap is found at the tip of the root and protects the meristematic zone as it grows.

B. Incorrect. Cell division occurs in the meristematic zone to create many undifferentiated cells.

C. Incorrect. The zone of elongation is where cells lengthen and extend the reach of the root.

D. **Correct.** Cells differentiate into specialized cells and tissues in this zone.

46)

A. Incorrect. Ground tissue is made of several types of cells. Parenchyma are a specific type of ground tissue that make up the bulk of a plant.

B. **Correct.** Parenchyma cells are very common cells that can quickly divide and differentiate to fill many vital functions within the plant.

C. Incorrect. Vascular cells, including xylem and phloem cells, have a specific purpose to transport food and water.

D. Incorrect. Collenchyma cells are specialized ground tissue that provide flexible support to new plant growth.

47)

A. Incorrect. Transport proteins like hemoglobin and cytochrome c convey molecules and nutrients from one place, in or out of a cell, to another place, in or out of a cell.

B Incorrect. Cells communicate with each other by producing and responding to signaling proteins, like the hormone glucagon.

C. **Correct.** Motor proteins convert chemical energy into mechanical work and play a role in processes such as muscle contraction and the movement of molecules across membranes.

D. Incorrect. Regulatory proteins, like p53, play a role in gene expression.

48)

A. Incorrect. Both fungal cells and plant cells have cell walls. One of the main components of the cell walls of fungi is chitin, whereas the cell walls of plants are mainly composed of cellulose.

B. **Correct.** This is the distinct difference between plants and fungi: Plants synthesize their own organic compounds through photosynthesis, while fungi acquire their organic sources of energy from the environment.

C. Incorrect. The opposite is true: Plants are primary producers; fungi are decomposers.

D. Incorrect. This answer is only partially true: Fungi include the yeasts and the molds. Molds are multicellular eukaryotes, but yeast cells are unicellular eukaryotes.

49)

A. Incorrect. Chromosomes are packaged differently in prokaryotic versus eukaryotic cells.

B. Incorrect. Only prokaryotic cells divide by binary fission.

C. **Correct.** Two genetically identical daughter cells are produced during the cell division of both prokaryotic and eukaryotic cells.

D. Incorrect. Microtubules play a role in the division of eukaryotic cells.

50)

D. **Correct.** Water will leave the cell through osmosis when the concentration of solute outside the cell is greater than that inside the cell. Water will leave the cell when it's placed in a 20 percent saline solution, decreasing the mass of the cell.

51)

A. Incorrect. Amino acids are joined to form proteins; DNA is transcribed into mRNA and translated into protein.

B. **Correct.** Proteins are the expressed products of a gene.

C. Incorrect. Fatty acids are components of lipids.

D. Incorrect. Monosaccharides are the subunits that comprise a carbohydrate.

52)

A. Incorrect. Oviparity is a mode of reproduction in which embryos develop in eggs outside the mother.

B. Incorrect. Viviovoparity is not an accepted scientific term.

C. Incorrect. Viviparity is a mode of reproduction in which embryos develop outside of eggs inside the mother, receiving nutrients directly from the mother instead of a yolk sac.

D. **Correct.** Ovoviviparity is a mode of reproduction in which young develop inside eggs inside the mother, hatch out and are born fully developed.

53)

B. **Correct.** Bacteria are prokaryotic organisms, which means they lack a nucleus with a membrane. The other choices are all eukaryotic organisms with a membrane-bound nucleus.

54)

A. **Correct.** Habitat restoration uses technology to make physical changes to restore habitats to their former state.

B. Incorrect. Waste management refers to the process of handling waste given off as a byproduct during human consumption of natural resources.

C. Incorrect. Species protection describes specific efforts to restore species to their habitats.

D. Incorrect. A conservation easement is a voluntary agreement between private landowners and the government to restrict human activities and protect habitats.

55)

A. **Correct.** Overgrazing leads to increased soil erosion and poorer soil quality.

B. Incorrect. Cover crops can enrich the soil during growing off-seasons.

C. Incorrect. Incorporating natural pest control can reduce pests and diseases while avoiding the use of chemicals.

D. Incorrect. Conservation tillage leaves plant residue behind after the growing season, which enriches the soil and reduces erosion.

56)

A. **Correct.** Gene cloning results in copies of individual genes or strands of DNA for research or genetic modification purposes.

B. Incorrect. Reproductive cloning is the cloning of an embryo with the intent of creating an organism genetically identical to the donor.

C. Incorrect. The organisms (GMOs) resulting from this technique have been genetically altered for a desired trait.

D. Incorrect. DNA fingerprinting is a specific laboratory technique that matches genetic information with an individual.

57)

A. **Correct.** The results of the Miller-Urey experiment provide evidence that it was possible for organic compounds to arise from inorganic compounds.

B. Incorrect. Genetic diversity among organisms is a result of evolution of life.

C. Incorrect. The rise of photosynthetic organisms led to an increase of oxygen in Earth's early atmosphere.

D. Incorrect. DNA replication is a process found later in Earth's evolution; it is believed RNA was actually responsible for replication in Earth's early organisms.

58)

A. Incorrect. Endosymbiosis is the theory that mitochondria and chloroplasts descended from bacteria that lived inside other cells.

B. **Correct.** Cephalization is head development among increasingly advanced organisms.

C. Incorrect. Embryology is the study of the development of organisms from fertilization to birth.

D. Incorrect. Multicellularity is the tendency of multiple cells to emerge and develop within an organism.

59)

A. Incorrect. Thirty-four molecules of ATP are usually produced during electron transport.

B. Incorrect. Two molecules of ATP are usually produced during glycolysis.

C. Incorrect. Two molecules of ATP are usually produced during the Krebs cycle.

D. **Correct.** A total of thirty-eight molecules of ATP are produced: two molecules from glycolysis, two molecules from the Krebs cycle, and thirty-four molecules from electron transport.

60)

A. Incorrect. All eukaryotic cells possess ribosomes.

B. Incorrect. Mitochondria are also found in all eukaryotic cells.

C. **Correct.** A plant cell is enveloped by a cell wall, but animal cells do not possess cell walls.

D. Incorrect. Both plant cells and animal cells carry a nucleus.

61)

A. Incorrect. Both are unicellular.

B. **Correct.** This is one of the major differences between these two groups.

C. Incorrect. Archaea do not go through photosynthesis; a few examples of bacteria do, however.

D. Incorrect. Although archaea are more likely to be extremophiles, both are found in a broad range of similar environments.

62)

A. Incorrect. The scientist is comparing *S. sponferus* with algae from other environments, so the existence of other algae species at this depth would not affect the hypothesis.

B. **Correct.** The results from these experiments show that the rate of growth does not change for this species of algae as the light changes, which directly contradicts the hypothesis.

C. Incorrect. The growth of *S. sponferus* on the ocean's surface would support the scientist's hypothesis.

D. Incorrect. The growth of other algae species does not affect the scientist's hypothesis about *S. sponferus*.

63)

A. Incorrect. Prokaryotes generally have a single chromosome, not a pair.

B. Incorrect. Not all organisms contain a cell wall.

C. Incorrect. Some viruses do not contain DNA, only an RNA core.

D. **Correct.** All living things, including viruses, contain nucleic acid in the form of either DNA or RNA.

64)

A. Incorrect. The parathyroid is a gland in the larynx that produces hormones to help regulate calcium levels.

B. **Correct.** The pancreas is a hormone-producing component of the endocrine system and produces insulin.

C. Incorrect. The testes produce both testosterone and estrogen in males in order to trigger sexual development and gamete maturation.

D. Incorrect. The thymus is located in the chest and produces thymosin to stimulate the production of white blood cells.

65)

A. Incorrect. This is the stage in which eggs mature.

B. Incorrect. This is the shedding of the uterine lining.

C. Incorrect. This term refers to the reproductive cycle of placental mammals and is not specific to humans.

D. **Correct.** Eggs are released into the fallopian tubes for fertilization during ovulation.

66)

A.   Incorrect. Taiga is dominated by trees and found in extreme northern areas.

B.   Incorrect. Estuaries are aquatic biomes located where rivers meet the oceans.

C.   Incorrect. The chaparral is a type of shrubland biome.

D.   **Correct.** The savanna is tropical grassland with nutrient-poor soil.

67)

A.   Incorrect. Gibberellins are plant hormones used to stimulate growth and cell elongation.

B.   Incorrect. Citric acid is not a plant hormone but is a weak acid found in fruits like oranges, lemons, and grapefruit.

C.   Incorrect. Cytokinins are plant hormones that promote cell division (cytokinesis).

D.   **Correct.** Ethylene is a gaseous plant hormone that promotes fruit ripening. In fact, many times fruit will be picked while it is still "green" and will be ripened artificially using ethylene so the fruit ripens right before it is placed in the grocery stores.

68)

A.   **Correct.** Red blood cells are created in bone marrow instead of through mitosis. They are the only type of cell to be created in this way. Without a nucleus, red blood cells are unable to undergo mitosis.

B.   Incorrect. Red blood cells do not have mitochondria and as a result have to produce ATP through glycolysis alone.

C.   Incorrect. Because red blood cells lack a nucleus, they are not able to repair damage.

D.   Incorrect. Red blood cells typically live for around 120 days before they die and are replaced.

69)

B.   **Correct.** Only II is true.

I.   False. mRNA accounts for the smallest percentage of RNA in the cell and its main function is to carry the copied genetic information from the DNA in a series of codons.

II.   True. tRNA is the key to decoding the codons from mRNA. The tRNA carries the information needed to transfer the amino acid and binds it to the appropriate polypeptide chain to form proteins.

III.   False. rRNA aids in the formation of ribosomes, which are the creation sites of proteins.

70)

A.   Incorrect. A gene is transcribed into mRNA and translated into a protein during this process.

B.   Incorrect. Feedback inhibition controls enzyme-substrate interactions.

C.   **Correct.** Cells are destroyed via this process.

D.   Incorrect. This process regulates the internal environment of the cell.

71)

A.   **Correct.** In addition to the condensation of chromosomes, the mitotic spindle forms during prophase.

B.   Incorrect. Spindle fibers attach to the sister chromatids in metaphase.

C.   Incorrect. The sister chromatids are separated during anaphase.

D.   Incorrect. Nuclear envelopes form around the two sets of sister chromatids during telophase.

72)

A   **Correct.** Because each offspring will inherit the dominant allele, all the offspring will show the dominant phenotype. The offspring would only show the recessive trait or a mix of the two phenotypes if they did not follow Mendelian inheritance patterns.

73)

A.   Incorrect. Analogous processes and structures stem from different common ancestors even though they are similar in function.

B.   Incorrect. This is the process of dissimilar species developing similar adaptations.

C.   Incorrect. This is the process of species of a common ancestor differentiating from one another.

D.   **Correct.** This is considered a homology because it is a process that is shared by all living things, indicating they stem from a common ancestor.

74)

A.   Incorrect. Allopatric speciation refers to the development of new species due to geographic isolation.

B.   Incorrect. Transitional fossils are considered evidence against the theory of punctuated equilibrium.

C.   **Correct.** The theory that species gradually change over time is supported by the existence of transitional (missing link) fossils.

D.   Incorrect. Adaptation refers to an inherited feature or behavior that gives an organism an advantage in its environment.

75)

A.   Incorrect. Large population is one of the five conditions.

B.   **Correct.** The Hardy-Weinberg equilibrium assumes that all mating is random.

C.   Incorrect. No natural selection is one of the five conditions.

D.   Incorrect. No mutation is one of the five conditions.

76)

A.   Incorrect. Producers are photosynthetic organisms that occupy the first trophic level.

B.   Incorrect. *Autotroph* refers to the energy pathway of an organism that creates its own food, not a trophic level.

C.   Incorrect. *Heterotroph* refers to the organism's energy pathway, not a trophic level.

D.   **Correct.** When an organism consumes another consumer, it is occupying the third trophic level of a secondary consumer.

77)

A.   **Correct.** Longer-lived plants are found in intermediate species stages and climax communities.

B.   Incorrect. Long roots are an adaptation that pioneer plants use to live in areas with sparse soil resources.

C.   Incorrect. Pioneer plants quickly reproduce to take advantage of new habitats.

D.   Incorrect. Pioneer plants are adapted to live in environments with little water.

78)

A.   Incorrect. An herbivore is a type of consumer, not producer.

B.   Incorrect. Secondary consumers are carnivorous.

C.   **Correct.** Herbivores feed on plants, which places them in the second trophic level after producers.

D.   Incorrect. Tertiary consumers are carnivorous.

79)

C.   **Correct.** Complementary base pairs always pair with the same base: adenine (A) will pair with thymine (T) and cytosine (C) will pair with guanine (G).

80)

A.   **Correct.** The last column of data can be used to determine which temperature is ideal for long-term survival. After ten days, almost all the individuals were still alive in the 20°C environment.

81)

B.   **Correct.** Based on the data given in the table, it is most likely that the population would continue to decrease as the temperature increased. After 20°C, the population continues to drop steadily as the temperature rises.

82)

A.   Incorrect. Predator and prey population numbers are interrelated.

B.   Incorrect. Prey provide nourishment for predators.

C.   Incorrect. The number of prey changes when the number of predators changes.

D.   **Correct.** Increased numbers of predators can cause prey numbers to decrease.

83)

A.   Incorrect. DNA polymerase adds new nucleotides to a growing, complementary strand of DNA.

B.   **Correct.** The synthesis of a strand of DNA complementary to the lagging strand is not continuous; therefore, the new segments of DNA must be joined together by DNA ligase.

C.   Incorrect. RNA polymerase opens the DNA helix during transcription.

D.   Incorrect. Helicases opens the DNA helix during replication.

84)

A.   Incorrect. Mitosis and cytokinesis produce two diploid (2n) cells.

B.   **Correct.** Four haploid (1n) cells are produced during meiosis.

C.   Incorrect. The daughter cells produced during mitosis are genetically identical to their diploid (2n) parent.

D.   Incorrect. Meiosis and cytokinesis result in four haploid (1n) cells.

85)

A.   Incorrect. Mutation of DNA can cause genetic variation.

B.   Incorrect. Sexual reproduction provides many opportunities for a variety of genes to enter a population gene pool.

C.   **Correct.** Codominance refers to two dominant alleles both expressing themselves in a phenotype.

D.   Incorrect. Crossing over, or recombination, of chromosomes allows for greater genetic variation than simple duplication.

86)

A.   **Correct.** Down syndrome is the result of an individual inheriting 47 chromosomes instead of the normal 46.

B.   Incorrect. Turner syndrome is a genetic disorder that arises due to a missing chromosome.

C. Incorrect. Sickle-cell anemia is the result of a genetic substitution, not an extra chromosome.

D. Incorrect. Cystic fibrosis arises due to the deletion of a gene.

87)

A. Incorrect. Migration is one of the mechanisms through which gene flow can take place.

B. Incorrect. Genetic drift is random change within a population.

C. Correct. Gene flow is the movement of genetic information from one population to another through successful reproduction of migrating individuals.

D. Incorrect. Evolutionary force is a term that describes the many ways genes move, including gene flow.

88)

A. Incorrect. Plants are primarily autotrophs.

B. Incorrect. Fungi are primarily heterotrophs.

C. Correct. Protists can fall into either of the two categories.

D. Incorrect. Animals are primarily heterotrophs.

89)

A. Correct. Classification is a broad term that refers to putting organisms into classes or groups. Taxonomy is the actual naming process based on this classification.

B. Incorrect. Taxonomy is the process of naming organisms, while classification is the broad grouping process.

C. Incorrect. All organisms can go through the processes of classification and taxonomy.

D. Incorrect. Classification is a concept that is much older than both Linnaeus and Woese; modern taxonomy was founded by Linnaeus and refined by Woese.

90)

A. Correct. Budding occurs when a protuberance on the parent plant generates a genetic clone.

B. Incorrect. Fragmentation occurs when a parent divides into multiple pieces that each mature into adult forms.

C. Incorrect. Sporulation occurs when parent cells undergo cell division to create genetic clones or gametes for release into the environment.

D. Incorrect. Binary fission occurs when one parent cell splits into two equal copies.

91)

A. Incorrect. Broad leaves are found among pteridophytes, gymnosperms, and angiosperms.

B. Incorrect. Angiosperms can be perennial or annual; gymnosperms are almost always perennial.

C. Incorrect. This is not the role of the fruit but rather the role of the endosperm, which is found in all seeds.

D. Correct. The attractive nature of the flower encourages animals to pollinate the plant.

92)

A. Incorrect. Animals are unlikely to consume non-fleshy fruit with a barb that could harm them.

B. Incorrect. This is an example of explosive dehiscence.

C. Correct. This is a form of animal-assisted allochory.

D. Incorrect. Wind-dispersed seeds are more likely to be lightweight, without a barb to weigh them down.

93)

A.   Incorrect. Organic molecules do contain carbon, but they also always contain hydrogen.

B.   Correct. An organic molecule is defined as a compound made of carbon and hydrogen.

C.   Incorrect. Although organic compounds can also contain oxygen, not all organic molecules contain oxygen.

D.   Incorrect. All organics are made from carbon and hydrogen; some organic compounds might also contain oxygen and nitrogen.

94)

A.   Correct. Ammonia is a good, inorganic electron donor and could potentially be a source of energy in a chemosynthetic reaction.

B.   Incorrect. Oxygen is more likely to accept electrons, not donate them.

C.   Incorrect. The electron donor for a chemosynthetic reaction is generally an inorganic molecule.

D.   Incorrect. Carbon dioxide is often "fixed" in a chemosynthetic reaction. In other words, carbon dioxide often serves as an electron acceptor and is reduced to sugar.

95)

A.   Incorrect. Cnidarians are simple but have more complex functions than sponges, such as stinging tentacles and simple tissues.

B.   Correct. Due to their lack of body tissues and organs, sponges in the Porifera phylum are considered very simple.

C.   Incorrect. Nematodes have more complex bodies than other phyla of animals due to having structures such as a pseudocel.

D.   Incorrect. Arthropods are more complex than other phyla of

animals, with bilateral symmetry, segmentation, and well-developed organ systems.

96)

A.   Incorrect. All reptiles, including the birds, lay hard eggs that contain amniotic fluid.

B.   Incorrect. All reptiles have scales. This includes feathers, which are modified scales.

C.   Correct. Hollow bones are a characteristic found in birds to help them attain flight.

D.   Incorrect. All reptiles, including the birds, have highly efficient lungs.

97)

A.   Incorrect. The space between genes acts as just that, "space filling," and is not used in coding proteins.

B.   Incorrect. Centromeres contain noncoding DNA and are used during mitosis to link sister chromatids.

C.   Incorrect. Telomeres are areas of repeating DNA at the end of a chromosome. They provide protection from deterioration of chromosomes during replication.

D.   Correct. Exons are a segment of DNA (or RNA) that contains the information needed for coding a protein.

98)

A.   Correct. mRNA is a sequence of nucleotides in which each triplet codes for a particular amino acid. The sequence of triplets in the mRNA would translate into the sequence of amino acids that make up a protein.

B.   Incorrect. The primary function of tRNA is to deliver amino acids needed for protein synthesis.

C.   Incorrect. Ribosomes are mostly composed of rRNA, which is used to help translate the information from mRNA into proteins.

D. Incorrect. DNA polymerase is an enzyme used to assemble the nucleotides during DNA replication.

99)

A. Correct. Equilibrium species tend to have higher rates of offspring success and greater mortality rates later in life.

B. Incorrect. Constant loss species produce moderate amounts of offspring and have a constant mortality rate.

C. Incorrect. Fecundity is the ability to produce offspring, so all species are considered fecund in some capacity.

D. Incorrect. Opportunistic species produce higher levels of offspring with lower levels of parental care.

100)

A. Incorrect. Intermediate filaments are composed of a large number of proteins.

B. Incorrect. Tubulin is a primary component of microtubules.

C. Correct. Actin is found in microfilaments.

D. Incorrect. Flagella are made of microtubules, but flagella are not considered fibers of the cytoskeleton.

101)

A. Incorrect. This is a form of passive transport.

B. Incorrect. This is also a form of passive transport, which does not require an input of ATP.

C. Incorrect. Although exocytosis does consume energy, molecules are released from a cell in this process.

D. Correct. Molecules or microbes are brought into a cell, with an input

of energy, through the process of endocytosis.

102)

A. Incorrect. Parasitism benefits the organism exhibiting the behavior and harms the other.

B. Incorrect. Mutualism occurs when both species benefit.

C. Incorrect. Territorialism is a behavior that drives organisms away from the chosen geographic area; it can bring benefits to the organism's population but has a negative effect on the species or individuals being driven away.

D. Correct. Altruism is a series of behaviors that benefits another organism at the cost of the organism displaying the behavior.

103)

A. Incorrect. Gymnosperms are not flowering plants.

B. Correct. Lilies are an example of a monocot within the flowering plant group.

C. Incorrect. Bryophytes do not have vascular tissue, flowers, or a true root system.

D. Incorrect. Pteridophytes are seedless vascular plants, such as ferns.

104)

A. Correct. This is considered a positive feedback loop because it exacerbates the stimulus rather than stopping it to return to homeostasis.

B. Incorrect. This allows blood pressure to rise and reach homeostasis.

C. Incorrect. Sweat cools the body and returns it to a normal temperature, stopping the effect of the external stimulus.

D. Incorrect. Insulin stores glucose to return the body's blood sugar levels to normal.

105)

A.   **Correct.** This is a function of the hypothalamus.

B.   Incorrect. The pituitary gland stimulates other glands to produce hormones.

C.   Incorrect. The posterior pituitary gland stores and releases hormones produced by the hypothalamus.

D.   Incorrect. The pituitary gland produces and transmits its own hormones in addition to trophic hormones.

106)

A.   Incorrect. The gastrula stage occurs after the cells of the blastula begin to separate and differentiate.

B.   Incorrect. The embryo is the resulting body of cells that occurs after cell division and specialization of embryogenesis occurs.

C.   **Correct.** Blastulas have a hollow cavity in the center of the body.

D.   Incorrect. The morula is a tightly packed ball of cells that gives rise to the blastula.

107)

B.   **Correct.** Plants always exist in multicellular adult forms. The other groups can contain unicellular organisms.

108)

A.   **Correct.** A neuron is a specialized nerve cell.

B.   Incorrect. A tissue is a collection of specialized cells that perform a similar function.

C.   Incorrect. Organs are composed of tissues that perform a similar function.

D.   Incorrect. Organ systems are composed of organs that work together to perform a similar function.

109)

A.   **Correct.** Problems like contaminating groundwater show the environmental impact of a landfill.

B.   Incorrect. Such chemical use usually occurs during material processing.

C.   Incorrect. Oil extraction is an example of raw material collection.

D.   Incorrect. Release of industrial byproducts usually occurs during material processing.

110)

A.   Incorrect. Transcription begins at the promoter region of a gene.

B.   Incorrect. A transcription factor can regulate expression of a gene by binding a region called the operator.

C.   Incorrect. Translation of a piece of mRNA begins at the start codon.

D.   **Correct.** The active site of an enzyme is where a substrate binds.

111)

A.   Incorrect. The orientation of the sugar-phosphate backbone of a nucleic acid determines its directionality.

B.   Incorrect. The sugar molecule of a nucleotide carries a hydroxyl group on the third carbon (3' carbon) of the 5-carbon sugar group; the sugar molecule is referred to as the 3' end of a nucleotide.

C.   **Correct.** The phosphate group is attached to the fifth carbon (5' carbon) of the sugar molecule and is designated the 5' end of a nucleotide.

D.   Incorrect. All of these comprise a nucleotide, but only the phosphate group represents the 5' end of the nucleotide.

112)

A. Incorrect. This would only refer to nucleic acids; this is not the property that is exploited in gel electrophoresis.

B. Incorrect. This would only be relevant to the separation of proteins; answer choice C is the best answer to this question.

C. **Correct.** The proteins and nucleic acids migrate through the gel based on their sizes: smaller molecules move more quickly than larger molecules.

D. Incorrect. The best response is answer choice C.

113)

A. Incorrect. The gene is the basic unit of heredity.

B. **Correct.** A genotype is the genetic makeup of an individual organism.

C. Incorrect. Alleles are alternate versions of the same gene, derived from different parents.

D. Incorrect. Chromosomes are the structures within a cell that carry genes.

114)

A. Incorrect. Transformation is the uptake of genetic information from outside the cell.

B. Incorrect. Transduction occurs when a viral phage absorbs genetic information from one host cell and incorporates it in another host cell.

C. Incorrect. This is not an example of genetic exchange in prokaryotes.

D. **Correct.** Conjugation is the only form of prokaryotic genetic exchange that requires cell-to-cell contact.

115)

A. **Correct.** DNA is first transcribed into mRNA.

B. Incorrect. DNA is transcribed, not translated, into mRNA.

C. Incorrect. mRNA is translated, not transcribed, into protein.

D. Incorrect. Although mRNA is translated into protein, this is not the first step in gene expression.

116)

A. Incorrect. Active transport requires energy to move molecules up their concentration gradient.

B. Incorrect. Energy is released by the oxidation of ATP; this energy drives active transport.

C. **Correct.** Oxidation of ATP is required for active transport.

D. Incorrect. Active transport occurs across the cell membrane.

117)

A. Incorrect. The structures and molecules needed to carry out photosynthesis are found in the chloroplast.

B. **Correct.** The nucleus is the organelle that carries the DNA of eukaryotic organisms.

C. Incorrect. Proteins are made at ribosomes.

D. Incorrect. The bacterial chromosome is found in the cytoplasm.

118)

A. **Correct.** Uniform dispersion is a pattern of dispersion that has individuals basically equally spaced. Animals that maintain defined territories will exhibit uniform dispersion.

B. Incorrect. Dandelions, as well as other plants that spread their seeds using wind dispersal, will exhibit random dispersion. The seeds will germinate wherever they happen to fall with no noticeable pattern.

C.   Incorrect. Elephants exhibit clumped dispersion patterns like most herd animals. This is due to habitat heterogeneity. This means that if there are favorable conditions in a localized area, populations will tend to clump around those areas.

D.   Incorrect. Oak trees exhibit clumped dispersion. Oak trees drop their seeds directly on the ground, with very little movement once they have landed. The result is a "clump" of oak trees.

119)

A.   Incorrect. Carbon atoms are not involved in the electron transport chain.

B.   Incorrect. Glycolysis is the first step of cellular respiration and is the process of breaking down glucose into two pyruvates in the cytoplasm. This process produces 2 molecules of ATP.

C.   Incorrect. The Krebs cycle occurs before the electron transport chain. During the Krebs cycle, acetyl CoA is modified within the mitochondria, making the "energy precursors." Electrons are given off that fuel oxidative phosphorylation.

D.   Correct. The electron transport chain is the last step in cellular respiration. It produces the most ATP.

120)

A.   Correct. Fructose is a simple sugar, or monosaccharide, like glucose.

B.   Incorrect. Lactose is a disaccharide and is made up of two monosaccharides bonded to each other.

C.   Incorrect. Sucrose is a disaccharide and is made up of two monosaccharides bonded to each other.

D.   Incorrect. Cellulose is a polysaccharide made up of many

monosaccharides bonded to each other.

121)

A.   Incorrect. Floodplains are found adjacent to rivers and may be temporarily flooded, but do not have ecosystems that exist submerged in water for a length of time.

B.   Incorrect. An estuary is an area where rivers meet the sea.

C.   Correct. Wetlands are covered with water, either seasonally or year-round.

D.   Incorrect. A lagoon is a shallow area of water separated from a larger body of water by a physical barrier.

122)

A.   Incorrect. Theories, not laws, are used to explain facts.

B.   Incorrect. This describes the relationship between hypotheses and investigations.

C.   Correct. While they are both rooted in confirmed observations, laws are broader and more predictive in nature than facts.

D.   Incorrect. Scientific laws are not explanatory; however, scientific facts are also not explanatory.

123)

A.   Correct. An anion is a negatively charged atom.

B.   Incorrect. A cation is a positively charged atom.

C.   Incorrect. An atom is electrically neutral.

D.   Incorrect. Answer choice A is the only correct response.

124)

A.   Incorrect. Methionine is an amino acid.

B. Incorrect. The centromere is a junction on a sister chromatid.

C. Incorrect. This enzyme catalyzes DNA replication during cell division.

D. Correct. The nucleosome is a chromosomal structure comprising two hundred nucleotides wrapped around eight histones.

125)

A. Incorrect. A germ-line mutation could occur in a cell that will differentiate into a gamete; these mutations are inherited.

B. Correct. Somatic cells are the nonreproductive cells of an organism.

C. Incorrect. This is a specific kind of mutation that could occur in a germ-line or somatic cell.

D. Incorrect. These types of mutations could affect either a germ-line or somatic cell.

126)

A. Incorrect. This gene mutation causes the normally round red blood cells to become crescent or sickle-shaped.

B. Correct. Sickle-cell anemia arises when a subunit of a gene is replaced with incorrect genetic information.

C. Incorrect. Sickle-cell anemia is not dominant and is instead inherited as an autosomal recessive disorder.

D. Incorrect. Low blood cell count is one of many symptoms of this disorder.

127)

A. Incorrect. The light-driven reactions of photosynthesis are generally considered to start when photosystem II captures sunlight.

B. Incorrect. The electrons generated in photosystem II are used in electron transport to generate ATP.

C. Correct. Photosystem II donates electrons to the electron transport chain; this drives the production of a proton gradient, which powers the synthesis of ATP.

D. Incorrect. ATP is generated by electron transport.

128)

A. Incorrect. Coral provides the structure for the coral reef biomes.

B. Incorrect. Detritus is the base of the food chain in estuary and wetland ecosystems.

C. Correct. These microscopic, floating organisms photosynthesize in the photic zone and are the primary producers in the ocean food web.

D. Incorrect. Zooplankton feed upon phytoplankton, which are the base of the ocean food chain in the photic zone.

129)

A. Correct. A habitat is a physical location with an organism's preferred biotic and abiotic conditions.

B. Incorrect. A geographic area refers to the physical parameters of a population; it does not account for the specific location in the geographic area with the conditions required for a species to survive.

C. Incorrect. A niche describes an organism's role within a specified area.

D. Incorrect. All biotic and abiotic factors in an environment characterize an ecosystem.

130)

A. Incorrect. Structural proteins provide strength to cells, tissues, and organs.

B. Incorrect. Signaling proteins move chemical messages from cell to cell.

C. Incorrect. Storage proteins provide energy storage.

D. **Correct.** Enzymes speed up a chemical reaction by lowering its activation energy.

131)

A. Incorrect. Microtubules play a key role in metaphase.

B. Incorrect. Sister chromatids are pulled apart to opposite poles of the cell during anaphase, a process performed by microtubules.

C. Incorrect. The two new nuclei form during telophase.

D. **Correct.** Actin filaments play a key role in the formation of a cleavage furrow during cytokinesis.

132)

A. **Correct.** This is the definition of biological fitness.

B. Incorrect. This is the definition of intersexual selection.

C. Incorrect. This can result in a species that is more fit than another, but the trait is not the biological fitness itself.

D. Incorrect. This is the definition of differential reproduction.

133)

A. Incorrect. Transformation refers to the exchange of genetic information among prokaryotes.

B. **Correct.** When large sections of chromosomes are deleted, the zygote is very likely to be miscarried.

C. Incorrect. Nondisjunction can lead to miscarriage, but it is a change to chromosomal number rather than structure.

D. Incorrect. Mutation is a general term that refers to any changes in chromosomal number or structure.

134)

A. Incorrect. *Kingdom* is still a part of the domain system.

B. Incorrect. The domain level does not exist in the kingdom system.

C. **Correct.** The domain system adds the domain level to the top of the classification hierarchy; this classification system is based on molecular evidence of evolutionary relationships between organisms.

D. Incorrect. The kingdom system has seven levels of classification (kingdom, phylum, class, order, family, genus, and species).

135)

A. Incorrect. This is true of some unicellular colonial organisms, however, each cell in a colony is capable of performing its own life functions.

B. Incorrect. This is one of many possible reproductive modes of unicellular organisms.

C. **Correct.** Unicellular organisms perform all life functions in the organelles within the cell.

D. Incorrect. All unicellular organisms are unspecialized cells.

136)

A. Incorrect. While members of the Echinodermata phylum display radial symmetry, they do not have specialized stinging cells to capture prey. Members of this phylum include sea stars and starfish.

B. Incorrect. All members of this phylum have embryos with a notochord, which, for most, will develop into a backbone. Included in this group are fish, amphibians, mammals, birds, and reptiles.

C. Incorrect. Animals that belong to this phylum all have a muscular "foot" for movement, a visceral mass to hold organs, and protective tissue called a mantle. Organisms such as squid, snails, and clams belong to this phylum.

D. **Correct.** Members of this phylum include jellyfish, corals, and sea anemones. All of these organisms have radial symmetry and have specialized cells to sting and capture their prey.

137)

A. Incorrect. Genes cannot physically be seen. It is the allele combination that is seen.

B. **Correct.** Alleles represent one of two or more forms of a gene for a particular trait.

C. Incorrect. A gene can be expressed by a single allele.

D. Incorrect. Recessive traits are not inherently bad; this just means that some traits will be expressed over others.

138)

A. Incorrect. The flower is the reproductive structure, which contains ovaries as well as other male and female reproductive structures.

B. **Correct.** A fruit matures after the ovule or ovules within it are fertilized and mature into seeds.

C. Incorrect. The seed contains the embryo and endosperm after the ovule is fertilized and is located within the ovary.

D. Incorrect. The ovule is the unfertilized egg of a flower.

139)

A. Incorrect. Apical and lateral meristem are both found in the root and shoot systems.

B. **Correct.** This is one of the primary differences between these two types of meristem.

C. Incorrect. Apical meristem is found in neither structure; lateral meristem is found in both.

D. Incorrect. Apical meristem produces both; lateral meristem produces neither.

140)

A. Incorrect. Controlled variables are variables that remain constant throughout the entire experiment.

B. **Correct.** Experimental variables, also known as independent variables, are the variables that are changed by the scientist.

C. Incorrect. Dependent variables are controls that change as a result of the manipulation of the independent variable.

D. Incorrect. There is no definition for a hypothetical variable.

141)

A. Incorrect. Gel electrophoresis separates molecules by size.

B. Incorrect. Microscopy magnifies a specimen so it can be observed.

C. **Correct.** Spectrophotometry transmits a certain wavelength of light through a sample; the amount of light absorbed by the molecules/microbes in the sample is measured.

D. Incorrect. This process is used to determine the sequence of bases in a segment of DNA.

142)

A. Incorrect. All species in the phylum Mollusca have a mantle.

B. Incorrect. Mollusks have a highly-developed circulatory system with a two-chambered heart to circulate blood.

C. Incorrect. Gills develop in the mantle cavity to take in oxygen.

D. **Correct.** Not all species of mollusks develop shells; slugs, octopuses, and squid are notable exceptions.

143)

A.   **Correct.** The allele for white fur is recessive, so only mice carrying two of the alleles for white fur will be white.

144)

A.   Incorrect. Parental cross refers to the cross breeding in the parent generation, not the number of traits for which the plants are being bred.

B.   Incorrect. Filial cross refers to the cross breeding in a filial (offspring) generation, not number of traits for which the plants are being bred.

C.   **Correct.** A dihybrid cross is selective breeding for two traits.

D.   Incorrect. A monohybrid cross is selective breeding for one trait.

145)

A.   Incorrect. Restriction enzymes recognize symmetrical sequences of DNA; this is not a symmetrical sequence.

B.   Incorrect. Symmetrical sequences read the same from 5' to 3' on one strand of DNA and from 5' to 3' on the complementary strand.

C.   Incorrect. This is not a symmetrical sequence of DNA.

D.   **Correct.** This is a symmetrical sequence of DNA; the complementary sequence to 5' GAATTC 3' is 5' GAATTC 3'.

146)

A.   Incorrect. Conceptual models are based on frameworks or diagrams, not equations.

B.   Incorrect. Population growth is a mathematical model that can be represented graphically but is not considered a graphical model because it is not probabilistic.

C.   Incorrect. Physical models are tangible, physical representations and are not based on mathematical equations.

D.   **Correct.** Population growth models are mathematical models because they use and apply equations to describe and understand the many variables involved in population size.

147)

A.   Incorrect. Trypsin is found in the small intestine and is used to digest proteins.

B.   Incorrect. Gastrin is a hormone that is useful for the entire process of digestion, but its main function is to stimulate the secretion of pepsin into the stomach.

C.   Incorrect. Secretin is actually a hormone that stimulates pancreatic enzymes to be released into the intestine.

D.   **Correct.** Pepsin is a digestive enzyme that breaks down proteins for digestion in the stomach.

148)

A.   **Correct.** Digestive juices are produced by the pancreas.

B.   Incorrect. The liver produces bile, along with the gall bladder, to help break down fats.

C.   Incorrect. The liver removes toxins that are ingested by the body.

D.   Incorrect. Blood travels through the liver for waste to be removed before it is dispersed throughout the body.

149)

A.   Incorrect. This is true. Monocots have a fibrous root system, whereas dicots have a taproot system.

B.   Incorrect. This is a true statement and is often easy to observe in plants.

C.   Incorrect. This is true. Often the single cotyledon is used up by the seed during germination.

D.   **Correct.** Monocots have scattered vascular bundles, whereas dicots exhibit ring formation of vascular bundles.

150)

A.   Incorrect. There is only a 1/16 chance that the resulting offspring will have the genotype wwss.

B.   Incorrect. There is only a 1/16 chance that the resulting offspring will have the genotype WWSS.

C.   **Correct.** There is a 1/4 chance that the resulting offspring will have a WwSs genotype.

D.   Incorrect. There is only a 1/8 chance that the resulting offspring will have the genotype WWSs.

	WS	Ws	wS	ws
WS	WWSS	WWSs	WwSS	WwSs
Ws	WWSs	WWss	WwSs	WsSs
wS	WwSS	WwSs	wwSS	wwSs
ws	WwSs	Wwss	wwSs	wwss

62. diff between virus and prokaryotes and eukaryotes

Biomes

Taiga - a forest of the cold subartic region

Tundra - Cold low amounts of precipitation

Estuary - partially enclosed coastal water body where freshwater from rivers & stream mix with salt from ocean

Chaparral - terrestrial biome woodland characterized by dry soil, hot weather mild winters and hardy shrubs

Taiga - tall plants and trees

Tundra - Flat

chaparal - small herbivores

post zygotic reproductive isolation occurs after members of two different species have mated and produced zygote

spermatozoa have flagella

motile cilia - epithelial cells of mammalian trachea

(48)

70

CPSIA information can be obtained
at www.ICGtesting.com
Printed in the USA
BVHW021147230323
661009BV00012B/816